Medieval Ireland

D1617537

This book is respectfully dedicated to the memory of Professor John O'Donovan, Bishop William Reeves, Goddard Henry Orpen DLitt, Hubert T. Knox, Professor Edmund Hogan SJ, Professor James Hogan, Father Paul Walsh, and Liam Ó Buachalla, and to all who work in the discipline of dinnseanchas today.

MEDIEVAL IRELAND

*Territorial, political and
economic divisions*

Paul MacCotter

FOUR COURTS PRESS

Set in 10.5 pt on 12 pt Bembo for
FOUR COURTS PRESS LTD
7 Malpas Street, Dublin 8, Ireland
www.fourcourtspress.ie
and in North America for
FOUR COURTS PRESS
c/o ISBS, 920 N.E. 58th Avenue, Suite 300, Portland, OR 97213.

© Paul MacCotter 2008

First published 2008
Paperback reprint 2014

A catalogue record for this title
is available from the British Library.

ISBN 978–1–84682–557–6

SPECIAL ACKNOWLEDGMENT

This publication has received support from the
Heritage Council under the 2008 Publications Grant Scheme.

AN
CHOMHAIRLE
OIDHREACHTA

THE
HERITAGE
COUNCIL

Printed in Ireland
by SPRINT-Print, Dublin.

Contents

Illustrations

Abbreviations

AB	Freeman, 'The annals in Cotton MS Titus A xxv' (Annals of Boyle)
AC	Freeman, *The Annals of Connacht*
A Clon	Murphy, *The Annals of Clonmacnoise*
AFM	O'Donovan, *Annals of the Four Masters*
AI	Mac Airt, *Annals of Innisfallen*
ALC	Hennessy, *Annals of Loch Cé*
AT	Stokes, 'The Annals of Tigernach'
AU	Hennessy and McCarty, *Annals of Ulster*
BB	*The Book of Ballymote* (facsimile edition)
BBCS	*Bulletin of the Board of Celtic Studies*
BF	Hennessy, *The Book of Fenagh*
BL	British Library, London
BSDC	RIA MS Book of Survey and Distribution, Co. Cork
BSDG	Mac Giolla Choille, *Book of Survey and Distribution, Co. Galway*
BSDM	Simington, *Book of Survey and Distribution, Co. Mayo*
BSDR	Simington, *Book of Survey and Distribution, Co. Roscommon*
BUPS	*Bulletin of the Ulster Placenames Society*
CCH	Tresham, *Rotulorum patentium et clausorum Cancellariae Hiberniae calendarium*
CDI	*Calendar of documents relating to Ireland*
CIH	Binchy, *Corpus Iuris Hibernici*
CIPM	*Calendar of inquisitions post mortem*
CIPRJ	*Calendar of Irish patent rolls of James I*
CJRI	*Calendar of the justiciary rolls of Ireland*
CLAJ	*County Louth Archaeological Journal*
CMCS	*Cambridge/Cambrian Medieval and Celtic Studies*
COD	*Calendar of Ormond deeds*
CPR	*Calendar of Papal registers and letters*
CS	Hennessy, *Chronicum Scotorum*
DIL	Royal Irish Academy, *Dictionary of the Irish language*
DKRI	Appendix, *Deputy Keepers reports, Ireland*
EHR	*English Historical Review*
Fiant. Eliz.,	*The Irish fiants of the Tudor sovereigns*, volumes ii and iii
FIA	Radnor, *Fragmentary Irish annals*

GO	Genealogical Office, Dublin
GT	Ó Raithbheartaigh, *Genealogical Tracts*, i
IHS	*Irish Historical Studies*
JCHAS	*Journal of the Cork Historical and Archaeological Society*
JGAHS	*Journal of the Galway Archaeological and Historical Society*
JKAHS	*Journal of the Kerry Archaeological and Historical Society*
Lec.	*The Book of Lecan* (facsimile edition)
LL	Best and O'Brien, *The Book of Leinster* (where page numbers as distinct from line numbers are given)
LPL	Archiepiscopal Library, Lambeth Palace, London
MIA	Ó hInnse, *Miscellaneous Irish Annals*
NAI	National Archives of Ireland, Dublin
NLI	National Library of Ireland, Dublin
NMAJ	*North Munster Antiquarian Journal*
OED	*Oxford English dictionary*
OSNB	Ordnance Survey Namebooks
PRC	MacCotter and Nicholls, *Pipe Roll of Cloyne: Rotulus Pipae Clonensis*
PRIA	*Proceedings of the Royal Irish Academy*
PRONI	Public Record Office of Northern Ireland, Belfast
RC 7/	National Archives, Record Commissioners Calendar of Plea Rolls, where * = volume no.
RC 8/*	National Archives, Record Commissioners Calendar of Memoranda Rolls, where * = volume no.
RIA	Royal Irish Academy, Dublin
SHR	*Scottish Historical Review*
TCD	Trinity College, Dublin, Library
TP	Carney, *Topographical Poems by Seaán Mór Ó Dubhagáin and Giolla na Naomh Ó hUidhrín*
TRIA	*Transactions of the Royal Irish Academy*
UM	*The Book of Uí Maine* (facsimile edition)
UJA	*Ulster Journal of Archaeology*
ZCP	*Zeitschrift für Celtische Philologie*

Acknowledgments

A very special word of thanks must go to three scholars who have played a significant rôle in the writing of this book. Firstly, the contribution of Professor Donnchadh Ó Corráin of University College Cork cannot be too highly acknowledged. This volume began life as a PhD thesis (NUI, 2006) which was researched under the supervision of Professor Ó Corráin. His profound knowledge of early Ireland – and further afield – was always made unstintingly available and served up in a sauce of wicked wit and genuine kindness, a most palatable mixture. Secondly, I wish to acknowledge the contribution of my good friend, Kenneth Nicholls of University College Cork, who has kindly made himself available to me as a mentor in the field of Irish Anglo-Norman studies over the years, a field in which he may well be the supreme authority. Important elements of the various methodological approaches adopted in this book originate with Kenneth, and it is no coincidence that he has the largest number of titles in the bibliography. Thirdly, I would like to acknowledge the contribution of Dr Marie-Therese Flanagan of The Queens University, Belfast. Following upon her rôle as external examiner for my thesis she kindly made a number of suggestions both for changes in presentation and for additional research which proved most helpful and stimulating.

A particularly challenging aspect of this work was the composition of my Atlas of the Cantreds of Ireland, and for assistance with this I wish to thank both Professor William Smyth of the Geography Department in UCC, and the department's cartographer, Michael J. Murphy. Another debt of gratitude is due to the staff of Special Collections, Boole Library, UCC, who met my constant requests for all sorts of material with unfailing courtesy. In this context a special word of thanks must go to Helen Moloney-Davis for assistances rendered 'beyond the call of duty'.

Others whose assistance must be acknowledged are Dr Catherine Swift of Mary Immaculate College, Limerick, Dr Diarmuid Ó Murchadha of the Locus project and Crosshaven, Dr Colmán Etchingham of NUI Maynooth, and Tomás O'Riordan, manager of the Multi-Text project, UCC. A special word of thanks goes to Dr Simon Taylor of the University of Glasgow, who kindly gave direct assistance as well as introducing me to several current authorities in the area of Scottish medieval and onomastic studies. I would also like to thank Martin Fanning and all of the staff at Four Courts Press.

Most importantly of all, I would like to give a very special acknowledgment for her support to my wife, Jo who, more than anyone else, knows the cost to family life of projects such as this (and the many others she has faithfully endured over the years). Without her loving support, and that of our children Niamh and Eoin, this book would not have been possible.

Baile an Chollaigh

Foreword

annálad and, is fír so,
cach rand rorannad hÉreo …
scél tellaig Temra, nach timm,
fis cech tríchat cét in hÉrind

(annals there, 'tis true,
every division into which Ireland has been divided …
the tale of the opulent household of Tara,
knowledge of every trícha cét in Ireland)

This, according to the medieval poet who described the activities at the Fair of Carman in valuable detail, was some of the business that occupied the time of the lords, lawyers and freemen assembled at the Fair. It is true to say that these matters have hardly concerned persons of this kind for some centuries in Ireland. And, with two notable exceptions, one can say much the same of the historians. The divisions of lordships and lands lie at the very heart of history – the descending order of *trícha cét*, *túath*, *baile biataig*, *tech*, and their levies, taxes and services that funded the early provincial kings and their late medieval successors. But the historiography is thin, uneven, and spatially vague.

Scholars talk airily about tribes and *túatha* but they may as well be counting them in baker's dozens. As one declares, 'there were probably no less that 150 kings in the country at any given date between the fifth and the twelfth centuries … Each king ruled over a tuath or tribal kingdom.'

Very odd: the tribe, as the anthropologists understand it, will have vanished with Neolithic agriculture; and the túath, now called theodum or the like, can be found all over the documents of the English administration in Ireland from twelfth-century charters to the seventeenth-century patent rolls of James I.

How, one may ask, do these divisions relate to the church's dioceses, rural deaneries, and parishes; to the cantreds, knights' fees, and manors of the later medieval English administration in Ireland? What are the elements of continuity, historical and prehistoric? Is there anything like this in Britain and continental Europe?

As a territorial unit, the *trícha cét* belongs to the eleventh and twelfth centuries – not to remote antiquity, archaic, immemorial or otherwise. By focussing on it and its successor, the 'cantred', Paul MacCotter brings order into the complex world of local denominations. He builds on the work of MacNeill and

Hogan but brings to the problem a much wider range of sources and greater methodological rigour. For the first time we have a well-founded mapping of the *trícha cét* and 'cantred', a detailed discussion of their historical relationship, and a convincing description of how they fit with other denominations, notably the changing *túath*. And the comparative aspect opens up interesting vistas, and poses even more interesting questions.

This is a major contribution to medieval Irish history and one that marks a new departure in Irish regional studies. It leaves us with more questions than answers, and that is what original historical writing ought to do.

Donnchadh Ó Corráin
12 October 2007

CHAPTER I

Overview

Cā līn thriūc[h]a i *n*-Ēirind āin?
Cā līn leith-triūc[h]a comlāin?
Cā līn baile? – monor nglē –
Cā līn congbas gach baile?

(How many *triúchas* in noble Ireland; how many complete half-*triúchas*; how many *bailes* – a bright toil – ; how many does each *baile* sustain?)

So wrote the anonymous poet, probably in the early twelfth century.[1] He goes on to attempt to answer these questions himself but, as we shall see, his efforts are not fully convincing.

In this study I attempt to answer his questions. A similar attempt was made seventy years ago by Professor James Hogan. Commenting on this, a modern authority on the period, Professor Donnchadh Ó Corráin, writes:

> It is a tribute to him [Hogan] – if not to the two generations of Irish historians who have succeeded him – that the *status quaestionis* is as he left it just over seventy years ago. A great deal more work must be done before we have any clearer idea of the history of the territorial divisions of Gaelic Ireland.[2]

While this book owes much to Hogan's work this is more in terms of inspiration than foundation, for Hogan's pioneering attempt falls short of the demands of today's historiography. He used fourteenth- and fifteenth-century material as a foundation for a reconstruction of twelfth-century boundaries, which is anachronistic, while his failure to use Anglo-Norman material proved a serious handicap.

More recently, Professor Francis John Byrne has written:

> Too many scholars have in the past been content to speak airily of tribes and kingdoms occupying certain areas without troubling to actually reconstruct a map or to visualize the situation of the ground.[3]

---

1 Pers. comm. Prof. Donnchadh Ó Corráin. See Appendix 1. **2** Ó Corráin, 'Hogan', 97. **3** Byrne, 'Tribes and tribalism', 157.

This work, in essence, tries to meet Byrne's requirements. In the course of various studies I had come to realize that many Anglo-Norman divisions seem to have been based on Gaelic precursors. If this is indeed true, it has large implications for the reconstruction of the socio-political spatial boundaries of Gaelic Ireland, for the material surviving from the colonial period is relatively full, and adequate for the task of reconstructing such boundaries. The first task, therefore, is to reconstruct the cantreds of Anglo-Norman Ireland. Once this is done a second survey is required, namely, to attempt to reconstruct the boundaries of the *trícha cét*s of pre-Invasion Ireland, a task for which the surviving evidence is not as full as for the earlier one, but for which, nonetheless, a significant quantity of evidence survives. In the course of doing a literature search for this work, it became clear to me that opinions varied wildly on the subject, for the simple reason that nobody since Hogan has made any attempt to do what Byrne indicated was required. Some held the opinion that cantreds were not found everywhere in Ireland, while others thought that the *trícha cét* was a mere imaginary product of twelfth-century antiquarianism.[4] My two surveys show that both cantred and *trícha cét* were both real and institutions of national distribution (see the gazetteer). The next question was what relationship each bore to the other. The answer is that the indigenous *trícha cét* was adopted without alteration and put to similar uses by the colonists, but under a new name. Another question I have attempted to answer is: Where did the *trícha cét* come from? Further investigations concern such entities as the rural deanery, *túath*, civil parish, manor, *baile* (*biataig*) and townland, and the relationship these entities bear to cantred and *trícha cét*. The largest section of this book comprises a gazetteer in which each cantred is described, whereupon an effort is then made to identify its corresponding *trícha cét*. Each such unit is given an identifying number prefaced by **C** (cantred) or **T** (*trícha cét*). Finally I have mapped the results of my cantred survey. This is what I have attempted to do; the reader will judge my efforts.

It is hoped that this work will be of value for a number of reasons. It represents the first attempt since 1929 to delineate precisely the local administrative structures and divisions of Anglo-Norman Ireland, with a corresponding value to scholars of that period. Given that I have shown that such divisions are merely those of pre-Invasion Gaelic Ireland as adopted by the colonists, this work possesses the significantly greater value of allowing the delineation of the local and regional boundaries and borders of pre-Invasion Gaelic Ireland, and thus should be of interest to historians and geographers of this earlier period. Indeed, my gazetteer can be said to represent, among other things, an effort to construct a compact political geography of pre-Invasion Gaelic Ireland. Furthermore, it attempts to give precise descriptions of superdenominations whose extent has hitherto often been only vaguely understood. Beyond toponomastic considerations, however, this work attempts to identify and describe the political and economic structures of eleventh- and twelfth-century Gaelic Ireland from a local

4 See p. 39.

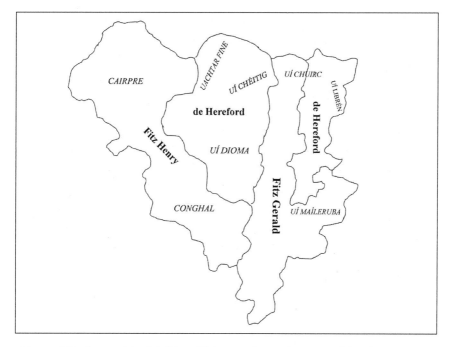

Map 1. The 'cantreds' of Offelan. This map shows the areas of the three original grants into which the kingdom of Uí Fáeláin was divided by Strongbow and/or Henry II. These were to Adam de Hereford, Maurice fitz Gerald and Meiler fitz Henry. Where the names and locations of irish *túatha* are known, these are given. Note how Uí Chuirc is divided between two grantees.

perspective – from the ground up, rather than from the top downwards, as it were. This is an area hitherto largely neglected by sociologists. The system which emerges from this study represents a schema unique in a European context, and adds yet another element of allure to the study of medieval Ireland. The effort to place the origins of this schema within its European context attempts to address this question for the first time in many years.

TERMINOLOGY AND GLOSSARY

Cantred

The early medieval cantred is the Gaelic *trícha cét* under another name. In Chapter 3 I adduce evidence in support of this. In England and Wales the Normans, in addition to adopting the pre-existing spatial units of local government, also adopted their terminology. In Ireland (and Scotland), the system was adopted but the terminology was not. The introduction of the term 'cantred', *cantredum* (sometimes feminine *cantreda*) in place of the Gaelic *trícha cét* is certainly attributable to the strong Cambro-Norman element in the original invasion forces. The term derives from the Welsh *cantref*, from *cant tref*, meaning one hundred *trefs* or vills.[5] The *cantref* was the principal division of local administration in Wales and, should there be any doubt on the matter, we have at least two examples from the 1180s of the use of the term *cantref* in Ireland. The *Song of Dermot and the Earl* speaks of the *cantref* of Athnurcher, while a later *inspeximus* of a deed of *c*.1180 speaks of the *canterefs* (sic) of the Barry family in Cork and Limerick.[6]

In the Welsh system the *cantref* was sub-divided into two or more *cymydau* (singular *cwmyd*), a term adopted by the Cambro-Normans as *commote* or *comodum*.[7] This term was introduced by the first invaders of Ireland along with 'cantred', and remained in use for several decades. It is used for the Irish *túath*, although eventually it was replaced by a Latinized form of the latter, *theodum*. Such usages of *commote* are recorded from Kildare (*c*.1173), Wicklow (1176), and Cork (*c*.1220). A reference to the *commote* of Odrone occurs before 1190; this was, in fact, a cantred rather than *commote*.[8] The term 'cantred' is a contemporary adaption of that of *cantref*, of uncertain etymology. The substitution of 'd' for 'f' may be the result of influence by the English term 'hundred'.[9]

There are two distinct usages of the term cantred by the colonists: (i) a replacement term for the Irish *trícha cét*; and (ii) a term meaning a distinct measure of land.

The first is by far the most general, and its use is in fact the main theme of this work. This matter is examined in detail in Chapter 3. The earliest examples of the second use of the term, namely, as a measure of land, can be seen in the sub-infeudation of the Irish kingdom of Uí Fáeláin (**T65**)[10] in what is now Co. Kildare. Here three grantees received equal measures of land called cantreds.[11] The *commote* of Ogurk was divided equally between two of these grantees. This is the Irish *túath* of Uí Chuirc (see Map 1). In this instance, therefore, two of these grants of cantreds ignored pre-existing spatial units. This shows that these three cantreds must have been the result of an arbitrary division of Uí Fáeláin made by the Lord of Leinster in favour of his three grantees. Further confirmation of this may be seen in the almost equal area of each of the three, averaging about 75,000 acres each. The fertile island of Anglesey in Wales was composed of three *cantrefi*, its total area being 176,630 acres (roughly 58,877 each). Allowing for the slightly less fertile overall nature of Uí Fáeláin, might we not here have the template for this colonial division, suggesting an idealized size for the Welsh *cantref* of around 60,000 acres?[12] An inquisition of *c*.1216 concerning the cantred of Kericuruhy (**C39**) makes the inter-

5 *Geiriadur Prifysgol Cymru: a dictionary of the Welsh language* (Cardiff, 1950–67), s.v. cantref. 6 Orpen, *Song of Dermot*, line 3138; Armagh Public Library MS KH II 24, f. 90; Davies, *Change in Wales*, 12. 7 *Change in Wales*, 20–2; *Geiriadur Prifysgol Cymru*, s.v. cwmyd; Latham, *Latin wordlist*, s.v. commotum. 8 COD, i, 29, 37; McNeill, *Alen's Register*, 17; Nicholls, 'Inquisitions of 1224', 111; Mills, *Gormanston*, 145, 193. 9 OED. The word cantred seems first to appear in the various works of Cambrensis. 10 Thoughout this book I use the reference style **T** to refer to the *trícha céts* and **C** to refer to the cantreds extended in the gazetteer. 11 See p. 175. 12 For the cantreds of Wales see Richards, *Welsh units*. Anglesey was the most fertile part of Wales and it will

esting comment that, when it was retained in the king's hand at the time of the infeudation of Desmond, it was not of full cantredal size (*et tamen perfectum cantredum non est*).[13] Kericuruhy comprised approximately 46,000 acres.

These are references to the cantred as an abstract measure of land. While many early references to fractions of cantreds occur, it is difficult to tell whether these relate to fractions of this abstract kind or to fractions of actual cantreds. In general, the evidence suggests that the latter is intended. However, there are some further unambiguous references to the cantred as a land measure. Muntyrmorghyth (**C21**) is described as two-thirds of a cantred in an early grant, the grantee being given one third of a neighbouring cantred to make up a full measure (*ad perficiendum ei unum cantredum*).[14] Nearby we have 'half a cantred in Fertyr & Clancowan' (**C17**). While such references usually have to do with one half of a full cantred, it is clear in this instance that this half-cantred did not have a corresponding half. Muntyrmorghyth contained around 61,000 acres, while Fertyr & Clancowan had around 77,000. Such acreages are of limited value for comparison in themselves, as they do not take into account land quality and productive capacity, something that medieval assessment systems certainly did. Fertyr & Clancowan by itself may simply have been a Gaelic *leth-trícha*. More than a half dozen of these occur in the sources, and the Gaelic term is translated as 'half-cantred'.[15] Unfortunately, none of these indigenous examples matches the dozen or so half-cantreds we find in the sources. This area requires at least passing notice, as the mention of 'complete half-tríchas' in the poem *Cā līn triūcha i nĒrind?* (Appendix 1, § 2) suggests that the *leth-trícha*, as distinct from full *trícha*, bore some kind of assessment function in the *trícha cét* system, whatever that might have been. In the case of some of the later half-cantreds we find possible evidence of linkage between both units, and it is possible that some, at least, of the half-cantreds originate in earlier *leth-tríchas*.[16] I cannot find any further certain instances of cantred used in the sense of a land measure – with one possible exception from 1279 – because virtually the whole of the remainder of such fractional references can be related, with varying degrees of certainty, to portions of full cantreds of varying sizes.

be noted that its *cantrefs* were among the smallest in area in all of Wales. This is what one would expect in a system which measured land not by area but by productive capacity. **13** Nicholls, 'Inquisitions of 1224', 111. **14** Idem, 'Charter of William de Burgh', 122. **15** GT, 191; Hogan, *Onomasticon*, s.v. leth-trícha. **16** The term 'half-cantred' occurs in a number of contexts. In two examples (**C31**, **C58**) it is used to describe discrete portions of cantreds made up of more than one section, while in another five examples (**C4**, **C18**, **C43**, **C50**, **C91**) it is used to describe cantredal moieties where a single cantred has been divided into two even infeudations. In these cases there is no indication of any linkage with earlier *leth-tríchas*. In another two certain (**C9**, **C62**) and one possible example (**C51**) we find cantreds divided into two halves where these halves each descend from what had been distinct local kingdoms, raising the possibility of some linkage with earlier *leth-tríchas*. In the case of the half-cantreds of Fertyr & Clancowan (**C17**), Omiled (**C89**) and Iffowyn (**C129**) there is no accompanying half, and the only explanations for these would appear to be that they correspond with what had been indigenously assessed as *leth-tríchas*. The reference cannot be to their size as they are all quite large cantreds.

The possible example from 1279 concerns the fourth part of a cantred in Sylmorne held by Henry de Rochfort. Earlier, Meiler de Rochfort was seized of a *theodum* in 'Selmoroni'. The cantred of Sylmolron (**C28**) had two constituent *theoda*, one of which was Síl Máelruainaid, now represented by the 25,000-acre parish of Kiltullagh. It may be, therefore, that this was being extended as a quarter-cantred in abstract measure as it certainly made up at least one half of the actual cantred here.[17] As to portional references to actual cantreds, a number can be found in the pipe roll of 1279 from Connacht.[18]

- Kerylochnarne, a fourth part of a cantred (elsewhere called a cantred), is later included as a *theodum*, one of four divisions in total, in the cantred of Sleoflow & the two Kerrys (**C26**) in 1333. Its exact extent is uncertain.[19]
- A fourth part of a cantred in Monterathy. This occurs as a *theodum* in 1333 within the cantred of Clantayg (**C10**), which was organized into one half-cantred and two *theoda*.
- Montyrmolynnan, Kenalethyn and Oloman occur as thirds of a cantred. The cantred of Muntermolinan (**C20**) as described in 1333 included all three territories.
- Half-cantred of Knockbeg. This appears to refer to Gnomore and Gnobeg, the western half of the cantred of Clanferwyll (**C9**). Many similar such examples of half-cantreds can be given where the other half is easily identifiable.[20]
- Elsewhere we find reference from 1205 to a third part of a cantred in Arclo (held of Theobald Walter).[21] Arclo appears to have been the southern part of the cantred of Arclo & Wykinglo (**C62**) and we should probably understand this reference in light of Walter's retention of the *commote* of Arclo itself in his own hand, an area that would thus have made up the remaining one-sixth to complete the half. From the same area references to the half-cantred of Offynglas are to be understood as an *alias* for the half-cantred of Arclo. The portional reference to the two and a half cantreds of Ardee (**C160**) makes no sense and must be in error.

The above examples are early, and it is clear that the usage of cantred as an abstract measure of land ceased early. Most tellingly, the three cantreds into which the Irish kingdom of Uí Fáeláin was divided did not last: by the 1290s all three formed the single cantred of Offelan (**C65**).

Medieval clerks were not always precise and occasionally one finds the term 'cantred' used for what were clearly *theoda* – smaller denominations, for which see below. Such examples are relatively rare but one must be careful to test the context of each reference in order to be sure that one is indeed dealing with genuine cantreds. Often such mislabelling was systemic, as, for example, in a list of 'cantreds' for Co. Kilkenny from 1375, where the term was used in an impre-

---

17 DKRI 36, p. 63. **18** Ibid. **19** NLI MS 760, p. 214. **20** Cf. Brooks, *Knights' fees*, 61; Nicholls, 'Charter of William de Burgh', 115–16. **21** COD, i, 43.

cise sense and included, in addition to four genuine cantreds, nine manors. This is clear from a study of the evidence. The *theodum* of Kerylochnarn in Connacht is once described as a cantred, once as one-fourth part of a cantred, and twice as a *theodum*.[22] Claneth in Limerick comprised one of the four constituent *theoda* of the cantred of Carbry Othrath (**C77**) but is described as a cantred in its own right in 1297.[23] Carbry and Tothemoy are described as cantreds in 1297, but the very same pipe roll makes it clear that they were in fact parts of the cantred of Offelan (**C65**). The first part of the name Tothemoy is derived from *túath*. A list of 1375 from Limerick describes what had hitherto been the cantred of Adare & Croom (**C77**) as the cantreds of Adare and Croom.

The colonial administration used the cantred in the administration of justice, tax collection and as a unit of paramilitary[24] levy in a way similar to that of the hundred in England. I have published on these topics elsewhere.[25]

Theodum

The colonists used the terminology 'cantred' and *commote* to refer to what had been the Irish *trícha cét* and *túath*. While *trícha cét* was never adopted as a term by the colonists, *túath*, in the forms *theodum, theudum, teod, theode, tweuth, teodh, toyth, toth, tothe* etc., soon replaced *commote*.[26] Just as in the Irish system where several *túatha* together comprised a *trícha cét*, so in the early colonial system several *theoda* together comprised a cantred. It would seem that early in the fully colonized areas – apart from those in Connacht – the *theodum* was largely replaced by, or renamed, the manor. Early evidence for the conversion of *theoda* into manors of identical size comes from Tipperary and Kilkenny, while from Limerick comes evidence that manors were based on half-*theoda*. Yet in several other regions there appears to have been little relationship between *theodum* and manor.[27] The exact relationship between the *theodum* and the later manor is unclear and needs further work. While in general the *theodum* disappears from colonial documentation as the thirteenth century progresses, in Connacht the term continued in common use into the fourteenth century while isolated examples continue to occur in all provinces. The *túath* can be found disguised under the form *teod* in the Meic Carthaig kingdom of Desmond in 1365, where it occurs several times, while the term continued in common usage into the sixteenth century in several uncolonized or reconquered areas, notably Thomond, Tír Conaill and the Glens of Antrim, but is also known from Anglo-Norman areas (as for example in Connello, Co. Limerick).[28] The *theodum* had little significance as a unit of spatial organization although in some cases it may have

22 CDI, iv, 258, and see fn. 19. **23** CJRI, ii, 449. **24** Paramilitary in the sense that each cantredal chief serjeant or keeper of the peace had the power to raise a posse composed of the free tenants from within his cantred at times of military crisis, once hue and cry was raised. See Frame, 'Commissions of the Peace', passim. **25** 'Functions of the cantred', passim. **26** The *theodum* is ubiquitous in colonial records of the thirteenth century. **27** See p. 48. **28** Armagh Public Library MS KH II 46, f. 195; Hogan, 'The tricha cét', 229, 232; Reeves, *Ecclesiastical antiquities*, 344–6; *Cal state papers Irleand, 1606–8*, p. 340.

formed the basis of the knights' fee or socage fee. The colonial units of civil administration in descending rank were: county – cantred – vill; neither the *theodum* nor the ordinary manor had any role.

Trícha cét

This was a spatial unit of royal tenure, taxation, local government, and military levy. In most cases it corresponded to the local kingdom (that is, as ruled by a petty king: see below) but this correspondence was not absolute. In a fairly small minority of *trícha*s evidence of leadership structure is lacking, a few others were ruled by *taísig* (see below), while a couple were ruled by governors (*airríg*) appointed by superior kings. The *trícha cét* system was national and probably became established during the eleventh century as a refinement of a pre-existing system. Certainly, the earliest evidence for the existence of this system dates to the eleventh century. Each *trícha cét* contained a number of *bailte* (see below), notionally thirty. Each *trícha* was also composed of a lesser number of larger units, the (late-)*túath* (see below). The units of fiscal relevance were the *trícha cét* and the *baile* (*biataig*). While *bailte* were grouped into late-*túatha*, such *túatha* did not have fiscal relevance. The late-*túath* may have been the unit by which military levy was organized. Thus tax was paid by each *baile* (*biataig*) but military service may have been levied from each *túath*. The meaning of the term *trícha cét* remains obscure. Two possibilities suggest themselves. The more likely arises from the probability that *cét* was a synonym for *baile* (*biataig*) and may thus refer to a numerical figure of tax assessment of some kind. The second possibility is that *cét* here has the meaning of 'troops' and the term *trícha cét* thus refers to a notional military levy of each unit or levy basis.[29]

Local kingdom (and regional and semi-provincial kingdoms)

In my new classification of eleventh- and twelfth-century Irish society, the local kingdom was the basic level of kingship, a kingdom ruled by a king who ruled no other kings and whose immediate subjects were *taísig túaithe* (see below). It was the lowest level in a hierarchy of kingdoms. Its kings were far from being totally independent and often, in reality, must have been mere lords under superior kings, to whom they owed allegiance and service. Above it were respectively: regional kingdoms (often with a mirroring diocese), (semi-) provincial kingdoms, the high-kingship.[30]

Túath

The *túath* has been described as 'a lordship, a unit of jurisdiction, a taxable denomination, a parish, a kingdom, people, community, country people, the laity as distinct from the clergy'.[31] The term could be applied to the first three levels on the lordship/kingship scale, namely late-*túath*, local kingdom, regional kingdom.[32] In essence, therefore, it meant a political community. By the

29 See pp 24, 93–4, 106.   **30** See p. 46.   **31** Ó Corráin, *Ireland before the Normans*.   **32** See pp 88–9.

twelfth century the term had largely become confined to the lowest level on the scale given above, that of late-*túath*.

Late-túath

I have coined this phrase to differentiate the twelfth-century *túath* from the broader range of meanings of the term as found at an earlier period. The late-*túath* was the smallest political community, the local community. It was the immediate sub-unit of the *trícha cét* and was ruled by the *taísech túaithe* (see below). It represents the lowest unit of authority and, perhaps, military levy. It was composed of a number of *bailte* (see below).[33]

Taísech túaithe

The *taísech túaithe* seems to have been the hereditary leader of an aristocratic *cenél*, sometimes of royal blood, whose jurisdiction coincided with that of his *túath*. He was thus the leader of the local community and military levy, presumably having the additional delegated functions of tribute collection and law enforcement. *Taísech túaithe* was a formal title in twelfth-century Ireland.[34]

Baile (biataig)

In Ulster and Bréifne the term used is *baile biataig*, while in Connacht, Munster and Mide it is simple *baile*. *AFM* (1176) does give one example of the usage *baile biataig* in Connacht, but we cannot be sure of what its exemplar read. Throughout this work, both terms refer to the same unit. The *baile biataig* has been described as 'the taxable unit of landholding, the economically independent estate of twelfth-century Ireland, the fundamental property unit of the lineage group, the mechanism by which property was allocated among the families of the sept'.[35] Such estates ranged in size from 700 to 7,000 acres or so. First attested during the eleventh century, the *baile biataig* appears to have had a national distribution. The *baile biataig* remained in operation in Ulster and parts of Connacht into the sixteenth century, when the term ballybetagh was used to denote this unit.[36] In Ulster parish boundaries usually coincided with those of ballybetaghs, with the external boundaries of a group of ballybetaghs corresponding with those of the parish in which the group lay. In some instances, parishes appear to coincide with groups of kin-linked 'ballybetaghs'. This suggests that such ballybetagh boundaries are older than those of parishes. In Leinster and Munster it is clear that many parishes, especially the smaller ones, were erected upon the boundaries of earlier *bailte*. Most ballybetaghs were held by family heads as freeholders. In the early centuries of the system, these heads were styled *biatach*, 'food provider', hence *baile biataig*. Other ballybetaghs were held by hereditary officer families, or as lords' demesne or as mensal land.[37] The ballybetagh

---

33 See pp 88–90. **34** See pp 46–7. **35** McErlean, 'Irish townland system', 332. **36** For what follows see McErlean, 'Irish townland system', *passim*; Duffy, 'Territorial organization', 7–8, 19; idem, 'MacMahon lordship', 135–6. **37** Mensal land was land from which food for the lords'

was a fiscal unit paying a rent to the territorial lord. It had precisely the same rôle as the earlier *baile biataig*, including that of being the mechanism by which property was allocated among the families of the kindred. This allocation was achieved by periodic re-distribution of the sub-divisions of the ballybetagh among related families. These divisions were the four quarters which in turn were sub-divided into a total of sixteen lesser divisions which sometimes formed the basis for the later townland. Generally, the ballybetagh contained a mix of arable land, grazing and turbary in related proportions which enabled it to function as an economically independent estate. In sixteenth-century Ulster, and no doubt earlier throughout Ireland, the ballybetagh and its sub-units represented a systematic organization of land resources, based on a method of assessment of land value, which functioned within the tenurial and inheritance conditions of Gaelic society. Notionally, each *trícha cét* was composed of thirty *bailte*. Therefore it would seem that the *cét* of the title is probably a synonym for the *baile biataig*. The origin and meaning of the term *cét* is unclear.[38]

Cóicráith Chétach
The *cóicráith chétach* of the early Laws is literally 'five *ráiths* possessed of a hundred'. Here the *ráith* is generally understood as the ubiquitous ringfort or homestead. This term is to be understood in the sense of a group of five substantial farms held by a kinship group. More importantly, this is a single kinship unit whose property confers on it a particular legal status, that of free-kinship. It is the fundamental property unit of the lineage group and may well be the ancestor to the *baile biataig* above.[39]

Acre
The acre as we have it derives from the Anglo-Norman acre which, in turn, derives from an Anglo-Saxon measure of the amount of land that can be ploughed in a day. As the *acra* this term is also found in use in immediate pre-Invasion Ireland, and may have been an earlier loanword from Anglo-Saxon. However, Irish sources also use a second word for the same concept, *iúger*, defined as *lá air* 'a days' ploughing', and clearly derived from the Latin *iugerum* or acre.[40] The Anglo-Norman acre varied in size according to local usage. The determining factor was the length of the rod, which eventually came to be standardized at 16.5' in the statute acre. The standard 'Irish acre' of the seventeenth century had a 21' rod, giving acres about 1.6 times the statute acre. There were, however, other variants. The sixteenth-century acres in use in Dublin had a 24' rod, while those found in Cork had a 29' rod, giving acres of respectively 2.15 and 3.1 times the statute acre (approximately).[41] Other examples can be given. A 'rule of thumb' of long standing among Irish medievalists has been to estimate medieval acres at around 2.5 times the size of the statute acre.[42]

household was provided as its rent. **38** See pp 22, 93–4, 106. **39** See pp 104–8. **40** DIL, s. vv. acra (for additional evidence for the existence of a pre-Norman Irish acre see Flanagan, *Irish royal charters*, 284), iúger. **41** I am indebted to Kenneth Nicholls for these observations. **42** Otway-

Carucate
The carucate is the ploughland, usually defined as the area one full plough-team could plough in a season. It originated in Normandy, and was introduced to Ireland by the colonists. Local usage determined the number of acres it contained, and from 60 up to 180 or more can be found. It was originally a fiscal unit but in time came to have the meaning of a fixed area of land. The Irish exchequer followed the English in taking the carucate to comprise 120 acres.[43]

Vill
The term vill is another Norman import, deriving from the Roman *villa*, a rural estate. It is used in several senses, principally that of the basic unit of agricultural freeholding. It was also used in the sense of a town, an urban unit. This accounts for the translation of the standard colonial phrase *villa[ta]m terrae* as townland.[44] The vill is the ancestor to the present townland.

Knights' fee
The knights' fee has its roots in the Anglo-Norman system of military tenure. In time it came to represent a fixed area or measure of land, but, as with the carucate, this varied from lordship to lordship. The number of carucates in a knights' fee lay in the range eight to thirty.[45]

Feudalism and Tribalism
There is a current movement away from using the term 'feudal' among medieval historians. I do not yet find the proposed alternatives satisfactory and will retain the traditional usages throughout this book as these are unambiguous and will be clearly understood in the context. The feudal system as introduced to Ireland by the Anglo-Normans had its immediate origins in the administrative and tenurial practices of Norman England and its ultimate origins in the fusion of Roman and Germanic cultures in the Frankish empire. Precise definitions of the Irish manor and feudal barony must await another day.

I will, however, avoid use of the term 'tribe', a usage surely more worthy of reprobation than that of feudalism. There were no tribes in Ireland – in the principal sense of the word – during the period studied in this volume.

Ruthven, *History of med. Ire.*, 109n. **43** Lennard, 'Fiscal carucate', passim; PRC, 25; DKRI 39, p. 43; McNeill, *Alen's Register*, 3. **44** PRC, 4, 84; MacNiocaill, *Red Book of Kildare*, 56. **45** Otway-Ruthven, 'Knight service', passim; PRC, 7.

CHAPTER 2

Methodology of cantred and
trícha cét reconstruction

In general the medieval Irish cantred is now long lost. Even where it was remembered little account was taken of its boundaries when the 'New English' con-
querors established their civil administration during the late sixteenth century.
This system involved the creation of administrative baronies with powers of local
government and local taxation. These were usually modelled on existing local
lordships, which might or might not preserve the shape of earlier cantreds.
Sometimes, indeed, the English seem to have followed the deliberate policy of
ignoring the old cantred names, as in the shiring of Connacht in the early 1570s.[1]
In some cases, the new administrative baronies agreed closely with earlier
cantredal boundaries, as, for example, in Co. Louth, but this was not the result
of any deliberate policy. This system of counties with their sub-divisions of
administrative baronies was further altered significantly in the reforms of the
early nineteenth century, culminating in those of 1836–7. In these reforms many
barony boundaries were altered significantly, while others were sub-divided into
north and south, east and west, upper and lower, divisions which thus have no
historical meaning.[2] The local government reforms of 1898 abolished any remaining local administrative functions retained by the baronies, rendering them redundant historical curiosities. In this book I will refer to these as 'modern baronies'
(in the sense that, cartographically, they remain important spatial units of reference). These are the strata below which are buried our ancient cantreds.

METHODOLOGY FOR CANTRED RECONSTRUCTION

I discuss here the nature and relevance of the various sources from which I
attempt to reconstruct the medieval cantreds of Ireland. (The cantred existed
from *c.*1170 until abolished as an administrative unit in the early fifteenth century.)[3] It should be remembered that, with a few exceptions, no actual extents

---

[1] PRO London SP/63/45/35.1; Falkiner, 'The counties of Ireland', 181–94. [2] Baronies began
to be sub-divided in the last decade of the eighteenth century but the major reforms were those
of 6 and 7 William IV, where acts of parliament gave baronial grand juries the power to re-organ-
ize 'inconveniently large' baronies for fiscal purposes. Detailed accounts of these changes will be
found in the *Report of the Commissioners for the Census of Ireland of 1841* (Dublin, 1843) at the end
of the general table for each county. See also p. vi. [3] MacCotter, 'Functions of the cantred', passim.

of the cantreds themselves survive, and it is accordingly necessary to reconstruct them indirectly from other sources. The sources themselves are eclectic and varied. This is due to the destruction of almost the entire volume of original source material from the Anglo-Norman period by the 'Irregulars' in 1922 in their wanton destruction of the Four Courts. Some calendaring had been published by then, but this represented an insignificant quantity of the total of the early Irish state papers. Sadly, the age of calendaring has largely passed, and it is to be regretted that so little of the not-inconsiderable quantity of calendared manuscripts which remain has been published. As most of the original material is lost, the scholar must content herself with the pursuit of the various unpublished calendar materials and other copies of the originals – not always accurately transcribed, made over a period of three centuries by various antiquarians and now scattered throughout various repositories in Ireland and Britain. One scholar particularly worthy of note in this context is Sir William Betham, who, in the early nineteenth century, made extensive notes from various genre of state papers now largely destroyed. The study of the location and provenance of such material is a discipline in itself, and outside of the scope of the present study.

Manorial extents

The manor is probably best defined as an estate which carries jurisdictional powers. Manors were organized into hierarchies. Capital manors (also styled 'chief manors' and 'feudal baronies') were manors with lesser manors appendant. These in turn sometimes had sub-manors appendant to them. For the purposes of cantredal reconstruction these capital manors concern us principally. Throughout much of medieval colonial Ireland, the pattern of primary infeudation was that the magnates or tenants-in-chief granted their dependent lords cantred- or half-cantred-sized fiefs. In essence this means that these capital manors contained all the lands in their cantreds or half-cantreds apart from the lands of the church. Often the location of the *caput* of these manors metonymically gave rise to an alternative name for the cantred. Where extents of such manors survive, these can be used to reconstruct the original area of the cantred or half-cantred, excluding the church-lands. In Ireland church-lands were widely distributed in fragmented parcels of varying sizes ranging from a few dozen acres up to several thousand acres. All church or cross-lands in each cantred were constituted into a distinct manor under episcopal authority.[4] It is clear from the evidence that for purposes of civil law and taxation these church manors were not treated separately but as an integral part of the cantred in which they lay.[5]

The survival of manorial extents is a matter of historical accident. A number of important collections have been published, especially those taken upon the death of the Brown Earl of Ulster in 1333,[6] and those included among the muniments of the Kildare and Ormond families as published in *The Red Book of the Earls of Kildare*, and *The Red Book of Ormond*. Other important collections

4 PRC, passim. 5 CJRI, i, 168. 6 See Knox, 'Connacht', and Orpen, 'Ulster'.

are that of the late thirteenth-century Shanid Geraldines, in volumes iii and iv of the *Calendar of Documents relating to Ireland*, and the Preston muniments in the *Calendar of the Gormanston Register*. Other individual extents have been published in various sources, while some significant material remains unpublished.

Ruridecanal extents

The rural deanery is an ecclesiastical administrative division comprising a group of parishes under the supervision of the rural dean or archpriest.[7] In a majority of cases, rural deaneries will be found to have an exact or approximate correspondence to cantreds – in many cases, even to bearing the same names. In a majority of dioceses it is clear that when constituted the ruridecanal spatial structure followed that of the pre-existing cantredal structure.[8] Appendix 4 contains summary results of a detailed study of the spatial and toponomastic relationship between rural deaneries and cantreds.

Patterns of monastic impropriation

A marked feature of the colony was the conferring by lords of the ecclesiastical tithes and rights of advowson of their lands on individuals or religious corporations as they saw fit. This activity was largely confined to the early decades of the settlement, after which most such benefices had been conferred. This, of course, has major implications for cantredal reconstruction. It was common for lords to grant the entire ecclesiastical revenue of their lordship to a single religious house, often founded by the donor and located within his lordship. Therefore – particularly in Munster and Leinster and to a lesser extent in Connacht – where we find a monastic house holding all the rectories in lay fee in a particular district, this can serve as a good indicator of the extent of early lordship and thus of cantredal extent when taken in conjunction with other indicators.

Only a few entire collections of monastic charters survive, especially those of St Mary's and St Thomas' abbeys, Dublin; Duiske and Kells in Kilkenny, and Tristernagh in Westmeath. Fragmentary charter references and partial transcripts survive, often unpublished, made by seventeenth-century antiquarians such as Sir James Ware. In the majority of cases, however, it is necessary to rely on sixteenth- and seventeenth-century material relating to the descent of such impropriations. This can largely be found in the published *Irish Fiants of the Tudor Sovereigns*.

Rurirectoral extents

The rural rectory was the spatial area over which a single rector had jurisdiction. Its boundaries were often independent of those of parishes. In origin the rural rectory would seem to represent, as Nicholls[9] has argued, an intermediate stage in parochial development where, in areas not invested by the invaders, var-

7 Thompson, 'Diocesan organization in the Middle Ages', 167–94.   8 MacCotter, 'Irish rural deaneries', forthcoming.   9 Nicholls, 'Rectory, vicarage and parish', passim.

ious Gaelic denominations (*túatha, leth-trícha cét* and full *trícha cét*) were constituted into rural rectories. That is, in areas not settled and thus fully emparished,
colonial lords granted the ecclesiastical benefices of pre-existing Irish civil divisions to monastic corporations. In most cases such rectories retained the names
of the territories they were based upon. Therefore rural rectories preserve the
spatial extent of earlier Gaelic super-denominations. Several bear the same name
as cantreds and can be shown to have been coterminous with cantreds. Many
rural rectories have been listed by Nicholls.[10] Records of rural rectories are found
largely in the *Calendar of Papal Registers* and the early Papal Taxations (see *CDI*
iv). Some survived as distinct tenures into the nineteenth century, enabling their
extents to be recorded in the Tithe Applotment Books (now held in the National
Library). These record the ownership of all ecclesiastical tithes held by the
Established Church on a townland basis and largely date from the period
1825–35. These enable the spatial extent of the rural rectories so recorded to be
described in detail. Rural rectories were mostly confined to Connacht and
Thomond with a few outliers in Tír Briúin and Uriel.

Justice
Some records survive of colonial court proceedings (of general eyre) where pleas
were heard before juries selected by cantred. It follows, therefore, that many of
the place-names occurring in these pleadings may relate to the cantred from
which the jury is drawn. It is clear, upon examination, that not all place-names
so recorded can have been located in the relevant cantred, and it would seem
that the place of residence of the accused rather than the location of the crime
was sometimes the determining factor. Again, a defendant may be accused of
crimes committed in several places not always within the same cantred.
Furthermore, an examination of these records indicates that the courts did not
adhere rigidly to the cantredal linkage between jury and criminal, and a significant number of such records yield no understandable pattern. Uncritical use of
this source may lead to serious error (see page 170). Pleadings with cantredal
juries relating to the medieval counties of Kildare, Tipperary, Limerick and Cork
survive.[11] These can be of use for cantredal area when read critically and taken
in conjunction with other sources.

Other court records survive which contain much of interest pertaining to several facets of the present study. These can contain manorial extents, pleadings relating to particular lands and their lords, and references to cantreds and their officers.
These can largely be divided into the records of the common and justiciars bench-
es. The former are – inexplicably – entirely unpublished and can be found among
the Record Commissioners' calendars of plea and memoranda rolls in NAI. Much
of the justiciary roll material is pubished in three volumes, and enough material for
another volume remains – again inexplicably – unpublished in NAI.

10 Ibid., Appendix A. 11 CJRI, i, 167–208; NAI MS Cal. roll justices itinerant 33–34 Edward I
(shelf no. 2/448/3); RC 7/2, 261–78; RC 7/8, passim.

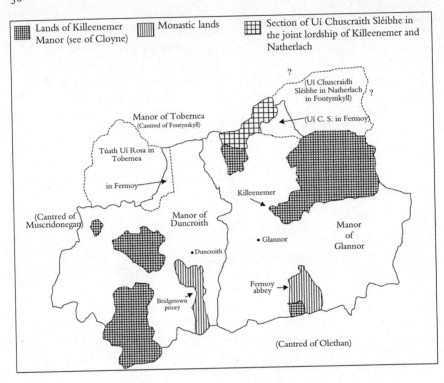

Lands of Killeenemer Manor (see of Cloyne)   Monastic lands   Section of Uí Chuscraith Sléibhe in the joint lordship of Killeenemer and Natherlach

?
(Uí Chuscraidh Sléibhe in Natherlach in Fontymkyll) ?

Manor of Tobernea
(Cantred of Fontymkyll)

(Uí C. S. in Fermoy)

Túath Uí Rosa in Tobernea

in Fermoy

Killeenemer

(Cantred of Muscridonegan)

Manor of Duncroith

Manor of Glannor

• Glannor

• Duncroith

Fermoy abbey

Bridgetown priory

(Cantred of Olethan)

Map 2. The cantred of Fermoy.

Cantredal extents

Undoubtedly, the Anglo-Norman administration kept written record of the extent of its cantreds, both for the purpose of taxation, where the basic unit of assessment was the carucate or ploughland consisting of 120 medieval acres of arable, and for amercement. Taxation was levied by carucate (hence the term *carucage* for such taxation) and lists of carucates within each cantred were maintained for this purpose. Amercements levied on entire cantreds were raised not by carucate but by vill, and the vill also acted as the smallest area upon which communal amercements could be levied.[12] The vill was the colonial rural townland, but, confusingly, could also mean an urban town. It is certainly the ancestor to our modern townland.[13] A number of cantreds in Co. Cork appear to have been subject to amercement levied on all of their vills in 1301.[14] No further examples of cantreds described by vill appear to have survived.

To demonstrate my methodology I treat fully of three reconstructions.

12 MacCotter, 'Functions of the cantred', 318, 320.   **13** See my forthcoming 'Townland origins in Munster'.   **14** See fn. 12 above.

EXAMPLE ONE: FERMOY (C32)

Our main source is the extent of the cantred contained in a plea roll recording the proceedings of the justices in eyre in Cork, in 1301 (hereafter the '1301 List'), when Fermoy was among the cantreds listed by vill (each vill being amerced). The gaps in this source caused by lost toponyms can be filled in with accuracy from the various records of the three superior manors of the cantred – the secular manors of Glannor (Glanworth) and Duncroith (Castletownroche), and the episcopal manor of Kyllenon (Killeenemer). The 1301 List for this cantred has been published with identifications by Ó Buachalla.[15] This example is illustrated in Map 2.

The manor of Glanworth
The history of the lordship of the cantred of Fermoy is complex and has been treated of elsewhere.[16] It is certain that the initial sub-infeudation here involved a division of the cantred into eastern and western moieties, with a chief manor in each. It is probable that the capital manor of the cantred was Glannor (Glanworth), while the manor of Duncroith was held of this manor. Extensive litigation, largely datable to the period 1280–1301, has left us an extensive list of lands held of the manor of Glannor.[17] These show it to have contained lands in the parishes of Glanworth, Kilcrumper, Macroney, Clondulane, Ballyhooly, Leitrim, Killathy, Kilworth and Litter. Early seventeenth-century sources,[18] listing chief-rents payable to the manor of Glanworth, add, besides places included in the above list, lands in the parishes of Marshalstown, Kilgullane, Carrigdownane and Ballylough.

Confirmation of this extent may be found in a study of the pattern of sub-infeudation in thirteenth-century eastern Fermoy, which echoes and, to some extent, supplements the above. In this connection, family land-ownership and family associations are pivotal. Glannor was originally a Caunteton possession, and branches of the family are found in possession of the manors of Athoul (Ballyhooly), Killathy, Litter, Ballyderown, Leitrim, Monuvanne (more or less

---

15 *Dinnseanchas* 2/2 (1966), 39–44. While most of his identifications are sound there are some obvious errors and further identifications may be made. The identifications of Gragurthyn, Thomaston, Mayghelesmenor and Rothan are unsound, fanciful or otherwise erroneous. The three vills associated with various Bekets should more likely be read in favour of Derryvillane and Kildorrery, the stronghold of the family in Fermoy (PRC, 246–7). Silvestreston is the Ballyhelester of BSDC, the present Ballyellis, Wallstown Parish. As to 'the vill of Michael Magnel', there are extensive references in the surviving period plea rolls to show that the Magnel manor here was located at Ballynahalisk (RC 7/9, 97; NAI unpublished Calendar of Justiciary Rolls, Pipe Roll no. 119, 39). Pembrokyston is now Ballynabrock, Brigown parish (JCHAS 97 (1992), 82). As to the vill of Milo le Walys, a pleading of the same year as the List associates this proprietor with Balymalmor, now Coolnanave in Brigown (RC 7/8, 369). 16 MacCotter, 'Sub-infeudation', ii, 89–94. 17 RC 7/4, 129; 7/5, 15, 169, 393; 7/6, 383; 7/7, 306; 7/8, 293, 391, 395, 402, 430, 442, 446–8, 451, 471; 7/9, 24, 38, 58, 77, 83, 133; CJRI, i, 353; CJRI, iii, 159–62. 18 CIPRJ, 209; RIA MSS Cork Ordnance Survey Inqs., i, 223.

the parish of Kilgullane), Carrigdownane and extensive lands in Glanworth parish. The de Sumery family possessed lands at Ballindangan – this family being known associates of the Cauntetons in Leinster. The manor of Marshalstown and the manor of Ballytandony (Ballyhindon) can also be linked to Glannor through the association of their Marshal and Talbot proprietors with the Cauntetons of Glannor.[19] This leaves only the Beket (which later became Pigott) manors of Derryvillane and Kildorrery unaccounted for, and, while I have been unable to uncover any reference linking these fees with Glannor, the association between Raymond le Gros – undoubtedly first lord of Glannor – and the Beket ancestor is most suggestive of the existence of such a link.[20] In any case, Derryvillane and Kildorrery occur in the 1301 List.

The manor of Duncroith

Alexander fitz Hugh built a stone castle here, around which his demesne lands were located. These are now the parish of Castletownroche. To the south lay the priory of Bridgetown, founded by fitz Hugh. Adjacent to the east is the parish of Kilcummer, also held by fitz Hugh.[21] The manors of Caherduggan, Mallow, Monanimy, Ballygriggin (that is, western Wallstown parish), Crogh/Doneraile (in southern Doneraile parish) and Dungleddy (in eastern Doneraile parish) were appendant to Duncroith, while there is indirect evidence to show that the manors of Carrigleamleary and Silvesterston (now Ballyellis: the lands in question lay in eastern Wallstown parish) were similarly held.[22] The possession of the manor of Shanaghgowan (probably commensurate with the parish of Templeroan) by a Roche family from an early period is suggestive of a similar tenure. The participation on the Roche side by the Magnel lords of the manor of Athliskmolag (Ballynahalisk) in the Roche/Caunteton war of 1315–17, again suggests that Athliskmolag was held of Duncroith. This leaves only Farahy unaccounted for, and this was certainly held 'of the manor of Duncroith *alias* Castletownroche' in the early seventeenth century.[23]

The manor of Kyllenon

This episcopal manor is described in detail in the *Pipe Roll of Cloyne*.[24] In this document it is noticeable that, without exception, all episcopal lands in each cantred are assigned to a single manor within that cantred. Kyllenon was the manor whose members lay in the cantred of Fermoy.

   To these three manors should be added the lands of the priory of Bridgetown and the abbey of Fermoy to give the full extent of the cantred. The area so described agrees precisely with that of the cantred of Fermoy as revealed in the 1301 List.

   In summary, then, all of the above sources agree in describing the cantred

19 PRC, 173, 186–7, 190. **20** MacCotter, 'The Carews of Cork' (thesis), 12. **21** MacCotter, 'Sub-infeudation', ii, 89. **22** RC 7/2, 250, 327; 7/3, 24, 170, 367, 373; 7/4, 4, 221; 7/6, 223; 7/8, 372, 412, 490; 7/9, 103; 7/13 (2 Edward II), 11; 8/19, 456; COD, iii, 34. **23** RC 7/10, 222; RIA MSS Cork Ordnance Survey Inqs. iii, 254. **24** PRC, 22–8, 104–10.

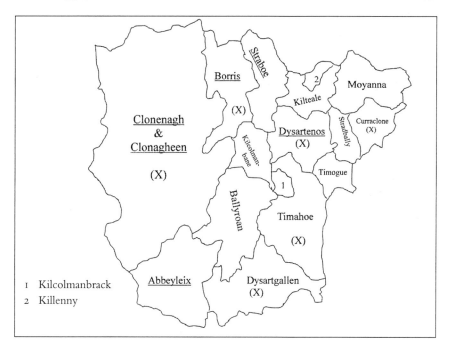

Map 3. The cantred of Leys. The area shown represents the reconstructed cantred of Leys. Parishes underlined contained lands known from direct evidence to have lain in the cantred. (X) indicates a parish impropriate in the priory of Great Connell. All parishes shown lay in the rural deanery of Leys.

of Fermoy as containing all of the modern barony of Fermoy excluding the portions of the parishes of Imphrick, Ardskeagh, and Ballyhay in the modern barony, and excluding the western and northern half of Doneraile parish. This cantred also contained all of the modern barony of Condons & Clangibbons apart from the parishes of Castlelyons and Knockmourne. The small portion of Leitrim parish in modern Co. Waterford was also in this cantred.

EXAMPLE TWO: LEYS (C63)

This cantred is parent to its namesake, Co. Leix, of which it forms the core. While this cantred was granted as a single fee to Meiler fitz Henry, in the 1170s, it escheated to the lords of Leinster when he renounced the world for the monastic life, and so no extent of its capital manor survives. The cantred can, however, be reconstructed from a variety of sources. This example is illustrated in Map 3.

The various feodaries of the Marshal heirs to Leinster gloss the fees of le Sydan, Ofithely and Dunsalach as lying in Leys. Dunsalach clearly lay on the south-western borders of the cantred but cannot be further identified. Ofithely

Map 4. The cantred of Omany (and rural deanery of Aughrim/Sogaun). The
area shown represents the reconstructed cantred of Omany. Parishes
underlined are those with lands explicitly known to have lain in the cantred.
(S) indicates those parishes which also lay in the rural rectory of Sogaun. (C)
indicates those parishes which also lay in the rural rectory of Clontuskert.
As cantred and rural deanery agree the area shown is also that of the deanery
of Aughrim. The cross lands of the diocese of Clonfert, dispersed in small
parcels throughout the cantred, are not shown.

lay in the parish of Clonenagh & Clonagheen.[25] Le Sydan is not, as Otway-
Ruthven thought (and this was partly responsible for misleading her about the
true shape of this cantred) one of the two townlands of Sheean in Co. Kildare
but is rather the medieval fee with corresponding parish, Sythan, the present
Shaen in Straboe parish, Co. Leix.[26] The parish of Abbeyleix (= 'the abbey of
Leys') must also have lain in this cantred as must that of Borris, whose derivation, *Buirgéis*, indicates that it was the borough (and parish) known to the
colonists as 'the new town of Leys'. The *caput* of Leys was at Dunamase. Finally
we should note the pattern of impropriation here. Meiler fitz Henry appears to
have granted the benefices of his land of Leys to his foundation, the priory of
Connell. Later, Connell is found to hold the impropriate rectories of Borris,
Kilteale, Stradbally (Nohoval), Curraclone, Kilcolmanbane, Dysartenos, Fossy

---

25 Otway-Ruthven, 'Fees in Kildare, Leix and Offaly', 176–7. **26** Fiant Eliz., 559, 1247.

(Timahoe), Clonenagh & Clonagheen, Straboe, Moyanna, and Dysartgallen.[27]
All of the above parishes lay in the rural deanery of Leys, which adds the parishes of Ballyroan, Killenny, Kilcolmanbrack, and Timogue to complete the extent
of the cantred.

The pattern of impropriation here represents a ghost image of the earlier
capital manor (of Leys), which it can be used to reconstruct, as fitz Henry's grant
to Connell would almost certainly have included the benefices of all the lands of
his capital manor. The extra parishes listed in the rural deanery, over and above
those likely to have been granted to Connell by fitz Henry, very probably indicate
cross-lands, the lands of the church. These would, of course, have lain within
the cantred for purposes of civil administration. This example illustrates the
importance of the rural deanery for purposes of cantredal reconstruction.

EXAMPLE THREE: OMANY (C113)

Colonial clerks use 'Omany' both to describe the specific cantred of Omany
and, in a more general sense, to describe lands in the area of what had been the
Irish regional kingdom of Uí Maine, so care is needed here. Lands which I shall
show to have lain in the cantreds of Moyhee (**C115**), Tyrmany (**C114**) and even
Sylanwath (**C27**) are stated to have lain in Omany.[28] We know from the few
certain records concerning this cantred that its court was at Aughrim, Co. Galway
(in 1323 'Athtrim Omany') and that it also included Clontuskert and Clonkeen
(both places which also gave their names to parishes).[29] As the deanery of
Aughrim *alias* Sogain in the diocese of Clonfert contained (*inter alia*) the three
parishes of Aughrim, Clontuskert and Clonkeen, this deanery immediately suggests itself as the ecclesiastical parallel to the cantred. This deanery contained, in
addition to the parishes mentioned above, those of Killoran, Kilgerril,
Ballymacaward, Kilconnell, Killalaghten, Fohanagh and Kilcloony.[30] The area
of the rural deanery of Aughrim is also exactly that of the combined area of the
rural rectories of Sogaun and Clontuskert.[31] Here these rural rectories, although
later found in monastic possession, must originally have represented tenures of
the colonial lords of the cantred. Such rectories have a completely different origin to the rural deaneries. The only possible explanation for the fact that both
deanery and rectory coincide exactly in area is that both were based on the same
template, which in this case can only be that of the cantred of Omany. As noted
above, all three places shown to have lain in this cantred were within the area
of the identical deanery and rectory. This example is illustrated in Map 4.

---

27 Ibid., no. 1216; 1622 Visitation in TCD MS 2158.   **28** COD, i, 97–8, 172; RC 7/7, 15, 150;
and cf. DKRI 37, p. 37.   **29** Harris, *Hibernica*, 69–70; COD, i, 99, 161, 172; Knox, 'Connacht',
ii, 285.   **30** CDI, v, 222 (where the parish identifications are: Othir = Aughrim; Erlyng = Killoran;
Kilgeridy = Kilgerril; Kilmolcosiny = Ballymacaward (Egan, 'Annates Clonfertensis', 55n; CPR,
xviii, 471); Kilconynny = Kilconnell); TCD MS 1066, p. 485.   **31** Nicholls, 'Rectory, vicarage
and parish', 72–3.

METHODOLOGY FOR 'TRÍCHA CÉT' RECONSTRUCTION

Evidence from the pre-Norman period is meagre when compared to that from after 1169. Nonetheless, more is available than would appear to be the case at first sight.

Precisely datable pre-Invasion material
This falls into three categories, annals, literary tracts, and monastic charters. Nothing need be said regarding the first, and just two literary tracts survive which mention *trícha*s and which can be dated with some precision: *Cogad Gaedel re Gallaib* (*c.*1100) and *Caithréim Cellacháin Chaisil* (1130s). One *trícha* reference occurs in a charter of 1157 (see **T164**).

Approximately datable pre-Invasion material
This varied material consists of references in the genealogies, such as those relating to the distribution of Clann Chuinn in Ireland,[32] the mention of *trícha*s found in such literary tales as *Táin Bó Cúailnge* and *Buile Suibhne* (where contemporary landscapes and spatial structures are described incidentally), and especially the poem dealing with the *trícha* system, 'Cā līn triūcha i nĒrind?' (see Appendix 1). These references are embedded in material generally considered to be of pre-Invasion date. The early martyrologies with their glosses can be taken to be a similar source.[33]

Topographical tracts
These are gazetteers or topographical dictionaries of individual *trícha cét*s. What marks them out as a distinct genre is the common spatial or landscape system they describe, by which estates (*bailte*) with their accompanying allodial proprietors are marshalled within each *trícha cét*. Typically, this system sees *bailte* identified with single- or multiple-family proprietors where the *bailte* are then grouped into *túatha* whose hereditary *taísig* are named. Though some of these tracts may have descended through centuries of recension before arriving at their present form, they all describe the same spatial and organizational landscape, one quite unlike anything found elsewhere and one featuring a distinct system of local and regional administration unique to pre-Invasion twelfth-century Ireland, distinguished by its three-tier communal system of *trícha cét*, *túath* and *baile* in descending order. The surviving tracts relate to the *trícha*s of Fir Maige (**T32**) and Trícha Meadhónach (**T50**) in Co. Cork, Cera (**T16**) and Bac & Glenn Nemthenne (**T6**) in Mayo, and Muintir Murchada (**T21**) in Galway. A related tract is that listing the *trícha*s of Mide as recorded in final form in a fourteenth-century manuscript (RIA MS D-iv-2).

Thirteenth- and fourteenth-century antiquarian material
While such material must be treated with caution, close examination suggests that it contains partly accurate memories of pre-Invasion structures. The well-known

32 GT, 190–1.   **33** As edited by Stokes.

so-called *Topographical Poems* are a case in point. Of course, the temptation to treat such sources as accurate must be avoided.[34] Some of this material also depicts the *trícha cét* structure in areas never colonized and where the system survived for some time after the Invasion, such as Thomond (*Caithréim Thoirdhealbhaigh*) and Tír Conaill (the poem 'Cairbre, Eogan, Énna éim' from *Leabhar Fidhnacha*).[35]

Material relating to local kingdoms

Many territories occur in the pre-Invasion Irish annals and literature in a context that suggests that these were local kingdoms. By 'local kingdom' I mean the political unit nearly always ruled by a king of the lowest level in the hierarchy of kingship, the basic king as distinct from the king of a regional kingdom and the king of a province.[36] The terms 'local kingdom' and 'trícha cét' almost always mean the same thing, and I use the terms interchangeably where permissible.[37] Due to scarcity of evidence, only a small number of local kingdoms are explicitly termed *trícha cét*s in the sources, but I do not doubt the correctness of the equation. What we see in the annals as local kingdoms are clearly the unit described in twelfth-century legal glosses as the *trícha cét*.

The main source of material for local kingdoms is annalistic references to kings (those entitled *rí, rex*) in the annals, largely for the period 600 to 1200. Here I have looked for kings of the lowest level, rather than kings of regional kingdoms or of provinces. The annals consulted are AFM, AI, ALC, MIA, AT, AU, CS, AB and FIA. AFM is used with caution because its rulership terms were subject to seventeenth-century editing of the exemplars.[38] Some additional sources are used, principally *Cogad Gaedel re Gallaib*, which incorporates otherwise unknown annalistic material, and *Lebor na Cert*. The latter is also used with caution since many of its polities do not have a corresponding annalistic record, and one suspects this work to have purposes other than creating an historical record, and that it does not represent the situation at the time of its composition *c.*1100.

---

34 The question of the historical accuracy of the *Topographical Poems* (Carney) is a complex one in need of further elucidation. Confining ourselves to the question of their references to *trícha*s, we note that only thirteen such references occur (13, 34, 41, 43, 47, 51–2, 57–8, 60). While most of these can be substantiated from other sources, at least one is clearly erroneous. This is that to the *trícha* of An Caladh, located near Limerick. This is preceded by a reference to the *túath* of Luimnech. Now, Limerick was a cantred (**C83**), not a *theodum*, and the reference to An Caladh cannot be reconciled with any other cantredal reference and there is no evidence for its existence. It seems likely that Ó hUidhrín has here confused a *túath* of An Caladh with the *trícha* of Luimnech. Note that a second *trícha* of An Caladh was claimed to exist much further up the Shannon in the partly fictional work *Nósa Ua Maine* (see **T135**), a claim which needs to be met with suspicion. Whatever lay behind such references seems to be entirely beyond recovery. A second *trícha* reference from the *Poems* (p. 13) also seems to be doubtful (see **T167**). Many of what were clearly *trícha*s are referred to by the contemporary term *críoch* in the *Poems*. It will be noted that of the eleven 'safe' *trícha* references nine are grouped in two distinct regional kingdoms (Osraige and Tuadmumu) suggesting that the 'poets' were drawing on some source which had the term *trícha* in these instances. **35** Pp 395–9. **36** See p. 22. **37** See p. 49. **38** McGowan, 'The Four Masters', 21–3.

Cantreds

Since it has been established, by various methods and by adducing large quan-
tities of supportive evidence, that the colonial cantred is the direct successor to
the indigenous *trícha cét*, it follows that, where evidence may otherwise be lacking, an onomastic relationship between cantred and local kingdom is enough to
infer with a high degree of certainty that a *trícha cét* of the same name previous-
ly existed which shared the same extent as the cantred in question.

CHAPTER 3

The relationship between cantred
and *trícha cét*

It will be helpful if, before addressing the subject of this chapter, we consider the relevant historiography. Hubert Knox, the pioneer of the medieval history of Connacht, most of whose writings were published in the first years of the twentieth century, was led to the conclusion that many Anglo-Norman land units must have been based on Irish precursors.[1] His illustrious successor, Goddard Orpen, in his seminal *Ireland under the Normans*, appears to have accepted without demur both the successor relationship between *trícha cét* and cantred and the number of these as given by Cambrensis and later Céitinn.[2] The first methodical attempt to address this question was made by James Hogan in 1929. He admitted that some relationship could be found between some *trícha céts* and early colonial cantreds, but in general he believed that most cantreds bore little relationship to any Irish precursor, being 'arbitrary creations' of the colonists.[3] The next general history to address this question was that of Edmund Curtis in 1938. He accepted that, as he rather confusingly put it, 'baile, tuath and trícha cét became township, hundred and barony', yet goes on, it appears, to contradict this statement elsewhere when he wrote that 'after the organization of shires was completed by 1297 the divisions of each county into cantreds became general'.[4] So much for clarity. His illustrious successor, Professor Otway-Ruthven, in the first systematic attempt to describe the institutions of Anglo-Norman shire government (1946), followed Hogan in the belief that 'some few of the Norman cantreds can be shown to have been identical with earlier trícha céts, but over the greater part of the country they seem to have been formed as settlement proceeded'.[5] Such an opinion must be the result of insufficient research, as was her mistaken belief that Wexford, Dublin and Meath had no cantreds. She had modified her position slightly by 1968, when she allowed that cantreds were formed by grouping *túatha* together.[6] This is clearly an opinion based on the virtually unique example of the division of Offelan into three new cantreds, and here Otway-Ruthven makes the basic error of making a single occurrence a general rule. In her treatment of the subject she was, of course, 'flying on one wing': her knowledge of pre-Norman Ireland was limited.[7] Given this rather confused *status quaestionis*, it is hardly surprising that since 1968 most general works have completely ignored this question.

---

1 'Tirechan's Collections', 27; *Tuam, Killala and Achonry*, 70–90.   **2** *Ireland under the Normans*, i, 110.   **3** 'The tricha cét', 181–2.   **4** *A history of medieval Ireland*, 76.   **5** 'Anglo-Irish shire government', 9 and fn.   **6** *A history of medieval Ireland*, 176.   **7** Flanagan, *Irish royal charters*, 2.

The only consistent voice crying in the wilderness has been that of Canon Adrian
Empey, who, since he first published on the subject of the cantred in 1970, has
held the position that the cantred is based on the pre-Invasion *trícha cét* and, more
generally, that much of the Anglo-Norman spatial organization is based on an
indigenous precursor.[8] In recent years he has been joined in this position by a
number of others, especially Marie-Therese Flanagan, Edel Bhreathnach, and I.
Of the above, only Hogan made a systematic attempt to examine the question on
a national scale, an attempt limited by an insufficient use of the sources for the
Anglo-Norman period. It is evident from the above survey that Hogan's conclusions on the question have had a significant effect on later opinion.

A consistent theme running throughout the history of the Anglo-Norman
invasion and settlement of Ireland is the establishment of the colonial feudal structure upon pre-existing indigenous models. This is true of the major political units
and also of the various levels of sub-infeudation below these, down to the hum-
ble fee consisting of no more than the simple freehold vill of a few hundred acres.
At the top, the Irish kingdoms became colonial lordships or counties, such as the
lordships of Meath and Leinster and the counties of Connacht and Desmond (later
divided into Cork and Kerry), for example. The colonial lordships of Connacht,
Leinster, Ulster, Limerick, Desmond, Meath, Breffny and Tyrconnell were all
based on Irish models. On the next level down, again we find Irish regional kingdoms and certainly *trícha cét*s becoming the foundations of feudal baronies. If we
look for grants in which the infeudated territory is specifically stated to have formerly belonged to a named Irish king, we find the example of the cantreds of
Aghaboe, Offelan, and Ofelmyth in Leinster, Ogenathy Donechud in Munster
and Lough Erne in Ulster.[9] Dropping down again to the next level, the occurrence of grants in which Irish *theoda* (*túatha*) and even smaller units of tenure are
given the name of the Irish 'forfeiting' proprietor are very common.[10]

Before turning to the main purpose of this chapter we should treat of the datable, pre-Invasion evidence for the existence of the *trícha cét*. An annal of 1106 indicates that all of Munster was divided into *trícha cét*s. A partial confirmation of this
comes from the tract, *Caithréim Cellacháin Chaisil*, datable to the 1130s, which
records the division of Desmumu (Desmond) into *trícha*s. A charter of 1157 describes
Ind Airthir in Ulster (**T164**) as a *trícha*. An annal of 1167 indicates that the regional kingdom of Uí Chennselaig in Leinster was divided into *trícha*s, while another,
of 1189, indicates that all of Connacht was also so divided. Yet another, in 1197,
describes Ciannachta in Ulster (**T141**) as a *trícha cét*. Other references to *trícha*s occur
in literature which can safely be dated to the pre-Invasion period, and which illustrates the existence of *trícha*s throughout Ulster and Mide, thus completing the picture, as it were.[11] An argument in favour of the ubiquity and importance of the

8 'Tipperary', 24; 'The Norman period', 73, 85; 'County Kilkenny', 76; 'Anglo-Norman
Waterford', 142. **9** Brooks, *Knights' fees*, 80; COD, i, nos. 29, 366; Scott and Martin, *Expugnatio
Hibernica*, 143; Hardy, *Rot. Chart.*, 77b; Flanagan, 'Mac Dalbaig', passim. **10** COD, i, 3–4; Brooks,
'Unpublished charters', 333, 342, 355, 361; McNeill, *Alen's Register*, 16–17; Orpen, *Ireland under
the Normans*, ii, 85; Ó Conbhuí, 'St Mary's', 46. **11** AU, 1106; AFM, 1167, 1189; Bugge, *Caithreim*,

pre-Invasion *trícha cét*s, is that notwithstanding the varying dates of colonial pene-
tration in different parts of Ireland between the 1170s and the 1250s, the *trícha cét*
remains the unit that is adopted by the colonists to their purposes.

In considering the direct evidence for the relationship between *trícha cét* and
cantred we may start with numbers. My surveys of the *trícha cét* and cantred have
demonstrated the close link between each at local level. This allows, for the first
time, the question of numbers to be addressed on a proper basis. As both Hogan
and Ó Corráin demonstrate, the various Gaelic sources ultimately derive from
a common source, the poem, *Cā līn triūcha i nĒrind*. Ó Corráin tentatively dates
this poem to the early twelfth century. The poem's variants list the number of
*trícha cét*s in Ireland as in the range 176 to 184. The higher figure gives 18 in
Mide, 30 in Connacht, 31 in Laigin, 35 in Ulster and 70 in Munster. This enumeration is followed, with varied degrees of accuracy, by the Cambro-Norman
historian of the Invasion, Gerald de Barri (*Cambrensis*), and by later historians
such as Seathrún Céitinn.[12] This schema has long been dismissed as fanciful, perhaps because evidence from the pre-Invasion period for the *trícha cét* was considered too sparse to test it.

My cantred and *trícha cét* surveys, in particular that of the cantreds, suggests
that these figures were based on an actual survey of the *trícha cét*s of twelfth-century Ireland, and are approximately accurate.

It has long been recognized that the thirty *trícha cét*s of Connacht must bear
some relationship to the like number of cantreds there, but this is as far as such
comparisons have gone.[13] We can now go significantly further. In Munster there
were 69 certain cantreds. My figure for Desmond, 30, is certainly missing one,
for this lordship was said to have comprised 31 cantreds.[14] When this unidentified cantred is added to the known cantreds it gives a certain total of 70 for
Munster, identical with the Irish tally. In Leinster (Laigin), we get a figure of 26
certain cantreds with an additional four probable cantreds (from 'Irish' north
Wexford and the original Kilkenny structure). This gives a possible total of 30,
one less than the Irish reckoning. In Mide, while only two definite cantreds can
be identified, the *trícha cét* structure, for which significant evidence survives, suggests that the total of 18 units is correct. Finally, in Ulster, we find 29 certain
cantreds and indicators of another probable eight, giving the figure of 37, one
less than the Irish reckoning. When these figures are tabulated nationally we find
159 certain cantreds and an additional 26 probable ones, giving a possible minimal upper figure of 185 (this includes the otherwise unknown additional cantred
in Desmond). This agrees well with the range given in Irish sources, 176–87.
Such coincidence of numeration should not be dismissed lightly, especially given
the detailed survey used to support it, and I have no doubt that the figures of
both Irish scholars and *Cambrensis* for the number of *trícha cét*s/cantreds in Ireland
is broadly correct and is a record of the actual situation at the time of the Anglo-

29; Flanagan, *Irish royal charters*, 292; O'Keeffe, *Buile Suibhne*, 62; Hogan, 'The tricha cét', 210; GT,
190–1. **12** Hogan, 'The tricha cét', 169–73; Ó Corráin, 'Hogan', 95. **13** Hogan, 'The tricha cét',
192. **14** Scott and Martin, *Expugnatio Hibernica*, 185.

Norman invasion, the leaders of which inherited a pre-existing system of local administration and taxation which they adopted largely unchanged. Such a conclusion should not surprise one, for this is exactly what happened in England after 1066 when the Norman invaders merely took over the existing system of Anglo-Saxon shire government unaltered. A similar development occured a generation later in parts of Wales.[15]

Support for these conclusions may be found in more detailed comparisons between the few surviving pre-Invasion topographical tracts and the colonial cantredal structure. By far the best comparison may be found in the case of the *trícha cét* of Fir Maige (**T32**) and the cantred of Fermoy (**C32**) in Co. Cork. The topographical tract, *Críchad an Chaoilli*, the exemplar of which can only be of pre-Invasion date, extends this *trícha* by listing about 180 place-names of which at least 113 can be identified. Again, the cantred of Fermoy has left abundant evidence for its extent. Comparison of both extents indicates that *trícha* and cantred were identical in area. Of particular significance are the references in *Críchad* to two *túatha* in dispute between Fir Maige and the polity of Fonn Timchill (**T84**) to the north. The colonial evidence indicates that both *túatha* were divided between the cantreds of Fermoy and of Fontymkill, thus demonstrating an exact inheritance both of area and of lordship dispute between *trícha* and cantred.[16] Similar inheritances or descents of pre- and post-colonial lordship disputes can be seen in a number of other areas.[17]

The second such example is that of the *trícha* of Cera (**T16**) in what is today Co. Mayo. An Irish extent of this lists about fifty-five place-names of which around two-thirds can be identified. While the corresponding colonial sources are not as full as those for Fermoy, the evidence for the cantred of Kerre (**C16**) again suggests that it was identical to its predecessor.[18] Again, the tract on Uí Fhiachrach in northern Connacht includes an extent of the *trícha* of Bac & Gleann Nemhthinne (**T6**) containing fifteen place-names. While sources for the cantred of Bac & Glen (**C6**) are less full, once again complete agreement is shown by the evidence.[19] A detailed extent of the *trícha* of Trícha Meadhónach (**T50**) in Corcu Loígde and its seven *túatha*, datable to the early decades of the twelfth century, again agrees with the outline of the later cantred of Rosselithir (**C50**) with the exception of two *túatha* which had become detached and joined with a neighbouring *trícha* in the interim.[20] Another example here concerns the four *tríchas* of Tír Conaill (**T136–9**), whose bounds agree in outline with the description from colonial sources of the four cantreds of Tirconyll (**C136–9**).[21] Another useful tract is that concerning the Uí Flaithbertaig (Muintir Murchada) lordship in Co. Galway, of pre-Invasion date, which simply names superdenominations without categorizing them. While this source is inconsistent in method and

15 Williams, *The Welsh church*, 16; Loyn, *The making of the English nation*, 100. **16** See Appendix 3. **17** Cf. the example of Saithne (**T53**) and that of the border conflict between Uí Briúin Aí and Uí Briúin Seola in east Galway (**T21**), both of which continued into the colonial period. **18** Knox, 'Connacht' i, 397; Ó Muraíle, *Mac Fhirbhisigh*, i, 610–14. **19** Ibid., 618. **20** Ó Corráin, 'Corcu Loígde', 63–8. **21** AI, 1311.3, 1313.1.

omits at least one important territorial component of this lordship, most of its thirty-two place-names can be identified and comparison made with extents of two manors which lay in the cantred of Muntyrmorghyth (**C21**) as well as in its rural rectory. Here we find close, if not exact, correspondence between the Uí Flaithbertaig native territory – and certainly *trícha* – of Muintir Murchada (**T21**) and two of the three manors comprising colonial Muntyrmorghyth. Another point of agreement here concerns the *túath* of Uí Briúin Rátha (**T7**) of the Muintir Murchada tract, whose extent agrees well with that of the cantred of Brunrath (**C7**). There are many other less complete examples. As an instance of what remains one might take the case of the half-cantreds of Wicklow and Offyneglas (**C62**) and their Irish precursors, the territories of Uí Garrchon and Uí (F)enechglais (**T62**). Just one source, the Irish martyrologies, list four places in Uí Garrchon which also lay in Wicklow and four in Uí Enechglais which also lay in Offyneglas (*alias* Arklow).[22]

Finally on this question we may turn to less direct evidence for the relationship between *trícha cét* and cantred. The remnant of territory left to the Uí Briain kings by the colonists formed the lordship of Tuadmumu or Thomond. This area experienced insignificant settlement of short duration, and colonial lordship was chiefly exercised *in absentia* in the form of cantredal rents levied on its Uí Briain kings. Material from the thirteenth and fourteenth centuries, from both Irish and colonial sources, contains many references to the *tríchas*/cantreds of this area in a context which again indicates that the units are identical.[23] The Irish *tríchas* are the colonial cantreds here, just as in Irish sources from this time forward until the end of the medieval period, throughout Ireland, the term 'cantred' is always translated as *trícha cét*, and so re-translated back into English as 'troghkyod', 'troghekahede', 'trohoked' and the like. The earliest example of such an Anglicization dates from 1201 and examples from as late as *c*.1600 can be cited for parts of Kerry, Clare and Donegal.[24]

Evidence of a more general nature for the correlation between *trícha* and cantred can be found in the naming pattern of cantreds. By taking all place-name elements occurring in cantred titles and sorting them by type we get the following table.

Table 1. Cantred names sorted by type (percentages)

Superdenomination	26
Metonym	15
Kinship–dynastic	57
Names in *trícha*	2

Superdenomination refers to names of territories, rather then single locations, without a personal name component (for example, Coran, Foniertheragh).

22 Price, 'Place-names, Arklow', 250, 258, 264, 271, 277; Stokes, *Félire hUí Gormáin*, 159; idem, *Félire Oengusso Céli Dé*, 55. **23** See pp 192–6. **24** Hogan, 'The trícha cét', 203, 228–9; NAI MS 5037, passim; Brewer and Bullen, *Cal. Carew MSS*, i, 447.

Metonym refers to a territory which takes its name from its chief place (for example, Shanid, Ardnurcher). Kinship–dynastic refers to ethnic terms and those indicating descent from, or kinship with, a named individual (names in -ne, -raige, Uí, Cenél, Síl, Fir, Corcu, Clann and so on).[25] 'Names in *trícha*' indicates where the term *trícha cét* occurs as part of the name.

The high percentage of Irish kinship and dynastic elements is significant. While many of these denote the pre-Invasion ruling or lordly family in the various cantreds, a significant number of such names relate to long-obsolete or long-extinct dynasties whose rule of the area in question may have ended as far back as the seventh or eighth century. Note, for example, the *trícha*s of Alltraige (**T56**), Uí Duach (**T70**), Cuircne (**T98**), Conmaicne Cúile Talad (**T12**), and Tír Meic Cáirthinn (**T142**). This demonstrates that these names – and, by extension, the denominations to which they referred – were territorial names of considerable antiquity at the time of the Invasion. If, as suggested, the Anglo-Normans had created new divisions bearing no direct relationship to what had gone before, why would the names of these new divisions perpetuate the names of long-obsolete dynasties or, even more significantly, the lineage names of the kings they had recently dispossessed? Another argument against the belief that the Anglo-Normans created the cantreds concerns metonymic names. By far the greatest number of colonial manors bear the name of their *caput* or chief place, and this naming pattern was clearly the norm among the invaders. If the cantreds were also fresh creations of the colonists one would expect a like naming pattern. Yet only 15 per cent of cantreds bore metonyms. Even here this figure is misleadingly large for many of these 15 per cent occur in cases of cantreds bearing two or even more names, one of its *caput* and the other a kinship or superdominational name. Cantreds named solely by metonym constitute only 8 per cent of the total. Even here evidence for the existence of some metonymic *trícha* names in pre-Invasion Ireland further weakens the value of this figure as an argument against the equation of *trícha* and cantred.[26] Consistently one finds that, where Irish pre-Invasion sources name a place as lying within a particular territory, the same place is almost always found in the subsequent cantred of the same (Anglicized) name, a comment that seems almost superfluous in the present context.

In conclusion, then, the evidence adduced above must show that the Anglo-Norman colonists inherited the topography of the Irish system of local administration, thus preserving – in amber, as it were – for centuries afterwards the boundaries of the *trícha cét* under the guise of cantreds and, in some cases, baronies. Of course, such preservation 'in amber' would appear to have already been the case with the indigenous system itself long before a Norman helmet appeared in Wexford, as we shall see.

25 MacNeill, 'Irish population groups', passim. **26** The eleven metonymic cantred or half-cantred names are Wykinglo, Shanid, Ardagh, Inyskyfty, Bruree, Limerick, Louth, Clones, Clogher, Athmethan and Dungarvan. The *trícha* of Esa Ruaidh is an indigenous example and several other probable *trícha*s in the same category occur in the annals, such as Loch Gabhair (Lagore), Cnodhbha (Knowth), Derlas, Telach Cáil, Telach Aird etc. (Flanagan, *Irish royal charters*, 133).

CHAPTER 4

Pre-invasion Irish political and territorial divisions: *trícha cét*, *túath* and *baile biataig*

OVERVIEW

What follows is a fresh attempt to describe the structure of the various tiers of kingship and local lordship in eleventh- and twelfth-century Ireland. I do not find any of the previous attempts at this task in the literature to be adequate for the purposes of the present study. I find this strange, for the structure I am about to describe is attested by abundant evidence. While what follows may draw accusations of unfashionable schematism, I would ask the reader to set the evidence presented below firmly within the homogenous culture of the Gaelic Ireland of the period. Such a contextualization suggests that cultural, linguistic and political homogeneity goes hand in hand in the present context.

The twelfth-century *trícha cét* was merely one part of a complex system of local administration for which good evidence survives. It represented one level in a hierarchy of such units, at the top of which were the eight or nine great semi-provincial overkingdoms which, in the eleventh and twelfth centuries, competed in shifting alliances for the high-kingship. Beneath these were the regional kingdoms, whose areas are often mirrored in that of the emerging reformed dioceses of the twelfth century, and whose kings sometimes distinguished themselves from those below by use of the term *árdrí*.[1] Beneath these in turn come our subject, the *trícha cét*, usually ruled by petty kings at the basic level of kingship, although there were a few *trícha*s containing two kingdoms. Regional kingdoms could consist of anything from two to a dozen or more *trícha*s. The *trícha* in turn comprised several *túatha*, each under the leadership of its hereditary *taísech* (= leader), under whom dwelt the free commoner population, whose allodial landholdings in severalty were represented by the unit known as the *baile* (*biataig*), and whose sub-divisions in turn often give us our modern townlands. Under this in turn came the *tech*, the house of the free individual.[2] We might represent this lordship structure schematically thus as Figure 1 (p. 46).

*Trícha*s could vary greatly in size – this point will be addressed below – as could the number of their constituent *túatha*. This structure can best be seen in *Críchad an Chaoilli*, the extent of the *trícha* of Fir Maige (**T32**).[3] This contained

---

1 This could also be used by provincial kings, see Ó Corráin's comments in 'Irish kings and high kings', 153–4. **2** Ó Corráin, 'Hogan', 96; idem, 'Nationality and kingship', 28. **3** See Appendix 3.

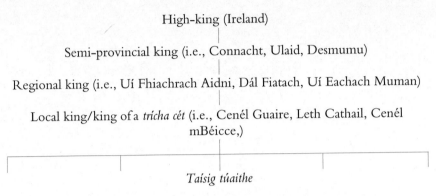

Figure 1. The lordship structures of twelfth-century Ireland

ten *túatha*, some of which had a single *taísech* while others were sub-divided between two or three *taísig* families. Each *túath* had its own church and resident clergy, which Sharpe and Ó Corráin[4] interpret as evidence for the existence of a pre-Invasion parochial structure. *Críchad* reveals a complex structure of sub-divisions and lordship structures suggesting an advanced level of spatial organization which can only have developed over a long period of time. Something of this is echoed in another well-known topographical tract, *Críchaireacht Muinntiri Murchada*, which reveals something of the *túath* stucture of eastern Galway before its colonization. In this, each *túath* has its *taísech*, apart from one shared between two *taísig* families.[5] A second well-known extent from Cork concerns Trícha Meadhónach (**T50**) and its seven *túatha*, each again with its hereditary *taísech*. Just north of this lay Múscraige Mittíne (**T42**), which had six named *túatha*, each with its *taísech*, in what is clearly an incomplete list.[6] In Mayo, the *trícha* of Cera (**T16**) appears to have had eight *túatha* and neighbouring Clann Chuán (**T17**) three.[7] The final Gaelic source of interest concerns the four *tríchas* of Tír Conaill, which contained three, five, six and two *túatha* respectively, most with named *taísig*.[8] Fainter traces of such a structure can be discerned in all corners of Ireland.

Taísech túaithe was a formal title, as can be seen in a document from Mide (1129 × 1146) and was Latinized *dux* (a direct translation), as can be seen in both pre- and post-Invasion charters from Ulster and Connacht.[9] The number of *túatha* contained in several additional *tríchas* is known: seven in Fir Manach (**T166**) and in Uí Failge (**T64**), four in Uí Chairpre Íochtarach (**T77**) and Muintir Máelfináin (**T20**), three (unsurprisingly) in Trí Túatha (**T116**). Again, a num-

4 Sharpe, 'Churches and communities', passim; Ó Corráin, *Ireland before the Normans*. 5 Hardiman, *Iar-Connaught*, 368–72. 6 Ó Muraíle, *Mac Fhirbhisigh*, iii, 276; TP, 114–15. 7 The tract names four *túatha* and their *taísig* and four additional *taísig* families in what were clearly unnamed additional *túatha*. See Ó Muraíle, *Mac Fhirbhisigh*, i, 610–15. 8 Dillon, 'Ceart Uí Néill', 4. 9 Mac Niocaill, 'Irish "charters"', 161; Nicholls, 'Reg. of Clogher', 392, 412; O'Flaherty, *Ogygia*, 30; Orpen, 'Irish Cistercian Documents', 306–7; Flanagan, *Irish royal charters*, 292, 350. Cf. Stokes, *Lives of the saints*, 61.2015.

ber of *tríchas* in the kingdom of Mide contained three or four *túatha* apiece. The regional kingdom of Eóganacht Chaisil, containing at least three *tríchas*, was said to have contained seventeen *túatha*. In Ostman Dublin, Túath Étair (Howth) and the two *túatha* of the foundation grant of the barony of Castleknock shows Ostmen overlordship to have made no difference to the equation.[10] *Taísig* of over one hundred *túatha* can be found in the annals, while the rank of *taísech* was one of those taxed during visitations of Cenél Eógain and Uí Thuirtre in the 1150s, showing it to have been an integral rank within society.[11] This evidence is merely the tip of the iceberg, while early colonial records are replete with references to *theoda*. Space does not permit an exhaustive survey. These twelfth-century *túatha* will be described as late-*túatha* in the remainder of this work in order to avoid confusion with other meanings borne by the term *túath*.

The *taísech túaithe* was in some cases clearly the hereditary leader of an aristocratic *cenél*, often of royal blood, whose territory seems to have coincided with that of his *túath*. He was thus a major landowner, local ruler, and the leader of the local military levy (*buiden*), presumably having the additional functions of tax or tribute collection and law enforcement, although evidence for these is lacking due to the early demise of the office. We may not be far wrong in seeing something of his rôle in relation to these functions preserved in that of the Scottish *tosheachdeor* and *tosheachdera*, whose rôles respectively came to be equated with those of feudal coroner and serjeant of the fee within what had originally been Gaelic spatial units of similar size to the Irish late-*túath* of the twelfth century.[12] We are reminded of a passage in the early Irish Laws where the *brithem* (judge), also called *ardmaor* (high steward), a royal official, is said to rule several *túatha* on behalf of his employer.[13] A later, concrete example of such a rôle appears to be that of Donnchad Mac Airechtaig, who, in the late twelfth century, acquired the *taisigeacht* 'between *tigernus* and *maeraigecht*' of several *túatha* in Connacht.[14] This reference illustrates the imposition of an outsider as *taísech* over several *túatha* by an overking, whose rôle, in addition to that of lordship (*tigernus*), included that of *maeraigecht*, which we may understand as royal steward and, no doubt, tribute collector.

The varying size of late-*túatha* can be partly explained by the quality of land, as originally only arable was assessed, resulting in bigger *túatha* on poorer land.[15] The same principle, of course, applies to the *baile* (*biataig*) estate and its function of common landholding within a perscribed degree of kinship. Clearly there was some threshold of agricultural wealth required to support such a kin-group, as evidenced by the clear relationship between *bailte* size and land quality. (The

10 Hogan, 'The tricha cét', 187; Bugge, *Caithreim*, 4; Todd, *Cogad*, 155; Brooks, 'Grant of Castleknock', passim. **11** AFM, 1150, 1151. **12** Byrne, 'Tribes and tribalism', 158–9n; Ó Corráin, 'Nationality and kingship', 9–10, 29; Jaski, *Irish kingship*, 50; Skene, *Celtic Scotland*, 279–81; Sellar, 'Scots law', 9–11. **13** CIH, 687.23–33, 1269.19–20. **14** Lec. 65rb. The lands were Clann Taidg and Clann Murrthaile. The latter was a *túath* in Mag Aí (**T115**) and the former, apparently, a *trícha cét* (**T10**) which contained several *túatha*. **15** McErlean, 'Irish townland system', 322; Duffy, 'Territorial organization', 3.

poorer the land quality, the bigger the *baile*.) This same principle then carried through to the *túath*, although not in as marked a fashion, but why this should be so is not easily discerned. There is no evidence, for example, to suggest that *túatha* were composed of a fixed number of *bailte*. Late-*túatha* are found composed of between four and twenty-four *bailte*.[16] At one end of the scale we have the two *túatha* upon which the feudal barony of Castleknock, Co. Dublin, was based. This contained approximately 16,500 acres, giving an average *túath* size of 8,250 acres.[17] At the other extreme we note the range of average *túatha* size in the four *tríchas* of Tír Conaill, 31,000–90,000 acres. In between these extremes we note the correlation between land quality and average *túath* size on a sliding scale, as follows. Uí Chairpre Íochtarach (**T77**) 13,000 acres; Fir Maige (**T32**) and Trícha Meadhónach (**T50**),[18] 17,000 acres; two *túatha* in Éile Uí Fhócarta (**T120**) of 19,300 and 13,000 acres each;[19] Trí Túatha (**T116**), 26,000 acres; Uí Failge (**T64**), 41,000 acres.

The belief that many late-*túatha* were erected into single manors by the Anglo-Normans, with corresponding parishes,[20] is far from an absolute rule, as may be seen in those examples from Dublin, Cork, Roscommon and Donegal adduced above. There was, however, an undoubted relationship between indigenous *túath* and colonial manor. *Theoda* feature extensively in early-colonial documentation in a context which shows that they represented an important unit of sub-infeudation. The most likely explanation for the non-concordance of parish and *theodum* boundaries is that, in such cases, single *theoda* were broken up into several parishes. This was certainly the case in the cantred of Shanid (**C80**), where many fees were based on half-*theoda*. Something similar may lie behind the example of the cantred of Adare & Croom (**C77**), which contained four *theoda* but twice that number of parishes. Further examples of half-*theoda* as the basis of fees come from Kildare, Wexford and Tipperary, and my search for these has not been exhaustive.[21] Where colonial settlement did not intrude we see a more direct relationship between *túath* and parish. This is especially so in the dioceses of Clogher, Derry and Armagh (*inter hibernicos*), where the *túath*, directly translated as *plebs*, formed the basis of many parishes down to the sixteenth century.[22] We will see in Chapter 5 that many parishes, particularly in the heavily settled parts of Leinster, are actually based on *bailte*.

16 Power, *Críchad*, passim; Ó Muraíle, *Mac Fhirbhisigh*, i, 613; Hardiman, *Iar-Connaught*, 368–9. **17** Brooks, 'Castleknock', passim. While no single extent of Castleknock survives the acreage of this barony can be reconstructed from a number of sources. One moiety was described in 1541 while references to many of its lands are contained in contemporary inquisitions. There is also thirteenth-century material on its ecclesiastical benefices. See MacNiocaill, *Crown survey*, 195–7; Gilbert, *St Mary's abbey*, pp ii, xxi, 18, 75; Griffith, *Inquisitions*, passim; White, *Dignitas Decani*, 17–18, 23–4; Gilbert, *Crede Mihi*, 138. **18** These figures are arrived at by dividing the acreage of each *trícha* by the number of its *túatha*. **19** Empey, 'Cantred of Eliogarty', 213. **20** Hennessy, 'Parochial organisation', passim; Empey, 'Cantred of Eliogarty', 211–13. **21** CDI, iv, 258; COD, i, 19, 135; Gilbert, *Reg. St Thomas*, 183. **22** CDI, v, 203, 212; CPR, viii, 9, 75; ix, 20, 193; x, 285, 287, 325, 445; xi, 220, 321, 674.

THE FUNCTIONS OF THE 'TRÍCHA CÉT'

The *'tricha cét'* had four functions: (1) unit of royal tenure; (2) unit of local government and law enforcement; (3) unit of collection of taxation or tribute; (4)
unit of military levy.

A large majority of *tricha céts* were local kingdoms ruled by petty kings.
Indeed such is the correspondence that legal glosses of the time equate *tricha cét*
with the earlier minimal polity *túath* (local kingdom) of the Laws, establishing
a definite link between *tricha cét* and local king.[23] Several of these local kingdoms
together comprised regional kingdoms, the kingship of which was often contested between the various local kings. Further up the scale came the semi-
provincial kingdoms comprised of several regional kingdoms. At both superior
levels of kingship, and especially at that of semi-provincial kings, we find the
exercise of a power whereby lesser kings are arbitrarily removed and replaced
by clients of the overking. This is especially so during the eleventh and twelfth
centuries. While the Laws and glosses maintained the political fiction which
denied such events, the reality was clearly different. It is certain therefore that
local kings held office with the consent of overkings. Thus, in an almost feudal
sense, it can be said that a *de facto* tenurial relationship existed where lesser kings
held their kingdoms/*tricha*s of their superior king. This must have been the practical outcome of the formal relationships of superiority and subordination, or
clientship, between kings. A similar reality may lie behind the replacement of
royal lineages by segments related to a superior king. Therefore, local kings held
their kingdoms at the pleasure of their superior kings – a form of tenure.[24]

The principal functions of local government in early medieval Ireland were
represented by the *airecht*, the king's court of justice, and the *óenach*, a meeting
attended by the general body of people where laws and royal pedigrees were
proclaimed, royal tribute collected, sporting and social events held (especially
horse racing), and commercial interaction occurred. These functions are described
in detail in the early medieval Irish Laws pertaining to the original *túath*, the
forerunner to the *tricha*. These indicate the existence of a judge within each *túath*,
the *brithem túaithe*, who assisted the king in holding the *airecht* in company with
the body of freemen or nobles, and they indicate that every free person had a
right to attend the *óenach* which was held on royal land at regular intervals.[25] To
what extent these gatherings continued after the early medieval period is unclear,
but there is some evidence to suggest some form of continuity. This is suggested by the many *óenaig* sites listed below as well as by the continued use of the
word *airecht* in toponyms (for example, Iraghticonnor barony, Co. Kerry, a territorial unit born of the Gaelic Resurgence of the late fourteenth century). Simms
suggests that the *oireacht* (*airecht*) continued to function as a royal council until

23 Ó Corráin, 'Hogan', 93–4. **24** Idem, 'Nationality and kingship', 10, 25; *Ireland before the Normans*; Jaski, *Irish kingship*, 99–102, 209–10. **25** Jaski, *Irish kingship*, 49–56 (description with extensive references); Kelly, *Irish law*, 193–4; Swift, 'Óenach Tailten', 118; Binchy, *Crith Gablach*, 73, 102, 109.

the mid-fourteenth century, after which the term developed the general sense of a collective of royal vassals. She is more pessimistic regarding the survival of the *óenach,* probably unduly so, given what follows below.[26]

Whether or not *airecht* and *óenach* were held at the same time, they are likely to have been held at a traditional meeting place, usually on a hill or mound, often in association with a sacral tree (*bile*), inauguration site or prehistoric hill-top centre. Each layer of kingship – local, regional and provincial – seems to have had its own such site. Provincial sites included Cashel, Carman and Tailtiu. Often overkingdom sites were located on the borders between the chief segments of the kingdom, such as Ráith Ua nEchach (Uí Echach Muman) and Ailech (Uí Néill an Tuascirt). Very many of these can be identified. While it has been suggested that each polity maintained distinct public assembly and royal inauguration sites some distance apart, this distinction is not always apparent.[27] It seems certain that each *trícha* had its own *óenach* site, many of which can be identified, but these were less significant sites and so tend to leave less record. That of Máenmag (**T19**) is mentioned in an annal of 1135 without further qualification. An annal of 1005 records Óenach Conaille, in the local kingdom of that name (**T161**), while *Vita Tripartita*'s references to Crúachain and the nearby Duma Selge (Shankill: significantly, a mound)[28] suggest the presence of provincial and local kingdom *óenaig* in close proximity within the same *trícha* (Mag Aí: **T115**). The nearby Cara na Trí Túath (Carranadoo) must surely represent the *óenach* site of the Trí Túatha (**T116**). *Onomasticon* lists several such sites. In Connacht we have Óenach Tíre Oilella (**T117**) at Carn Oilella near Lough Arrow, Óenach Ua nAmolngid at Carn Amolngid (Mullagh Carn near Killala: **T29**), and Óenach Locha Gile for Cairpre Mór (**T8**). In Munster, Óenach Cairpre (**T76**) gives Monasteranenagh, and Óenach Téte *alias* Óenach Urmuman gives Nenagh (**T118**), while Óenach Áine lay at the heart of the *trícha* of Uí Énna Áine (**T85**). In Ulster we note Telach Óc and Óenach Fir Aendarta in Mag Line (**T148**).[29] The later Burke inauguration sites at Rathsecer near Kilmaine and 'Caher na nIarla' in Dunkellin probably represent the relict usage of what had earlier been *óenaig* sites. The former must represent the *óenach* of Conmaicne Cúile Talad (**T12**) while the latter has been identified with Ruaidbheitheach, the sacral tree site of the *óenach* of the regional kingdom of Uí Fhiachrach Aidni. Significantly, a second inauguration site existed in the south of this territory high on Slieve Aughty: was this the *óenach* site of the *trícha* of Cenél Áeda na hEchtge (**T22**)? Other later inauguration sites may similarly have occupied older *óenaig* sites. Does the Clann Aodha Buidhe site at Castlereagh perhaps derive from the *óenach* of Uí Blaithmeic (**T152**)?[30] Some of

26 Simms, *From kings to warlords*, 62–70. **27** Warner, 'Royal mound', 39. See, for example, the location of the inauguration and assembly sites of Carn Fraích and Cnoc na Dála in Roscommon, which seem to be identical (FitzPatrick, 'Royal inauguration mounds', 48–50). **28** Cf. FitzPatrick, 'Tír Fhiachrach?', 83–4, 86. **29** AT, 1135; AU, 1005; Stokes, *Tripartite Life*, 106; Hogan, *Onomasticon*, 558–9. **30** FitzPatrick, 'Assembly and inauguration places', passim. Kilmaine was at or near the *caput* of the *trícha* of Conmaicne Cúile Talad (ALC, 1225). For more likely examples

these sites, such as the probable *óenach* site at Aughris in Tír Fhiachrach (**T30**), continued as local meeting and sporting venues, associated with such festivals as *Lughnasa,* into the nineteenth century.[31]

While the greater portion of *trícha*/cantred names derive from kinship or dynastic terms, 15 percent derive from the names of single locations or metonyms.[32] In many cases the names are those of cantreds whose preceding *tríchas* are anonymous. We must suspect, however, that many of these names are inherited from the preceding *tríchas* as we know that some *tríchas* were named metonymically. One such category are likely to be cantred names in *dún*: 'fortress', of which there are seven.[33] One of these is also that of the earlier *trícha,* that of Conmaicne Cenéoil Dubáin or Conmaicne Dúna Móir (**T11**). While *óenaig* sites may well have been located adjacent to royal fortresses, of greater interest are names deriving from natural phenomena such as waterfalls (**T138**), fords (**C97**) and lakes. Two lake examples are known, Lough Sewdy (**C98**) and Lagore (**T111**), although the latter rather refers to a royal crannóg site. Of special interest are those metonyms derived from hills or heights, of which there are ten, at least six of which are certainly pre-Invasion.[34] As we see, two of these, Telach Óc and Cnoc Áine, were certainly *óenaig* sites, and one must suspect the remainder to have been so. Another must be that of Shanid, Co. Limerick, a remarkable hill-top site commanding an extraordinary view with extensive pre- and post-Invasion structures and earthworks. Not alone does this site give its name to a cantred (**80**), it occurs as a strategic location as early as the 830s and its name derives from *seanad,* a word for an important assembly place.[35]

The *trícha cét* functions of tribute collection and military levy are closely related. On a superior level we find details of these recorded in *Lebor na Cert,* a source of perhaps the late eleventh century. Here we find a relationship between provincial kings and their regional and sometimes local underkings in which the lesser kingdoms pay annual livestock tributes or *císa,* mostly of cattle, and the overking fulfills the relationship by payment of *tuarastla* or stipends, sometimes of luxury items but mostly of military material such as horses, weapons and ships. This form of relationship has its roots in the principle of clientship or *célsine,* a fundamental feature of relationships among the middle and upper classes of Irish society as illustrated in the early Laws. From the early medieval period onwards a dual currency operated in Ireland, that of livestock – especially cattle – and silver and gold bullion. The early Irish Laws speak of the *cís flatha* 'royal tribute' and the profits of justice as income rightfully due to kings.[36] *Cís* can mean rent, tribute, tax, and what exactly is meant by the Laws here is unclear.[37] Evidence for royal taxation on every household – as distinct from royal income from the king's own free- and base-clients (including sub-kings) and from royal estates – can be found from the ninth century onwards.[38] Evidence for royal taxation of

see FitzPatrick, 'Royal inauguration mounds', *passim.* **31** FitzPatrick, 'Tír Fhiachrach?', 71–2, 75–8, 85–6. **32** See Table 1, p. 43. **33** 9, 11, 33, 59, 154, 161, 170. **34** 85, 106, 110, 112, 122, 125, 130, 140, 146, 173. **35** DIL, s.v. seanad. **36** CIH, 219.5. **37** DIL, s.v. cís. **38** Gerriets, 'Kingship and exchange', 68–9; CS, 1005.

landed estates can be found from the eleventh century onwards.[39] The evidence
suggests that both forms existed side by side in the twelfth century. Estates (*bailte*)
were subject to a number of impositions, principally *cís*, *slógad* 'hosting' and *coinmed* 'billeting', and it would appear that both king and *taísech* were entitled to
levy these, no doubt in specified measures and in clearly ordained circumstances.
Such taxes were levied from ecclesiastical as well as from lay estates, and free-
dom from these could be purchased, usually for a bullion payment.[40] The term
biatach 'food provider' suggests that the principal form of *cís* paid by *bailte* was
livestock, while prepared food and cereals must have been provided for royal
consumption at cosherings or as an additional form of tribute. Cattle remained
the chief form of currency in pre-Invasion Ireland, and the annals contain numerous examples of semi-provincial kingdoms paying *eric* and other fines in cattle,
often in very large numbers, to the high-king.[41] These must have been levied
internally from each *trícha*. *Císa* were clearly collected by the officials of the king
or governor (*airrí*) of the *trícha*. Presumably some of these were kept locally and
some passed up the line to the layers of kingship above. Annals of 1106 and 1227
indicate taxation by *trícha*, where each contributed the same amount in cattle or
bullion, regardless of size. [42] While this may have been the practice on occasion,
*trícha*s varied greatly in size and little is known about the detail of how tribute
was levied. The *trícha cét* must have been the primary collection unit for taxation by the great kings, where all local taxes were gathered together before being
sent onwards. Within the *trícha cét* the collection system may have been one
where each *taísech* collected the tribute from each *baile* within his *túath* and duly
forwarded a portion of these to his king.

The final function of the *trícha* was that of military levy. It seems to have
been the norm for each local king to lead a hosting (*slógad*) drawn from the
freemen of his *trícha* in the service of his overking(s). The annals are replete with
such references. Perhaps each late-*túath* contributed a contingent under its *taísech*,
a term sometimes understood as having military leadership connotations.[43] In
the case of coastal kingdoms military activity often had a naval aspect. Material
from the approximate period 1090–1130 contains significant references to the
naval levy or *laídeng*, both term and substance of which indicate Scandinavian
influence.[44] As with the terrestrial military levy, such arrangements were based
on the principle of *tuarastal*, where the acceptance of gifts from the overlord
bound the retainer to his service. In the case of naval levies, it appears that gifts
of ships were bestowed by the overking on lesser kings who were then required
to staff these and operate them in the service of the overking, and where spoils
of war or tribute were shared between both in fixed proportions, just as with
terrestrial levies.[45] While *Lebor na Cert* notes several examples of the number of
ships given to each regional kingdom by its provincial overking, *Caithréim*

39 Mac Niocaill, 'Irish "charters"', 157, 159; AFM, 1089 (where the king of Mide is joined in a
land-sale as the superior lord). **40** Mac Niocaill, 'Irish "charters"', 159. **41** See AFM, 1166, 1168
for several examples. **42** AU, 1106; ALC, 1227. **43** Byrne, 'Tribes and tribalism', 158–9n. **44**
See p. 122. **45** Swift, 'Royal fleets', passim.

Cellacháin Chaisil (*c.*1130) is more specific, mentioning a naval levy of ten ships due from each *trícha cét* of the coastal kingdoms of west Munster as part of the provincial army. A very much earlier example is the naval levy exacted from Dál Riata in Scotland in the seventh century (?) as evidenced in *Senchus Fer nAlban*.[46] Of course, there were other kinds of levy, such as the labour levy for maintaining roads and especially the fortifications of powerful kings. A striking example is that of Toirdelbach Ua Conchobair's diversion of the River Suck for defensive purposes in 1139, an effort which required significant levels of manpower, raised perhaps through the *trícha cét* system.[47]

THE 'BAILE BIATAIG' ESTATE SYSTEM

As we shall see below, the term is *baile biataig* in early references occurring in Ulster and Bréifne, and in a single and unreliable early reference from Connacht. This gives the sixteenth-century Anglicized form 'ballybetagh' as found in Ulster. Generally in Connacht, Munster and Mide however, the style is simply *baile*. There are thus two styles in use to refer to this unit, and I use these interchangeably.

Any study of the *trícha cét* would be incomplete without addressing the question of the *baile biataig*, for both units are inextricably linked. The very name *trícha cét* possibly derives from a collective of *baile biataig*. The *baile biataig* was the taxable unit of landholding in pre-Norman Ireland and was an economically independent estate.[48] This is suggested both by the surviving contemporary evidence, as well as by the practice of the system as found in those parts of sixteenth-century Ireland where it had survived. In a study of the sixteenth-century *baile biataig* pattern in Co. Monaghan, Duffy defines this unit as 'the fundamental property unit of lineage groups, the estate of Gaelic society, the mechanism by which property was allocated among the families of the sept'.[49] Evaluation of earlier evidence for this system is difficult because *biatach* has several meanings. However, the colonial equation of *betagius* (*biatach*) with *villein* is not an insurmountable difficulty.[50] In the light of what follows, I suggest that the decline in status of the *biatach* from that of Irish gentlemen or freemen (*maithi*) to *nativus* tied to the land is a perfectly understandable transformation in Anglo-Norman Ireland when viewed in the light of the general treatment of the Irish in the early colony. Note that the original, superior, meaning of *biatach* (as discussed below) continued to prevail in Gaelic areas for centuries after the Invasion. Evidence from Ulster, Connacht and Mide for the period 1100 to 1350 clearly describes elements of the *baile biataig* system as defined by Duffy, that is, the basic unit of free-kinship landholding, the rents of which were paid in food renders and cattle to the overlord. Here the *biatach* is the head of the kin-group holding each *baile biataig*. Sometimes

46 Bugge, *Caithreim*, 29; Bannerman, *Dalriada*, 132, 140. **47** AT, 1139. **48** McErlean, 'Irish townland system', 332; Duffy, 'Territorial organization', 7–8. **49** Duffy, 'Territorial organization', 7. **50** Price, '*Betagius*', 187–190; Mac Niocaill, '*Betagh*', passim; Nicholls, 'Anglo-French Ireland', 378–80.

the term *lánbiatach* 'full *biatach*' is used to describe the kin-group or *baile biataig* leader, presumably to differentiate him from lesser persons with their lesser share of the *baile biataig*. Another related term was *fir ba[i]le*, apparently 'men of the *baile*', as found in *Betha Colmáin* in relation to *bailte* in Mide.[51]

The lands of the *baile biataig* appear to have been divided periodically among the kin-group into sub-divisions upon which lived each nuclear family of the kin-group, under whom would have dwelt the unfree or leaseholders, the actual tillers of the soil. Such a social gradation is recorded in an annal of 1150 (AFM), recording an archiepiscopal visitation of Tír Eógain and its accompanying dues. In this, each *rí* gives twenty cows, each *taísech* one horse, each *biatach* half of a cow, each *sáerthach* one third of a cow, and each *dímaín* one quarter of a cow. Note the grades under the *biatach* here. *Sáerthach* means 'freeman', and surely pertains to a member of the kin-group under the *biatach*, while *dímaín* 'idler, waster' is a derogatory term for what must have been tenants-at-will. The ratio of such kin-group sub-divisions was very often that of 1:4:16 (or 12), where 4 represents the four quarters of the *baile* and 16 (or 12) a further layer of sub-division of these quarters, usually into a further four divisions, whose name varies by region (cartron, ballyboe, tate etc.). Exactly how this triple-layered structure related to how the *baile* was divided among the kin-group requires further investigation. In many instances, at least in Ulster and Connacht, these 16 (or 12) sub-divisions in turn give us our modern townlands, but this is far from an absolute rule, as we shall see. The reference to a fixed number of cows and *seisrig*s which each *baile* is said to support, in the twelfth-century poem, 'Cā līn triūcha i nĒrind', indicates that the *baile biataig* had a fixed or notional area, and thus was an assessment system as well as an estate system. This is further indicated by the reference to a half-*baile* or *leathbhaile* in the poem (and elsewhere in contemporary pre-Invasion literature).[53] In the *baile* system of sixteenth-century Connacht we find sub-divisions of the *baile*, particularly the *dhá bhaile* (double *baile*), *leathbhaile* (half *baile*), and *ceathramh* (quarter *baile*). The latter could be further divided into four 'cartrons', a word deriving from the Norman-French *quarteron* (a quarter). Similarly, in Ulster the ballybetagh was also divided in the ratio 1:4:16, where each of the four quarters was further divided into quarters, known in most parts as the ballyboe or *baile bó*, a name probably deriving from its annual rent of one cow. The term *dhá bhaile* is recorded in Connacht as early as 1223.[54] The *leathbhaile* division occurs throughout Ireland, as can be seen in townland names containing the element 'levally' or 'lavally', and seems to have been used in many cases as an assessment term for a small estate, rather then a halving of a full *baile*, although this latter usage can also be found.[55]

The poem 'Cā līn triūcha i nĒrind' gives an insight into the internal organization of the *baile* by the twelfth century.[56] The ideal *baile* was thought to have

51 AU, 1178, 1179 (pp 190, 195); Meyer, *Betha Colmáin*, 88, 94. **52** The term *seisreach* originally carried the meaning of plough-team, later coming to assume that of ploughland (DIL, s.v. seisrech). **53** DIL, s.v. baile (c). **54** McErlean, 'Irish townland system', 318, 320, 328; Nicholls, 'Gaelic society and economy', 408. **55** See Chapter 5. **56** 'Cā līn triūcha i nĒrind', § 5.

300 cattle, eight *seisrig* – although whether this bears the meaning of a unit of measurement or a plough-team is unclear – and 'ceithri h-imirchi dóib de'. While this has been been translated 'four full herds' by O'Curry, it may be more correct to read 'four migrations' based on an alternative meaning of the word *immirge*, thus giving a possible reference to transhumance.[57] This line should perhaps be understood in light of the common attachment of upland pasture to *bailte*, especially in Connacht and Ulster, sometimes in the form of a discrete portion of upland, as revealed by the sixteenth-century surveys.[58] Can this reference also be interpreted as indicative of the existence of the ubiquitous quarter so early? This can certainly be traced in immediate post-Invasion Connacht and is perhaps earlier.[59]

'Cā līn triūcha i nĒrind' gives an approximately accurate number of *tríchas*, and says that each contained thirty *bailte*.[60] This is demonstrably untrue and appears to be schematic.[61] It is clear, however, that the *baile biataig* was an intrinsic part of the *tricha cét* system. The *tricha cét* is always composed of a definite number of *bailte*. The evidence may be recited here. The earliest datable reference to the *baile biataig* I can find occurs in *Cogad* (of *c*.1100).[62] In this narrative Brian Boraime gives a gift or *tuarastal* 'to each *biatach* of every *baile*' of the Ulaid during his circuit (*cuairt*) of 1005. In another passage the *baile* is shown as the unit immediately under the late-*túath* in a schema of society. At a minimum these references show that the *baile biataig* must have existed in living memory at the time of *Cogad*'s composition. In *Betha Colmáin*, written perhaps during the 1120s, we find the *fir baile* representing the social grade immediately below that of *taísech tuaithe* in Mide just as, in 1150 and again in 1178, we find the *biatach* in a similar rôle in Tír Eógain. Another such reference occurs in Fir Manach in 1278, while a reference to *betaxiorum* in a charter of the Ua Floinn king of Uí Thuirtre in 1260 is similarly suggestive. The Annals of Ulster contain a reference to the donation of a named *baile* near Drogheda to Mellifont by Muirchertach Mac Lochlainn in 1157, and of a *baile biataig* to the church of Derry, in 1177, in reparation for a breach of its sanctuary. A similar grant is recorded in AFM in relation to a *baile biataig* near Roscommon in 1176, and the grant of a *baile* to the clergy of Saul by the king of Ulaid in 1165 'for the luck of the reign of Mac Lochlainn'.[63] *Betha Colmáin* shows much of what is today Co. Westmeath divided into a network of *bailte* (most of which, unfortunately, cannot be identified), and goes on to suggest that Uí Failge was similarly so divided.[64] Even more impressive is the evidence provided by two pre-Invasion topographical tracts, *Crichad an Chaoilli*, relating to a part of Co. Cork, and *Críchaireacht Muinntiri Murchada*, relating to a part of Co. Galway. Both preserve

---

57 DIL, s.v. immirge. The meaning 'herd in transhumance' is probable but not certain. **58** McErlean, 'Irish townland system', 332. **59** See DIL, s.v. cethramtha(e); Hogan, 'The tricha cét', 230–1. **60** 'Cā līn triūcha i nĒrind', § 4. **61** Hogan, 'The tricha cét', 197, 203. **62** Todd, *Cogad*, 49, 136. **63** AU, 1157 (p. 130), 1177 (p. 188); AFM, 1165, 1176; Meyer, *Betha Colmáin*, vi, 88, 94; Nicholls, 'Anglo-French Ireland', 379. **64** Meyer, *Betha Colmáin*, 62–5, 88; Doherty, 'Vikings in Ireland', 317–18.

remarkable evidence for the existence of the *baile biataig* system, as we shall see shortly. A fifteenth-century account of the inauguration of an Uí Conchobhair king of Connacht, but which contains much earlier material, shows Síol Muireadhaigh divided into *bailte*, each ruled by a *brughaidh baile*, where the word *brughadh* is used in its alternative sense of *biatach*. *Leabhar Fidhnacha* contains a poem, apparently of fourteenth-century date, which claims for the monastery of Fenagh 'a cow from every *baile biataig* from Drogheda to Sligo' (that is, from Bréifne). A prose passage of the same work, written in 1516 but based on an earlier exemplar, regards the *biatach* in the sense of the references of 1150, 1178, 1260 and 1278 noted above.[65]

The topographical tracts noted above provide significant evidence for the operation of the *baile* system in both Connacht and Munster before the Invasion.[66] Both documents show the sub-division of *túatha* into *bailte* and *leathbhailte*, while *Críchad* further extends some of its *bailte* by naming sub-denominations. Some passages in *Críchaireacht* suggest the same interpretation but, as the toponyms are mostly obscure, it is impossible to be certain. *Críchad* is not consistent in its method, sometimes naming families without *bailte* and sometimes *bailte* without families. Both are named in 58 instances, and 44 of these *bailte* are associated with just one family or surname. In eight cases *bailte* have two associated families, in three cases three families, and in three other cases *bailte* have more than three families (in one case 12 are named). In *Críchaireacht* 18 *bailte* are associated with just one named family, while four are associated with two families. Another family is associated with three *leathbhailte*, at least one of which lay discretely to the others. It is not clear whether we are dealing with related families in these instances of multiple-family *bailte*. It will be noted that one family per *baile* appears to be the norm. The term *baile* is found affixed only to such units, that is, no sub-denominations bear the element *baile* in their names. Another point of agreement between both tracts is the similar size of *bailte* in each, as we shall see in Chapter 5. Comparison of both tracts shows that what was essentially the same system operated in two widely separated parts of Ireland in the pre-Invasion period. When we add to this the charter evidence cited in Chapter 5 demonstrating the existence of the *baile* system in all its facets in parts of Munster and Leinster in the immediate pre-Invasion period, the conclusion is that the system illustrated in these tracts was universal in pre-Norman Ireland.

The *baile biataig* system survived in Connacht, in much of Ulster, and probably in Thomond into the sixteenth century as a significant method of area organization, enabling detailed study.[67] In Ulster the unit bore the title ballybetagh while in Connacht it was simply the *baile*. As a unit of assessment of agricultural output rather than a simple land-measure the average size of the *baile* varied according to the nature of the terrain and local practice. Good-quality

65 Hennessy, *Book of Fenagh*, 47, 81; O'Daly, 'Inauguration', 346; Simms, 'Gabh umad a Fheidhlimidh', 136, 141. 66 Power, *Críchad*, 45–9; Hardiman, *Iar-Connaught*, 368–72. 67 McErlean, 'Irish townland system', passim.

agricultural land produces more than poorer-quality marginal land; therefore the *baile biataig* of good land will have a smaller acreage than one of poorer. MacErlean has estimated the average size of the *baile* in Monaghan and Fermanagh to have been under 3,000 acres and in Connacht, around 1,350. In Tyrone and Derry his figure is nearer to 6,000 acres.[68] While MacErlean notes the difference in unit-size averages between Ulster and Connacht he concludes that the similarities between the systems in both provinces is such as to indicate that they descend from the same ancestral system. The above studies have assumed, rather than demonstrated, that the system as found in the sixteenth century is a direct descendant of the twelfth-century one, and that the *baile biataig* system was not confined to those areas where it is found in the sixteenth century but was once national.

In Chapter 5 I show that these assumptions are correct, and go much farther. There I show that the *baile*, often disguised under its new name of 'villate', became an important unit of sub-infeudation throughout the colony, especially in the earliest settled areas, as well as in much of Connacht. In the latter province the early *baile* system becomes the colonial villate system which in turn becomes the sixteenth-century *baile* system, a seamless descent differentiated only by the name of the units involved, which themselves remain largely changeless throughout. In Leinster and Munster examples of *bailte* becoming manors and parishes are numerous and, in many cases, allow us to describe these and thus provide examples of *bailte* sizes immediately post-Invasion. This research shows a range of approximate *bailte* sizes from 700 to 7,000 acres, but with regional variations suggesting the existence of localized norms. In Galway the average figures agree broadly with MacErlean's estimate for Connacht (1,350 acres), but larger *bailte* are found in Roscommon and Mayo, while in east Cork the average was nearer to 2,000 acres. In Kilkenny and Wexford the average size was around 2,400 acres. The relevance of the sub-divisions of the *baile* for townland development are also explored. These certainly became the template for the sixteenth-century townlands of Connacht and much of Ulster, although the situation in the other provinces is less clear.

---

68 Ibid., 323–4; Duffy, 'Territorial organization', 7.

CHAPTER 5

The *baile*-estate and its descendant, the villate

This chapter demonstrates that the *baile* estate-system in Connacht, Munster and Leinster derived from a pre-Invasion model and indicates that the same was probably true in Ulster. Additionally, it demonstrates the survival of the system in Munster and Leinster during much of the Anglo-Norman period, a survival not hitherto noticed.

The missing link in the evidence between pre-Invasion *baile* (*biataig*) and sixteenth-century *baile* and ballybetagh in Connacht and Ulster is the Anglo-Norman period. The key to uncovering the existence of the *baile* (*biataig*) system in these areas (and in all other parts of Ireland) is the Latin term *villata*, Anglicized 'villate'. This appears to be an early-medieval formation deriving from the Latin *villa*: farmstead, rural estate. It gives, through Norman-French, the English word 'village'. It is the usage of this word in Ireland that concerns us here, and we note a range of meanings.

The medieval Latin words *vill* and *villata* share a common root. It is, therefore, no surprise to find both used interchangeably. Context will indicate the correct meaning. Vill can mean (a) a townland, (b) a town[1] and (c) a villate in its various senses. Villate can mean (a) a town,[2] (b) a fixed measure of land (in the same way that carucates and knights' fees do), (c) a vill or townland,[3] and (d) a spatial unit significantly larger than the vill or townland. Many references to the villate as a fixed measure of land survive. Typical examples will read 'two-parts of a villate of land in A', 'two villates of land in A, B, and C', 'one-quarter of one-half of a villate in A, B, and C'; 'three-quarters of a villate in A'; 'he holds in said vills [six are named] two villates of land'. Respectively, the provenance of these examples is: Thomond, 1297; Connacht, 1307; Waterford, 1280, 1298; Dublin, 1305.[4]

The fourth meaning of 'villate' is of greater significance for the matter at hand. An examination of the evidence shows that, throughout Anglo-Norman Ireland, there was a hierarchy of spatial units. While this may vary in its upper layers according to local practice, the two basic layers are always vill and above that villate. Nowhere do we find a listing of vills per villate, but the conclusion is inescapable. The standard unit of agricultural reference in colonial sources in Leinster and Munster is the vill, typically composed of roughly 400 statute acres

1 DKRI 38, pp 66, 92; 45, p. 39. **2** DKRI 38, p. 92; 42, pp 42, 70; 44, p. 26; 54, p. 27. **3** COD, i, 50; DKRI 36, p. 34; RC 7/2, 265–6. **4** DKRI 38, pp 39–40; COD, i, 109; CJRI, ii, 30, 341.

or so,[5] but in both provinces a larger mensuration and assessment unit, the vil-late, is known and employed. In Connacht the villate is of common occurrence in the sources, almost as common as the vill, and both have the same meaning as they do in the other provinces. While the term 'villate' will often have the sense of a fixed unit of mensuration (measure of land), the same does not appear to have been the case with the vill. In Munster and Leinster, the context in which villate occurs leads to the conclusion that, while the vill may have been the standard unit of reference, local knowledge of superior levels of spatial hier-archy, including the villate, survives everywhere.

While the terminology 'vill' and *villata* is colonial, the system can hardly be so. No such system is found in medieval Britain. One is led to the conclusion that the vill and *villata* hierarchy is yet another terminological re-christening of an indigenous system, as with *theodum* and cantred. Can we find direct evidence of this? Apparently. The purpose of the Domesday Book in English history is well understood. Such a national record of royal revenue also existed in Ireland, in the Dublin exchequer. By 1281 this had been destroyed in a fire, and a replacement had been composed by around 1298.[6] The prologue to this con-sisted of an enumeration of the cantreds and lesser land-units of Ireland. This prologue is none other than a version of the order in the indigenous schematic poem 'Cā līn triūcha i nĒrind'.[7] While the various indigenous recensions of this work are content to give a total number of *bailte* in Ireland, based upon the fixed rule of thirty *bailte* per *trícha cét*, the version in the exchequer goes further, and gives the number broken down by province, again based on a multiplier of the *trícha cét* by thirty. Significantly, this source uses the colonial terms 'cantred' and 'villate' in place of the indigenous *trícha cét* and *baile*, but the numbers make it certain that the terms refer to the same units.[8] Thus, no less a source then the Anglo-Norman exchequer in Dublin uses the term *villata* to refer to the *baile*. Here we have the Anglo-Norman administration – whose area of control cov-ers the greater share of the island – including among its most important fiscal records a computation giving a total number of cantreds and a corresponding number of villates contained within these cantreds, which is merely adopted unaltered – apart from a change in terminology – from an earlier indigenous computation of *tríchas* and *bailte*. Of these computations the first, that of *tríchas* and cantreds, is certainly accurate, while the second, that of *bailte* and villates, is schematic, theoretical and inaccurate. Despite this, the conclusion to be drawn here is that the *baile* estate, a socio-economic spatial unit found throughout pre-Invasion Ireland (as we shall see), was still a nationally distributed theoretical reality to the colonial administrators of Ireland more than a century after the Invasion. As we shall see presently, the 'villate' was, in fact, much more than this. We should also note the continued use of the term villate to refer to the *baile* in Connacht as late as the early seventeenth century.[9] In order to illustrate

5 See my forthcoming 'Townland development in Munster'. **6** Bateson, 'Irish Exchequer mem-oranda', passim; Otway-Ruthven, 'Knight service in Ireland', 11–12. **7** See Appendix 1. **8** Bateson, 500. **9** NAI RC 9/16, no. 20.

the identification of the *baile* (*biataig*) with the villate, and to demonstrate the parallel existence of vill and villate, it will be necessary to provide a number of examples. These are best adduced by province.

CONNACHT

Villates occur markedly more often in records relating to Connacht than to anywhere else in Anglo-Norman Ireland.[10] We even have an example of the term being used in its Norman-French form, village.[11] One suspects that the prominence of the villate in Connacht may be due to the pattern of infeudation here, where colonial settlement occurred later than elsewhere and where it was clearly less dense over much of the province. It may have been the case that here the colonial settler simply replaced the *lánbiatach*, and so was lord of a small estate otherwise entirely populated by Irish. So much is suggested by the bulk of the surviving manorial extents. Of course, parts of Connacht did get a heavier layer of colonial settlement, and these may be represented by those areas where holdings were normally measured by the smaller assessment units of carucate and acre. Here, as elsewhere, we find evidence of the existence of the spatial layers vill (that is, townland) and villate (that is, *baile*), although these are sometimes obscured by the usage of the term 'vill' in reference to both units. A pertinent example is seen in the extent of the *theodum* of Clanconway in north-eastern Galway, which contained twenty vills containing in all twenty-one carucates of land.[12] A reference to both layers occurs in that of 1281 to 'two vills of land in the moiety of the vill[ata] of Lusmath'.[13] This reference suggests that we are here dealing with a single *baile* and two of its four quarters.

Certain evidence of continuity from the pre-Invasion period for the *baile*-villate system is shown by the tract, *Críchaireacht Muinntiri Murchada*, which relates to the Headford area of Co. Galway.[14] At least four of its *baile* occur in colonial records as villates, and as much is implied in the case of another few.[15] Evidence of onomastic development also occurs. Two of the three *leathbhailte* of Meic Giolla Ceallaig, as named in *Críchaireacht*, occur in 1284 as the implicit villate of Balimachgillekally.[16] It is possible to identify the actual size of some of the *baile* of *Críchaireacht*, just as it is possible to identify the size of some colonial villates in Connacht. The *baile* system remained intact in Connacht until the second half of the sixteenth century. After this its disintegration was gradual and, on occasion, where a single *baile* remained in sole ownership, the 1654

10 NAI RC 7/1 to 7/12. 11 Curtis, 'Feudal charters', 290. 12 CDI, ii, 491. 13 Knox, 'Admekin', 170, 179. This place is the parish of Lusmagh, Co. Offaly, elsewhere described as containing two villates. It lay originally in Connacht. Knox was unable to identify it. (Cf. CDI, ii, 378, 560; COD, i, 166–7.) 14 Hardiman, *Iar-Connaught*, 368–72. 15 The explicit *bailte*/villates are Muine Inradain/Munynrethan (now Bunanraun), Baile Uí Cholgain/Balycalqyn (now Ballycolgan), Ráith Buidhbh/Rathboygh (now Rafwee), and Baile Uí Máelmuine/Balymoumun. 16 Hardiman, *Iar-Connaught*, 371; Knox, 'Admekin', 171.

Civil Survey records all of its sub-divisions. By using this survey, assisted by Petty's maps, it is possible to plot exactly the size of such a unit on the modern Ordnance Survey maps.[17] Just two of the *bailte* of *Críchaireacht* can be extended in this way. The *baile* of Cill Leabhair gives Killower (also a parish). Its trians give a total acreage of 1,114.[18] The *baile* of Beitheach gives Beagh (Donoghpatrick parish).[19] This is today represented by both townlands of Beagh, with an acreage of 2,678, about one-third of which is bog.

A further example of a *baile*-descent from the pre-Invasion period comes from the same area. This concerns the grant of the *pagus* of 'Lismacuan [read Lismacnan] in Clonfergale' to Abbeyknockmoy (*Collis Victoriae*: Co. Galway) by a *comes* of Muintir Murchada, probably during the early 1190s. In this Latin charter, of which only a partial abstract survives, *pagus* 'country district' is clearly used for *baile* (in this case a half-*baile*).[20] Clonfergale is the later cantred of Clanferwyll (**C9**) and the descent of Lismacnan can be traced as it was a discrete portion of the abbey-land. This is the 'half-villate' of Lysmakenan from which the abbot of Knockmoy was claiming rent in 1293 from David de Barry. By 1582 this was represented by the 'two quarters of Lismeckenan', described three years later in more detail as the three half-quarters of Lismakinnan and the half-quarter of Uranebegge, the former in the possession of the French family, and from all of which 'the abbey and convent of Knockmoy' had been seised of a chief rent.[21] Today Lismakennan has become Frenchfort, containing 1,379 acres, while the remaining half-quarter, Oranbeg, contains 519 acres, in total giving 1,898 acres for this half-*baile* in Oranmore parish.

A final such example concerns the *baile* of Leamore, granted to the hereditary physician family Uí Maoltuile by Cathal Crobderg Ua Conchobair (d. 1224) as payment for services. This was still retained by the 'Tully' family in 1641, and contained 824 acres of better-quality land.[22]

The de Burgh inquisitions of 1333 give a good flavour of mensuration practices in Connacht and contain useful references to the villate.[23] Everywhere lords' demesne is extended in acres and carucates. These carucates contained 120 acres.[24] Carucates and acres are rarely found outside demesne-land, apart from in the most heavily settled cantreds in eastern Galway. In all cantreds the villate is the standard unit of mensuration, along with its sub-divisions, the half-villate, the quarter, the half-quarter (the *leathcheathramh* or lecarrow), and the third (the *trian* or treen). It is easy to recognize the sixteenth-century *baile* system in these inquisitions. Many villates or portions thereof are held by colonists, but some by

17 For the Civil Survey see the various published *Books of Survey and Distribution* for Galway, Mayo and Roscommon, and for Petty see W. Petty, *Hibernio Delineatio: Atlas of Ireland* (1685: reprint Newcastle-upon-Tyne, 1968). **18** BSDG, 95–6. Its *trians* became the townlands of Killower, both Treanbauns, Tulrush and Goldenpark. **19** BSDG, 102. **20** O'Flaherty, *Ogygia*, 30. **21** NAI RC 7/10, 87; Freeman, *Compossicion Booke*, 34–5, 51; NAI RC 9/14, nos. 12, 23. **22** Nicholls, 'Gaelic society', 432; BSDR, 52. This *baile* contained the present townlands of Leamore and Emlaghglasny in Ballinakill parish, Co. Roscommon. **23** Knox, 'Connacht' i and ii. In these inquisitions Knox translates *villata* as townland (Connacht, i, 137). **24** Ibid., 133.

'betagii' and gavillors. Outside of the most heavily colonized cantreds we find *theoda* occuring as single fees. The burgagery of Galway is said to have contained three and a half villates while that of Loughrea three.[25] The burgagery of Galway appears to be represented by the area of St Nicholas' parish, containing 3,767 acres, suggesting that these villates contained around 1,100 acres each.[26]

It is possible to trace the area of some other villates occurring in these inquisitions, by using the methodology described above. A small number of denominations occurring in 1333 from the area of the later county of Galway survived until 1654. These included one full villate, that of Rathgorgyn, later recorded as the *baile* of Rathgorgin (Kilconierin parish), containing 1,073 statute acres; and two half-villates, the later half-*bailes* of Lickerrig (also a parish), containing 744 acres, and Cahercrea (Killeenadeema), with 677 acres.[27] While these were in fertile areas still within the colony by 1333 we also find references to villates west of Lough Corrib, in the stony and boggy area which had recently been lost to colonial control. From here we can identify at least two villates which survived intact into the late sixteenth century. The Balymackolvew of 1333 had become the *baile* of Ballymacgillewye by 1593, but cannot now be described. Tologhkoygan had become the *baile* of Tollykhane by 1631, the modern Tullokyne and surrounding townlands (Moycullen parish). This villate/*baile*, with its castle on the western shore of Lough Corrib, contained 1,942 acres of rather boggy land.[28]

Further evidence is provided by the extent of Kilcolgan manor made in 1289.[29] In this what are certainly villates are called 'vills', and the typical *baile* divisions two (*dhá*), one, half, and quarter occur. Again, several survived as recorded *bailte* down to 1654. We have the villate of Coythill held by the Croke family, which Nicholls identifies with the *baile* of Cloghroak (Ardrahan parish: *Cloch an Chrocaigh*), containing 849 acres of good-quality land; and the half-villate of Balymagrey, later a *leath-bhaile*, now the townlands of Castletaylor in Ardrahan parish, containing 698 acres.[30] Of particular interest due to its naming pattern is the villate of Belsychauch, Cathersordaly & Lochomyr. Nicholls has identified these places with Caherawoneen and Loughcurra in Kinvarradoorus parish, and with the 1654 *baile* of Caherseral and Loughcurro, with an acreage of 1,923 of mixed-quality lands.[31]

Similar examples can be found in Co. Mayo. The manor of Lehinch *alias* Muntercreghan was described in 1299 and again in 1308.[32] This seems to have

25 Ibid., 135, 397. **26** In 1609 the burgesses of Galway owed various services to St Nicholas' parish 'according [to] the olde ancient custome' (Hardiman, *Iar-Connaught*, 236–40). **27** Knox, 'Connacht', i, 134–5; BSDG, 237, 241, 334. The modern townlands for these units are 1) Rathgorgin and Deerpark; 2) both Cahercreas and Curheen; 3) Lickerrig, Crossderry, Lecarrow, Coolraugh and Laughil. **28** Knox, 'Connacht', i, 397; NAI RC 9/14, no. 50; NAI Lodge MSS Rolls i, 257; NAI RC 5/29, 133; BSDG, 78; Petty's map, Co. Galway. **29** MacNiocaill, *Red Book of Kildare*, 53 ff; Knox, 'Kilcolgan', 170–7. **30** 'Kilcolgan', 172; Nicholls, 'Red Book of Kildare', 29–30; BSDG, 247. The *baile* of Cloghroak contained the townlands of Cloghroak, Ballyglass, Shantallow and Ballyboy. **31** Knox, 'Kilcolgan', 171; Nicholls, 'Red Book of Kildare', 27–8; BSDG, 45. This *baile* contained Cahercarney, Turloughkeeloge, both Caherawoneens and both Loughcurras. **32** Knox, *Mayo*,

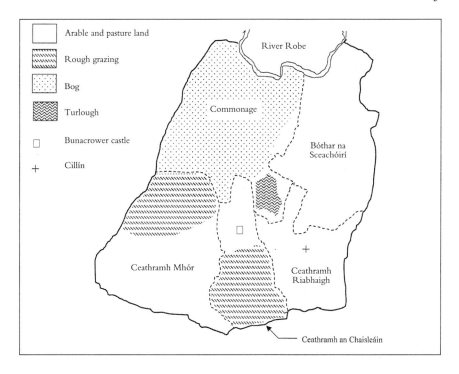

Map 5. The 1,221-acre *baile* of Muine Creabhair (Bunacrower, Co. Mayo)

corresponded to the parish of Kilcommon. These extents can be compared with that of Pobal Muintire Creacháin, which lists all the *bailte* in the territory and which dates from the 1560s or 1570s.[33] The manor contained sixteen vill[ate]s and one half vill[ate]. As many as eight of these villates can be identified in the *bailte* list.[34] The villate of Moneycrower *alias* Baile Muine Creabhair (now Bunacrower) is of special interest as it survived intact until 1654 and in that its area is further demarcated by its forming a detached portion of Kilmainmore parish. Most of its half-quarters became distinct townlands, seven in all, giving a total acreage of 1,221 on land with some bog.[35] As a typical example of a Connacht *baile* this is illustrated in Map 5. At least one further villate here can be described in the same way. Lehinch becomes Baile na Leithinse, containing 1,575 acres.[36] In other cases it is clear *bailte* in the list must correspond with earlier villates even though there is now no evident onomastic relationship.

106–8. **33** TCD MS 1440, which describes all the mensal lands of the MacWilliam Burkes. This was printed, with errors, by O'Reilly in his 'Historia et Genealogia Familiae de Burgo'. **34** Dericoul/Baile Doire Cola, Baliblohagh/Baile Blaedhach, Coolcon/Baile Cúlacon, Skeaghloghan/Baile Sciathlochain, Moneycrower/Baile Muine Creabhair, Coolishel/Baile an Chuilísill, Kilglassan/Baile Cille Glasain, Lehinch/Baile na Leithinse. **35** BSDG, 42. This *baile* contained Bunacrower, Carrowreagh, Carrowmore, Lecarrow, Mweelis, Ballinla and Cloonkeeghan. **36** O'Sullivan, *Strafford Inq.*, 70–1. This *baile* contained Lehinch Demesne,

Further to the north, an extent of around 1240 lists the villates of the *theodum* of Moyntirlathnan.[37] Just one survived down to 1654, the villate of 'Lothbrothry', the *baile* of Lough Brohly (now in Lissard More, Kilgarvan parish). Its four quarters are now represented by seven townlands comprising in all 4,580 acres.[38] The land here is a mixture of lowland low-grade pasture and mountain bog. The 1333 inquisitions provide further identifications in Mayo. The villate of Knappaugy gives the *baile* of Knappagh (Aghagower parish). Its three *trians* became townlands, giving an acreage of 1,627 on pasture with some bog.[39] Of interest is the quarter-villate of Corbeggan. This gives the quarter of Carrowbiganny of 1654, the modern townlands of Corraveggaun (Ballynahaglish parish) containing 414 acres.[40] In this example we find a portion of land in *ceathramh* described as a quarter-villate in 1333, a quarter in 1654, and which survives as a modern townland. The element *ceathramh* is present throughout its onomastic history.

Even when the *baile* system does not survive until the era of cartography, other methods can be used to uncover *baile* extents. A grant of 1282 names the villates of Unchen, Tasrather, Dondermod and Thoburalgyly 'on the east side of the [River] Suck' in a context which indicates they lay conterminously.[41] Unchen is now the townlands of Funchionagh, Tasrather gives the parish name Tisrara, the church of which lies in Mount Talbot, while Dundermot lay around Lisgillalea in the north of Tisrara parish.[42] From their distribution within the parish it is clear that all four villates together comprised the entire parish of Tisrara (Co. Roscommon), containing 8,482 acres, giving an average of 2,120 acres per villate in this lowland and somewhat boggy parish.

A similar example concerns lands in Co. Sligo. Around 1265 the castle of Rathardkrath with its villate and the adjacent villates of Ronelan and Clarath were the subject of an enfeoffment.[43] These places are now Ardcree, Ranaghan and Claragh in Kilvarnet parish. These places occur at either end and towards the middle of the parish, and it seems clear that, once again, the total area of these three agrees with that of the entire parish (incidentally giving additional evidence for the agreement of parish and manor). The acreage is 6,696 acres, giving a villate average of 2,230.

An example of considerable interest involves a grant made by King Ruaidrí Ua Conchobair no later than 1236, of lands in the *túath* ('theud') of Clann Uatach. In this he grants three *villatae terrae* to St Mary's abbey, Dublin. These are named as Fininagh/Fynchmahc, Desert *juxta* Briolem, and Soynemaneran/Macsynemenan. He also granted one and a half carucates at Kilkarch. These lands, in the parishes of Dysert and Cam, Co. Roscommon, were subsequently confirmed to St Mary's by their new colonial lord, in 1270. The *Book of Survey*

Knockalegan, Clareen, and Robeenard.   **37** MacNiocaill, *Red Book of Kildare*, 60 (and cf. 167). **38** BSDM, 155. This *baile* contained Lissard More, Graffy, Carrowcastle, Carrowcrom, Craggera, and both Ellaghs. **39** Knox, 'Connacht', ii, 58; BSDM, 113–14. This *baile* contained Knappagh More and Beg and Knappaghmanagh. **40** Knox, 'Connacht', ii, 58; BSDM, 180. **41** COD, i, 102. **42** BSDR, 112–15; Petty's map of Roscommon. **43** MacNiocaill, *Red Book of Kildare*, 69.

and Distribution and its accompanying maps records the *baile* of Feevagh, containing 3,723 acres, much of which was bog, while we can also reconstruct the *baile* of Desert and its 2,552 similarly boggy acres. By this time 'Syvannanan' has become a half-*baile*, whose area is now represented by the 861 acre, largely bogless, townland of Curry. Kilkarch is now the townland of Kilcar, containing 776 acres. Does this deed indicate that the colonial carucate had already spread to pre-colonial Connacht, or does the carucate here do duty for an unnamed indigenous unit, perhaps the *seisreach*?[44]

More general estimates can be made where we know the total area of a cantred and its total of villates. One such example is that of the cantred of Sylmolron (**C28**: now in Co. Roscommon), whose secular lordship was extended at twenty-four villates in 1305.[45] This cantred contained approximately 58,000 acres and, allowing for its cross-land, suggests an average acreage per villate of something above 2,000 on lowland with much bog.

The survey cited illustrates the continued existence of a largely static *baile* system in Connacht from the twelfth to the seventeenth century, unaffected by political mastery or colonial settlement. While many of the above examples (see that of Lismakennan), clearly illustrate continuity in mensuration from the Anglo-Norman period into the seventeenth century, such continuity should not be seen as an absolute. The example of the 988-acre holding of Ballinamanagh (Ballynacourty parish) is a case in point. This appears to have been an early possession of St Mary's abbey, Dublin. While its size suggests that it may originally have been a half-*baile*, it is described as a quarter in the seventeenth century. Indeed, the variations in quarter size experienced at this time by jurors empanelled by the court of chancery in an inquisition concerning the barony of Kiltartan, Co. Galway, led them to draw attention to gross inconsistencies in the system.[46] They found quarters ranging in size from 50 up to 436 acres (statute measure), giving probable *bailte* sizes in the range 200–1,744 acres. This suggests that, over time and subject no doubt to variations in local practice, the older system of *bailte* and *ceathramha* had become subject to further sub-division and so corrupt in places. Factors such as demography and the spread of blanket-bog must be noted. Nonetheless, the general evidence leans more towards continuity than change over this period in the *baile* system in Connacht.

McErlean's estimation method – in which he takes the townland as representing the quarter – gives an average *baile* acreage for Connacht of 1,350.[47] As shown above, however, such an estimate only holds for good-quality agricultural land, while *bailte* of up to 5,000 acres existed on uplands. These examples suggest an average of nearer to 2,000 acres for Connacht. The correlation between the quarter and townland in Connacht is not absolute, and it is clear

44 Ó Conbhuí, 'St Mary's', 82; BSDR, 102, 105–6, map of Athlone Barony; CIPRJ, 238. Feevagh contained the three Feevaghs, Ballyglass, Ardcolman, Cartronkilly, Derrycahill, both Breeole's (the Briolem of the title), and Porteen. Desert contained Commeen, Cuilleenoolagh, Cuilleenirwan, Bredagh, Cooldorragh and Milltown. **45** RC 7/11, 133. **46** BSDG, 231; NAI RC 4/14, no. 8. **47** McErlean, 'Irish townland system', 322–4.

that many townlands consisted of one, two, or more cartrons, itself the quarter of the quarter.

ULSTER

Little material survives from this province for the Anglo-Norman period. The Ulster inquisitions of 1333 employ the standard colonial system of measure: acres, carucates and knights' fees. One of the few exceptions to this rule occurs in the inquisition on the county of Coleraine, where we get a list of vills.[48] A few of these can be identified, such as Maynfauour, now the 825-acre townland of Moyaver (Armoy parish), the vill of Le Crag, now the 1,722-acre townland of The Craigs (Finvoy parish), and Clontfynan, now the 755-acre townlands of Clontyfinnan (Loughguile parish). These examples suggest that *baile biataig* sizes here were towards the smaller end of the scale. Reference to the villate here is relatively frequent, despite the paucity of evidence generally. The close corre-lation between *baile biataig* boundaries and those of parishes in much of Ulster (that is, several coterminus ballybetaghs form a single parish) indicates the antiq-uity of the ballybetagh system here and its descent from the earlier *baile biataig* system.[49]

MUNSTER

McErlean found some evidence for the *baile* system in Co. Clare, while Ní Ghabhláin has shown that the townland system in the area of what was Corcu Modruad descends from this system.[50] Further evidence can be found in the 1287 extent of the manor of Bunratty which found that it contained twenty-three vill[ate]s in addition to several hundred acres of demesne. Most of its place-names can be identified, and they show that the manor coincided with the cantred of Traderi (**C88**), an area containing around 29,000 acres.[51] Allowing for demesne and cross-land, it seems clear that the average villate size in this area of relatively rich land was around 1,100 acres. Gaelic land rentals of the late four-teenth- and early sixteenth-centuries demonstrate the continued existence of the system in Thomond.[52]

Remnants of the *baile* system in sixteenth-century Munster are not confined to Clare, however. The 'Desmond survey' of Connello – the western half of Co. Limerick – survives from 1584.[53] The basic unit of mensuration in this is

48 Orpen, 'Earldom of Ulster', iii, 128. 49 Ibid., passim; COD, i, 106; McNeill, *Anglo-Norman Ulster*, 138; Duffy, 'Territorial organization', 7; idem, 'Social and spatial order', 135. 50 McErlean, 'Irish townland system', 324, 327; Ní Ghabhláin, 'Kilfenora', passim. 51 Westropp, 'Wars of Turlough, 191–95. 52 Hardiman, 'Ancient deeds', 36–9, 43–5. The 'McNamara rental' seems to date from the late fourteenth century, while the 'O'Brien rental' is probably of early sixteenth-century date (Pers. comm., Mr Kenneth Nicholls). 53 Begley, *Limerick*, ii, 96–131.

the quarter, and half-quarters also occur with regularity. Many quarters bear names in Carrow (*ceathramh*). This survey bears some resemblance to those of the Civil Survey for Connacht, in that, while the quarter is the customary unit of mensuration, a few *bailte* still survive, usually represented by a singular denomination consisting of four quarters. Examples include Moynerly (Askeaton parish) containing 1,086 acres, and Tomdeely, a two-townland parish, containing 1,082 acres. Another interesting example is that of Ardnacrohy (Monagay parish). While this is estimated to contain one quarter (arable land only), it was divided in fact into *trian*s to give a total acreage of 670.[54]

Clear evidence for the presence of the system elsewhere in Munster can be had by the simple expedient of noting the distribution of townland names containing the element lavally or levally (*leathbhaile* 'half-*baile*'). All Connacht counties and several Ulster ones contain examples, but so do counties Tipperary and Cork, while obsolete examples are known from Limerick.[55] More significantly, south Tipperary alone in Munster retained a large assessment unit, the colp, into the sixteenth century. The evidence indicates that this unit was largely similar in size to our *bailte*.[56] Yet another remnant of the *baile* system in topography is the element trien, trean or trian (*trian* = third). This occurs widely in townland names in Connacht (see examples above) and Ulster, and is also found in most Munster counties and in several Leinster counties. In some of these instances the townland is quite small, often with acreages of less than two hundred. This suggests that some *trian*s were later divisions of quarters, made perhaps during the fifteenth and sixteenth centuries. Others, however, are quite large, and would seem to represent portions of *bailte*. Some of these consist of upland, such as the neighbouring townlands of Treanamanagh (600 acres) and Treangarriv (570 acres) in Glanbehy parish, Co. Kerry (where the final *trian* cannot now be identified). Bigger again is Trienearagh, a townland of 1,708 acres in Duagh parish in Kerry, and where again the remainder of the original unit cannot now be identified. An educative example is the similarly-named Trienieragh, a 270-acre townland in Kilbolane parish, Co. Cork. The Down Survey parish map shows that, in 1656, this townland was much bigger than it is today, containing much of the neighbouring townlands of Prohust and Cromoge to give an approximate acreage of *c*.750, and thus an original *baile* in excess of 2,000. This example suggests that there may be many other similar examples, where the element *trian* does indeed preserve memory of the *bailte* fraction. Of course, the term *trian* is not confined to *bailte* divisions, and was commonly applied to all sizes of spatial unit, such as monastic towns, *trícha*s, *túatha* and even provinces.[57]

The topographical tract, *Críchad an Chaoilli*, discussed above, preserves remarkable evidence of *bailte* size in pre-Invasion Cork. Thirteen *bailte* occur with sub-denominations and, where these toponyms can be identified, it is possible to estimate fairly exactly the size of such estates. The following acreages

54 Ibid., 109, 119, 124. **55** NAI RC 7/3, 289. **56** McErlean, 'Irish townland system', 322, 324. **57** See Hogan's *Onomasticon*.

are based on those of the townlands identified and their linking townlands and, while approximate, cannot be that far off the mark. It is clear that most of these *bailte* were undivided or concrete. The royal *baile* of Gleannamhu or Gleanndomain (Glanworth) contained around 1,576 acres.[58] Other approximate *baile* sizes were: Mag Drisein (Monadrishane), 1,056 acres;[59] Feic Beg & Ráith Siadail (Mount Rivers and Rathealy), 1,730;[60] Daingin Eóganachta (Ballindangan), 1,684;[61] Cill Ghallain (Kilgullane), 875.[62] These figures suggest a range of average size for *bailte* here on good quality land, and this can be confirmed to some extent by further examples established by other methods. Baile Uí Ghormain (now Ballyviniter) can be reconstructed simply by reference to the shape of the present three townlands bearing this name, giving an acreage of 1,554, again on high-quality land. In only a single *túath* of Fir Maige (Uí Cuáin) can all the constituent *bailte* – seven in all – be identified, and this *túath* has the added advantage of lying on the edge of the *trícha cét*, bounded by uplands to its south and riven by the Blackwater. The townland pattern here is uniformly on a north-south axis, with the toponym-giving section lying on the rich lands north of the river and a much larger section comprising uplands on the south bank. This has enabled Ó Buachalla to reconstruct the original *bailte* structure here, giving an average acreage of around 2,200 per *baile*.[63] The acreage figures quoted so far are consistent with land quality and show a pattern, but there are some exceptions. The *baile* of Lios Leithísel & Doire Uí Thnúthghaile seems to have contained only about 600 acres,[64] but the *leath* of the toponym is suggestive of *leathbhaile* status, although this is not stated. At the other extreme we have two examples. The *baile* of Leathnocht (Ballynoe), with twelve named families each located within their own sub-denomination, contained around 3,000 acres, on good quality land.[65] The Baile idir dá Abhuinn (Ballyderown) contained a small area of good land between the eponymous rivers (Funchion and Araglin) and then an extensive area of upland and mountain lying on the north bank of the Araglin, in all about 7,500 acres.[66] In summary, *Críchad* provides unique evidence of the *baile* structure in Fir Maige. Its value goes well beyond this, however. Features such as the general range of *bailte* size (700 to 7,000 acres) and the onomastic patterns displayed agree well with the fragmented evidence for the *baile* system elsewhere in Ireland, and, in *Críchad*'s *bailte*,

---

58 Power, *Críchad*, 45. For onomastic identifications from *Críchad* see Appendix 3. Gleanndomain, as extended in *Críchad*, contained the townlands of Glanworth, Cuppage and Clontinty, and so must also have contained all or part of the linking townlands of Dunmahon, Rathdaggan, Boherash and Ballyquane. **59** Ibid., 47. From its description it probably contained the eponymous Monadrishane, as well as Ballynacarriga, Maryville, Moorpark and Gortroe. **60** Ibid. Contained Mount Rivers, Rahealy and Strawhall, and so must also have contained Gearagh, Carrigabrick and Ballyvadona. **61** Ibid., 45. Contained Ballindangan and Curraheen, so also must have contained Flemingstown. **62** Ibid. Contained Kilgullane and Broomhill, and so also Curraghbowen and Johnstown. **63** Ó Buachalla, 'Townland development', 92. **64** Power, *Críchad*, 45. **65** Ibid., 46. Contained Ballynoe, Cornhill, Killeagh, Ballyvoskillakeen, Boherderoge, Loughnahilly, Manning, and Garraunigerinagh, and so also at least Ballyclough and Knocknacappul. **66** Ibid., 47. It contained Ballyderown, Macroney and Gortnaskehy, and thus everything in between.

we may see a glimpse of what may have been the typical topography of pre-Invasion Gaelic Ireland.

The presence of the *baile* system in pre-Invasion Munster can also be demonstrated from charter evidence. This comes from a charter of Diarmait Mac Carthaig, king of Desmond, granting lands to Gillabbey (*de Antro*) in Cork. While doubt has been cast on its authenticity, Flanagan, following upon exhaustive investigation, accepts it as genuine.[67] She dates the charter 1167 × 1175, a period probably preceding the arrival of colonists in Cork. In this charter King Diarmait confirms grants of vills by relatives, and makes one fresh grant. Of relevance here is the description of these denominations as *vills*, a term which can only be a direct translation of *baile*. One of these vills, Killinacannigh (Killeens, St Mary's Shandon parish), being located near Cork City, descended intact down to the eighteenth century, and its acreage thus computed at 1,545. These lands, much on north-facing hills, were of average agricultural quality.[68]

Another example, on the surface, appears to suggest that some early *bailte* may have been very small, but closer investigation disproves this. Among the lands granted to Holycross abbey by Domnall Ua Briain, probably during the 1170s, was Bali Icheallaich. This is now Ballykelly (Ballysheehan parish, Co. Tipperary), a mere 243 acres. In its present boundaries this townland formed a detached portion of Holy Cross parish in the seventeenth century, appearing to confirm its small size. However, lying adjacent to its north are the townlands of Grange More and Grange Beg. The former belonged to the abbey of Cahir while the latter was held by the Sall family of Cashel. While the term 'grange', given its customary sense of monastic out-farm, suggests links to Ballykelly, these links are proven by the quitclaim by John Sall of all rights 'in Balycally' in 1429. The original Baile Uí Cheallaig must have contained all three townlands.[69]

In Munster, while the typical colonial mensuration of acre, carucate and knights' fee was the principal system, a parallel system of quarter, villate and *theodum*, reflecting the indigenous system, can also be found. The latter is especially common in Limerick and Waterford, but *theoda*, villates and quarters can be found everywhere in colonial Munster.[70] In Waterford, the large honour of Dungarvan made extensive use of the villate and of half- and quarter-villates in late thirteenth-century extents.[71] This is perhaps due to the large size of this fee, which covered about half of the county, contained extensive uplands, and in which the Irish retained some lands well into the thirteenth century. Some vil-

67 Flanagan, *Irish royal charters*, 175–210, 333–42. **68** Flanagan and Ó Murchadha (Flanagan, *Irish royal charters*, 33, n. 9) misconceive the extent of this estate. In addition to their sources, an early eighteenth-century rental exists (UCC MS U/251) which denotes precisely the Boyle lands here. Killinacannigh contained the modern Killeens, Knocknaheeny, both Knocknacullens and that part of Commons in St Mary's parish. It cannot have contained Ballycannon, which was part of the Blarney estate. **69** Flanagan, *Irish royal charters*, 308; Fiant Eliz., 391; MacCotter, 'Salls of Cashel', 218. **70** CDI, ii, 420–8; CDI, iv, 257–62; RC 7/1, 149, 198, 285, 323; RC 7/2, 72, 83, 235; RC 7/3, 408; White, *Book of Ormond*, 71; COD, i, 9–10, 18, 135; DKRI 38, p. 39; 44, p. 30; CJRI, i, 32. **71** CDI, iv, 261–2; DKRI 38, p. 40.

lates here, and elsewhere in Munster, can be described. (Most of the following examples relate to lands in Co. Waterford.)

• That of Ballyeelinan & Ballyguin (Lisgenan parish) has a fifteenth-century perambulation which allows us to extend it at around 1,075 acres of good land.[72]
• The fee of the Fews, whose area certainly corresponds to the parish of the same name, is said to contain two villates; this had remained in Irish hands well into the thirteenth century.[73] The parish contains 6,817 acres of pasture and mountain land.
• The villates of Clonkoghen (now Clooncogaille) and Seskinan must correspond to the latter parish, which contains 16,867 acres of largely mountain land.[74]
• The quarter-villate of Rathnameneenagh (Ardmore and Ringagonagh parishes) must equate with the present townlands of the name, containing 618 acres, of which about 60 per cent is upland bog.[75]
• The townland structure of the parish of Lickoran suggests that it preserves the area of the villate of Farnan (Farnane).[76] The parish contains 2,414 acres, equally divided between lowland pasture and mountain land.
• The villate of Bolydysert (sometimes described as a half-villate) must now be represented by the 5,396-acre – largely mountainous – parish of Dysert. Its descent as a sub-manor of Kilsheelan can be traced.[77]
• An extent made in 1234 of a portion of the cantred of Obride lists seven vill[ate]s containing a total of forty nine carucates, or around 2,100 acres per villate.[78]
• A reference to 'a quarter of half a villate' in the cantred of Offath, Co. Waterford, may indicate a *leathceathramh* as found in Connacht.[79]
• The Dene estate in Offergus was measured at five villates in 1302.[80] Ofergus lay in medieval Cork but lies in modern Waterford, being that area west of the River Blackwater and south of the River Bride. The Denes held an even moiety of Ofergus through inheritance, the remainder being held by their co-parceners, the de Exeters. Such partitions involved a careful division of lands and both moieties were discrete and interspersed. Extensive records allow us to extend Ofergus at a total of around 24,400 acres of intermediate quality land.[81] Thus the average villate size here was 2,440 acres.
• In 1294 John le Poher of Shanagarry, Co. Cork, a free-tenant of the manor of Inchiquin, was impleaded for dower in 'two villates of land in Sengarthe' by the widow of his late lord. While these Powers held extensive lands in the area, much of these lands were held of the see of Cloyne. The lands referred to in the

72 CDI, iv, 262; Nicholls, 'Mandeville deeds', 12; PRC, 145. Additionally, this villate formed a detached portion of Lisgenan parish. It contained the eponymous Ballyeelinan and Ballyguin, as well as Glenwilliam and Tonteeheige. 73 CDI, iv, 262; Curtis, 'Sheriffs accounts', 3. 74 DKRI 38, p. 40. 75 Ibid. 76 CDI, iv, 262. 77 CDI, ii, 298; DKRI 36, p. 62; COD, i, 133; COD, iv, 112–13. 78 CDI, i, 327. 79 COD, i, 109. 80 CJRI, i, 403. 81 Brooks, *Knights' fees*, 222; NAI RC 7/1, 434; 7/2, 64; 7/4, 245; 7/5, 457; 7/9, 212; 8/1, 120–1, 237.

above pleading can only be their holdings at Shanagarry and at Inch, both of which occur regularly in the contemporary Inchiquin inquisitions, and both of which are extended at three knights' fees. These were distinct sub-manors, whose area is represented by the parishes of Kilmahon (2,849 acres) and Inch (3,822 acres). A similar example concerns 'half a villate of land called Drumkohel' of 1250 or so. This is Dromcolloher, a Limerick parish of 4,846 acres. One of its townlands is Carroward (644 acres), which suggests that this early reference may have related only to a moiety of this *baile*. Thus, even where colonial mensuration is the norm, knowledge of the villate remained.[82]

Our final examples are from Desmond. The MacCarthy entail of 1365 lists the lands of the MacCarthy kings of Desmond.[83] This list includes four holdings which were divided into quarters, and which seem to represent royal demesne lands. Of these four, two remained in MacCarthy hands into the seventeenth century as discrete portions surrounded by non-MacCarthy holdings. While these may earlier have been Anglo-Norman demesne manors this is far from certain: any colonial presence in these areas was early and of very brief duration.[84] The context, especially the reference to quarters, indicates that these estates originated as indigenous *bailte*.

- The first of these is described as *quatuor quarteriis de Iruelagh, viz. Drumdymhir unacum aliis tribus quarteriis ibidem*. This is Airbhealach or Castlelough, on Lough Leane in Co. Kerry, one of the chief castles and demesne manors of the later MacCarthaigh Mór, descendants of the earlier kings of Desmond. The evidence suggests that this *baile* came into MacCarthy possession during the third quarter of the thirteenth century, and remained the location of their principal seat for over a century after.[85] This was thus a royal *baile*. By the sixteenth century this MacCarthy enclave consisted of the lands of the manor of Castlelough – which included Drumhumper, the earlier Drumdymhir (Druim Diamhair) – and those of the Franciscan friary of Muckross, founded by the MacCarthys during the fifteenth century. By this time these lands were measured in ploughlands and we can identify only two of its original four quarters: Druim Diamhair and its surrounding townlands, and the townlands of Irelagh (now Castlelough, Carrigafreaghane and eastern Muckross). In total, these lands amount to around 4,770 acres, of which around 1,450 acres are arable and pasture-land while the remainder is mountain grazing, oakwood and lakeside scrubwood liable to seasonal flooding.[86] As a large royal *baile* showing a typical pattern of mixed land-use, this example is illustrated in Map 6.
- The second such estate is described as *quatuor quarteriis Castri de Berra*. This is the estate of Castletown or Castledermod, the castle of Castletown Bearhaven,

82 RC 7/3, 408; Caulfield, *Youghal*, xxxv; CIPM, ix, 131; PRC, 80, 145; COD, i, 48. **83** Armagh Public Lib. MS KH II 46, p 195. **84** Nicholls, 'Lordship, Co. Cork', 164; MacCotter, 'Anglo-Norman Kerry', 60. **85** MacCotter, 'Anglo-Norman Kerry', 50; AI, 1302, 1391; BL Add MS 4821, f. 99. **86** CIPRJ, 82; BSD, Co. Kerry; LPL MS 625, f. 27; Petty's map.

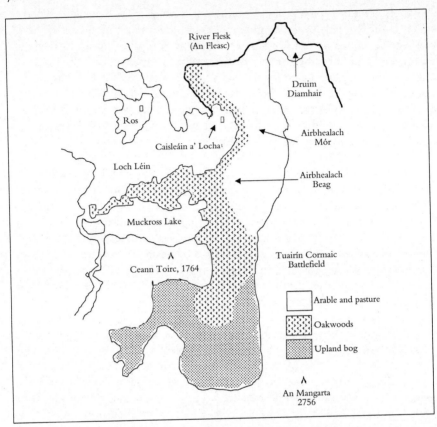

Map 6. The 4,770-acre *baile* of Airbhealach (Castlelough, Co. Kerry)

Co. Cork. By the sixteenth century this estate had passed to a junior branch of MacCarthaigh Mór, Clann Diarmada, when it is described as 'the four quarters of Clandermodie'. As with Castlelough, its precise extent can be established from sixteenth and seventeenth-century sources, which record its quarters.[87] The Castledermod estate contained around 5,500 acres. One of its quarters occupied the western end of Bear Island, facing Castledermod across the harbour, while the other three were on the mainland. Again, about one-third of the estate was land of some agricultural quality while the remainder was mountain land of limited value.

This survey indicates clearly that the *baile* system was universal in Munster and of pre-Invasion origin.

87 Butler, *Gleanings*, 60–2; Down Survey parish map, Killaconenagh (NLI MS 713).

LEINSTER

Evidence for the existence of the *baile* system in pre-Invasion Leinster comes from a charter of King Diarmait Mac Murchada, in which he granted lands to St Mary's abbey, Ferns, Co. Wexford.[88] This can be dated to 1160 × 1162. The relevant section reads *scilicet Ballisufin, Ballilacussa pro una villa, Borin et Roshena et Kilbride pro duabus villis* 'namely Ballisufin, Ballilacussa as one vill, Borin and Roshena and Kilbridi as two vills'. Of these names only Kilbride (a parish in northern Wexford) can be identified. Here we have direct evidence for the existence of an assessment system based on *bailte* (vills), just as we find in contemporary Connacht, and using exactly the terminology later found applied to the villate by the colonists, as demonstrated above. Evidence for the sub-divisions of the *baile* is also found here. The place-name element 'levally' is found in Leix, while the cartron, the quarter of the quarter as found in Connacht, is also present in sixteenth-century Leix, Offaly, Westmeath and Longford.[89] Further evidence for this sub-division system is found in ecclesiastical grants concerning lands in Dublin, Kildare and Carlow from the period 1179–86. In these grants several denominations in *leth-* and *lath-* and *trian-* occur. These are the familiar fractions *leath* and *trian* as found elsewhere – especially in Connacht – as fractions of *bailte*. Lest there be any doubt, one of the latter, Trianch[l]ochiar, occurs elsewhere as *tertia pars de Clochair* 'the third part of Clochair'. This was part of the lands of Christ Church, Dublin, in whose possession it remained into the seventeenth century. It is now represented by the townland of St Doolaghs (202 acres) and possibly that of Burgage (78 acres), both in Balgriffin parish, Co. Dublin.[90] Clochar appears to have been the original name for this *baile*.

  Further evidence for the existence of the *baile* system in Leinster in the pre-Invasion period is provided by references to a group of four denominations in *baile* which lay in Glencree, Co. Wicklow, part of the de Ridelesford honour of Bray.[91] These are first mentioned in a confirmation of the 1180s, when each .is measured, supiciously, at one carucate apiece. This mensuration was formulaic. Further evidence shows them to have been considerably larger.[92] Some were later granted to various monasteries, leaving a considerable paper trail. In the early 1200s two were subject to an exchange, the third part of Balibedan was traded for half of Balisenechil, once again showing usage of the familiar fractions. Part of the bounds of Balibedan are recorded, and show it to be ancestor to Ballybrew (Stagonell parish). From these bounds it is clear that Balibedan contained at least a couple of thousand acres of land, if not more, much of it upland.[93] The deed giving the bounds dates from the early 1200s, and states that

88 Flanagan, *Irish royal charters*, 88, 284. **89** McErlean, 'Irish townland system', 317. **90** McNeill, *Alen's Register*, 2–5, 15–16. **91** Brooks, 'The de Ridelesfords', i, 121–3, 127–8, 132–3. **92** Ibid., ii, 52. **93** Gilbert, *Chart. St Mary's*, i, 387–9; Nicholls, 'Miscellanea', 37 n. 15; Ó Conbhuí, 'St Mary's', 61. While Balibedan cannot have contained Killegar, which was episcopal land, it is clear that it contained at least Ballybrew and Kilmalin, and may well have contained Monastery, Cookstown, and other townlands to the south.

these were made by loyal men, English and Irish, *audivi eas antiquitus fuisse in tempore Hiberniencium* '[as] I have heard them to have been in the time of the Irish, anciently'.[94]

Our best Leinster evidence for the *baile* comes from Dublin. In at least four cases we can trace *bailte* boundaries from the pre-Invasion period down to that of the Ordnance Survey. The first of these features in the small collection of charters given by pre-Invasion Irish kings which has recently been published in a detailed study by Dr M. T. Flanagan. One charter concerns the lands of Baldoyle, Co. Dublin, granted to All Hallows priory by Diarmait Mac Murchada, king of Leinster and Dublin, around 1162.[95] The grant concerned *Balidubgaill cum hominibus suis scilicet Melisu Macfeilecan cum filiis et nepotibus suis* 'Balidubgaill with its men, namely M. M. with his sons and grandsons'. Flanagan shows that the Mac Feilecans were the kin-group holding Baldoyle and believes that they were not serfs but a free kin-group whose overlordship was the subject of the donation.[96] This is exactly the situation pertaining to a *baile*. The descent of the lands of Baldoyle is easily followed.[97] The lands of this grant are today the area of the civil parish of Baldoyle, comprising 1,235 acres. This is well within the size range we expect for a *baile* of good-quality land. Melisu Mac Feilecan was probably its *biatach*, the head of the kin-group whose land Baldoyle was.

Another example of an ancient estate from Dublin concerns Cloghran Swords. This was the estate of the FitzRery *alias* MacCynan family from at least 1222 until the extinction of the mainline of the family in the male line after 1378. These were a branch of the Welsh royal family of Gwynedd. The Welsh geneal-ogists derive the family from Gruffyd ap Cynan, whom they say was born in Cloghran, an estate that his father, a royal exile in Ireland, was said to have obtained. This was in the 1040s.[98] Flanagan accepts that the family were certain-ly established at Cloghran before the Anglo-Norman Invasion, and therefore this is a pre-Invasion estate.[99] The six carucates of the FitzRery family here were held *in capite*, and it is almost certain that this estate is coterminous with the parish of Cloghran, whose descent can be traced from the early thirteenth cen-tury onwards, and whose rectory was a possession of the family.[1] This parish contains 1,557 acres, making Cloghran of similar size to its near neighbour and fellow ancient estate, Baldoyle.

The third example concerns the estate of Ballyboghil (Baile Bachaill). This *baile* takes its name from the *Baculum Iesu*, an ancient relic associated with St Patrick and originally venerated in the church here. This estate was part of the *paruchia* of Armagh in pre-Invasion times, a status of some antiquity. Before 1180 it was sold by the see of Armagh to St Mary's abbey, Dublin, in whose posses-sion it descended. The area of this estate is preserved in that of its parish, with

94 Gilbert, *Chart. St Mary's*, i, 388–9. **95** Flanagan, *Irish royal charters*, 271. **96** Ibid., 79–80, 272 n. 4. **97** For a list of references see *Dinnseanchas* 3/3 (1969), 80–2. **98** Doherty, 'Vikings in Ireland', 300. **99** Flanagan, 'Origins of Balrothery', 84–94. **1** White, 'Reportorium viride', 193–4; McNeill, *Alen's Register*, 33.

an acreage of 2,789. Another possession of this abbey was Raheny. This estate appears to have been the subject of rival claims, and was certainly in St Mary's possession by 1172. A contemporary charter, by Strongbow, names its pre-conquest owner as one 'Gilcolman', showing it to have been a pre-Invasion estate. It remained in possession of the abbey until the Dissolution, and consisted of 910 acres.[2]

Further examples of the descent of pre-Invasion estates from elsewhere in Leinster can be found, most in grants made by King Diarmait and his *reguli*. Several occur in a grant of lands to the abbey of Baltinglass (Co. Wicklow: *de Valle Salutis*) made in 1148 × 1151, and the work of identification has been done by Nicholls.[3]

- The abbey itself lay at the centre of a block of land comprised of seven denominations, and now represented by Baltinglass parish and the southern half of that of Rathbran. Some of these are described as 'lands' while others follow the formula villa Ua X, representing the typical *baile* formula Baile Uí X. Two of the 'lands' also feature sept names, and it seems clear that all were *bailte*. The lands in question total around 10,800 acres, suggesting an average *baile* size of 1,540 acres. A number of outlying estates or granges can also be traced.
- Ros in alvein is now Grangerosnolvan parish, Co. Kildare (1,392 acres).
- Cluain Melsige is now the parish of Clonmelsh, Co. Carlow (3,146).
- Rath hargith corresponds to the contiguous townlands of Grangebeg and Kennycourt (Gilltown parish, Co. Kildare), acreage 2,565.
- Insi o Breslein corresponds to the parish of Brannockstown and the townlands of Gilltown and Grangemore in Gilltown parish, acreage 2,728.
- Magafin almost certainly corresponds to the parish of Monksgrange, Co. Leix, of 863 acres.
- Another example of the descent of a pre-Invasion secular estate concerns the vill of *Ballifislan in Fotherth*, granted to St Mary's abbey, Ferns, in 1160 × 1162. This is the fee and manor of Ballifistlan *alias* Ballycushlane, in the cantred of Fothard (**C178**), Co. Wexford, held of the lords of Leinster by service of one-quarter of a knights' fee. The claim of St Mary's to this appears to have been reconciled by their being left in possession of the rectory of Lady's Island parish, the ecclesiastical parallel to the manor. From the descent of this manor we know it to have comprised around 880 acres.[4]
- Baliucutlane occurs among the lands of the diocese of Glendalough in a confirmation of its lands by Strongbow given a few years after the Invasion. This

---

2 White, 'Reportorium viride', 195; Gilbert, *Chart. St Mary's* i, 141–2; ii, 64–8; Ó Conbhuí, 'St Mary's', 36–7, 46. **3** Flanagan, *Irish royal charters*, 383–4; Nicholls, 'Baltinglass charter', passim; White, *Extents*, 127–30. **4** Flanagan, *Irish royal charters*, 284; Brooks, *Knights' fees*, 117–19. While the parish contains only 597 acres the manor, as described in the early seventeenth century, contained an additional 280 or so acres as it extended into southern Kilscoran parish. This suggests that the manor – in an area whose feudal boundaries remained largely unchanged since the conquest – preserves the true area of the *baile*.

list clearly relates to the pre-Invasion lands of the diocese. Baliucutlane is grouped
with those lands 'in the land of Ufelann': the cantred of Offelan. The tithes of
the single townland parish of 'Cotlandstown' still lay with the diocese of Dublin
in 1654, and this *baile* is now represented by the 1,515 acre parish of
Coghlanstown, Co. Kildare.[5]

• A final example may be that of the *baile* of Finnabhair na nIngen, granted to
Mellifont in 1157 (AU), and which was said to lie near Drogheda. This is, perhaps, to be identified with the 1,127 acre parish of Fennor, Co. Meath, which lies
seven miles west of Drogheda, although this identification is far from certain.

Another example concerns the lands of the abbey of Killenny (*de Valle Dei*),
Co. Kilkenny. In this grant (early 1160s) fourteen denominations represent the
main land-block of the abbey. Only five of these are in 'Bale', others beginning
in *druim*, *ráith*, *cill*, *muileann* and *ard*. From this it would appear that sub-denominations are included, just as we have seen happen in *Crichad*. The lands in question appear to be represented by the area of the parish of Grange Silvia – representing the lands of Killenny at the time of the Dissolution – and perhaps some
of northern Powerstown parish, with an acreage that cannot have been much
in excess of 5,000.[6]

The lands of Jerpoint abbey (*Jeripons*), Co. Kilkenny, provide further evidence. Unfortunately the original grant, made by King Domnall Mac Gilla
Pátraic of Osraige (d. 1185), only survives in summary in a later confirmation
by John, of *c*.1192. Domnall's grant contains a fine list of toponyms of similar
form to that of the Killenny grant, containing six denominations in *baile* – including *Balleochellam … in qua monasterium ipsum situm est* – and several others. Most
of these are unidentified toponyms, giving a graphic example of the lost onomastic heritage underlying such heavily colonized areas. Two safe identifications
can be made here, that of the land of Baley Longsiu, which descended as a grange
and is represented by the 1,167-acre parish of Ballylinch; and the land of
Raichellela, now represented by the bulk of the parish of Grangemaccomb
(*c*.3,000 acres).[7]

One final such example comes from Meath, where St Mary's abbey, Navan,
included amongst its pre-Invasion possessions *Grange juxta ffoghyn*. This is now
Grange (Ardbraccan parish), containing 493 acres.[8]

While references to villates in Leinster are less common than in either
Connacht or Munster, once again they can be found everywhere.[9] In 1290 we
hear of 'half a villate in Portroyn'.[10] This suggests that the parish of Portraine
may have constituted a full villate. Its acreage is 2,185. The common-law practice of uniting adjacent places in groups of four and holding them legally respon-

5 McNeill, *Alen's Register*, 2, 21; *Civil Survey*, viii, 56–7.   **6** Flanagan, *Irish royal charters*, 252–3;
Bernard, 'Charters of Duiske', 9; White, *Extents*, 194–5.   **7** Flanagan, *Irish royal charters*, 386;
Langrishe, 'Jerpoint abbey', 180; Carrigan, *Ossory* ii, 321–2.   **8** Brooks, 'Charter of John de
Courcy', 39, 42.   **9** NAI RC 7/2, 229; 7/3, 223; COD, i, 44; DKRI 43, p. 37; 54, p. 35.   **10** RC
7/2, 229.

sible for failure to apprehend felons is well-known in England.[11] In 1271 the villates of Lucan, Esker, Palmerstown and Ballyfermot were fined in such a way.[12] These are fees which have corresponding parishes, giving respective acreages of 1,125, 2,366, 1,517 and 1,183. The spatial pattern here is clear.

While most manorial extents in Leinster follow the standard mensuration of acre, carucate and knights' fee, one significant omission is that of the large feudal barony of Overk, Co. Kilkenny, in which villates feature prominently, and which dates from 1314.[13] Like Dungarvan, Overk contained much marginal land, in this case woodland as much as mountain. As with Dungarvan, a number of fees here are extendable, while similar examples can be found elsewhere in Leinster.

- The five villates of Donkyt most likely equal the parish of Dunkitt, with an acreage of 6,773. This averages 1,355 acres on good quality lowland.
- Another lowland parish is Pollrone. Its 3,596 acres must represent the two villates of Polrohan.
- The five villates of Ownyng can be equated with the parish of Owning, containing 4,030 acres, much of which is good-quality lowland, giving an average of 800 acres per villate. Again, this extent lists several half- and quarter-villates, none of which can now be described.
- In 1312 the Carlow villates of Thamolyng (St Mullins) and Ballycrinnigan were fined for trespass.[14] From the context it is clear that these lay adjacent, and the geography here helps us to estimate their area, given that these were the southernmost two villates in the county. Each villate seems to have been over 3,000 acres in extent, and both contained a mixture of quality land and mountain.
- Two of the post-Invasion estates granted to Jerpoint abbey can be described, that of 'the entire ville of Clohan', now represented by the 529-acre parish of Garranamanagh, and 'the vill of Kell Rudi', now represented by Grangekilree parish, of 991 acres.[15] Kilree boasts a round tower and high-cross, indicators of some pre-Invasion importance. Can its estate be of similar date? Both lie in Co. Kilkenny.
- Elsewhere, mention of 'a quarter of Ballmagorin' in 1336, also in Kilkenny, is noteworthy, as is mention of 'a quarter of land' in Omayl (in Wicklow: *c.*1300).[16] These references attest to the presence of the quarter in parts of Leinster from where it subsequently disappears.
- It is possible that the assessment unit called the martland, found in sixteenth-century Carlow and northern Wexford, may preserve something of the older *baile* system of Leinster as these martlands varied in size from around 600 acres on good quality land to as much as 6,000 acres or so on mountain land, a range similar to

11 See my forthcoming 'Townland development in Munster'. 12 DKRI 36, p. 25. 13 White, *Book of Ormond*, 131–5. 14 DKRI 39, p. 4. 15 Flanagan, *Irish royal charters*, 386; Langrishe, 'Jerpoint abbey', 179–80; White, *Extents*, 182–3; Carrigan, *Ossory*, ii, 258; iii, 372. 16 COD, i, 139 and 290.

that of the earlier *baile*. This was the territory of the Kavanagh lineage, an area in which older indigenous practices may well have survived for longer.[17]

In summary, once again we can trace the *baile* system in all its facets in Leinster from the pre-Invasion period well into the Anglo-Norman period. Average *bailte* acreages again agree with those elsewhere, especially in Munster.

FROM 'BAILE' TO VILLATE

As we have seen, the *baile biataig* system survived in Connacht and Ulster into the sixteenth century, but disappeared much earlier in Leinster and Munster. McErlean concluded that the survival of the *baile* system in these provinces was due to the weakness or absence of Anglo-Norman settlement, just as the extinction of the system in Munster and Leinster was due to the strong presence of such settlement. However, the survival of the *baile* system in Connacht, with its significant colonial settlement, suggests that this argument does not explain all.

If my conclusion that the *baile* system was originally national is correct, then why does it disappear so early in the south and east? The Irish concept of kin-based land-holding or estate management, upon which the *baile biataig* system was based, was completely alien to the Anglo-Normans, to whom land was best managed by a hierarchy of nuclear families of freemen and nobles. It is clear that colonial settlement was most dense on good-quality tillage land, and considerably less so on marginal land, even in otherwise heavily settled areas of Munster and Leinster. Such heavily settled areas, made up of the better-quality agricultural land, came to support a tillage-based manorial economy of significant density, where less land was needed to produce the same amount of food as would have been generated under the indigenous *baile* system. Here the *baile* system would not have served the density of population well, which may explain why it disappeared early in favour of the significantly smaller vill, while, in adjacent but much less settled areas, such as the honour of Dungarvan and in Overk, elements of the system survived under the guise of the villate, at least into the fourteenth century. A similar dilution of settlement density must explain its survival in Connacht. Therefore, it might be supposed that the *baile* fell into disuse earlier as the primary estate in the areas of most intense colonial settlement.

Given the necessary practice among the first colonists of using indigenous spatial units, should we not find evidence of the *baile* in the earliest grants, say in the period before 1210, just as we find evidence of the *theodum* and cantred there? In terms of early secular grants, it will be noted that these are not of common occurrence and, where they occur, usually confine themselves to units of higher rank than the *baile*, such as cantred, knights' fee, and *theodum*, or fractions of these. Manorial extents or even listings of lands at the level of the vill are almost

---

17 Pers. comm., Mr Kenneth Nicholls.

unknown from the early period. An important exception here are the Leinster feodaries, especially in relation to parts of counties Wexford and Kilkenny. The situation is better in the case of ecclesiastical grants, a substantial body of which survive from this early period, largely from grants made in Leinster to Dublin monasteries, in addition to the earliest series of all, those made in Cork to St Nicholas' abbey, Exeter. However, such grants run the gamut of tenurial size, ranging from (the benefices of) entire cantreds to mere urban messuages. Within the broad body of such grants it is possible to isolate a stratum of donations concerning what appear to be vill[ate]s. Within this, however, only a significantly lesser number can be traced down to the sixteenth century, the period of commencement of cartographic record. Examples can be divided into lands entirely donated, and those where only the ecclesiastical benefices were given.

To the first category belong the following examples.

- Tullachani. This is mentioned in the foundation charter of Duiske abbey (*Vallis Sanctus Salvatoris*), of *c*.1207. An extent of 1541 shows this grange to be represented by the parish of Grange, Co. Kilkenny, with an acreage of 1,934.[18]
- Annamult. Included among the original lands of Duiske, pre-1204, and descended intact as a grange. A single modern townland of 1,351 acres (Danesfort parish, Co. Kilkenny).[19]
- Rosrehil/Toberogan. This vill was granted to St Mary's abbey during the 1170s. It is said to comprise five carucates. It descended intact until the Dissolution, with its castle and church, and contained around 1,300 acres. (Toberogan, Kilcullen parish, Co. Kildare.)[20]
- All the 'land of Baliomorchechad' and a parcel of that of Balivkerde, all lying together, were granted to St Mary's abbey around 1185 by two donors. The lands in question descended intact, and can be shown to be represented by the parish of Brownstown and most of that of Monktown, Co. Meath. The lands total around 2,250 acres.[21]
- The foundation grant of Bridgetown priory (*Villa Pontis*), Co. Cork, from 1201, donated the eight carucates of *villa de Ponte*, upon which the abbey itself was built. From the bounds given in the charter it is clear that these lands are now represented by Bridgetown parish. This example is of especial interest as the toponomy of this area is earlier recorded in *Crichad*. The parish encompasses two earlier *bailte*, Cill Laisre, apparently where the priory itself was built, and Cill Cuáin, now Killquane. The acreage of the parish is 3,239.[22]
- Between 1177 and 1182 'the land called Murivechimelan and the land called Balilannocan (? read Balinlecan: *Baile an Liagáin*)' were donated to St Nicholas', Exeter. These were clearly adjacent and possessed significant fisheries, and are

18 Bernard, 'Duiske charters', 17–18, 21–2, 164–7. **19** Ibid., 14, 17–18; White, *Extents*, 195. **20** Gilbert, *St Mary's*, i, 67–8; White, *Extents*, 22; Ó Conbhuí, 'St Mary's', 68; *Civil Survey*, viii, 77–8; Fiant Eliz., 6010. From these references it is clear that Toberogan, with its church and castle, contained the modern townlands of Toberogan, Castlefish and Gormanstown. **21** Ó Conbhuí, 'St Mary's', 76–8. **22** Rawl. B479, fos. 57v–60; Power, *Crichad*, 49.

to be identified with the parishes of Marmullane (529 acres) and Monkstown (1,523 acres), on the shores of Cork Harbour. The descent of the five carucates of 'The Legan', later Monkstown, a monastic grange possessed by the priory of Bath, in Somerset, is clear.[23]

The second category, of grants of parochial tithes, contains many examples, but once again a much lesser number whose area can be established with certainty.

• A most illustrative example concerns a grant made by Hugh de Swordeval before 1224, in which he donated the benefices of his fee, 'Balimacleri and Baliodacaran'. A few years later this grant was confirmed by his lord, William, baron of Naas, when the fee is described as 'the vill of Hugh de Swordeval'. This illustrates the process by which many *bailte* names must have disappeared. This fee, originally a distinct parish, is now represented by the detached portion of Kill parish (Co. Kildare) which includes (*inter alia*) both Swordlestowns, with an acreage of 1,447.[24]

• The benefices of the five carucates of the vill of Balibaldric were donated by Nicholas de Verdon in the early thirteenth century. This is now Ballybarrick parish, Co. Louth, with 1,018 acres.

• A similar example is that of the benefices of the vill of Macglassewein, granted by Hugh de Lacy around the same time. This is now Ballymacglassan parish, Co. Meath, acreage 3,476. It shows a similar pattern to that of Ballymadun below, with the original *baile* estate name surviving, but almost all internal townland names deriving from colonial tenants.[25]

• By the time other contemporary grants were made the original names had already been lost, as in the case of 'Villa Crike', now the parish of Crickstown, Co. Meath, acreage 1,431. (Crick is a colonial surname.) Many grants, of course, do not explicitly state that the fee is a vill (*terra*: land, is often used) but there is an implication of this in many cases. For example, the grant of 'Strupho', given probably during the 1190s, is to be identified with the single-townland parish of Straboe, Co. Carlow, acreage 1,104.[26]

• The early Exeter grants contain further examples. The tithes of the vill of Chilmahanoc are to be identified with the parish of Kilmonoge (3,060 acres), and those of Balicornere with that of Ballintemple (2,659 acres), both in Co. Cork. Evidence of sub-divisions also occur, such as that of the *dimidietatem ville* of Balivfian, now the Cork suburb of Ballyphehane.[27]

• An instructive case is that of Ballymadun, Co. Dublin. As the etymology (*Villa MacDun*) suggests, this was a manor erected upon the *baile* of the MacDun

23 Brooks, 'Unpublished charters', 326–7; Gwynn and Hadcock, 105, 107–8; JCHAS 30 (1925), 15–19, 90–7. The western lands and rectories granted to Exeter, including Legan, soon passed into possession of the Benedictine abbey of Bath, England and, more immediately, to that of Bath's cell in Waterford City, while those in eastern Cork remained with Exeter. Cf. White, *Extents*, 352; Nicholls, 'The Anglo-Normans', 104–5. **24** Gilbert, *Reg. St Thomas*, 92, 95; CDI, v, 245. **25** Gilbert, *Reg. St Thomas*, 8. **26** Ibid., 39, 73, 115. **27** Brooks, 'Unpublished charters', 321, 328, 340, 344.

family, who still held here in around 1185. By 1200 or so it had passed into colonial possession and its subsequent feudal descent is clear.[28] As with many manors
in colonial Ireland, its area is mirrored in that of the parish of the same name,
with an acreage of 3,438. Most of its townlands bear the family names of its early
colonial tenants (Borranstown, Nutstown etc.) and here we have a single *baile*
erected into a colonial manor, whose sub-divisions were in turn probably the
basis for its sub-infeudation.

We must now turn to early secular evidence for the *baile*/villate. The only major
source appears to be that of the earlier Leinster feodaries, beginning with that
of 1247, and which are confined to Carlow, Kilkenny and Wexford.[29] Fees held
directly under the lords of Leinster vary greatly in size. Many are small, however, and a study of all of those of one-half fee or less reveals interesting results.
These are mostly located in southern Wexford and in parts of Kilkenny, and a
small number around the seignorial manor of Ferns in northern Wexford. Those
which lie in the baronies of Shelburne, Forth and Bargy are of early date, especially those in the latter baronies, which represent the fees of the lordship of
Hervey de Montmorency which escheated to the chief lord when Hervey
became a monk in 1183, and so must pre-date this event. The Kilkenny fees can
be no earlier than 1192 and those around Ferns may post-date 1207 and the
arrival of the Marshals. It is possible to reconstruct the size of several of these
fees, especially in southern Wexford, where the feudal structure descended largely unaltered into the sixteenth century. That these fees represent pre-Invasion
bailte seems very probable, as has already been demonstrated in the case of one
of them, Ballycushlane (see above). Sometimes *biataig* families may have retained
a portion of their *baile*, as in the case of the O Dermods of Balidermod, an obsolete fee of uncertain extent in Old Ross parish.[30] Where estimates of size occur
in the early sources they are usually of five carucates or smaller. Examples from
Wexford follow.

• Slievecoltia, consisting of lands in central and southern Whitechurch parish,
*c.*2,800 acres.[31]
• Balybrasil, now Ballybrazil, fee and parish identical, 2,370 acres.[32]
• Balikeroch, descended as Ballykeeroge and Ballykeerogebeg (Kilmokea
parish), with a combined acreage of 693. Here we have a rare example of modern townland boundaries preserving much earlier ones, for there are three townlands of Ballykeeroge. The third, Ballykeerogemore (759 acres), appears to have
been part of the fee of Balybrasil above. This suggests that the fee of Balybrasil
consisted of that *baile* and half of that of Balikeroch, while the fee of Balikeroch
contained the remaining half of its *baile*. Balybrasil minus Balikeroch would thus
have contained *c.*1,600 acres while both moieties of Balikeroch – as preserved
in the three townlands of the name – 1,453 acres.[33]

28 McNeill, *Alen's Register*, 14, 219; Mills, *Gormanston*, 129–38.   **29** Brooks, *Knights' fees*, passim.
30 Ibid., 18–19.   **31** Ibid., 10–12.   **32** Ibid., 14–16.   **33** Ibid., 16, 166.

- Balydufathely, now Ballyhealy, a fee probably identical to the area of the parish of Kilturk, 2,206 acres.[34]
- Carrickbyrne, consisting of the northern half of Newbawn parish, including Carrickbyrne Hill, *c.*2,400 acres.[35]
- Ballyregan, which occurs under an alternative name, Ballymore, after it escheats to the chief lord in 1292, certainly equates with the latter parish, of 2,523 acres.[36]
- Balliatan (Ballyanne) *alias* Disertmachen, parish and fee identical, 4,577 acres including some uplands.[37]
- Ballyconick, parish and fee identical, 1,610 acres.[38]
- Ballyteige, a fee comprising most of Kilmore parish, of *c.*3,400 acres.[39]
- Kylcouan, now Kilcowanmore, parish and fee identical, 2,760 acres.[40]
- the land of Balymakaterin, originally in two moieties, united by 1324. Descends as the manor of Ballymacane (Tacumshin parish), of *c.*2,300 acres.[41]
- Ballybrennan, parish and fee identical, 1,041 acres.[42]
- Carn, fee and parish almost identical, *c.*1,800 acres.[43]
- Balyconewy, now Ballycanew, manor and parish probably identical, an acreage of 3,627 with some upland and bog.[44]
- Balliduykir (Ballydusker: Killinick parish), fee and parish identical, 1,283 acres.[45]
- Killesk, parish and fee probably identical, although the Barrons, descendants of its ancient proprietors, only held around 1,100 acres of the 2,820-acre parish by 1641.[46]

When we turn to the Kilkenny examples we note a similar pattern, although the manorial descents are less certain. This can be remedied to some extent by the clear parallels between manor/fee and parish here. One significant difference between fees in Kilkenny and those in Wexford is in the occurrence of names in *baile*, which are much less frequent in the Kilkenny fees. Why this should be so is unclear. The example of the fee of Dunmore may be instructive. When first mentioned, during the 1190s, this fee is called Balimucchin but, when next encountered, around 1215, it is called Dunmore. These names occur in monastic grants which show that Balimucchin is now represented by the 2,379-acre parish of Dunmore. One of these grants contains a list of its lands, none of which are in *baile*, suggesting that here we have an example of a *baile* and its sub-denominations, just as in *Críchad* earlier.[47] This example reinforces those above in which names in *baile* are seen to be subject to early replacement by the

34 Ibid., 33–4. **35** Ibid., 100–1. **36** Ibid., 101–2. **37** Ibid., 109–13. **38** See preceding note. **39** Brooks, *Knights' fees*, 113–15; Hore, Wexford ii, 71, 85. The lands of Tintern in this parish were not part of the fee. **40** Brooks, *Knights' fees*, 115–16. **41** Ibid., 119–20. The manor did not contain all of the parish, as Tacumshin itself and some surrounding townlands had been retained as fees appendant to the seignorial manor of Wexford. **42** Ibid., 123. **43** Ibid., 119–20, 127–9. The Ring of Carn was not part of the manor, an ancient arrangement. **44** Ibid., 152–3. **45** Ibid., 154–8. **46** Ibid., 158–60. **47** Gilbert, *Reg. St Thomas*, 127–9.

colonists. In this connection it is interesting to note those manors/parishes occurring among the south Wexford fees adduced above whose names have already been 'colonized' by 1247, for example, Tullerstown and Ambrosetown.[48] At least nineteen Kilkenny and Leix parishes occur which can be shown to have been formed of the ecclesiastical benifices of fees occurring among the Leinster feodaries, that is, these parishes share the same area as the secular fees they derive from. Most of these fees were held of the lords of Leinster by half a knights' fee or less.[49] Their acreages range from Kilferagh, 964, to the largely upland parish of Kilmacar, 4,815. All nineteen give an average acreage of 2,561. This compares to an average acreage of 2,386 for the seventeen Wexford examples adduced above. I think by now we can answer the question as to whether *bailte* were adopted by the colonists in a similar way to cantreds and *theoda* in the affirmative. However, the evidence for the adoption and use of *bailte* by the colonists appears to be much more extensive than this.

Astute readers will have noted that in many of the examples given above the *baile*/villate formed the basis for a subsequent parish. Sixty such examples from counties Louth, Meath, Dublin, Kildare, Carlow, Kilkenny, Leix, Wexford, Waterford, Cork and Limerick are adduced above. Given the lack of evidence for the ultimate origins of many parishes, a figure of sixty parishes formed from villates suggests that there must be many more parishes of similar origin. Most of these examples are drawn from areas featuring a high proportion of parishes of similar size to the exemplars cited. Such areas can be classed as those where at least half of the parishes are smaller than about 3,500 acres. Such a situation can be found in the Ards Peninsula and Lecale in Down, parts of southern Antrim, in Louth, eastern Meath, Dublin, Kildare, northern Carlow, parts of Leix, much of Wexford, the hinterland of Waterford City, north-western, central, and south-western Kilkenny, centrally in the South Riding of Tipperary, eastern Limerick, and coastal Cork as far west as Rosscarbery. These areas have a second link in common, that of representing the area settled by the Anglo-Normans before AD 1200. Of course not all parishes in these areas are so small, and some were clearly based on *túatha* or half-*túatha*,[50] or on the ecclesiastical estates of indigenous mother-churches, or on seignorial manors. Nonetheless, the clear conclusion to be had is that, in these areas, many parishes in their bounds preserve the area of earlier *bailte*, and that the *baile* was a favoured unit of infeudation.

One final proof can be offered for this statement. No indigenous topographical tract survives from areas within the qualifying parameters above, that is, areas with a high number of smaller parishes and which were colonized before 1200. In one case, however, we have an example where, although settlement probably did occur before 1200, the number of smaller parishes here is somewhat less than half. This is the cantred of Fermoy (**C32**) with its pre-Invasion extent,

48 Brooks, *Knights' fees*, 12–14, 108–9.   **49** Ibid., 182–7, 210–16, 226, 229–33, 240–3, 253–4, 260–4.
50 Flanagan, *Irish royal charters*, 386; Langrishe, 'Jerpoint abbey', 179–80; White, *Extents*, 182.

Crichad. In Fermoy we have a complete list of *bailte* which can be compared with the subsequent parish structure. Unfortunately, the parish structure here appears to have changed considerably since its inception, some changes occurring as late as the 1830s.[51] This probably has something to do with the endemic warfare which existed over several centuries between its Roche and Condon lineages, which saw the cantred divided into two conflicting lordships. Nonetheless, much is known of the history of these parish boundary alterations and, when these are taken into account, it is possible to perform a study. Despite Fermoy's borderline status in our parameters, the results are interesting.

- The parish name St Nathlash derives from a ridiculous Anglicization of the *baile* name, Echlasca Molaga, later Baile na hEchlaisc or Ballynahalisk. The parish probably represents the area of the manor of Athlyskmalag of 1315. This is the only *baile* from *Crichad* which can be located within this 1,024-acre parish.[52]
- The parish and manor of Derryvillane appear to have been identical. Only one *baile* can be located within its 1,826 acres, the eponymous Daire Faiblig.[53]
- The 3,217-acre parish of Killathy appears to have contained only the eponymous *baile* of Cill Achaidh. This parish shares a pattern with several of its neighbours, with a smaller portion of good quality land north of the Blackwater and a larger portion south of the river where the ground rises sharply into the Nagle Mountains. This pattern suggests that these parishes retain their original boundaries.[54]
- The single townland parish of Aghacross (355 acres) was much larger in the fourteenth century, and certainly contained in addition Ballyshurdane and part or all of Graigue and Cullenagh, an area of at least 1,100 acres. The only *baile* occurring within this area in *Crichad* was that of Áth Cros Molaga.[55]
- The early de Sumeri fee of Dengeneaghnach & Acheradloski mirrors precisely the terminology of the *baile* of Daingen Eóghanachta and its sub-denomination of Achadh Loiscthe. This became the manor of Ballindangan, its rectory the subject of a donation to Duiske abbey, Co. Kilkenny. This fee contained precisely 1,684 acres. Here we have a rectory without a mirroring parish preserving the extent of a *baile*.[56]
- The *baile* of Feic Beg & Ráith Siadail (Mount Rivers and Rathealy) contained around 1,700 acres. While these lands now lie in the parish of Clondullane, 'Fegbeg' formed a distinct parish in 1302.[57]
- The early fourteenth-century secular fee of Dungleddy had a corresponding parish which bore the *alias* Cloustoge, thus helping to locate it in the Ogeen valley in eastern Doneraile parish. This was a mixed lowland and mountain fee with an acreage of around 3,500 acres. The name Cloustoge derives from the *baile* of Cluas Doigi, the only one in this area in *Crichad*.[58]

51 See PRC, 185–6. 52 PRC, 172, 186; Power, *Crichad*, 49. 53 Power, *Crichad*, 52. 54 Power, *Crichad*, 46; Ó Buachalla, 'Townland development', passim. 55 PRC, 185–6; Power, *Crichad*, 52. 56 Power, *Crichad*, 45; PRC, 186–7, 241. 57 Power, *Crichad*, 47; CDI, v, 276, 313. 58 NAI RC

As a final illustration of the linkage between *bailte* and small parishes we might note the percentage of parishes smaller than 3,000 acres per county as we move in a direct line westwards from Dublin:

Dublin	72%
Meath	46%
Westmeath	22%
Longford	8%

While the figure of 3,000 may be arbitrary, we have seen that, while *baile* sizes can be found in the range *c.*700 to *c.*7,000 acres, most of the examples adduced above were of *bailte* smaller than 3,000 acres in extent.

THE ELEMENT 'BAILE' IN TOPONYMS

An important question in the present study is how to interpret the occurrence of toponyms in *baile* in relation to those not in *baile*. We have seen how, in *Críchad*, some *bailte* are listed with their component sub-denominations. Furthermore, it is clear from both *Críchad* and *Críchaireacht* that many *bailte* do not feature the element *baile* in their names. At a minimum it seems clear that any pre-Invasion toponym in *baile* must represent a *baile* (*biataig*). The presentation pattern in *Críchad* is reminiscent of those early-colonial examples in which the ecclesiastical benefices of a fee are granted to a monastery before parish formation has occurred. Such grants are, of course, the basis for subsequent parish formation, and are valuable as a very early source for lists of vills or townlands. As an example we might note the confirmation of the 1170s concerning Ballyboghil, Co. Dublin.[59] In describing the lands of this parish Ballyboghil itself is followed by three denominations, none in *baile*, indicating that we are here dealing with a single *baile* and its sub-denominations, just as we see in *Críchad*. Another useful example concerns the lands which duly came to be represented by the parish of Clogher, Co. Tipperary. A grant datable to around 1200 lists all eleven vills in what became this parish. Four of these are in *baile*, suggesting that this 8,119 acre parish had at least four *bailte*. One of these was Balibrenan. Around 1281 we find mention of the vill of Lethbalibrenan here, as well as a villate called Midletun.[60] This reference demonstrates that the sub-divisions of the indigenous *baile* system sometimes became the template for colonial vills. It also suggests that the memory of the *baile* system and its sub-divisions remained alive well into the Anglo-Norman period, even where *bailte* have been renamed in colonial style.

7/4, 221, 225; 7/8, 372, 404, 428, 490; CDI, v, 276, 313; Power, *Críchad*, 49. The Down Survey barony map shows that Cloustoge then included both modern Cloustoge and Garryhintoge. In the latter townland lies the ruined church of Aglish, which must locate the parish church of Dungleddy *alias* Cloustoge. This fee probably ran northwards from Park South on the Awbeg to the summit ridge of the Ballyhouras. **59** Gilbert, *Chart. St Mary's*, 141–2. **60** Brooks, *St John Baptist*, 332–43.

A final aspect to be considered is the later debasement of the term *baile*, and the origins of this. While many original *bailte* names survived into the colonial period and later, as we can see from *Crichad* and *Crichaireacht*, they usually come to refer to only a portion of their original area. The Anglo-Normans brought their own languages and naming patterns. The Anglo-Saxon term *toun* or *tūn* (town) occurs widely in Leinster, Meath, Munster and in the Ulster colony, usually in association with a surname, and usually referring to a rural landholding or minimal freehold. This term descends into our *town*land. In Leinster and Meath such names usually remained in *town* (for example, Kerdiffstown, Follistown, Horetown, Palmerstown) while in Munster and Ulster they are usually translated into *baile* (for example, Trewedyeston = Ballindridden; Brouneston = Ballybrowney; Priourtoun = Ballyprior).[61] Here it is clear that, as Irish came to replace English as the *lingua franca*, the term *toun* is directly translated into Irish as *baile*. Quite independently of this usage, however, the term *baile* had degenerated from its classical meaning to give the sense of a simple rural settlement or farm name, and early post-Invasion evidence of this can be found.[62]

Ó Conbhuí has shown that the vill of Balimacheilmer was part of the possessions of St Mary's abbey as early as 1172, and that it is probably now represented by the 184 acre townland and parish of Kilmahuddrick, Co. Dublin. If, as seems possible, if not indeed probable, this was a pre-Invasion *baile*, its small size raises many questions. Nothing as small as this occurs in our series of reconstructed *bailte* adduced above, which show a range of between 700 to 7,000 acres approximately. The one exception in this series is Grange, belonging to St Mary's abbey, Navan, a pre-Invasion estate of around 500 acres. We do not, however, have its original name or the record of its donation. It may perhaps have been a fraction of a *baile*, as indeed may Balimacheilmer. We have at least one example of a fraction of a *baile* being subject to monastic donation (St Doolagh's). Again, while Ó Conbhuí's methodology appears to be sound, we should not invest it with powers of infallibility. One swallow does not make a summer. A second relevant example concerns the 140-acre townland of Ballyfouloo in Monkstown parish, Co. Cork. This first occurs in 1226 when in dispute between the Benedictines of Waterford and the local secular lord. As shown above, Monkstown was originally the vill of *Balinlecan, a monastic grange of 1,523 acres donated no later than 1183. Ballyfouloo lies within *Balinlecan but on its border with the surrounding secular lordship. Therefore, this early vill/*baile* already has another lesser *baile* within its borders by 1226. A date for the creation of this lesser *baile* is suggested by the circumstances of ownership here. While originally granted to St Nicholas' abbey in Exeter, sometime before 1204, *Balinlecan passed into the ownership of the Benedictine priory of the Apostles Peter and Paul at Bath. Bath controlled *Balinlecan through its sub-priory in Waterford. Ballyfouloo certainly derives from Baile Uí Foghladha, and Uí

---

61 *Dinnseanchas* 2/1 (1966), 11; 2/3 (1967), 61; JRSAI 43 (1913), 139. **62** For a useful – if sometimes misleading – discussion on aspects of this question see Price, 'The word *baile*', passim.

Foghladha were originally a Co. Waterford sept with no apparent Cork connections.[63] What may have happened here is that sometime within the period
1183–1226 a new family arrived in *Balinlecan, as retainers of the new proprietors, to become tenants of a portion of the estate which thereafter assumed a
toponym with the family name in *baile*. Whatever of this, here we have a certain example of a new and debased usage of the term *baile* occurring within two
generations of the Invasion.

Taken in its entirety, the evidence suggests that in the immediate pre-Invasion
period the term *baile* refers to a large freehold kin-based estate within the range
700–7,000 acres – a range relating to land quality, and that, shortly after the
Invasion, the term became debased, perhaps paralleling the similar process involving the term *biatach*, and came to refer to a range of holdings, from large colonial *touns* to any rural farm or landholding, especially one tenanted by Irish. Of
course, more research is needed to confirm these conclusions.

---

63 For early material on the history of Uí Foghladha in Waterford see TP, 46; Curtis, 'Sheriffs
accounts', 7; CDI, iii, p. 94; CJRI, i, 205; ii, 293; iii, 190, 262.

CHAPTER 6

Origins

'TÚATH', LATE-'TÚATH' AND 'TRÍCHA CÉT'

Scholars have advanced various views on the origin of the *trícha cét*. Hogan believed that it was the Irish version of an ancient Indo-European military levy with roots in prehistoric times, while Patterson sees the *trícha* system as a method of assessment for military levy imposed by the provincial overkingdoms on their constituent parts, developed in response to the Viking threat. Byrne and Ó Corráin take the more balanced view that the *trícha* is merely the descendant of the earlier *túath* or local kingdom of the early medieval Irish Laws, the minimal polity of the period.[1] Therefore the *túath* is clearly central to the quest for the earlier history of the *trícha cét*.

In the current understanding of the term (especially D.A. Binchy's), the *túath* is the basic socio-political and jurisdictional unit of society, the basic unit of citizenship, outside of which an individual lacked full legal rights. In the Laws each *túath* is described as having its own king, bishop, judge and scholar. These minimal polities arranged themselves into hierarchical structures with a triple layer of kingship, beginning with the *rí túaithe*, the king of the single *túath*. In addition the Laws record two superior grades of king, the *rí túath* or *ruiri* (king of *túatha*) and *rí cóicid* or *rí ruirech* (provincial king, 'king of overkings').[2] This view presents many problems. In a forthcoming work,[3] Ó Corráin describes this view as simplistic, and draws attention to a broader range of meaning for the term *túath*. His definitions include *túath* as 'a lordship, a unit of jurisdiction, a taxable denomination, a parish', and elsewhere 'kingdom, lordship, people, community, country people, the laity as distinct from the clergy'. Many of these descriptions clearly relate to what I have called the late-*túath*, the *túath* ruled by a *taísech*, the unit several of which together comprise a *trícha cét*. These late-*túatha* had no kings and so bear little resemblance to the minimal polity of the Laws, the *túath* with its local king. What is going on here?

The terms *olltúatha* and *mórthúatha*, 'great *túatha*', which occur alongside that of *túath* in the Laws and other sources, demonstrate that the term *túath* was not

---

1 Hogan, 'The tricha cét', 154–9; Patterson, *Cattle lords and clansmen*, 170–73; Byrne, 'Tribes and tribalism', 158–60; Ó Corráin, 'Nationality and kingship', 9–11; idem, 'Hogan', 94–6. 2 Ó Cróinín, *Early medieval Ireland*, 111–12; Jaski, *Irish kingship*, 37–40, 89, 99–102; Kelly, *Irish law*, 3–6; Binchy, *Celtic and Anglo-Saxon kingship*, 4–8, 31–3; Byrne, 'Tribes and tribalism', 132–3. 3 Ó Corráin, *Ireland before the Normans*.

confined to a single layer of spatial organization.[4] Texts from Munster, probably of ninth-century date, use the term *túath* to refer to what are certainly regional kingdoms (Uí Fhidgente, Corcu Duibne etc.).[5] As late as perhaps 1100, *Cogad*,
in describing the lordship structure of Munster, mentions 'rígi ocus toeseach for
cach tuaith', thus describing both *rí* of *trícha cét* and *taísech* of late-*túath* as rulers
of *túatha*. Thus the term *túath* is applied to a parish-sized area ruled by a *taísech*,
to a local kingdom (*trícha cét*) ruled by a basic-grade *rí*, and to a regional kingdom ruled by a *rí túath*.

These three levels of spatial organization, all of which are composed of units
sometimes called *túatha*, can be distinctly identified in the sources throughout
most of the historical period. The regional kingdom is best documented and
needs no further comment. The local kingdom is to be identified with rulership by a king of lowest level and again occurs throughout the period of record,
especially in the annals. This is the unit which eventually, in most cases, comes
to bear the designation *trícha cét*. Its defining characteristic is that it is almost
always ruled by a king who does not rule over any other king but rather over a
collection of *taísig*. The lowest level is the late-*túath*, usually ruled by a *taísech*.
Strangely, this unit has been completely ignored by scholars, content to follow
Binchy's inappropriate schema in which the late-*túath* finds no place.[6]

These late-*túath* first occur in the annals in perhaps the tenth century. This
is more likely to reflect a poverty of sources rather than to suggest that the late-
túath comes into existence only when it begins to be recorded. The occurrence
in the annals of the title *taísech* for the leader of the late-*túath* provides valuable
evidence. In the Latin portions of the annals *taísech* is usually rendered *dux*, a
direct translation. The term *dux* begins to occur in AU as early as 756, and *taísech*
in 869. However, for well over a century, references to both terms are either
inexact or relate to rulers of local and regional kingdoms. By the period 911–16
we begin to find *dux* referring to the leader of an aristocratic *cenél*, such as Cenél
Máelche, Uí Chernaig, Clann Chathail and Uí Lomáin Gaela.[7] In very many
cases these *cenéla* bore names which can be shown by the twelfth century to refer
to the late-*túath*, such as Oloman (Uí Lomáin Gaela), still one of four *theoda*
comprising the cantred of Muntermolinan (**C20**) in 1207. A later example relates
to Clann Murchada (AFM, 953, 971). These early *duces/taísig* must represent the
earliest record of the twelfth-century *taísech túaithe*. In 924 a Viking fleet arrived
on Lough Erne 'and they raided the islands of the lake and the *túatha* round
about'.[8] Does this not suggest the usage of the term *túath* in the sense of smaller late-*túatha* rather then earlier local-kingdom *túatha*? References to *taísig* occur
with increasing regularity as the eleventh century progresses. A second term,
muire (lord, leader),[9] occurs less frequently, first appearing in the annals in 1018,

4 Ibid. **5** Meyer, 'The Laud Genealogies', passim; Fraser, Grosjean and O'Keeffe, *Irish Texts*, i,
19–22. **6** Binchy, *Celtic and Anglo-Saxon kingship*, 4–5, 7; Ó Cróinín, *Early medieval Ireland*, 111;
Jaski, *Irish kingship*, 37–9, 210. Professor Ó Corráin's forthcoming second edition of *Ireland before
the Normans* will attempt to address the issue. **7** AU, 912, 914, 916; CS, 916. **8** AU. **9** DIL,
s.v. muire.

and is confined to the northern half of Ireland. This shows the same range of meaning as *taísech* and in some cases the terms are interchangeable.[10] The rank of *taísech túaithe*, and the term *túath*, may have been subject to further gradation. Cenél Máelche, whose *taísech* was recorded in 914, were one of four *prím-thúatha* of the Monaig of Ulster and it, in turn, was divided into four *túatha* as was each of its other *prím-thúatha*. Another of the Monaig *prím-thúatha* was Cenél Laindúin, one of its *túatha* being Cland Ailebra, a *taísech* of which was recorded in 1172.[11] A few late examples occur where *dux* refers to a king of a local kingdom.[12] In these cases the term is always used where a superior king monopolizes the style *rí*, and shows that in these examples *dux* has a different meaning, that of an indicator of subservience.

While the annals are silent on the late-*túath* before the tenth century, the early Laws, apparently, are not. A number of passages referring to the archetypical king indicate that he ruled, not over a single *túath*, but over several *túatha*, just as did the later local king.[13] Such passages can only be integrated into Binchy's schema if they are assumed to relate to higher levels of kingship to the exclusion of the most numerous category, that of local king. Further passages of relevance relate to various categories of royal officials.

One set of these refers to the '*brithem* [judge] who is the *ardmaor* [high steward]', said to rule over many *túatha* and lords (*iltúatha & ilmuire*), who has the same *eneclann* (honour price) 'as the king who employs him'.[14] The term *maor* occurs but rarely in the annals, beginning in 1072, and usually refers to stewards of regional or provincial kingdoms. In one certain and one possible reference, however, the term refers to late-*túatha*.[15] I suggest that these references to *ardmaoir* in the Laws are best understood as referring to officials having responsibility for several late-*túatha*. Another reference from the Laws describes the *bóbriugaidh cétach* 'cow-*brugaid* of hundreds', also called *righbriughaidh* 'royal *brugaid*', 'with *túatha* under his yoke' (*túatha fo mam*).[16] This is the *brugaid* or hospitaller, probably here again acting as some kind of royal manager or official over late-*túatha*. Another important early noble grade was that of *aire tuísea*. This was the grade schematically represented in *Críth Gablach* as having at least fifteen free base-clients and may have been the highest grade open to those outside of the king's kindred.[17] One suspects that here we have the origin of the later office of *taísech túaithe*. Ó Corráin, in a forthcoming work, adduces evidence of relevance from ecclesiastical sources which may be as early as the seventh century.[18] This indicates that one form of *túath* or *plebs* was of parish size and had a resident priest, while bishops were often described as *epscop túath* 'bishop of *túatha*'.

10 *Muire* can refer to leaders of late-*túatha* (ALC, 1018), local kingdoms (ALC, 1059) and regional kingdoms (ALC, 1100). For evidence of interchangeability see AU, 1059, 1067, 1073, 1081, 1086, 1095.5, 1095.9, 1155; AFM, 1122. 11 Lec. 132rc 45–va29; AT, 1172; Ó Corráin, *Ireland before the Normans*. 12 Cf. Flanagan, *Irish royal charters*, 254. 13 Ó Donnchadha, 'Advice to a prince', §17, §22; Gwynn, 'An Irish penitential', 166; CIH, 219.5–19. 14 CIH, 687.23–33; 1269.19–20. 15 AU, 1081 (Cenél Fergusa), 1086 (Clann Sínnach). 16 CIH, 955.9–11. 17 Charles-Edwards, 'Críth Gablach', 58, 61–2. 18 Ó Corráin, *Ireland before the Normans*.

When all of this evidence is considered together it leads to the conclusion that the late-*túath* may well have been as prevalent in the seventh and eighth-centuries as in the twelfth, although the subject of the *túath* remains in need of further elucidation. Therefore, Binchy's definition of the *túath* must be qualified. The term *túath* should not be seen in the narrow sense of relating to one spatial layer. Rather, it can be applied to all political communities as Ó Corráin suggests, from late-*túatha* through local kingdom (the *trícha cét*) and on upwards to regional-kingdom level.

The material for discussion in this section is best summarized in tabular form. Table 2 concerns the linkage between *trícha* and local kingdom. To the 122 *trícha*s comprising a single polity can be added twenty-three almost certainly of similar nature, but lacking explicit evidence. These examples concern *trícha*s without record of a king but in regional kingdoms where sister *trícha*s with kings occur. These are mostly in Munster where the annalistic record is poorest and I believe that records of their probable kings do not survive. This table shows that, in most cases but not all, *trícha* equals local kingdom. The figure of eight *trícha*s each with two minimal polities should be treated with some caution. Some of these reflect *trícha*s/cantreds whose status appears ambiguous owing to contradictory evidence, while others, such as Trí Túatha (**T116**), where the kingship may have rotated between each constituent late-*túath*, must have arisen due to particular local circumstances.[19] Some, however, clearly did comprise two polities, one always subservient to the other, such as Fir Manach (**T166**), containing Fir Manach and Fir Luirg; and Inis Eógain (**T144**), containing Cenél Eógain na hInnse and Carraig Brachaide.[20] Fir Maige (**T32**) was perhaps another similar example but conclusive evidence is lacking. In such cases the dominant king must have fulfilled the duties normally associated with the leadership rôle in those *trícha*s with only one king. Then we have the case of Cenél Áeda na hEchtge (**T22**), where a single polity of long standing was divided between

Table 2. Political structure of *trícha cét*s

*Trícha*s comprising a single kingdom	122
*Trícha*s probably comprising a single kingdom	23
*Trícha*s apparently comprising two kingdoms	8
*Trícha*s apparently without a resident king	6
*Trícha*s with insufficient data to assess	27

19 Another such example may have been that of the Trí Commain in Loígis. **20** The others in this category were **T16**, **62** and **163**.

two *leth-ríg* around 1170, this division being maintained by their descendants even though the *trícha* remained undivided.

Table 2 also lists six *tríchas* apparently without a king. Caution should be exercised here lest the apparent lack of kings is the result of deficiency in the historical record. These are found in two groups of three and may again reflect local particularism. Bac & Glenn Nemthenne (**T6**), Fir Tíre & Clann Chuáin (**T17**), and Crích Fer Tíre (**T15**), all originally lay in Uí Fhiachrach Tuascirt. There is no record of local kings and these *tríchas* seem to have been made up of individual late-*túatha*, perhaps grouped together for administrative purposes, whose *taísig* had a direct vassal relationship with the overking. Cuircne (**T98**), Mag Asail (**T105**), and Corcu Raíde (**T104**) are the other three, all in Mide. Corcu Raíde again shows a grouping of *túatha*. The *trícha* of Síl Máelruanaid & Ciarraige Maige Aí (**T28**) seems to represent two late-*túatha*, again apparently without a king. A final example may be Uí Moccu Uais (**T100**), in Mide, which again groups four late-*túatha*, two of which appear to have been royal demesne. Other examples occur where a local kingdom is grouped with one or more late-*túatha*, apparently not subject to its king, to constitute a *trícha*. Clann Taidg & Uí Diarmata (**T10**) was one such, others being Sliab Luga (**T26**), as well as Fir Tulach (**T101**), and Delbna Mór & na Sogain (**T106**), both in Mide. Caution is again needed regarding this conclusion due to the scanty nature of the evidence. That such untypical arrangements occur only in Connacht or Mide indicates that these are clearly local administrative usages, possibly of relatively late date. Twenty-five of the single-polity *tríchas* of the twelfth century had earlier comprised two or more local kingdoms (Clones had four). This suggests that the number of original local kingdoms in Ireland in the early historical period may have been as many as two hundred or more.

We see, therefore, that *trícha cét* does not always equal local kingdom. While the correspondence holds true in the large majority of cases there are enough exceptions to the rule to illustrate that *trícha cét* and local kingdom are not necessarily one and the same entity. In particular, the examples from Mide and Connacht cited above, where these *tríchas* appear to represent administrative units imposed from above where local political boundaries seem to be ignored, are telling. The usage of affixes such as *uachtarach*, *íochtarach*, *iartharach* and *oirthearach* in several Munster *tríchas* without record of kings[21] is again indicative of some kind of administrative structure imposed from above. All of these examples indicate the existence of some kind of spatial assessment or taxation system of some complexity. Where possible this system seems to choose local kingdoms as assessment units but where these are fragmented or no longer exist the system creates similar sized units to meet the need. It might be better to speak of several such assessment systems, perhaps with one or more in each province. This may account for the localized phenomena noted above in relation to Mide, Connacht and Munster. The term *trícha cét* is certainly related to this system or

21 **T**38, 76–7, 92–3.

group of related systems, and, in the history of the term *trícha cét*, we may perhaps discern something of the history of this underlying structure.

The earliest certain annalistic reference to the term *trícha cét* dates from 1106. Earlier entries for 919 and 1014 occur in interpolated verse and are of limited value.[22] *Caithréim Cellacháin Chaisil*, datable to the 1130s, contains a verse giving the units of society in the descending order *trícha – túath – baile – tech*. This is based on a similar verse in the earlier *Cogad Gaedel re Gallaib*, datable to around 1100, but here the word *tír* is used in the sense of *trícha*.[23] Possibly the earliest safe use of the term *trícha cét* occurs in a poem attributed to a poet who died in 1024.[24] More generally, the term occurs in the saga literature and in legal glosses of the eleventh and twelfth centuries, but this literature is difficult to date precisely.[25] The widespread use of the term in the saga literature, as for example in the older recension of *Táin Bó Cúailnge* (which can hardly be older than the eleventh century), can mean no more than that the *trícha cét* is widespread at this time.[26]

A study of individual *tríchas* provides further clues as to the age of the spatial system I am discussing. Cuircne (**T98**), had borders which seem to originate in those of a local kingdom which disintegrated during the tenth or, at the latest, early eleventh century. No less than five *tríchas* of the kingdom of Airgialla had borders which had become politically redundant before 1170, most of which seem to preserve the outlines of local kingdoms as they had existed in the second half of the eleventh century.[27] In these cases the evidence suggests that these *tríchas* were established during the eleventh century, using local kingdoms as templates, and that later changes in the borders of the local kingdoms did not result in any matching change of *trícha* borders. This indicates that, at least in Mide and Airgialla, the *trícha* structure was established during the eleventh century and remained largely unaltered by subsequent political boundary changes.

'BAILE BIATAIG', 'TRÍCHA CÉT' AND THE
DEVELOPMENT OF SURNAMES

A similar chronology can be suggested for the *baile biataig*, a component unit of the *trícha cét*. The familial relationship between these units requires us to give close study to the *baile biataig*. The term *trícha cét* was understood in its literal sense of 'thirty of hundreds' by the literati, who saw it primarily as a unit of military levy consisting of 3,000 fighting men and, secondly, as a unit of territory where this levy was raised. Such figures do not sit well with the estimates of population for the period nor with the unambiguous references in several places in the early Laws to the figure of 700 as the adult male levy or *slógad* typical of a *túath*.[28] The term *cét* is often used to denote 'troops', not necessarily one hun-

22 AU, 919, 1106; AB, 1014. **23** Bugge, *Caithreim*, 1; Todd, *Cogad*, 48–9. **24** Ó Corráin, 'Hogan', 91–5. **25** Hogan, 'The tricha cét', 159–69. For a useful survey of the occurrence of the term *trícha cét* in contemporary literature see DIL, s.v. trícha cét. **26** Ó Corráin, 'Hogan', 92–3. **27** T163–7. **28** Bannerman, *Dalriada*, 146–7; Kelly, *Irish law*, 4, 19.

dred, and perhaps this is the meaning we should take here, that is, *trícha cét* as some kind of military muster. It was seen thus in the saga literature.[29] As against this the schema of the literati saw the *trícha cét* as comprising thirty *baile biataig* and it has long been seen that the *baile biataig* is probably the *cét* of the title ('thirty of *céts*').[30] I suggest below (p. 106) that *cét* may be a synonym for *baile biataig* and may derive from a numerical figure of assessment levied upon each *baile*. No certain derivation of *cét* can be offered at present, however.

The evidence shows that the term *trícha cét* first occurs during the eleventh century and allows us to date the origins of some *trícha* boundaries to the same century. (Many *trícha cét*/local kingdom boundaries are, however, likely to be much older.) The term *baile biataig* seems to be of broadly similar date, as we shall see presently. Both spatial units were components of the same system. This suggests that this system may originate in the eleventh century, and is unlikely, given the dating evidence for the onomastic emergence of the term *baile*, to have been any earlier.[31] We must now turn to that evidence. Toponyms in *baile* constitute twenty two per cent of all toponyms recorded in our small collection of pre-1169 indigenous charters.[32] These date to the period *c*.1150–65 and show how well established the term *baile* was by then. When we turn to earlier evidence, however, we note something remarkable. A search of the annals for occurrence of the settlement terms *baile*, *achadh*, *ráith* and *lios* show that all occur with regularity throughout the period of record apart from that of *baile*, which first occurs as late as 1164 (in Ulaid).[33] When we look in the early martyrologies we fail to find one single reference to a place-name in *baile*. Examination of our only pre-Invasion monastic cartulary, that of the Columban house of Kells, Co. Meath, gives similar results.[34] This source contains grants of lands spanning the period *c*.1040–1160. The only grant containing places in *baile* can be dated to 1133.[35] A couple of dozen *bailte* are mentioned in *Betha Colmáin*, only a few of which have names in *baile* itself. This source, whose composition may date from as early as the 1120s, shows the existence of a network of *bailte* occupying much of central Westmeath, and further suggests that Uí Failge was also so divided.[36] As we have seen above, the earliest occurrence of the term *baile biataig* in datable literature is to *c*.1100. When we search the Laws and literature we find only a few references and glosses to the *baile* as an estate, none of which can be dated to before *c*.1100.[37] This chronology is repeated (and thus confirmed) in the contemporary Irish cultural province of Scotland, where the earliest datable reference to a place-name in *baile* occurs in the late eleventh century, and in Man, where the earliest examples appear to date from the mid-twelfth century.[38]

29 Ó Corráin, 'Hogan', 89–93; Hogan, 'The tricha cét', 155. **30** Hogan, 'The tricha cét', 175. **31** Doherty ('Vikings in Ireland', 317) dates the emergence of the *baile biataig* system to the tenth century, but without adducing any evidence for this. **32** Flanagan, *Irish royal charters*, 252, 270, 284, 292; Nicholls, 'Baltinglass charter', 189–91. **33** MIA, 1164.3. **34** MacNiocaill, 'Irish "charters"', passim. **35** Ibid., 154–5. **36** Meyer, *Betha Colmáin*, vi, 62–5, 88, 94. **37** DIL, s.v. baile; *Ancient laws of Ireland* v, 50, 348; Kelly, *Irish law*, 124. **38** Broderick, 'Baile', 16–17; *Liber Cartarum*

This evidence indicates two items of significance. Firstly, the term *baile* emerges as a place-name element no earlier than the eleventh century and, secondly, once it emerges it comes into widespread use very rapidly. This remarkable situation can only be explained if *baile* is understood as a technical term coined to refer to an assessment unit which is part of a new taxation system. This is further suggested by the origin of the term, for *baile* in its original sense has the meaning of place in such senses as physical location, a spot, or passage in a book (*ball*). Its sense of a piece of land or an estate is clearly a later development, perhaps mirroring the development of the Latin word *locus* into the Catalan *lluc*. We may even see something of this process in action in the grant of 1133 referred to above, where the donation concerns *Ard Camma . i. Baile [U]i hUidhrín ocus Baile Uí Comgáin*. This may be interpreted as meaning that the estate of Ard Camma had, within living memory, been converted into two *bailte* as part of a new assessment system, or at least that memory of an older spatial structure where the two *bailte* of Ard Camma did not exist as a division survived. (I cannot identify these places, said to be located in Luigne Connacht: **T18**). An intermediate stage in this development is suggested by an annal of 1011, in which a *baile* is associated with a royal *dún*, and appears to have the sense of a royal residence.[39]

One avenue of exploration bears on the adoption of surnames. It may not be coincidence that the adoption of surnames in Ua (plural Uí) as distinct from its literal and patronymic meaning of 'grandson', broadly occurs around the same time as the introduction of the new assessment term *baile* for estate. In a recent survey Ó Murchadha demonstrates that the practice of turning *ua* from its literal meaning into that of a surname can be dated to the period *c*.925 to 1125.[40] Of the fifty-two examples he adduces, however, thirty or 59 per cent show this process of surname adoption to have occurred during the eleventh century.[41] A significant number of *bailte* feature the formula Baile Uí X. We see both the emergence of the term *baile* in its new sense of a taxable estate, and the new surname style Uí X, emerging at the same time and linked together regularly in toponomy. One example of interest concerns the place-name(s) *Bali ichorcrain et Iconligain* which occur in a charter of Domnall Ua Briain to Holy Cross abbey, datable to the period 1168 × 1185.[42] It is not clear whether we are here dealing with two distinct *bailte* or perhaps two *leathbhailte* occupied by the respective families, but the scribe clearly associated these surnames. The place-names cannot be identified with certainty but they clearly lay within what had earlier been the regional kingdom of Eóganacht Chaisil. Among the genealogies of Eóganacht Chaisil is that of the Cenél Conaill segment, whose ruling king, Lorcán, son of Conlígán son of Corcrán, became king of Caisel in 922. Therefore we may assign the adoption of these forms as surnames (Uí Chonlígáin and Uí Chorcráin) to

Prioratus Sancti Andree in Scotia (Bannatyne Club, 1841), 115 (which records a name in *baile* from Fife in a charter of 1070 × 1093. This reference was kindly supplied by Dr Simon Taylor.) **39** AU, 1011. For a useful discussion of the origins of the term *baile* see Flanagan, '*Baile*', passim. **40** 'The formation of Gaelic surnames', passim. **41** Ibid., 42–3. **42** Flanagan, *Irish royal charters*, 308–10.

no earlier than the last years of the tenth century, and the subsequent association of these surnames with the term *baile* in these places near Cashel can be no earlier. This apparent linkage between the emergence of surnames and estates in *baile* is certainly worthy of further investigation. It will be remembered that several theories exist to explain the unique emergence of surnames in Ireland at this time, none being entirely satisfactory.[43] The *baile* began its life as a definition of the basic unit of kinship-based, taxable landholding. Can it be that a new style was adopted at the same time whereby the associated kin-group also received or adopted a new name-form in Uí X or Mac Y as part of this new or reformed taxation system? In other words, just as *baile* became the new technical term for the estate, did Uí X or Mac Y become the new technical term for the kin-group?

In summary, then, the *status quaestionis* leads to the firm conclusion that the *trícha cét* system with its constituent unit, the *baile biataig*, emerges no earlier than the eleventh century as a new assessment and taxation system.

One can speculate as to why this might have been so. The most marked feature of political development during the eleventh century was the increasing power of the few provincial kingdoms at the expense of the many lesser kings in a development mirroring that of the feudal system in other parts of Europe. To quote Ó Corráin, 'the greater kings of eleventh-century Ireland partitioned kingdoms, appointed subordinate rulers, granted away whole territories [often *trícha céts*], expelled royal dynasties, made dependant lords of their subordinate kings, and developed power-based territorial lordships'.[44] Such a situation had arose directly from the increasing militarization of Irish society which had occurred during the ninth and tenth centuries, at least partly as a result of the Viking incursions.[45] At the core of such enhanced royal powers lay the control of wealth and an efficient taxation system must have facilitated this control. This was the *trícha cét* system. I believe that what probably happened was that this system was introduced in some fashion during the eleventh century as a development or refinement of the existing system of taxation and military levy by a powerful king or kings. It is clear that Irish politics changed markedly during and after the reign of Brian Boraime (d. 1014). After this the chief dynamic was one where a single powerful king arose who, while unable to achieve total dominance over all of the island, nevertheless managed to extend his rule over the greater portion of the island in a significantly more effective way then hitherto. Such was the case with Diarmait Mac Máel na mBó between 1058 and his death in 1072, and later with both of his Uí Briain successors down to 1114 or so. Such dominance by a single king became even more marked after this in the shape of the Uí Chonchobair kings from Connacht. The exercise of such dominance over the subservient provinces took the form of tribute taxation in cattle and the enforcement of a military levy in order to swell the ranks of the premier

43 For a useful discussion see Ó Canann, 'Ua Canannáin', 114–19. 44 Ó Corráin, *Ireland before the Normans*. 45 Doherty, 'Vikings in Ireland', 312–14, 318–22.

king's army. These are precisely the functions we find associated with the *trícha cét* system. This may have been introduced in one province and later spread nationwide, perhaps as an export from the native province of such a dominant king. As we have seen, the system had provincial variations of structure. Can we perhaps speculate that the system originated in Munster under Brian Boraime, given that that province shows the most developed application of the *trícha cét* system with its seventy *tríchas*? Whatever of this, I believe that the *trícha cét* system arose directly as a result of the greater power of the high-kingship, as manifested from Boraime's time onwards, with its centralizing and feudalizing tendencies, and its need for greater wealth and resources.

This chronology finds further confirmation in a study of the question of the economic aspects of the *trícha* system. While little direct evidence for the operation of this system survives we do have one well-documented example. This concerns the national collection of tribute or donation by the head of the Patrician church of Armagh on his *cuairt*, an event which appears to have occurred shortly after the ordination of each new incumbent.[46] In one case, that of 1106, we are specifically told that seven cows, seven sheep, and a half-ounce of silver was collected from every *trícha cét* in Munster. Such national collections appear to have been an innovation made possible by the growing power of the office of the high-kingship and, I would suggest, the existence of a new system of assessment and taxation which facilitated such collections. This was, of course, the *trícha* system and it is hardly coincidental that the first such Patrician collection is recorded in 1068, perfectly within the chronology argued above for the creation of the *trícha cét–baile biataig* system.

LOCAL KINGDOM, ANCESTOR TO THE 'TRÍCHA CÉT'

It is important to remember that the functions of the *trícha cét* system and of its component parts are certainly much older than the establishment of the system itself. Local polities, military levy, public assembly, taxation, and local jurisprudence all existed long before the *trícha cét* and the *baile biataig* came into existence. Most, if not all, *trícha céts* were based on pre-existing local kingdoms, of which as many as 200 may have existed at one time. Such kingdoms, with their kings of the lowest level of kingship, must have been the subject of lordship by more powerful kings throughout the historical period. At the basic level such lordship consisted of the consuming of food rents by kings peripatetically, as well as by participation in the *slógad*. For larger kingdoms this meant the extraction of animal rents, especially cattle.[47] Higher up the political scale we might find taxes being paid in silver, for Ireland seems to have had a silver bullion currency long before the arrival of the Vikings and their coinage.[48] The *trícha cét*

---

46 AU, 1068, 1094, 1106, 1120, 1162. **47** Charles-Edwards, *Irish and Welsh kinship*, 368–9. **48** Ó Corráin, *Ireland before the Normans*.

system, in essence, was merely a further development of the age-old system of levying wealth and military service from the local kingdoms by the greater powers. This system must be of similar antiquity to that of the kingdoms themselves. Down to the Invasion most *trícha céts* were also local kingdoms, and the history of both are inextricably linked. Evidence of the antiquity of the local kingdom structure can be found in three areas.

Table 3. *Floruit* of the 95 *trícha* eponyms with dynastic form

Before AD 600	67
7th century	8
8th century	9
9th century	5
10th century	1
11th century	1
No pre-colonial record	4

Firstly, Table 3 dates the men (and a few women) who gave their names to *tríchas*. The results are striking. These local kingdoms surely cannot have been formed more than two or three generations after the death of their eponyms, if indeed they formed them at all. It may be more likely to envisage the same eponyms taking over pre-existing local kingdoms which duly became renamed by the immediate generations descending from the eponym. As to the pre-historic section, some of these eponyms may be considerably older than AD 600, although there cannot be any certainty. Some of those of Uí Néill can be placed roughly in the late fifth century while the genealogies and proto-historical tales suggest that some eponyms of Connachta, Ulaid and Laigin may also have been of fifth-century date.[49] A fourth- to sixth-century date may be assigned to those eponyms or associated eponyms recorded on ogam stones. At least eight *trícha* names can be dated in this way.[50] Some of the genealogies are even older in claim then this, and several derive from an apical ancestor who would have lived in the early fourth century.[51] Such claims are, of course, very speculative. To go back even further, Ulaid and Uaithne (Uaithne give their name to two *tríchas*) appear to be recorded by Ptolemy in the second century. All of this suggests that many *tríchas* bear names originating in the pre-historic period.

A second test may be applied to this question. MacNeill's classification system for early Irish population groups, though nearly a century old, has not been superseded.[52] One can apply this system to *trícha* nomenclature. I have analysed all *trícha* names and assigned these to MacNeill's various classifications as follows.

49 Byrne, *Kings and high kings*, passim.   **50** Uí Liatháin, Uí Enechglais, Corcu Duibne, Alltraige, Ciarraige (of Kerry), Conaille, Luigne (of Meath), and Sogain (MacNeill, 'Irish population groups', 72–4).   **51** Such as those of the Osraige, Múscraige, Loígis etc.   **52** MacNeill, 'Irish population groups', passim.

Table 4. MacNeill's system applied to *trícha* names

1st Class	Plural names	10.0%
2nd Class	Collective singular names	22.5%
3rd Class	Sept names in Uí	34.5%
4th Class	Cenél names	9.0%
5th Class	Clann, Muinter etc.	24.0%

His first group are plural names. These are the oldest known stratum of nomenclature and this was the standard form of naming in Celtic Continental Europe and in Ptolemy's second-century map of Ireland. This system of naming can safely be dated to the very first centuries AD.

The second group, collective names, are again prehistoric, if perhaps a later development then the first group.

The third group, sept names in Uí, are dated by MacNeill to the period from prehistoric to seventh century. When examining *trícha* names in Uí, most can only be dated by their place in the genealogies, and by this method can be attributed to the fourth and fifth centuries. The latest can be dated to the eighth century.

The fourth group, names in *cenél*, are dated by MacNeill from the fifth century onwards. *Trícha* names in *cenél* can be dated to the fifth to seventh centuries, agreeing with MacNeill.

The fifth group, names in all other lineage terms, is dated by MacNeill to the sixth century onwards. *Trícha* names in this group generally agree with MacNeill's dating, which might, however, be a century late in beginning.

Therefore the results of Table 4 confirm those of Table 3. We can say that *trícha* names show a development beginning perhaps as early as the second century AD, with new names being formed on a continuous basis until the Invasion. Significantly, the clear majority of *trícha* names with dynastic form originated in the period before record begins, that is, before AD 600. The results of Table 5 below indicate that a similar conclusion can be drawn in the case of *trícha* names with toponomastic form.

Table 5. Date of first record of *trícha*s with toponomastic form

7th century or earlier	25
8th century	7
9th century	13
10th century	10
11th century	9
12th century	9
13th century[53]	2
No pre-colonial record	19

53 These examples are from pre-colonial Connacht.

A third class of evidence for local kingdom antiquity is perhaps to be found in that of the archaeology of boundary ditches or linear earthworks, although this approach is in its early stages. Several miles of the so-called 'Black Pig's Dyke' in Co. Monaghan, which has been dated to the last centuries BC, agree precisely with a boundary of the *trícha* of Clones (**T165**). 'The Dorsey', a large earthwork dated to the second-century BC, lies a couple of miles north of the southern boundary of the *trícha* of Ind Airthir (**T164**), in Co. Armagh. Again, the Claidh Dubh linear earthwork, which divides the *trícha* of Fir Maige in Co. Cork (**T32**), has been dated to the early centuries AD. Its line agrees approximately with the boundary between both divisions of Caoille – said to represent two former *trícha*s – as extended in the *Críchad* tract.[54] I suspect further excavations will result in more such examples in the future.

Table 3 above suggests the existence of considerable political stability throughout the period of record. This is particularly so in Munster – even allowing for the poverty of annals here. Other areas of marked stability over centuries were Mide, Tír Conaill, Uí Fhiachrach Tuaiscirt, Uí Failge, and most of Airgialla. Where political change does occur it involves a brief period of expansion of ruling elites, again followed by stability and continuity. In Laigin Uí Chennselaig polities mostly became established during the sixth/seventh centuries leaving a ring of older polities surrounding them, just as Uí Dúnlainge did a century later, at the same time as a marked Dál Fiatach expansion in Ulster. Brega was somewhat similar. Spectacular and continued expansion of an elite at the cost of surrounding polities over a long period is seen only in the examples of Cenél Eógain, Uí Briúin Aí and, somewhat later, Dál Cais. Even in such cases the local kingdom often seems to have remained unaltered apart from a change of ruler at the top. They were infiltrated as much as conquered. Many *trícha*s bear the names of polities long extinguished. Most of the Ostmen *trícha*s bear the names of their original Irish lords, all superseded by 900 or before.[55] Dál Riata of Scotland probably lost influence in north Antrim during the eighth century, yet the *trícha* called from them (**T150**) survived until the Invasion and beyond. Dartraige Coninse (in **T165**) had been replaced as lords of their polity by at least 946, Uí Ailello after 800 (**T117**), Uí Dróna (**T4**), Uí Duach Argatrois (**T70**) and probably several of the Conmaicne polities of Connacht during the eighth century, and Tír Meic Cáirthinn (**T142**) as early as 677. And what are we to make of the probable thirteenth-century Leinster cantred name Kenalahun (***C183**), which derives from a line, Uí Aithemon Mestige, so long fallen from power and sunk in obscurity that they were almost forgotten by the genealogists? In all of these cases, as well as in such twelfth-century ones as Caílle Follamain (**T107**) and Eóganacht Chaisil, the political change did not alter nomenclature or boundaries. Such onomastic alteration appears to have been very unusual and just two examples are found. Uí Thuirtre (**T140**, **T151**) was a name which crossed the

---

54 Walsh, 'Black Pigs Dyke', passim; Baillie, 'Navan Fort and the Dorsey', passim; Cooney, 'Reading a landscape manuscript', 28; Power, *Críchad*, 9–13. **55** See **T39**, **T171**, **T178**.

Bann, apparently during the eleventh century, and, during the twelfth century, Múscraige Tíre (**T118**) became Urmumu.

The individual local kingdom usually took its politics and alliances from its ruling elite or royal family. Many local kingdoms were ruled by related kindreds who competed for the regional kingship (*ríge túath*) of a polity comprised of several individual local kingdoms and whose joint eponym was the alleged common ancestor. Well documented examples include Uí Chennselaig and Uí Maine but the same system can be seen in operation over much of Ireland. Other clear examples are Dál Fiatach, Cenél Conaill, and Osraige, although the latter were dominated by a single line from an early period. Indeed, retention of kingship by a single line became the norm in many regional kingdoms, particularly during the tenth and eleventh centuries. Often older or unrelated lineages continued to rule their own local kingdom/*trícha* as a client of the regional kingdom, but without the right to compete for the overkingship. We have already noted how many local kingdoms were simply taken over by an outside regional kingdom which then placed a lineage of its own in charge. This suggests that local kingdom/*trícha* boundaries had a tendency to endure. In this context we may note Uí Bairrche Mara (Bargy, Co. Wexford, **T179**), whose twelfth-century boundaries can first be identified *c*.AD 800. Sometimes *trícha*s were forcibly detached from one regional kingdom by another but usually without boundary alteration. Note the incorporation of Fir Arda (**T159**) into Airgialla during the 1130s, the long rivalry between Cenél Conaill and Connacht for Cairpre Mór (**T8**), the even division of the Uí Fhidgente kingdoms along *trícha* boundaries between the semi-provincial kingdoms of Tuadmumu and Desmumu during the 1150s, and the contemporary transfer of the entire regional kingdom of Ciarraige Luachra from Tuadmumu to Desmumu.[56] Sometimes the political change was internal but again without boundary change. The boundaries of Cuircne (**T98**) reflect the political situation of not later than *c*.AD 1000, after which extensive immigration into the *trícha* by Fir Thethba greatly reduced the area retained by its original rulers. Similarly Mugdorna Maigen (**T163**) has boundaries which became politically obsolete in the late eleventh century as Fir Fernmaige colonized the southern half of the *trícha*. Again, the *trícha* of Ind Airthir (**T164**) experienced extensive settlement by segments of Cenél Eógain after 1150 which occupied its northern third. The common factor in all three examples is that these political movements were *internal* to large semi-provincial kingdoms (Mide, Airgialla, Cenél Eógain).

Where border warfare resulted in territorial alterations between semi-provincial kingdoms *trícha* border changes could ensue, where typically only a portion of a *trícha* was conquered. The disputed border between Fonn Timchill (**T84**) and Fir Maige (**T32**), and the shape of the *trícha* of Uí Énna (**T85**), both probably owe much to the ebb and flow of warfare between the provincial kingdoms of Tuadmumu and Desmumu after 1150. Similarly southwards aggression

56 MacCotter, 'Anglo-Norman Kerry', 40.

by Uí Briúin Aí at the expense of Uí Briúin Seola caused uncertainty about borders, resulting in significant border alterations occurring in what is today northeast Co. Galway during the twelfth century. The conquest of territory in Laigin: Crích na Cétach, by Mide, probably in the early twelfth century, resulted in the creation of what was probably a new *tricha* (**T108**). The ecclesiastical *civitas* of Derry originally lay in Tír Énna (**T136**) and was transferred to Inis Eógain (**T144**) after Derry came under Cenél Eógain control around 1100. Peaceful change could also occur. The internal *tricha* borders of Corcu Loígde seem to have been re-arranged during the twelfth century. Lugmad (**T158**) may have been a new demesne *tricha* carved out of Conaille Muirthemne by its Uí Cherbaill overlords during the 1130s. While we can discern general rules with wide application the diverse results of local particularism must be studied.

The unit which first emerges as the local kingdom later comes to be called *tricha cét*. This relationship offers some clues to the reasons why *tricha*s varied greatly in size. One of the largest *tricha*s, Uí Failge (**T64**), contained over 300,000 acres. This ancient kingdom, with several important dynastic segments, was largely dominated by one line which, certainly after the eleventh century, reserved the title *rí* to itself, relegating the others to the humbler title *flaith*. A similar development can be seen in the case of the neighbouring kingdoms of Uí Muiredaig (**T66**) and Uí Fáeláin (**T65**). These were late in origin, developing from the mid-eighth century onwards. In the course of this expansion they each absorbed and extinguished several other local kingdoms and created relatively large kingdoms, later regarded as single *tricha*s. Significantly, their cousin kingdom, Uí Dúnchada, whose expansion north-eastwards may have taken place somewhat later, did not manage to extinguish all the local kingdoms within its boundaries, resulting in the survival of two *tricha*s here (**T51**, **T52**). Ind Airthir (**T164**), probably the largest *tricha* in Ireland (approximately 315,000 acres), has a strange history of kingship. From the sixth to the early ninth centuries this was a single kingdom. Then it appears to divide into three segments forming distinct kingdoms. Occasionally, however, one of these claimed the title to all of Ind Airthir. By the 1150s we again find reference to a single kingdom, held now by a stranger in sovereignty, Murchad son of King Donnchad Ua Cerbhaill of Airgialla.[57]

Mide and Connacht had strong centralising dynasties, perhaps resulting in the peculiar *tricha* structure noted above where the relationship between *tricha* and local kingdom was weaker then elsewhere. We may also note the existence of several Conmaicne *tricha*s, only one of which retained its indigenous kings (**T13**). In all other cases these were ruled by collaterals of ruling branches of Uí Briúin. Even when one of these *tricha*s, Muintir Angaile (**T135**), finally broke free of Uí Ruairc rule during the 1170s, the annalist gives its leaders only the intermediate title of *rígthaísech*.[58] In the cases of Uí Maine and Uí Chennselaig the component *tricha*s tended to be of similar size, suggesting perhaps a contem-

57 Flanagan, *Irish royal charters*, 292. 58 This title seems to have been borne by leaders of new polities of junior rank emerging in the chaos of the post-Invasion period. See ALC, 1196, 1207, 1212, 1215, 1218; AU, 1172, 1181, 1185, 1238.

porary origin. The norm is widely differing *trícha* sizes on an apparently random basis that is likely to derive from an organic development over a long time chiefly influenced by the individual local circumstances (as with the English *hundred* and the Welsh *cantref*). Thus we get wide variations from the large *trícha*s noted above to the smallest, such as Dungarvan (**T170**: 9,400 acres) and Críoch na Cétach (**T108**: *c*.20,000).

To summarize, we see that the twelfth-century *trícha cét* bears names the majority of which originate before AD 600, appears to be a spatial unit which has undergone little alteration for centuries, in some cases with borders relevant only to an earlier political era, and is almost always ruled either by a petty-king of the lowest order of kingship or is a demesne (native or private) lordship of a king of higher order. Therefore, the twelfth-century *trícha*s are largely older units under a new name. This older unit can only be the local kingdom or *túath* of the early Irish Laws (of *c*.700). This is confirmed in the later glosses to these Laws, where *trícha cét* occurs as a gloss on the earlier *túath*.[59]

ORIGINS OF THE 'BAILE BIATAIG'

As we have seen, *baile biataig* is a new term coined no earlier than the eleventh century. The reality behind this term, the basic unit of free-kinship landholding, is surely of much greater antiquity, although little or no work has been done in this area. One suspects that many such estates were merely re-named in *baile* rather then created at the time the *trícha cét/baile* system was introduced. Nicholls suggests that the estate network behind the *baile* system may have its origins as far back as the period of population peak preceding the great plagues of the late seventh century, and suggests that a similar estate system operated in parts of Scotland, which may date to the first centuries BC.[60] A useful avenue of inquiry here may be that of the large ditches which often mark townland (and *baile*?) boundaries. References to such ditches occur in colonial documentation as well as in the pre-Invasion Kells 'Charters'.[61] This is, of course, an avenue for archaeological exploration.

There is an avenue of inquiry which moves the question of the age of such estates beyond mere conjecture. However, lest what follows be criticized for being overly schematic, I should sound the cautionary note that the early Irish Laws are more likely to represent idealized norms then actual conditions in eighth-century Ireland, and this should be born in mind as we progress. Again, what follows are tentative conclusions. *Baile biataig*, *trícha cét*, and late-*túath* with its *taísech túaithe*, were components of the same system of wealth generation and social organization. Just as the *trícha cét* was successor to the local kingdom, and probably *taísech túaithe* to the *aire túisea*, so the *baile biataig* also may have had a

---

59 Ó Corráin, 'Hogan', 93–4. **60** 'Gaelic society and economy', 407, and pers. comm. **61** PRC, 72; MacNiocaill, 'Irish 'Charters''.

precursor in the early Laws. In these we find intermittent usage of the set phrase *cóicráith chétach*, 'five ráiths possessed of a hundred'. Sometimes *treb* is substituted for *ráith*, as in the term *cóicthreb*.[62] Here the *ráith* is the ubiquitous ringfort[63] while *treb* has the meaning house or homestead. This term is to be understood in the sense of a group of five substantial farms corporately held by a kinship group or *derbfhine*. More importantly, this is to be understood as a single kinship unit whose property confers a particular legal status, that of free kinship, giving a meaning close to that of Duffy's definition of the later *baile biataig*. This unit of five farms held in common ownership by a single kin-group formed the basic unit of clientship as illustrated in *Críth Gablach* and elsewhere: noble status is defined by the number of such units of clientship a noble possesses. Each of the five farms represents the homestead of the *bóaire*, the basic grade of Irish freeman. The *bóaire* was the substantial farmer, possessed of a full plough-team of oxen, who had various grades of unfree or semi-free men under him working his land.[64] The term *cétach*, here to be understood as 'one hundred [cattle]', is used elsewhere in the Laws to denote a legally qualifying threshold of wealth, such as in the case of the *brigiu cétach* 'hospitaller', or more generally as a superlative not to be taken literally, and may even occur in toponomy: compare the *trícha* of Crích na Cétach (**T108**). Its usage in the term *cóicráith chétach* may perhaps be taken in the sense of a legally qualifying wealth threshold in livestock rather then as literally one hundred cattle. However, it is remarkable that *Críth Gablach* assigns a herd of twenty cows to the strongest grade of *bóaire*, the *mruigfher*.[65] The first meaning, that of wealth, is found in an early fourteenth-century poem from Connacht, which refers to a *biatach* possessed of a *baile* as *brúghaidh bó chéadach baile*.[66]

Early Irish land measurements and currency units, as revealed in the Laws, are difficult and ambiguous. The exact meaning of the units called *cumal* and *tír cumaile* remain matters of debate. Many scholars prefer not to enter the tangle.[67] One who has is Stout.[68] He concluded that to qualify as a *bóaire* one had to possess between 60 and 70 acres, while a king would have had to possess 245 acres. This is based on a passage in *Seanchas Már* which states that the lowest grade of freeman, the *ócaire*, possesses a *tír cumaile* of land 'and every grade from that up to the king of a *túath* has respectively a *tír cumaile* of land in excess over each preceding one'.[69] For a number of reasons, I believe these latter figures are unacceptably low and are, in fact, in error.

The *bóaire* or *mruigfher* was the strongest grade of free commoner, the archetypical freeman. He possessed a full plough-team, twenty cattle and two bulls, in addition to pigs, sheep, horses and poultry, and would have had unfree (*muga*,

62 Charles-Edwards, *Irish and Welsh kinship*, 319–23, 549. 63 Stout, 'Ringforts', passim. 64 Charles-Edwards, *Irish and Welsh kinship*, 320–3, 344–6, 408; Kelly, *Early Irish farming*, 428–30, 445–7; idem, *Irish law*, p. xxiii; Charles-Edwards, 'Kinship, status', 18. 65 Kelly, *Irish law*, 37; Jackson, 'Book of Deer', 55–6; Byrne, 'Tribes and tribalism', 140; Charles-Edwards, 'Críth Gablach', 68. 66 O'Daly, 'Inauguration', 346. 67 Charles-Edwards, 'Críth Gablach', 67–8; Kelly, *Irish law*, 422–3. 68 Stout, 'Ringforts', 231. 69 *Ancient Laws of Ireland*, ii, 13.

senchléite) or semi-free (*fuidri*) tenants on his lands or as labour.[70] His Anglo-Saxon counterpart, the *ceorl*, possessed, similarly, a full plough-team, around the same number of cattle, unfree tenants and slaves, and had an estate of 120 medieval acres, perhaps as much as 300 statute acres or more, in addition to woodland and perhaps turbary.[71] In *Críth Gablach* the *ócaire*, the lower level of freeman, is stated to have had seven *cumals* of land while the *bóaire* (*mruigfher*) is possessed of twenty-one *cumals*.[72] The *cumal* was originally a unit of value or currency of account equal to a female slave. Estimates of the value of the *cumal* vary, probably because her value was variable over several centuries or may have possessed different values in different parts of Ireland at the same time.[73] Similarly, the value of the *tír cumaile* 'land of a *cumal*', also varied over time. We may accept that, eventually, it came to represent a standard value of around thirty-four acres.[74] Again, opinions differ as to whether the *cumal* and *tír cumaile* are identical.[75] We must now address this situation.

The best approach is by measuring grazing levels for livestock. In one passage the *ócaire* is said to reserve three of his seven *cumals* of land for grazing his stock, namely seven milch cows, three dry cattle, ten sheep, five pigs, two horses, and assorted fowl.[76] The *mruigfher* has twenty milch cows, two bulls, and at least as much other stock as the *ócaire*, and probably at least twice more, given that his land was theoretically three times bigger than that of the *ócaire*. It is possible to assign an area of grazing to these amounts of livestock. At 1861 levels the *ócaire*'s stock would have required about sixty-three acres of land of average quality.[77] Earlier agricultural practices may have been less effective, and this would, of course, result in larger acreages per beast. One estimate for the twelfth century gives average grazing of 4½ acres per cow on land of average quality, a figure similar to that of 1861.[78]

A source not hitherto used is the unpublished Strafford Survey of Co. Sligo of 1636, which gives cattle grazing totals per townland.[79] According to this survey the annual grazing acreage per cow on best-quality land was three and on poor quality mixed mountain and bog-land as high as twenty. It seems clear from this survey that a figure of 4½ acres per beast is too low and that a truer average for Sligo in 1636 was six or seven acres per beast. Applying an acreage of six acres per beast to the three *cumal* stocklist above gives an acreage of 90 for three *cumals* of land, close to the figure of 34 acres per *tír cumaile*. Therefore, the *ócaire*'s three *cumals* of grazing must represent between 60 and 90 acres of land, and his total area of seven *cumals* between 140 and 210 acres. Accordingly, Stout's figures must

70 Charles-Edwards, 'Críth Gablach', 67–9; Brady, 'Labor and agriculture', 128–30. **71** Charles-Edwards, 'Kinship, status', 9, 12–15. **72** Idem, 'Críth Gablach', 67–8. **73** Kelly, *Early Irish farming*, 574–5; McLeod, 'Status and currency', 64–5, 78. **74** Mac Niocaill, 'Tír cumaile', passim. **75** Ibid., 84n; McLeod, 'Status and currency', 65; Kelly, *Early Irish farming*, 574–5. **76** Kelly, *Early Irish farming*, 422–3. **77** Jones, *Graziers, land reform*, 57. **78** Lucas, *Cattle in ancient Ireland*, 238; Feehan, *Farming in Ireland* , 57. **79** BL Harleian MS 2048. My figures derive from a survey of two parishes, Ahamlish and St Johns (ff 129–31, 134–6). I an indebted to Mr Kenneth Nicholls for drawing this source to my attention.

be wrong (based as they are on a single passage in the Laws). These figures suggest that the *tír cumaile* of 34 acres is that meant more often then not by the various references to *cumals* of land in *Críth Gablach* and elsewhere in the Laws.

It is, nonetheless, safer to continue to interpret references to grazing in the Laws by historical grazing levels. The *mruigfher*, with twenty cows, is clearly the grade referred to in the *cóicráith chétach* kinship unit, with each of its homesteads theoretically containing twenty cows. Based on the livestock levels of the *mruigfher* as indicated above, he would have possessed at least 180 acres of grazing, in addition to arable (ploughed with his full plough team), wood and perhaps turbary. The twenty-one *cumals* of land held by the *mruigfher* therefore contained somewhere in the range 420–630 acres of land of average quality, and that of the next grade below him, the *bóaire febsa*, with his fourteen *cumals* of land, in the range 280–420 acres. For this grade Stout's figures give a farm size of sixty-eight acres. Based on the estimates for the *mruigfher* above, the *cóicráith chétach* unit would have contained somewhere in the range 2,100 to 3,100 acres. These estimates are based on average grazing levels, but the figures could be reduced downwards where high-quality land is concerned, giving a *cóicráith chétach* unit of not much more than 1,000 acres. These figures agree well with those given elsewhere for the size of the *baile biataig*.[80] In the twelfth century, the ideal *baile biataig* was thought to support a herd of 300 cattle which, at the average Sligo level of six cows per acre, would require 1,800 acres of grazing, or perhaps 900 acres on best-quality land.[81] When arable and woodland are added, this theoretical *baile biataig* would be between 1,800 to 3,600 acres in extent. Therefore a number of sources combine to suggest that the *cóicráith* unit of kinship was approximately similar in size to the later *baile biataig*.

The size of the seventh-century *cóicráith* unit and the twelfth-century *baile biataig* unit seem similar. I believe that this five-farm unit, the *cóicráith chétach*, may perhaps have evolved into the later *baile biataig*. While it might be thought that some memory of this evolution was preserved in the name of the new term, *trícha cét*, it is hard to see how the term *cóicráith chétach* could have evolved into the term *cét*. It may be that some reflex of the evolution from *cóicráith* to *baile biataig* was preserved in the term *cét*. It may be of some relevance to note that the early twelfth-century *Betha Colmáin* uses the terms *baile* and *ráith* interchangeably to refer to what were clearly *baile biataig*.[82] It is probable that *cét* was an alternative term for *baile biataig*, but its origins must remain obscure. It may have had something to do with 100 units of some kind, assessed or taxed. The *cóicráith* kinship unit displayed the structure 1–5–? (Figure 2) and the *baile biataig* unit 1–4–16 (Figure 3), as illustrated.

We cannot be sure just how many subservient households lived under the *bóaire* (*mruigfher*), clearly several. Examples of this five-farm kinship unit are not confined to the Laws but occur in *Senchus Fer nAlban*, an early genealogy of Dál Riata in Argyll, a Gaelic kingdom which originated as an Irish colony in Scotland.

80 See Chapter 5. **81** 'Cá līn triūcha i nÉrind', § 5. **82** Meyer, *Betha Colmáin*, 64.

Figure 2. The *cóicráith chétach* unit

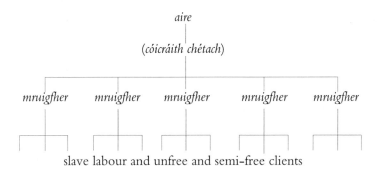

This genealogy has embedded within it a remarkable fragment of what is clearly some kind of register of military levy in which the basic unit is the house (*tech*), these being grouped into units of five, multiples of which are in turn placed under the lordship of various nobles. Bannerman has argued convincingly that these five-house units are the same as those theoretically illustrated in *Críth Gablach*, that is, the *cóicráith chétach* unit discussed above. While the dating of this fragment remains controversial, it is certainly a genuine record and can be no later in date then the arrival of the Scandinavians in Scotland. The *Senchus* survey provides a unique opportunity to test my conclusions relating to the size of the *cóicráith chétach* unit, as it gives a figure for the total number of *taige* on the island of Islay, 350, which in turn represents a total of 70, five-house units. By dividing this into the total area of the island we get a figure of approximately 2,200 acres per five-house unit. This agrees well with the range arrived at above for the theoretical *cóicráith chétach* unit (between 1,000 to 3,000 acres). A further practical value of the *Senchus* survey is in its numbers of men raised by military levy, which give figures close to the 700 men of the Irish Laws for the *slógad*.[83]

Figure 3. The *baile biataig* unit (based on MacErlean)

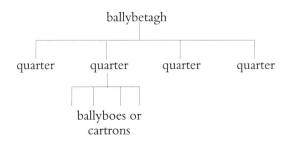

---

83 Bannerman, *Dalriada*, 42–3, 130–40, 146–7; Hogan, 'The tricha cét', 165. There are problems with Bannerman's dating of *Senchus*, not least the presence of a Norse loanword (for a discussion see Williams, 'Ship-levies', 300–3).

If indeed the *cóicráith chétach* represents an earlier stage in the development of the *baile biataig*, this developmental process may owe much to centuries of population variation. Such a development, from fortified *ráith* to unfortified *baile*, agrees well with current thinking on the origins of the *baile* and recent archaeological research on the abandonment of the *ráith* after AD 1000.[84]

THE ORIGINS OF THE LOCAL KINGDOM

What of the origins of the local kingdom? Binchy suggested that the description of the *túath* in the early Laws as the primary unit of citizenship and jurisdiction already reflected an obsolete situation and that this description might better relate to the period before 600.[85] Indeed, it is hard to reconcile Binchy's understanding with the common picture presented by the existence of overkingdoms made up of *túatha*, these being led by related ruling families. Can it be that the Laws in reality reflect the situation before the period of expansion of the great dynasties (Uí Néill, Laigin, Eóganachta etc.) during the fifth century? I have shown above that many local kingdoms can probably be traced back into the sixth century and, if this is indeed the case, surely by implication we may be dealing with perhaps a significantly older unit again? Etymologically *túath* derives from a common Indo-European root meaning 'people', and it has the secondary sense of a territory, and thus is a usage of considerable antiquity across Europe.[86] During the Dark Ages Ireland was never culturally isolated, and we should look to other models for evidence both for the evolution of the *túath* as local kingdom and its development into the *trícha cét*. Such a quest needs to be integrated into the larger picture of a general development throughout Europe, in which we see movement from a position of multiple petty-kingdoms with their concomitant judicial, commercial and military-levy structures to that of national kingdoms whose local administrative functions are discharged through a system broadly similar throughout the area, which we may call 'the hundred system'.

---

84 As summarized in Doherty, 'Vikings in Ireland', 315–18. 85 Binchy, *Celtic and Anglo-Saxon kingship*, 1–3. 86 Ibid., 4 –7.

CHAPTER 7

The 'hundred systems' of northern Europe

SURVEY BY COUNTRY

WALES

Close relationships existed between Ireland and Wales during the eleventh century, and probably earlier.[1] In Wales, the parallel unit to the Irish *trícha cét* was the *cantref* ('100 trefi', a Welsh term cognate with the Irish *treb*). Wales was divided into something above fifty *cantrefi*. By the eleventh century at least, each *cantref* had its fiscal and administrative court. Gerald de Barri, an acute observer of both Welsh and Irish society, writing in the 1180s, says that 'the word cantred is the same in Welsh and Irish'.[2] This suggests that he saw many similarities between both units. These similarities must explain why a Latinized form of the Welsh term, *cantred*, came to be used instead of that of *trícha cét* in Ireland. Both units were probably the templates for the new ecclesiastical division, the rural deanery, in each country.[3] Cantred and *cantref* were primarily spatial units of taxable lordship and of justice. A further similarity can be seen in the constituent parts of each. The sub-division of the *cantref*, the *cwmwd*, in the form *commote*, was the first term used by the Cambro-Norman invaders of Ireland for the Irish late-*túath*, again suggesting some similarities between these units.[4] Hogan made much of the apparent similarity between the Welsh *maenol* (estate) and the *baile biataig* and their respective sub-divisions.[5] However, this comparison was based on a north-Welsh schema which gave each *maenol* four *trefi* of 256 acres each, which Hogan compared to the Irish quarter. Hogan was unaware that the actual statute acreage represented here per *maenol* was a mere 300 or so for these were much smaller acres. Furthermore, in South Wales, the *tref* seems to have comprised around 125 statute acres (similar to some English *hides*) and to have been grouped into estates of seven or thirteen *trefi*.[6] Therefore Hogan's comparison appears to have little value.

The main problem with further comparison here is the lack of evidence for Welsh administration before the tenth century. There are, however, indications that the spatial aspect of the cantrefol system in Wales is early. The cantrefol nomenclature and boundary structure of Glamorgan appears to have seventh-

---

1 Duffy, 'Ostmen, Irish and Welsh', passim. **2** Richards, *Welsh units*, 229; Smith, *The itinerary of John Leland* iv, 1–9; Thorpe, *Gerald of Wales*, 186, 223–4. **3** Williams, *The Welsh church*, 16. **4** See p. 18. **5** Hogan, 'The tricha cét', 178–9. **6** Jones, 'Multiple estates', 15, 17; Davies, *Llandaff charters*, 33–4, 39; Jones, 'Post-Roman Wales', 327–8.

century origins, and something like the later *cantref* structure seems to have existed in Dyfed by the ninth century. Furthermore, there is evidence to suggest that
some *cantrefi* used administrative centres whose roots go back to the Roman
period. A further indicator of the likely antiquity of the cantrefol structure in
Wales is the pattern of nomenclature exhibited both by *cantref* and *cwmwd*.
Significant numbers of each bear names incorporating that of an ancestor of the
ruling lineage. Where these can be dated they refer to persons who lived during the period AD 400–800.[7] Further light can be thrown on the origin of the
cantref by a study of legal and kinship terminology. It is clear from the terminology of the Welsh Laws, especially relating to the word *tud* (cognate with the
Irish *túath*), that the early jurisdictional system as described in the early Irish Laws
also existed in Wales, where the *tud* had once been the legal and jurisdictional
unit. By the eleventh century, the *tud* had evolved into the *cantref*, just as in
Ireland the local-kingdom *túath* became *trícha cét*. Charles-Edwards, drawing on
developments in the usage of the word *tud* and its derivatives in addition to several kinship terms, has demonstrated that the *tud* became obsolete as the primary
jurisdictional unit in Wales by around AD 400 if not even earlier, during the
Romano-British period. Thus similar developments occurred in Wales and
somewhat later in Ireland. Does this suggest the possibility of some element of
common inheritance or common development? While the existence of extensive Irish colonies in Wales from the fourth century – if not earlier – and the
continued close relations between both countries after that date is suggestive,
there were also significant differences between the political (kingship) structures
of both countries, at least by the tenth century, and we should be cautious about
making too much of what may have been a cognate development.[8]

ENGLAND

Wales also had close ties with Anglo-Saxon England. Here the parallel unit was
the hundred, theoretically composed of 100 *hides* just as the *cantref* was theoretically composed of 100 *trefi*, each representing the homestead of the basic grade
of freeman (in England the *ceorl*). Thus the hundred has a schematic derivation
similar to the *cantref*, although, as shown below, the term 'hundred' is likely to
have an entirely unconnected derivation. This schema was just that however:
the area of the English hundred varies greatly, just as does that of the *cantref* and
trícha cét. In the thirteenth century there were over 600 hundreds in England.
The chief function of the hundred was to administer local justice and regulate
taxation by means of its court, which met every three weeks in a fixed meeting
place. The earliest direct evidence for the existence of this system comes from

7 Jenkins, 'Regions and Cantrefs', 41–50; Charles-Edwards, 'The Seven Bishop-houses', passim;
Jones, 'Multiple estates', 19–24; Richards, 'Early Welsh territorial suffixes', passim.   8 Charles-
Edwards, 'Celtic kinship terms', 114–122; Davies, *Conquest, coexistence and change*, 19–22; Jones,
'Multiple estates', 17; Davies, *Patterns of power*, 19, 83–4, 89–90; Lloyd, *History of Wales*, i, 300ff.

the middle of the tenth century but it would seem to be somewhat older.[9] Certainly, by the early ninth century at the latest, the Anglo-Saxons had an established tradition of public assembly and of constructing meeting-places to serve early administrative units that were similar to (and often co-extensive with) the later hundreds. This chronology can be confirmed by the existence of a system similar in all but name to the hundred system in the Danelaw, the wapentake system. The undoubted links between both systems must pre-date the Danish settlement in the Danelaw, which began during the late ninth century.[10] Turner has drawn on a wide variety of historical, onomastic and archaeological evidence to show that some features of the hundred system are significantly older again. He has shown that most hundreds bear the name of their meeting place, usually a mound or hill, often with associations with pagan ritual sites, sacred trees and criminal execution cemeteries. Many hundred mounds appear to have been raised specifically for the purpose of public assembly, while some hundred names are derived from early Anglo-Saxon dynasties or social groups.[11] The early existence of a complex system of local assessment in England is illustrated by the Mercian 'tribal hidage', a detailed territorial taxation of much of England by *hide*, which has been dated to the late eighth century.[12] Turner concludes that:

> In ninth-century Anglo-Saxon England there was a well-established system of meeting-places and administrative organisation which had grown out of the social, political and economic developments of the seventh century, and which may have had its origins in the earliest territorial and religious organisation of the Anglo-Saxons.

We should, however, note the counter-argument which suggests that the Anglo-Saxons simply took over pre-existing Celtic units. This argument is based on the shared tenurial practices in Wales and several parts of eastern England, which has led to the suggestion that some hundreds, especially those whose chief church bore the title *eccles*, late Brittonic for 'church' (from Latin *ecclesia*), preserve the memory of pre-Germanic Romano-British spatial units. While such hundreds can be found east of the Pennines, especially in Kent and Yorkshire, they are more often found west of the Pennines, especially in Lancashire, Staffordshire and Cheshire, areas which remained British into the seventh century. It is clear that some hundreds, at least, may derive remotely from pre-Germanic units.[13]

There are some similarities between this English hidage system and that in Ireland. The size of some *hides* may have been up to 300 acres or more when

9 Campbell, *The Anglo-Saxons*, 172–6; Pollock and Maitland, *History of English law*, i, 556–8; Stenton, *Anglo-Saxon England*, 292–3, 296–300; Finberg, 'Anglo-Saxon England', 478; Cam, *Hundred rolls*, 137. 10 Turner, 'Public assembly in the Danelaw', passim; Stenton, *Anglo-Saxon England*, 296, 298. 11 Turner, passim; Loyn, *Making of the English nation*, 27–9; Stenton, *Anglo-Saxon England*, 293–4. 12 Campbell, *The Anglo-Saxons*, 59–61; Stenton, *Anglo-Saxon England*, 295–6. 13 Jones, 'Multiple estates', 25–8, 35, 40; idem, 'Continuity despite calamity', passim; Barrow, *Kingdom of the Scots*, 7–68.

grazing and woodland are added to the arable. More important, the Irish *cóicráith* kinship unit of five *bóaire* holdings is paralleled by an English *five*-hide unit which operated – at least in the earlier period – in a similar way. Both represent a system linking an area of land quantified by ploughing time, kinship, and status, as Charles-Edwards has shown.[14]

SCOTLAND

Scotland is especially worthy of scrutiny given its very close cultural relations with Ireland. Such scrutiny, however, is greatly complicated by Scotland's extremely complex ethnic and linguistic history and the relative absence of early source material. Whatever of the dating problems with *Senchus Fer nAlban*, it seems clear from this source that late seventh-century (?) Dál Riata was a *mórthúath* whose internal political structure followed the Irish model. Dál Riata was divided into at least three local-kingdom *túatha*. At least two of these, Cenél nGabráin and Cenél Loairn, had kings of their own who also competed for the overkingship.[15] The eulogy, *Amra Choilm Chille*, generally accepted as dating to the saint's death *c.*597, mentions the *túatha* of the Tay Valley in southern Pictland. While this may be a non-technical use of the word (to be translated 'peoples'), the context suggests that the writer understood these as being units similar to the Irish local-kingdom *túath*.[16] These Pictish *túatha* were perhaps the forerunners of the minimal polity in Pictland as represented by the areas which later came to be ruled by *mormaers* but which were originally kingdoms in their own right.[17] These units were certainly in existence by the eighth century, and may have contained within them additional sub-kingdoms ruled by *reguli*, as we find in Ireland. Centralizing tendencies are evident much earlier in Scotland than in Ireland and in time these original polities seem to have become earldoms in the feudal system. Evidence for the early spatial structures of the Celtic-speaking areas of the western Lowlands (Strathclyde and Galloway) is lacking, but Barrow notes the size of the newly created twelfth-century feudal baronies here as being similar in size to the Welsh *cantref*.[18]

Bannerman's belief that the reference to a *céttreb* in *Senchus* represents an early Irish version of the *cantref*/hundred unit may, as Ó Corráin suggests, be making too much of a single unsupported example of dubious provenance.[19]

14 Charles-Edwards, 'Kinship, status', 3–33; Finberg, *Agr. hist. England and Wales*, 480–2.   **15** Bannerman, *Dalriada*, 111–15, 130; Anderson, *Kings and kingship*, 156–7, 162–5, 230.   **16** Stokes, 'Amra Choluimb chille', 164; Skene, *Celtic Scotland*, 210–11.   **17** While the principal source for the existence of such kingdoms, the tract *De situ Albanie*, is now treated with much caution (see Broun, 'Seven Kingdoms'), the existence of many petty-kingdoms in early Scotland is beyond doubt. At various times kings of Fortrenn, Athol, Argyll, Orkney, the Hebrides, Strathclyde, Galloway and Moray occur in addition to those of Dál Riata in the very sparse records. This list is certainly not exhaustive.   **18** Barrow, *Kingdom of the Scots*, 36; Anderson, *Kings and kingship*, 139–45, 171, 173–5, 242; Duncan, *Scotland: the making of the kingdom*, 110–11, 164–7; Watson, *Place-names*, 107–9.   **19** Bannerman, *Dalriada*, 56, 142–3; Ó Corráin, 'Studies, Dalriada', 171–3,

However, similarities of kinship/administrative terminology between Ireland and parts of Scotland during the eleventh to thirteenth centuries suggests that Gaelic Scotland had, by the eleventh century, adopted some aspects of the Irish *trícha cét* – *túath* – *baile biataig* system in name if not always in substance. This development should be viewed in light of the contemporary status of both Ireland and the greater part of Scotland as a single cultural province (as for example in possessing a common language, literary culture, surname fashion and the simultaneous appearance in both countries of the newly-coined and important place-name element *baile*). These close cultural links between both countries are seen at the very time the *trícha cét* system was evolving in Ireland. One cannot, of course, speak of a politically or even culturally unified Scotland during the eleventh century.

There is no evidence whatsoever for the export of the *trícha cét* unit to Scotland. The same cannot be said for its component parts, however. The only evidence for any hundred system in Scotland comes from the toponomastic evidence for the existence of the Norwegian *herred* system in the Hebrides and northern Isles.[20] This evidence awaits investigation but can hardly imply more than that such a system was introduced in these parts by the Norwegian kingdom during the twelfth or early thirteenth century.

Dropping a level (in an Irish context) to the spatial layer below that of *trícha cét*, we come to the late-*túath* and the search for such a similar layer in Scotland. By the time records of substance begin we note the presence of a pre-feudal unit called the shire or thanage throughout Scotia and the Anglo-Danish south-east, terms deriving from the Old English *scir* and *thegn*. The entire region may well have been divided into such units, although this supposition requires further investigation. These units display a range of between 10,000–50,000 statute acres, averaging towards the higher end of this scale, and were characteristically units whose food renders were collected in a common centre from its various villages.[21] Thanages were essentially royal shires controlled by a steward ('thane') originally appointed for a limited period, but this office later became hereditary in many cases. Shires can be found as early as the seventh century in Northumbria and Barrow interprets the evidence as suggesting that the shires of Scotia date back to the time of the Brittonic-speaking Pictish kingdom, conquered by the Gaelic-speaking Scots during the ninth century (?).[22] Whatever of this, the term *scir* is the source of the Gaelic *sgíre*, a word first recorded during the late eleventh century and which came to mean 'parish'.[23] Does this suggest that this term had already spread to Pictland before its Scottish conquest? The adoption of the ministerial term 'thane' may have come later: Grant suggests that this was introduced by Malcolm II (1005–34).[24] There is an emerging

---

180. **20** Crawford, *Scandinavian Scotland*, 84. **21** These figures are based on Barrow's reconstructions of several shires in his *Kingdom of the Scots*. **22** Barrow, *Kingdom of the Scots*, 14, 22–4, 32, 41–50, 59–68; Grant, 'Thanes', passim. **23** Dr Simon Taylor (pers. comm.) **24** 'Thanes and Thanages', 47.

consensus that shires may have formed the template for many parishes in Scotia during the period of parish formation during the twelfth century.[25]

While the term *scir* was adopted by Gaelic, *thegn* was not, its Gaelic equivalent being *taísech*.[26] The meagre evidence from both Scotia and Galloway for the 'High-Gaelic' eleventh century illustrates the existence of spatial units featuring terminology similar to that of the contemporary Irish late-*túath*. In Buchan at this time several *taísig* of territories whose names included the term *clann* occur. In Ireland many late-*túatha* also feature the term *clann* in their names. These *taísig* clearly formed a lower layer of administration under the *mormaer* just as the Irish *taísig túaithe* did under the local king. In Galloway and Carrick we find *taísig* of territories whose names feature the terms *clann*, *muintir* and *cenél*, again echoing Irish practice.[27] A further similarity concerns the *mormaer*. Each *mormaer* was also *taísech* of his own local territory as well as being lord over the other *taísig* and their territories, the combined areas of which comprised his lordship. This is identical to the Irish practice where each local king was *taísech* of his own late-*túath*, as well as king of the entire *trícha cét*.[28] Scottish evidence only becomes abundant once the process of feudalism is well advanced under David I and his successors. Detailed evidence for the lower levels of the socio-political spatial structure of Scotland before AD 1100 is meagre in the extreme. The references to entities in *clann*, *muintir* and *cenél* adduced above, given their broad geographical distribution, are likely to represent rare survivals of what once may have been common terminological usages in eleventh-century Gaelic Scotland. In addition to the usage of the Irish term *taísech*, we find shires and thanages originally paying rent in the form of tribute and food renders called 'cain' and 'conveth' which are, of course, the common Irish estate renders of *cáin* (tribute, tax) and *coinmed* (billeting).[29] One suspects that we are here dealing with a spatial unit, the *scir*, once found throughout Scotia east of Druim Alban, as well perhaps in Galloway and Strathclyde, deriving from the time when all of these regions spoke a Brittonic language, and which was subsequently adopted and Gaelicized during the period of Scottish expansion.[30] Furthermore, there may be direct evidence for this. The entity in *muintir* referred to above from Galloway is 'Muntercosduf', which occurs during the late twelfth century as the territory of the Uí *Choisduibh sept (the ancestral Kennedys).[31] Here the patronym contains the Cumbric element *quas*, the equivalent to the Gaelic *gìolla*. Thus we would seem to have a lineage of recent Cumbric descent, using the contemporary Irish surname style *ua*, and ruling a territory in *muintir*.

25 Barrow, *Kingdom of the Scots*, 54; Ross, 'Dabhach', 68; Dr Simon Taylor (pers. comm.)   **26** Barrow, *Kingdom of the Scots*, 65; Grant, 'Thanes', 42.   **27** Jackson, 'Book of Deer', 32, 102–14; Skene, *Celtic Scotland*, 214; J. Maitland-Thomson (ed.), *Reg. of the Great Seal of Scotland*, i (new edition, Edinburgh, 1912), nos. 912–14, 982; *Charters of the abbey of Crosraguel* i (Edinburgh, 1886), pp 26–7. Scottish commentators have perhaps failed to appreciate the territorial dimension implied by such usages. In Ireland the terms *clann*, *muintir* and *cenél*, as well as relating to a kindred or lineage, refer to a concrete territory subject to the lordship of the lineage.   **28** Power, *Críchad*, 45–6.   **29** Grant, 'Thanes', 48–9.   **30** *Kingdom of the Scots*, 66–8.   **31** MacQueen, 'Laws of Galloway', 140 (fn. 13).

Evidence from the same period is completely lacking from the west of Druim Alban but Skene suggests that the often hereditary office of *tosheachdeor*, found from the fourteenth century onwards, attached to specific lands with well-known and clearly long-established boundaries in much of Scotia, as well as in Galloway and Man, is a remnant of what had earlier been something resembling the Irish late-*túatha*. This merits consideration.[32] A further similarity of nomenclature involves the Scots legal term *ogethearn*. Twelfth-century Scots law displays a hierarchy of legal status for the freeman, clearly inherited from the earlier and more shadowy laws of the Gaelic kingdom. At the top is the king, under whom is the earl/*mormaer*, under whom comes the *ogethearn*. The latter is the primary free-tenant. *Ogethearn* derives from the Gaelic *ócthigern* 'young lord', a term clearly related to that of *óclach*, the like level (under the *taísech túaithe*) in the Corcu Loígde tract in twelfth-century Co. Cork. *Óclach* 'young warrior' also has the meaning 'vassal', just as does *ogethearn*. (Cf. feudal *iuuenis*.)[33]

The primary unit of land assessment east of Druim Alban was the davoch (*dabhach*, Gaelic 'pot, cauldron'; but the term may in fact be Pictish and not bear this etymology).[34] This unit has, since the nineteenth century, been understood as originally referring to a measure of cereal output, and later to have become a fixed land measure, and these interpretations remain orthodox.[35] Recently this orthodoxy has been challenged by Ross, whose work has involved the first detailed topographical reconstructions of the davoch structure in northern Scotia, initially in Moray.[36] He has shown that the term probably first occurs during the reign of Malcolm II (1005–34). Ross' findings may be summarized as follows. Davochs occur within the size-range 2,500–16,000 acres and the davoch system underlies and so pre-dates the establishment of the parish system. *Coinmed* was levied by davoch and each davoch contributed a number of men to the military levy, who would then be equipped and provisioned by the remainder. The davoch is described as an 'economically independent estate' and, while many *dabhaichean* lay concretely, others are found in two portions. Ross also concurs with Williams' dating of the origins of the system to perhaps the tenth century as a Gaelic adoption of an earlier Pictish unit.[37] These conclusions go a long way to confirming Nicholls' view, referred to above, that the Irish and Scottish pre-feudal estate structure is similar in nature and is of considerable antiquity, for the significant similarities between the *dabhach* and *baile biataig* estate systems are immediately apparent. We must suspect that *dabhaichean* were originally held in

---

32 Skene, *Celtic Scotland*, 279–80, 300–2; Broderick, 'Tynwald', 90; Sellar, 'Celtic law and Scots law', 9–11. *Tosheachdeor* may derive from *taoiseach díre*, 'indemnity officer' or 'compensation officer', and gives the Manx 'toshiagh jioarey'. The office operated something like that of coroner. **33** Skene, *Celtic Scotland*, 219–20, 282; Ó Corráin, 'Corcu Loígde', 65–6; McKerral, 'Ancient denominations', 53. **34** Williams, '*Dabhach* reconsidered', 27n. **35** Zupko, 'Weights and measures', 127; Connor and Simpson, *Weights and measurements*, 647–56; Williams, '*Dabhach* reconsidered', 23–4. **36** Ross, 'The Dabhach in Moray', passim. I am grateful to Dr Ross for a discussion of the issue in advance of the publication of his forthcoming work on the *dabhach* in Scotland. **37** Williams, 'Land assessment', 38–75.

free-kinship as allodial landholdings in severalty, just as the Irish *bailte* were, but this remains to be established. Again, it would be interesting to study the naming pattern of *dabhaichean*. Taylor notes that in twelfth-century feudal Scotland *baile* seems to have become the indigenous word for estate (*villa*), in the process replacing such older equivalent terms as the Pictish-derived *pett*.[38] How does such a process relate to the davoch structure?

Crossing Druim Alban we come to the political region consisting of the Western and Northern Isles and the west coast. This region formed a politically cohesive unit under Norse domination between the tenth and thirteenth centuries. At the level of estate taxation it displays a complex series of related and overlapping systems, concerning the origins of which much ink has been spilled.[39] In the Norse-speaking areas, the principal estate unit was the *eyrisland* and in the Gaelic-speaking areas the *tír unga*, both meaning 'ounceland', and probably of common origin. The *eyrisland* was sub-divided into eighteen 'pennylands' and the *tír unga* into twenty. Apart from these pennyland divisions we find the ounceland divided into quarters (called *skattland* in the Norse areas, *ceathramh* in the Gaelic) and sometimes eighths. All divisions are not present uniformly: pennylands alone occur in Galloway while ouncelands are not found in Argyll nor pennylands in Islay and its surrounding islands.[40] Ouncelands and davochs are specifically related in medieval charters and the evidence suggests that the ounceland had by then come to represent a similar unit to the davoch in size and function, although this does not necessarily mean that both units share a common origin. The term 'davoch' appears to have been introduced into the ounceland region after it became part of the kingdom of Scotland (1266). This size comparison is illustrated on mountainous Skye, where its probable total of fifty-five ouncelands give an average of *c.*6,000 acres per unit. Ouncelands, like *dabhaichean* and *bailte*, were units of agricultural output rather than simple fixed measures of area, as may be seen in the single-ounceland island of Rum and the five-ounceland island of Eigg. Rum contains around 22,000 barren acres, while the more fertile Eigg only around 7,000. Indeed, there appears to be major regional variations in the size-pattern of these units.

The origins of the ounceland/pennyland system are obscure. These may have originated as distinct systems and it has been suggested that the pennyland was of Hiberno-Norse origin, deriving from the Dublin penny, first coined at the end of the tenth century.[41] An alternative interpretation sees pennylands as originating in English fiscal influence on Man during the late 1100s.[42] Whatever of this, it has been established that this system does not originate in Scandinavia.[43] The term 'ounceland' suggests that this system may be older than the penny-

38 Taylor, 'Generic-element variation', 10–12. 39 For discussions see Crawford, *Scandinavian Scotland*, 86–91, and Williams, '*Dabhach* reconsidered', 18–20. For much of what follows I am indebted to Mr Denis Rixson for a discussion concerning his ongoing researches into the spatial divisions of the western coast and islands. 40 McKerral, 'Land divisions', passim; idem, 'Ancient denominations', passim. 41 Crawford, *Scandinavian Scotland*, 90; Denis Rixson (pers. comm.) 42 Andersen, 'Regular, annual taxation', passim. 43 Williams, 'Ship-levies', 300.

land one, if indeed both are distinct. The most recent work on this question has been done by Williams, who suggests a date sometime before *c.*1050 for the introduction of the pennyland system, and believes it to originate with the Anglo-Saxon penny, by far the most dominant element in Scottish coin-hoards.[44]

Bannerman equated the ounceland with the Irish *baile biataig* estate, as well as with the davoch.[45] In this I believe he may have been correct, but not for the reasons given. The early Irish genealogy *Senchus Fer nAlban*, which treats of the kingdom of Dál Riata in Scotland in the period before the arrival of the Norse, has embedded within it a remarkable fragment of a military-levy record. This reveals a social system in which the basic unit was the house (*tech*), these being grouped into kinship-units of five, singles or multiples of which are in turn placed under the lordship of various nobles, and all of which represents an actual record of this very same system as described in the early Irish laws.[46] Beguiled by the coincidence of twenty pennylands per ounceland and the twenty houses (4×5) assessed for naval levy in the fragment, Bannerman derived the twenty-penny ounceland from this earlier Dalriadan assessment, a view largely accepted by others.[47] Elsewhere in this volume I have attempted to demonstrate that this early Irish estate sometimes bore the technical term *cóicráith chétach* 'five ráiths possessed of a hundred (cattle)', and consisted of five free-households held by a single kin-group under a noble.[48] The key point is that these early Irish and Dalriadan estates were five-house, kinship based units and not twenty-house units. If I am correct here, it follows that there can be no connection whatsoever between these early units and the twenty pennylands per ounceland. Furthermore, the *Senchus* fragment allows us our only actual survey of this early estate unit, in the case of Islay, where we obtain an average of *c.*2,200 acres per five-house unit on this modestly fertile island, whose total number of five-house units is known. This figure agrees well with both my interpretation of the theoretical area of the five-house unit of the Irish Laws and with the size-range of the later ouncelands.[49] *Senchus* shows that this five-house unit was distributed throughout Dál Riata, a large area consisting of much of the western coastlands and islands of Scotland. Did this unit survive the arrival of the Norse, descending perhaps, in company with its Irish cousin, into the later *baile* estate? This question remains to be answered, as does that of the pre-feudal internal structure of the ounceland. One argument against such a descent is the absence of the ounceland/davoch from Argyll and Lennox, the heart of ancient Dál Riata, although quarters are found here.[50] One is reminded of the Irish province of Munster, where sixteenth-century records reveal no trace of the earlier, well-documented *baile* estate, whose quarters however still remained omnipresent.[51] Another argument against is that of the relative scarcity and often late date of

44 Idem, '*Dabhach* reconsidered', 27, and pers. comm. **45** *Dalriada*, 141. **46** See p. 107. **47** *Dalriada*, 141. **48** See p. 104. **49** The size range of units such as the davoch and ounceland has been largely ignored by historians to date, along with their internal dynamics. The identification of a size-range per unit type has diagnostic and comparison value (see pp 104–7). **50** McKerral, 'Land divisions', 18–19; idem, 'Ancient denominations', 43–5, 72. **51** See pp 66–72.

places named in *baile* in Argyll. To which it can be answered that many Irish
bailte bore names which did not include the element itself. Should we see ouncelands, *daibhaichean* and *bailte* alike as descendants of an older common estate system? And should we add the early Anglo-Saxon five-hide unit to this list? Many
questions remain to be answered.

ISLE OF MAN

Broderick has argued that Man was originally administered as a single *trícha cét*
during its period as an Irish colony (which came to an end during the ninth century), and that its present governmental organization descends from this structure. The parliamentary assembly at Tynwald is said to descend from the *óenach*
of the *trícha*.[52] That Man was governed as an Irish-style local kingdom in the
pre-Scandinavian period is entirely likely. Again, cultural contacts with Ireland
remained strong throughout the Scandinavian period and after – notwithstanding the untenable view that Norse speech entirely obliterated Gaelic during the
Norse period – so Broderick's argument is entirely plausible, if not proven. If
one feels that this position is too kind to Irish influence on Man, then Andersen
presents the opposing view, one that sees the entire Manx administrative structure as being of Nordic derivation.[53] While such institutions as Tynwald and the
islands' sheadings are undoubtedly Norse in etymology, by the same token the
island coroners bear the Gaelic term *taoiseach*, and other important spatial units,
such as *treen*, *balla* and *kerrow* are also of Gaelic derivation. Again, the ceremo-
nial at Tynwald retains some Celtic features, and accordingly cannot be seen as
entirely Nordic in origins.[54] A recent archaeological survey suggests that Tynwald
(Cronk Keeill Eoin) was an important public assembly site *before* the Viking
Period began.[55]

The principal estate unit on Man was the treen, a unit divided into quarters
(*kerrow*). Surviving land records only begin in the late-fifteenth century, and so
are of limited use in investigations of the pre-feudal period. We know that estates
here were burdened with the Gaelic taxes of cain and conveth during the second half of the twelfth century, while the Manx for parish is *skeerey*, of similar
derivation to the Scots Gaelic *sgíre*, discussed above, all of which suggests strong
links with pre-feudal Gaelic Scotland.[56] The spread of the term *baile* to Man
(where it became ubiquitous), first recorded in probability during the mid-twelfth
century, is a clear indicator of continued Irish influence as this term only evolved
in Ireland during the eleventh century – and incidentally must prove that Gaelic
remained the *lingua franca* of the island at this time.[57] The earliest comprehensive treen rental, of 1511, shows the treen to comprise between one and seven

52 Broderick, 'Tynwald', passim.   **53** Andersen, 'Isle of Man', passim.   **54** Megaw, 'Norseman
and Native', 24.   **55** Darvill, 'Tynwald', passim.   **56** Megaw, 'Norseman and Native', passim.   **57**
Broderick, '*Baile* in Manx nomenclature', passim.

quarters, four being the most common number. This suggests that the system was then of considerable age, and this is confirmed by other references.[58] Marwick and Marstrander abandoned the received wisdom which derived treen from the Gaelic *trian* 'third', and instead derived it from the Scottish *tírunga*, a derivation uncritically followed since.[59] This is both a philological impossibility and equally void on spatial grounds, as the treen, with its average acreage of *c*.450, is much too small to be an ounceland or, as has been suggested, a version of the Irish *baile*.[60] Treen must derive from *trian*, and the term must also give some clue to the original pre-feudal estate structure of the island, now long lost, for an acreage of *c*.1,350 is well within the size range of both Irish *baile* and Scottish ounceland. As we have seen, the *trian* is a common division of the Irish *baile* estate.

SCANDINAVIA

Substantial records of government in the Scandinavian kingdoms begin only in the twelfth and thirteenth centuries. These illustrate the existence of hundred-style systems in all three kingdoms, with local divisions each with an assembly place (*ting*) usually located on a mound or hillock. The Swedish unit bore the name *hundare*, a term found on eleventh-century runic inscriptions.[61] Kraft shows that the *hundaren* system in Sweden appears to be of pre-Christian origins and so can be no later in origin than the tenth century.[62] Little is known about Scandinavia's internal affairs before the emergence of its principal kingdoms, a process which began in Denmark during the eighth century and in Sweden in the ninth century. Before this power lay with a congeries of what historians usually term 'chiefdoms' or 'tribal leaders' (of smaller polities). Some of these were known to the Franks in the sixth century while earlier, during the Roman Iron Age, the Romans record Scandinavia as being divided into a series of petty kingdoms, each ruled by a *rex* or king. This term was adopted by the Goths to give their *reiks*. This accords well with later descriptions of early Scandinavia as containing many '*reges* and *reguli*'.[63] Kraft has found evidence which suggests that Iron Age Sweden was divided into at least sixty seven such early polities or 'chiefdoms'. By the eighth century groupings of such 'chiefdoms' are found ruled by a king. In some cases *hundaren* appear to have been based on single 'chiefdoms', while in others each 'chiefdom' was divided into several *hundaren*. It is clear from the archaeological evidence that the *ting* mounds of some *hundaren* are much older than the tenth century. During the high-medieval period, the Swedish *hundare* was partly replaced by the *herred*, the Danish hundred unit. This Danish unit

---

58 Talbot, *Manorial roll*, passim; Megaw, 'Norseman and Native', 34–5. **59** Megaw, 'Norseman and native', 38. **60** Davies, 'Treens and quarterlands', passim; McKerral, 'Land divisions', passim; Bannerman, *Dalriada*, 141. **61** Sawyer, *Medieval Scandinavia*, 85. **62** See three works by Kraft: *Ledung och sockenbildning*, passim; *Hednagudar och hövdingdöme*, passim; *Tidiga spår av Sveariket*, passim; Helle, *Scandinavia*, 72–3. **63** Helle, *Scandinavia*, 181–2; Sawyer, *Medieval Scandinavia*, 86.

seems to originate in an administrative re-organization of the eleventh century which may have seen an older system replaced. A variant of this *herred* system was later exported to Norway which, however, also possessed a larger unit of administration, the *fylki*, whose relationship with the *herred* is in need of elaboration. Once again, public assemblies featuring some of the elements of the later *herred* appear to have existed in Denmark, at least by the early ninth century.[64]

A COMMON ORIGIN?

The Irish *trícha cét* and its earlier manifestation, the local-kingdom *túath*, as well as their sub-divisions, did not exist in isolation but bore a resemblance to similar systems, especially in Britain, Scandinavia and the Frankish empire (the *centena*, see below). These systems had much in common and were clearly subject to some kind of mutual influence or shared some element of common development. The general pattern is the same throughout the region. Comprehensive systems of local and regional lordship, primarily dealing with issues of taxation, justice, commerce and military levy by means of public assembly, and based upon a spatial unit of relatively modest size, are found to emerge during the period between the ninth and eleventh centuries. These units, variously called hundred, cantref, hundare, herred, huntari, centena, and trícha cét, all of broadly similar size, occupy a similar position in a hierarchy of spatial administrative units. We may classify these similar systems as variants of a common hundred system. Of course, such systems did not emerge from nowhere, and many of the features they exhibit clearly had a long history at the time these systems came into existence, a point to which I shall return below. The key point is that this generic hundred system represents a new and more comprehensive method of dealing with fundamental aspects of government and lordship, and its emergence must be directly related to the increasing agglomeration of kingdoms and the parallel development of royal authority and of national kingdoms, in other words, to the development of feudalism.

Such connected developments within a relatively cohesive cultural area and within a broadly similar time-span cannot have occurred in isolation, and clearly some element of influence from a central core-region to peripheral regions was involved. The traditional view, especially favoured by English and German historians of earlier generations, derives this hundred unit from an imagined Germanic unit of 'tribal' democracy, based on comments of the Roman historian, Tacitus, writing in his *Germania* (AD 98). Tacitus describes a unit which he states the Germans called *centeni* ('the Hundred').[65] This unit schematically provided both one hundred warriors for the royal army and one hundred freemen to advise and counsel the elected judge of each hundred. All later hundred-type

---

64 Sawyer, *Medieval Scandinavia*, 81–2, 85; Andersen, *Samlingen*, 262. **65** Handford, *Tacitus*, 106, 111.

units are said to descend from this unit, and the glaring historical gap of several centuries between AD 98 and the emergence of the later hundred systems is never satisfactorily explained.

In recent decades this subject has been looked at afresh. These researches show with near certainty that the territorial *centena* of the Frankish empire bears little relationship to any Germanic unit but is rather of late-Roman origin.[66] The term ultimately derives from *centenarii*, an officer-rank in the later Roman army, who was in charge of 100 soldiers (the popular *centurion*). In addition this rank also had jurisdiction over the civilian population within a particular area under the form of martial law which operated in the late Empire. The Frankish invasion of Gaul saw a continuation of such arrangements as the Franks, originally employed as Roman *foederati*, adopted both the terminology and practices of the Roman army. Between the sixth and eighth centuries a development occurred in Francia where various officer ranks and their duties came to have a comprehensive administrative territorial application. In this way the old Roman *pagus* (region) became the county (*comitatus*) ruled by a count, a term deriving from the *comes*, a more senior officer to the *centenarii* in the Roman army. At the same time the sub-division of the county became the *centena*, controlled by a *centenarii* who presided over its assembly, the *mallus*, in a rôle bearing some similarities to that of the later Anglo-Saxon hundred bailiff.[67] While this system originated in the Romance-speaking part of the empire (France) it soon spread to the Germanic-speaking areas (Netherlands, Germany, Switzerland), and by the end of the eighth century we find record of the *gau* (county) and *huntari* (*centena*) here, the latter a direct translation. The later terms *hundertschaft* and *canton* are derivatives.[68] While the *mallus* has traditionally been seen as a court of justice, recent research suggests that it also bore public assembly functions, one of which bore a similarity to the later Anglo-Saxon frankpledge system. The *mallus* may even have had a commercial function. In time, the term *centena* appears to have replaced that of *mallus* as a term for the hundred unit.[69]

While further detailed study of the spread of the *centena/huntari* is awaited, it is a likely supposition that it is this Frankish unit which acts as the exemplar for the further spread northwards of the hundred unit. Note the Swedish *hundare* and, of course, the Anglo-Saxon hundred.[70] While some English scholars accept that the hundred must indeed derive from the *centena*[71] many still choose to derive it from an indigenous hundred-hide unit of assessment, which either appears from nowhere or is thought to descend from Tacitus' hundred.[72] Proponents of the latter view ignore the evidence for the usage of the related term *comes* in Anglo-Saxon charters of the period and the existence of the *centena* in pre-Scandinavian Normandy.[73] Having spread from Francia to England,

66 For most of what follows see Murray, 'graphio in Merovingian Gaul', passim, and eadem, 'centenarii and centenae', passim. See also Barnwell, 'Frankish mallus', 242–4. 67 Barnwell, 'Frankish mallus', 236–7. 68 *Deutsches Rechtswörterbuch*, s.v. huntari; Fick, *Worterbuch*, s.v. huntari. 69 Barnwell, 'Frankish mallus', 237–8, 241–3. 70 *Lexikon Des Mittel Alters*, s.v. hundert. 71 John, *Reassessing Anglo-Saxon England*, 15. 72 Campbell, *Anglo-Saxons*, 176. 73 Stenton, *Anglo-Saxon*

I would suggest that further research may indicate that an onwards movement into Wales gave the *cantref*, the Welsh version of the hundred system. In the case of the Danish *herred*, while this term bears no etymological relationship to the Frankish *centena*, both systems clearly bear strong resemblances, and, given the close geographical and political linkages between the Frankish empire and the Danish kingdom from at least as early as the ninth century, a developmental link is likely.

What of the origins of the *trícha cét* in all of this? A significant piece of evidence comes from the Irish word *laídeng*. This term refers to a form of naval levy imposed on *trícha*s, a system which appears to be broadly similar to that of the Scandinavian *leiðangr*, and the Irish word is clearly derived from this Scandinavian term. As we have seen,[74] this Irish usage can be dated to at least the last years of the eleventh century, just as the earliest reference to its Danish equivalent, the *leding*, also occurs.[75] The *leiðangr* system involved the division of the land into districts called *skipreiður*, each of which contributed a fixed amount of manpower to the national naval levy. (Unlike in England and Ireland however, this form of Scandinavian military levy was not directly related to the hundred system but had its own spatial divisions.) The etymology of the Irish word *laídeng*, when studied along with that of *leiðangr*, suggests that this borrowing into Irish can be dated to no later than around AD 1000, a dating which agrees with that of the apparent beginnings of the Norwegian *leidang* system in the mid-tenth century.[76] If this dating is correct, then the Irish were already exposed directly to an element related to the Scandinavian hundred unit during the late tenth century, a period immediately before the likely emergence of the Irish *trícha cét* system. This suggests an influence on the Irish *trícha* system by the Scandinavian hundred system. It is notable that the Anglo-Saxon equivalent of the *leiðangr*, the shipsoke, leaves no trace in Irish.[77] The very term *trícha cét* itself may provide further evidence of such a link. As we have seen,[78] the term *trícha cét* may derive from a reference to a form of military muster. Unlike the Swedes, the Danes and Norwegians choose a different term to describe their hundred unit, the *herred*, a term meaning 'war band'. This reminds us of the term for hundred used in the English Danelaw: *wapentake*, the 'weapon taking' or brandishing, a term also known from Denmark, where it represented a method of indicating consent at the *herred*.[79] Can we see in this preference for military terminology by the Danes and Norwegians in reference to their hundred unit a possible origin for, or influence on the formation of, the term *trícha cét*? Whatever of this, it is clear that the only certain foreign influence on the formation of the Irish *trícha cét* system comes from Norway and perhaps Denmark, and may ultimately and indirectly derive from practices of the late

England, 302–6; Haskins, *Norman institutions*, 25, 46. **74** P. 52. **75** Helle, *Scandinavia*, 189. **76** Williams, 'Norwegian *leiðangr* system', passim (where, however, his acceptance of Bugge's early dating for *Caithreim Ceallachain Caisil* is unsafe). **77** Campbell, *Anglo-Saxons*, 172–3. **78** See pp 93–4. **79** Hellquist, *Svensk Etymologisk Ordbok*, s.v. härad; *The concise Oxford dictionary of English etymology*, s.v. wapentake; Sawyer, *Medieval Scandinavia*, 81–2.

Roman administrative system. The extent of this Scandinavian influence is, of course, unclear.

The above survey suggests that many of the features which came to make up the generic hundred system throughout northern Europe were older by several centuries than the system itself – in particular, the element of public assembly at a dedicated hill or artificial mound, as organized by the ruling power, with its functions of jurisprudence, taxation, commerce, and military muster. We have seen this to have been the case in Britain and Scandinavia, while the most substantial evidence of all for such functions comes from the early medieval Irish Laws, which feature both *airecht* and *óenach*, public assemblies which therefore must be at least of seventh century date, if not earlier.[80] This is suggestive of a common pattern in such pre-hundredal units. The history of politics and power in Europe is one of gradual evolution from a myriad very small polities to the emergence of nation-states (with the obvious exception of the Roman period). We are familiar with the petty kingdoms of ancient Greece and of the Italian peninsula in the centuries before the rise of Rome. Very small 'kingdoms' continued to be a feature of the societies of both Celts and Germans, in the latter case down to the fall of the Western Empire, and perhaps even later in England.[81] In these societies kingdoms were often organized into hierarchies, of two or even three levels. Ireland provides the most graphic example of this structure, with as many as perhaps 200 local kingdoms forming the base level of a four-tiered hierarchy of kingship which lasted until the introduction of the hundred-style *trícha cét* system during the early eleventh century, when the lowest level of kingdom became the template for the new hundred unit. Of course, in Ireland the *rí* of the *trícha* must have been *rí* largely in name only. These were, at best, local lords retaining a lofty title worth little beyond prestige. While Ireland is not a unique case of such an archaic survival in Europe it certainly provides the best documented example.[82] In the case of Ireland we can demonstrate the descent of its local kingdoms without interruption for five hundred years to the period when it acquires its hundred system. Given the evidence adduced above, such an origin for many of the hundred units of Britain and Scandinavia – as representing the area and public assembly functions of what had originally been small kingdoms of the lowest rank – remains a viable hypothesis.

The component functions and sub-divisions of the hundred system were also, of course, subject to international developmental trends. The primary level of taxation within the Irish *trícha cét* system appears to have been at that of estates, that is, the basic unit of taxation was the *baile biataig*. This represents a departure from an earlier system, where royal taxation began at the level of the individual household. Such a development, that of taxation being levied by land assessment unit rather than individual household unit, occurred in north-west Europe at different times. It first appears in Anglo-Saxon England, probably during the ninth

80 See pp 49–51. **81** Loyn, *English nation*, 27–9. **82** Cf. the case of Latvia in the fourteenth century and even later, for which see E. Christiansen, *The Northern Crusades: the Baltic and the Catholic frontier* (London, 1980), 202.

century, and spreads to Scotland and Norway by the twelfth century.[83] Given the known Anglo-Saxon influences in both countries, it is probable that 'spread' is the correct word to use in this context. Ireland also maintained close links with Anglo-Saxon England before 1066, and the introduction of taxation by *baile* estate in Ireland may well be due to Anglo-Saxon influence, as in the case of the Mercian penny, adopted by the Irish as their first coinage.

There would seem to be much older international links and similarities, however. As illustrated above, the early Irish spatial system of estate organization was certainly exported to Argyll, probably during the sixth century or before, and there is clear evidence of continued Irish influence on the Scottish system before AD 1100. The evidence of mutual influence between Ireland and Wales is not at all so strong but cannot be entirely ruled out. On a more systemic level, however, the parallels between Welsh *tud* and Irish local-kingdom *túath* are dramatic.[84] In the case of the *tud*, its jurisdictional status in law pre-dates any Roman influence within Britain, and thus must date to the period before the Roman invasion. The common *tud/túath* system is only one facet of a heritage shared between early Ireland and the British in Britain and Brittany. They also shared important kinship structures and terms, legal terminology, and, of course, a common linguistic heritage. These must derive from a time when culturally, socially, legally and linguistically, both were very close together indeed. Therefore it would appear that, at the very least, the common *tud/túath* legal system must derive from sometime in the pre-Christian era. Furthermore, the parallel between the Irish *cóicráith* unit and the Anglo-Saxon five-hide unit raises the possibility that such spatial organization may have its roots in an older time again when Celtic and Germanic cultures lived in close association in Continental Europe. Charles-Edwards has demonstrated that the *cóicráith* unit had an exact parallel in that of the five-hide unit, and he has argued that in both cases these represent an inheritance from ancestral Celtic and Germanic systems, rather than as a result of cultural intercourse between Ireland and England within the historic period.[85]

In conclusion, we can say that the Irish *trícha cét* system of spatial landscape organization preserves the outline and some of the substance of a much older system of spatial organization featuring a hierarchy of kingdoms where the lowest level consisted of many miniscule kingdoms. This kingship system clearly has archaic origins in the pre-historic period and something like it appears to have been general throughout much of Europe in the pre-Roman period. Thus that historical curiosity, the Irish barony, must be, in many cases, the descendant of an ancient unit of civil administration with communal/dynastic origins linking us to our very distant ancestors.

83 Andersen, 'Regular, annual taxation', passim. 84 Charles-Edwards, 'Celtic kinship terms', 114–22. 85 Ibid., 'Kinship, status', 3–33.

GAZETTEER

of the cantreds, *trícha céts* and local kingdoms of Ireland

The following survey proceeds by Anglo-Norman county or lordship. Each cantred is described, and then the history of the indigenous spatial unit(s) upon which the cantred is based are given. Each cantred is given a number prefixed by **C** in order to facilitate easy cross-reference. The format *C indicates a probable cantred for which explicit ascription is not found. Where possible each heading consists of a set of ascriptions of the cantred name as they occur in original sources, usually up to a total of five in all. Normally this listing will contain approximately the earliest and latest chronological examples of the name. Occasionally references are given where the term cantred does not occur in association with the toponym. In these cases the cantredal status of the toponym is implicit. Such toponyms are denoted by not appearing in bold format, unlike explicit cantred references. Each *trícha cét* is given a number prefixed by **T**. References to annalistic dating usually appear as in the published annals. I have not thought it necessary to correct the slight errors in some of these.

CONTENTS

Medieval Carlow, significantly bigger than its modern descendant, had five cantreds which bear the same name as, and appear to be quite similar in extent to, five of the six rural deaneries of the diocese of Leighlin.[1]

C1: *Fotheret Onolan* (1188); *Fotherid Onolan* (1252); **Fotherd** (1282); **Fothryd** (1300); *Forde* (1420)[2]
Granted in its entirety to Raymond le Gros, escheated to the lord of Leinster upon his death without heirs. The extent of this cantred can be reconstructed with the help of a significant amount of surviving charter and other evidence. These reveal that lands in the parishes of Barragh, Fennagh, Ballon, Kellistown, Urglin, Aghade, Gilbertstown, Ardristan, Killerrig, Grangeford (that is, the grange of Fothryd), Straboe, that part of Ardoyne and those sections of Ballyellin in the modern barony of Forth lay in this cantred.[3] All of these parishes occur in the rural deanery of Fothryd, which adds the parishes of Myshall, Templepeter, and Ballycrogue to complete this extent.[4]

T1: *Fotharta Fea*
The cantred of Fothryd (Onolan) derives from Fotharta Fea *alias* Fotharta Tíre, and all ten kings recorded in the annals between 737 and 1133 were of this branch of Fotharta.[5] Two distinct lines of kings can be noted who unite at Eochu mac Báeth who seems to have lived during the seventh century. The second line, who replaced the first after 863, were ancestors to the later ruling family, Uí Nualláin, whose name the Anglo-Normans initially incorporated into their cantred.[6]

C2: *Obarthi* (1177); *Hubargay* (1204); **Abargy** (1282); **Obargy** (1300); *Obargy* (1420)[7]
This cantred covered north-western Co. Carlow and the adjacent parts of Kilkenny and Leix. Most of it lay in the feudal barony of Obargy, an extent of which, from 1349, survives.[8] This included lands in the parishes of Carlow (the town of Carlow

1 DKRI 36, p. 72; 38, p. 71. 2 Scott and Martin, *Expugnatio Hibernica*, 194; COD, i, 27; DKRI 36, p. 72; 38, p. 71; Richardson and Sayles, 141. Where name references are already contained in the body of the article these are not repeated in the example references. 3 MacCotter, 'The Carews of Cork' i, 61–3; idem, 'Carews of Cork' (thesis), 6, 10–11, 17–18, 25; Gilbert, *Reg. St Thomas*, 106–7, 111–12, 114–15; Brooks, *Knights' fees*, 51, 62–4, 67, 69, 71–4; Nicholls, '*Pontificia*', 86; idem, 'Carlow and Wexford', 33–4; idem, 'Baltinglass charter', 190, 196. 4 In the course of this book, when dealing with the ruridecanal structure of the dioceses of Leighlin, Ferns, Ossory, Kildare and Dublin, I have used an unpublished MS synoptic table and accompanying map of the various deanery lists in these dioceses as compiled by Mr Kenneth Nicholls from all surviving pre-1634 deanery lists. I am grateful for permission to use this source. 5 AT, 737, 753; FIA, 865, 908; AFM, 854, 863, 1017, 1018, 1022, 1133. 6 O'Brien, *Corpus*, 82–5. 7 Sheehy, *Pont. Hib.* i, 129; Orpen, *Song of Dermot*, l. 3070; fn. 2 above. 8 LPL Carew MS 606, f. 92–3. (In this extent Leighlin, Shankill and Rathornan in Tullowcreen are easy enough to identify while many other denominations are obscure. Hydestowne is now Ballyhide in Killeshin while either of the fees of Gragroham and Gragneshowka may be represented by Graig in the same parish. The fee held by

was assessed with Obargy in a subsidy of 1301), Ballinacarrig, Tullowcreen, Oldleighlin, Cloydagh and Killinane in modern Carlow, Kilmacahill and Shankill in Kilkenny, and Killeshin and Sleaty in Leix. All of these parishes occur in the rural deanery of Obargy, which adds the parishes of Painestown (partly in Kildare today) and Wells to complete the extent.

T2: *Uí Bairrche Tíre*
The cantred of Obargy derives from the kingdom of Uí Bairrche Tíre. The eighth-century (?) Laigin genealogical construct, Timna Catháir Máir, makes the eponym one Dáire Barrach. Indications in the earliest literature suggest that Uí Bairrche estab-lished several kings over Laigin in the sixth and early seventh centuries. The loca-tion of a branch of Uí Bairrche in Moyacomb which diverged from the royal line in the mid-seventh century may indicate, perhaps, that Uí Bairrche were then dom-inant over Uí Dróna and may have included much of the latter territory. As con-sistent allies of Uí Dúnlainge against Uí Chennselaig, their territory may have suf-fered subsequent reduction due to its 'front-line' position. [9] At least twelve later kings occur in the annals between 856 and 1124 and its ruling family, Meic Gormáin, retained power into the 1170s. [10]

C3: *Obowi* (1188); **Oboy** (1282, 1300, 1317); *Oboy* (1335) [11]
This cantred contained the modern barony of Ballyadams, much of that of Slievemargy, and parts of Stradbally, Co. Leix. We know it to have contained land in the parishes of Ballyadams, Killabban, and Shrule while the parish of Tullomoy, which derives from *Tulach Ua mBuidhe,* must also have lain in this cantred. Its *caput,* the colonial Castelloboy, is now Castletown in Killabban. All of these parishes (except Shrule) occur in the deanery of Oboy, which adds the parishes of Rathaspick and Tecolm to complete the extent. [12]

T3: *Uí Buide*
The cantred of Oboy derives from the kingdom of Uí Buide. Although associated with Eochu Timmíne son of Catháir Már in the synthetic Laginian schema, (inci-dentally acknowledging the importance of Uí Buide at this time), the true Uí Buide pedigree may be found among those of Dál Cormaic Loisc. These may have been one of the leading powers in proto-historic Laigin whose territory was said to stretch

John Martell is probably represented by Morterstown in Carlow parish and that held by Philip Stacboll by Staplestown in Ballincarrig. Chiuerson, held by the heirs of Simon Sutton, must be Closutton in Killinane. For further identifications here see Brooks, *Knights' fees,* 56–8, 76, 82–3, and cf. Nicholls, 'Pontificia', 86–7.) For the assessment of 1301 see DKRI 38, p. 71.   **9** Dillon, *Lebor na Cert,* 152; O'Rahilly, *Early Irish history and mythology,* 37–8; Mac Shamráin, *Glendalough,* 10–11; Kelleher, 'History and pseudo-history', 124; O'Brien, *Corpus,* 46, 54; Ó Muraíle, *Mac Firbhishigh,* ii, 246–8.   **10** FIA, 858, 869, 908; ALC, 1042; AU, 1057; AT, 1040, 1141; AFM, 856, 866, 884, 896, 900, 943, 1008, 1042, 1103, 1124; Nicholls, 'Baltinglass charter', 188.   **11** Scott and Martin, *Expugnatio Hibernica,* 194; COD, i, 216; DKRI 44, p. 56; see fn. 2 above.   **12** Brooks, *Knights' fees,* 83, 88; Nicholls, 'Pontificia', 87; Pender, *Census of Ireland,* 500. Typerkathan 'in Oboy' is now Ballintubbert (Brooks, *Knights' fees,* 83; Nicholls, 'Red Book of Kildare', 62).

from Dublin to Carlow. Their power appears to have been broken in the sixth century and their polity fragmented into smaller units scattered around the caldera-like rim of its previous border. One such was Uí Buide whose eponym, Buide mac Laignén, is a guarantor to Cáin Éimíne Báin and thus lived around 700. Uí Buide appear to have constituted one of the Three Commain ('The three allies'?), a grouping sometimes acting independently of, and at other times under, the lordship of the Loígis. This is especially suggested by the reference to a king of the Three Commain who died in 969 and who occurs at the head of the Uí Buide genealogy. Uí Buide appear to have dissociated themselves from this alliance subsequently. Kings of Uí Buide were recorded in 1010 and again in 1012 (the former with a suspiciously Uí Dúnlainge-like name) and, while the Three Commain were eventually absorbed into Loígis, the continued existence of Uí Buide as a polity is demonstrated by its inclusion in *Lebor na Cert* (late eleventh century?) and, I would suggest, its later status as a cantred.[13]

C4: *Odrone* (1176, 1189); **Odron** (1282); **Odroon** (1300)[14]
This cantred contained the baronies of Idrone East and St Mullin's Lower, Co. Carlow, and parts of Kilkenny to the west across the Barrow. Both the feudal baronies of Odrone and Tachmolyng (Tech Moling: St Mullins) — the latter described as a 'half-cantred' in 1171 — are associated with different branches of the Carew family during the thirteenth century, heirs here, no doubt, of Raymond le Gros of Carew who was granted 'all of Odrone' in fee by Strongbow. While the later history of Tachmolyng is somewhat ambiguous, it was still paying a chief rent to the feudal barony of Odrone in 1350. No extent of this barony appears to survive. The *caput* of Odrone was at Dunleckny and two of its members were Alanbegstown (now Ballyellin), and Powerstown. The lords of the barony also claimed the fee of lands in Tullowmagimma. The parishes of Lorum, Clonygoose and Kiltennell must also have been in this feudal barony: these were impropriate to Glascarrig priory, Co. Wexford, a foundation either of Le Gros or of his de Caunteton nephew, William, and were said to have been donated to that foundation by members of the Carew family. Another Carew donation was probably the rectory of Agha: we know that William de Carew donated the rectory of Dunleckny to the nunnery of Graney which also held neighbouring Agha at the Dissolution.[15] Furthermore, it is possible that Kiltennell represents the knight's fee in Odrone granted by Raymond le Gros to de Caunteton.[16] Tachmolyng, at a minimum, is represented by the parish of St Mullins (a large part of which lies in Wexford). All of these parishes are in the dean-

---

13 O'Brien, *Corpus*, 29–30, 34, 66; Dillon, *Lebor na Cert*, 108; Todd, *Cogad*, 146; Ó Murchadha, 'Laígis', 50–1; Poppe, 'Cáin Éimíne Báin', 45; AFM, 1010. **14** Scott and Martin, *Expugnatio Hibernica*, 85; Orpen, *Song of Dermot*, l. 3067; see fn. 2 above. **15** Brooks, *Knights' fees*, 60–2; idem, 'The de Ridelesfords', i, 127; MacCotter, 'Carews of Cork' i, 63–4; idem, 'Carews of Cork' (thesis), 19, 21, 23–4, 38; Nicholls, 'Baltinglass charter', 199; RC 8/6, 390. **16** While this fee is described as that of Balygolan and Delgy in 1334 (CCH, 40), both obsolete place-names, it contained a township called Balylegan (CJRI, ii, 250), which is perhaps to be identified with Leighan of the *1659 Census* (358), the modern Lackan in Kiltennell.

ery of Odrone, which adds the parishes of Sligduff, Nurney, and Clonmelsh in Carlow, Grange Silvia in Kilkenny, and the shared parish of Ullard, to complete the extent. It will be noted that the Irish *trícha cét* of Uí Drona (**T4**) similarly extended westwards across the Barrow, and contained lands in the parishes of Powerstown and Grange Silva.[17]

T4: *Uí Dróna*

A major Uí Chennselaig segment were Síl Cormaic whose eponym was a brother to Eógan Caech, a king of Uí Chennselaig who may have lived around the middle of the sixth century (see **T177**). The only *trícha* associated with them was Uí Dróna, from which derives the cantred of Odrone. Both lines of Síl Cormaic contributed thirteen kings of Uí Chennselaig between 624 and 978. Colgu mac Bresal (d. 722) of Síl Cormaic is described as *rí Arda Ladrann*, now Ardamine in the territory of Uí Dega.[18] This territory in north Wexford gives the later deanery of Oday but it does not appear to have been a cantred (from which it follows that its status as a *trícha cét* is also uncertain). Uí Dega is of interest as the earliest recorded homeland of Síl Cormaic who must already have subordinated its original rulers. A later Síl Cormaic dynast, Cellach mac Dondgaile (d. 809), is described both as *rí Rátha Etain* and *taísech Uí Dega*. This is Rathedan in Uí Dróna. These entries indicate that Síl Cormaic, while still established in Uí Dega, may already have replaced the original rulers of Uí Dróna, whose line henceforth disappears from the record. In the genealogical schema of Uí Chennselaig, probably datable to the eighth century, the eponyms Drón and Daig are made brothers to Énna Cennselach.[19] Uí Dróna and Uí Dega were probably originally totally independent of Uí Chennselaig.[20] The later Síl Cormaic rulers of Uí Dróna were Uí Riain.

C5: Ofelymeth (1192); *Ofelmyth* (1220); *Ofelmeth* (1300); *Felmythe* (1420)[21]

This cantred contained most of Rathvilly barony, Co. Carlow, and northern Shillelagh, Co. Wicklow. Again, it formed a single unit of sub-infeudation, as the barony of Tullowphelim, when granted to Theobald Walter. An extent, made in 1303, defines its boundaries. This shows the cantred to have contained the parishes of Tullowphelim (from *Tulach Ua bhFelmedha*), Rathmore, Rathvilly, Haroldstown and Clonmore, all of which lie in modern Carlow, those parts of Ardoyne – shared by both Carlow and Wicklow – outside of the barony of Forth, the similarly divided parish of Crecrin, and the Wicklow parish of Aghowle.[22] Indeed, Ofelmyth's

17 Bernard, 'Charters of Duiske', 4; Flanagan, *Irish royal charters*, 254. **18** For the kings of Uí Chennselaig I have relied upon Ó Corráin's 'Irish Regnal Succession', passim. **19** Hogan, *Onomasticon*, 42, 571; O'Brien, *Corpus*, 343, 346–7, 350, 430–1. **20** The original ruling line of Uí Dega made a rare recovery and the name of its king as recorded in 908 suggests that he was of these, as were the later ruling family, Uí Áeda. Uí Dega gives the deanery of Oday which seems to have formed half of the cantred of Kenalahun (O'Brien, *Corpus*, 429; Dobbs, 'Ban-Shenchas', 193; eadem, 'Uí Dega', passim. **21** Brooks, *Knights' fees*, 79; COD, i, 23. **22** White, *Book of Ormond*, pp 1ff. The identifiable locations are: Tullowphelim, Rathin = Raheen in Clonmore, Archethyll = Aghowle, Crescroyn = Crecrin, Villa Tancardi = Tankardstown in Tullow, Ballyconnell in Crecrin, Villa Oliveri = Ballyoliver in Rathvilly, Rathvilly, Rathmore, Nican =

sub-fee, Ardoyne, originally stretched eastwards into part of Kilcommon parish and so must also have included that of Mullinacuff, while much if not most of the Wicklow parish of Kilranelagh also lay in this cantred.[23] All of these parishes, apart from Kilcommon, occur in the deanery of Ofelmyth, which adds the parishes of Rahill in Carlow and Liscolman in Wicklow to complete the extent. While the Wicklow parishes of Baltinglass, Rathbran, Rathtoole and Ballynure also lay in this deanery, they were part of the cantred of Omurthi (**C66**) in Kildare and not of that of Ofelmyth.

T5: *Uí Felmeda Tuaid*

The Uí Chennselaig dynasty was originally located around Ráith Bile (Rathvilly) in Uí Felmeda Tuaid and its early kings were of this segment, suggesting that some credence can be given to the genealogies here.[24] The last of these kings, Crimthann mac Ailella, died around 630 and was fifth in descent from the eponymous Fedelmid, who is said to have lived during the fifth century (his brother, Crimthann is given an obit of 483). This was the chief territory of Uí Felmeda. A secondary and smaller one, Uí Felmeda Thes, lay on the north-east Wexford coast. The cantred of Ofelmyth derives from Uí Felmeda Tuaid. The only early king of Uí Felmeda on record (in 906) is not recorded in the Uí Felmeda pedigrees. The pedigree of the Uí Murchada lords of Uí Felmeda Thes is titled *Ríg Húa Murchada* yet these descend from an earlier line styled *Uí Felmeda Tíre*, an *alias* for Uí Felmeda Tuaid. It may be that both territories, though thirty miles apart, sometimes shared the same king. To further confuse matters, by the late eleventh century Uí Felmeda Tuaid was ruled by a family, Uí Gairbíd, of uncertain lineage (when described in the *Banshenchas* as 'Ríg Ua Felmeda'). By early in the twelfth century this line had been replaced as kings by Dalbach Ua Domnaill (cousin of Diarmait Mac Murchada), and his descendants.[25]

CONNACHT

It is possible to reconstruct most of the boundaries of the twenty-five cantreds which are known to have comprised the medieval county, which covered an area approximating to the present counties of Galway, Mayo and Sligo.[26] Our principal sources are the de Burgh inquisitions taken in 1333 after the death of the Red Earl, extents of individual cantreds, some incomplete cantredal lists and, lastly, details of the unusually large number of rural rectories which are found in Connacht and which preserve the outline of some ancient cantreds and manors.[27]

Acaun in Tobinstown in Rathvilly, Villa Johannis = Ballyshane in Crecrin, fisheries on the River Deryn = the Derreen river which is the boundary between Rathvilly and Haroldstown. Cf. Brooks, *Knights' fees*, 79–80, and COD, i, 143. Another source includes Knockevagh in Rathvilly parish (Nicholls, 'Baltinglass charter', 195). **23** Nicholls, 'Baltinglass charter', 195; idem, 'Medieval Anglo-Ireland', 580n. **24** O'Brien, *Corpus*, 344. **25** Ibid., 353–5, 430; Dobbs, 'Ban-Shenchas', 193, 234; Flanagan, 'Mac Dalbaig', passim. **26** DKRI 35, p. 47. **27** For the de Burgh inquisitions see Knox, 'Connacht' i and ii. This source does not, however, list all the cantreds: further

C6: *Le Bak & le Glen* (1299); ***Bak & Glen*** (1299, 1333)[28]
This cantred is attested in the 1333 inquisitions and in earlier litigation concerning its lordship, and must be the second of the two cantreds in Tiramli (Tirawley) noted in the 1195 de Lacy grant. Only a few of the place-names mentioned in 1333 can be identified here, and these lay in the parishes of Crossmolina and Ballynahaglish. Of the territorial names here 'the two Bacs' refer to territories on both sides of Lough Conn while 'Glen' is Gleann Nemhthenne, the glen south of Nephin Mountain. A useful guide to the southern limit of this cantred is the boundary of the diocese of Killala here. A detailed extent of the Irish *trícha cét* of Bac & Gleann Nemhthenne (**T6**) enables us to fill in the gaps here and we may conclude with some confidence that this cantred contained the parishes of Ardagh, Addergoole, Kilbelfad and Kilmoremoy, in addition to those named above.[29]

T6: *Bac & Glenn Nemthenne*
Mac Firbisigh's *trícha* of Bac & Glenn Nemthenne gives the cantred of Bac & Glen. While Mac Firbisigh's tract notes a *taísech* of this *trícha* no record of kings survives.[30]

C7: *Brunrath* (1308); ***Brounrath*** (1333); ***Brunrath*** (1347, 1353)[31]
The capital manor of this cantred was Clare[galway]. Extents of this cantred were made in 1348 and again in 1353. These suggest that Brunrath contained the parishes of Claregalway, Lackagh and Annaghdown, Co. Galway.[32]

T7: *Uí Briúin Rátha*
Uí Briúin Rátha is listed under its own *taísech* in the Muintir Murchada tract (see under **C21**). Uí Briúin Rátha, clearly long established here, are derived from an early and assuredly spurious son of Brión (*a quo* Uí Briúin).[33] From these derive the cantred of Brunrath.

C8: ***Carbridrumclef*** (1195); ***Carebre Drumclef*** (1235); ***Karbridrumclef*** (1240); ***Crycarbri*** (1295)[34]
An extent of 1289 shows that the manor of Sligo consisted of lands in all parishes of the modern barony of Carbury except Rossinver. This parish was, of course, in the

useful lists may be found in GO MS 192, p. 27, and RC 7/13 (2 Edward II), 4. For lists of cantreds in the de Lacy third of northern Connacht see Mills, *Gormanston*, 191–2; CDI, i, p. 37. For the rural rectories of Connacht I have relied mostly on Kenneth Nicholls' excellent 'Rectory, vicarage and parish'. **28** RC 7/7, 389; CJRI, i, 227. **29** Knox, 'Connacht' ii, 58–9; MacCotter, 'Carews of Cork', i, 65–6; Ó Muraíle, *Mac Firbhishigh*, i, 568, 616–8. **30** Ó Muraíle, *Mac Firbhishigh*, i, 568, 616–18. Mac Firbhisigh's 'Genealogy of Uí Fhiachrach' can be dated to the fourteenth century but is clearly based on earlier material, as confirmed by thirteenth century annalistic references to several of its kingly families. For a discussion see Ó Muraíle, 'Settlement and place-names', 233–7. **31** RC 7/7, 4; Knox, 'Connacht' i, 396; GO MS 192, 27; see following note. **32** PRO SC/6/1239/30. These extents list the burgagery of Clare[galway], Cregricard [Creg in Annaghdown?], Crisbarry [?], Island of Kyltarrok [Kiltroge in Lackagh], Toine [Tonamace or Tonagarraun in Annaghdown], Curlarkan [?] and Drumgryffin [in Annaghdown]. **33** Ó Muraíle, *Mac Firbhishigh*, i, 437, 449. **34** Mills, *Gormanston*, 143; MacNiocaill, *Red Book of Kildare*, 26, 60.

diocese of Kilmore. The remainder of Carbury preserves the northern outline of the diocese of Elphin and agrees exactly with that of the rural deanery of Carbury. The cantred was therefore all of Carbury except Rossinver.[35]

T8: *Cairpre Mór*
The earliest lordship in this territory to appear in the record was that of Cenél Cairpre, descending from Cairpre son of Niall Noígiallach. He is traditionally believed to have held lands around Sligo from where his descendants expanded the kingdom. At its greatest extent this stretched south eastwards from Cairpre Mór around Sligo to Cairpre Gabra around Granard in Tethba (north Longford). No doubt the lands in between were subject to the overlordship of Cenél Cairpre. I suggest below that the southwards expansion into Tethba did not occur until the early seventh century. Both main lines of Cenél Cairpre derive from grandsons of Cairpre. The early kings use the designation Cenél Cairpre for the kingdom, and kings from both lines, Cairpre Mór (**T8**) and Cairpre Gabra (**T103**), hold office. Conaing ua Dubdúin, *rí Cairpre Tethba* (d. 751), is connected to the Cairpre Mór line by Mac Firbisigh, while the last king of Cenél Cairpre from the Tethba line, Laegaire, died in 812. Conall Menn, the last king from the Cairpre Mór line to bear the title, died in 718. It is hardly coincidental that this fracture into separate kingdoms by both main lines is contemporaneous with the rise of Uí Briúin Bréifne whose north-westwards expansion from Mag Aí targeted the very centre of Cenél Cairpre power. After the period 750–800 the former unity is gone and there are two separate kingdoms. Dúnadach (d. 871) is the last king of Cairpre Mór to occur in the pedigrees but Áed mac Garbíth (d. 953), *rí Cairpre Móir & Dartraige*, and probable ancestor of Uí Garbhítha, was likely also of this line. An earlier king had used the same title in 770, which suggests that before the eleventh century this kingdom consisted of the area of the later *trícha* of Cairpre Mór (**T8**) and the probable *trícha*/cantred of Dartry (**T132**) in north Leitrim. By 1029 Uí Ruairc had taken over Dartraige. The lineage of Murchad mac Serraig, *rí Cairpre Móir* (d. 1033), is uncertain; by the latter twelfth century this *trícha* was in dispute between the kings of Connacht and Tír Conaill. From it derives the cantred of Carbridrumclif (**C8**: the second element is the parish name, Drumcliff).[36]

C9: *Dungalue* (1200); *Clanargely* (1309); *Clannargyl* (1333); *Clanferwyll & Methry* (1347)[37]
The 1333 inquisition takes this cantred and that of Clantayg (**C10**) together, as is clear from even a superficial reading of the document, intermixing details of both and giving a rental total only at the end. It is necessary, therefore, to adduce additional evidence to clarify exactly what lay where. The inquisition is clear enough about locating lands in and around Galway itself in Clanargyll as well as those to the

35 MacNiocaill, *Red Book of Kildare*, 113–15; TCD MS 1066, 489 ff. 36 O'Brien, *Corpus*, 166; Pender, 'O Cleary Genealogies', 71ff; Ó Muraíle, *Mac Firbhishigh* i, 377; Ó Duíbhgeannáin, 'Bréifne', 132–3; Knox, *Mayo*, 59; BF, 396; AU, 648, 665, 670, 770, 812; AT, 739, 751, 975; CS, 953; AFM, 718, 747, 871, 1033. 37 CDI, i, 24; CJRI, ii, 90; GO MS 192, 27.

west, showing that the baronies of Moycullen and Galway must have lain in this cantred. Indeed, this cantred appears to be that first referred to as Dungalue (*Dún Gaillmhe*) in 1200.[38] The inclusion of Methery in the cantred title on occasion adds the parish of Meary *alias* Ballynacourty while there is also evidence for the inclusion of Oranmore parish in this cantred. The half cantred of Clanargyll proper seems to have included the parishes of Galway, Rahoon, Oranmore and Ballinacourty while the half cantred of Gnomor and Gnobeg (*Gnó Mór, Gnó Becc*) included all of Moycullen barony.[39]

T9: *Clann Fhergail & Meadraige*

The Muintir Murchada tract (see **C21**) lists Clann Fhergail and Meadraige each under its own *taísech*. Clann Fhergail are derived from an early and assuredly spurious son of Brión, (*a quo* Uí Briúin). From these derive the cantred of Clanargyll & Methery, which also included lands west of Galway which were not within the overlordship of Uí Briúin Seóla when the Muintir Murchada tract was being composed. These lands were occupied by Delbna Tíre dá Locha (Gnó Mór and Gnó Becc) whose king is recorded in 1142 and whose pedigree is remotely linked into the greater Delbna lineages. Does the fact that only one local kingdom is found within the area of the later cantred suggest that these Delbna were kings of the entire area, under Uí Briúin Seóla? Reference in an Irish charter of *c*.1190 to a named *pagus* **within** 'Clonfergale' appears to be the earliest reference to Clann Fhergail as a *trícha*.[40]

C10: *Clantaie O Dermod* (1200); *Glantayg* (1308): *Clantayg* (1333, 1347)[41]

See my comments above regarding Clanferwyll (**C9**). This confused return begins with a half cantred in Clantayg which is not further identified; this must have contained at least the parishes of Athenry – which we know to have lain in Clantayg – and Monivea, an eighteenth-century creation hived off from Athenry, and the location of the early Bermingham castle of Tiaquin. The inquisition goes on to locate unambiguously the territories of Corca Mogha and Uí Diarmata in Clantayg, adding the parishes of Kilkerrin and Moylough respectively (and giving the *O Dermod* of 1213). To these should be added the *theodum* of Munteraghy, misplaced in the inquisition, to bring in the parishes of Killererin and Ballynakill-Aghiart, the latter originally a parcel of the former. (In the seventeenth century the rectories of Killererin and Kilkerrin were claimed by the Bermingham barons of Athenry.) It will be noted that this extent agrees well with the southern and eastern boundaries of Tuam diocese, which would perfectly delineate these borders of Clantayg with the addition of the parish of Killoscobe, impropriate to Abbeyknockmoy. Furthermore, the location of the western, detached portions of Athenry parish suggest the inclusion of Abbeyknockmoy parish in Clantayg, as does its pattern of impropriation. In 1467 Machaire Clainne Taidhg is used as an *alias* for Machaire Riabhach, the later Maghere

---

38 For a second reference to Galway as 'Dungaluy', from 1294, see RC 7/11, 7. 39 DKRI 36, p. 63; RC 7/4, 357; 7/10, 130, 499; 8/11, 143; Knox, 'Connacht', i, 396–7. 40 Ó Muraíle, *Mac Firbhishigh*, i, 437, 449; ii, 265; AFM, 1142; O'Flaherty, *Ogygia*, 30. 41 Nicholls, 'charter of William de Burgh', 122; CJRI, ii, 61; GO 192, 27.

Reogh, those eastern parts of Clare barony in the parishes of Abbeyknockmoy, Kilmoylan and Cummer. While Cummer seems to have been borderland this reference certainly allows us to include Kilmoylan to complete the extent of Clantayg.[42]

T10: *Clann Taidg & Uí Diarmata*

The cantred of Clantayg O Dermod must derive from the *trícha* of Clann Taidg & Uí Diarmata. This *trícha* seems to have been a late formation uniting two distinct Síl Muiredaig waves of expansion. Uí Diarmata descend from Diarmait Finn, king of Connacht (d. 833). An early tract on Uí Diarmata suggests that this was a kingdom carved out of parts of Cenél Dubáin, Clann Choscraig and Sogain in the time of Uatu, grandson of Diarmait Finn, and thus in the latter ninth century. Confirmation of this may be had in the eponym of Muintir Fhathaig, a *túath* in western Uí Diarmata, named from Fothad son of Uatu.[43] Kings of Uí Diarmata are recorded regularly in the annals from 971.[44] Clann Taidg seem to represent an even later expansion here. While there is no direct evidence of an etymology, Kelleher is probably correct in identifying the eponym with Muiredach son of King Tadg (d. 956) mac Cathail of Connacht. From Muiredach descend the lineage of Uí Thaidg an Teaglaig, an important lineage of Síl Muiredaig recorded from 1048 onwards.[45] Their *túath* cannot otherwise be identified. Clann Taidg may have invested this country – probably earlier part of Uí Briúin Seóla – around the mid-eleventh century just as Áed in Gaí Bernaig was doing in Tuam. Clann Taidg was not a kingdom, however. Donn Cathaig (or Donnchad) Mór Mac Airechtaig of Síl Muiredaig, who flourished towards the end of the twelfth century, was said to have usurped the lordship (*taoisidheacht*) of Clann Taidg, no doubt with Uí Chonchobair support.[46]

C11: *Connacdunmor* (1308); *Conmacdonmor* (1308); **Condunmor** (1333); **Conyk Dunmor** (1347)[47]

No extent of this cantred appears to survive. Its *caput* was the de Bermingham manor of Dunmore and it is ancestor to the later barony of Dunmore, Co. Galway. It included the archiepiscopal seat of Tuam. It must have consisted of all the barony of Dunmore (apart from the portion of Killererin parish therein) and much of that of Ballymoe to its east. This is suggested by those parts of Dunmore and Tuam parishes in Ballymoe, by the prebendal arrangements of the chapter of the diocese of Tuam, as well as by the eastern border of that diocese in Ballymoe. Conmacdunmor, therefore, must have included the Ballymoe parishes of Templetogher, Boyounagh, Clonbern and those parts of Dunmore and Tuam in it, as described above.[48]

---

42 Knox, 'Connacht', i, 396–7; idem, *Tuam, Killaha and Achonry*, 243; O'Doherty, 'annates Tuamensis', 57–8, 70; Orpen, *Ireland under the Normans*, iii, 246; Nicholls, 'Rectory, vicarage and parish', 69 (n54); AC, p. 2n. 43 Ó Muraíle, *Mac Firbhishigh*, i, 537, iii, 403. 44 CS, 971, 990; AI, 1105; ALC, 1067, 1188, 1200; AT, 1037, 1093, 1167; AU, 1181. 45 Kelleher, 'Uí Maine', 111; AFM, 1048, 1132; ALC, 1225. 46 Ó Muraíle, *Mac Firbhishigh*, i, 505, 526; Lec. 65rb. 47 CJRI, ii, 61; RC 7/7, 4; GO 192, 27. 48 Hogan, *Onomasticon*, 289; Knox, *Tuam, Killaha and Achonry*, 242.

T11: *Conmaicne Cenéoil Dubáin*

The Conmaicne formed three kingdoms in Connacht lying in a continuous belt from Connemara to Tuam. The *trícha* of Conmaicne Cenéoil Dubáin or Conmaicne Dúna Móir gives the later cantred of Conmacdunmore. These Conmaicne occur as a dynasty in 1095 and one of their constituent *túatha* had its *taísech* recorded in 1162.[49] Their pedigree does not come down much beyond 700. Their rout at the hands of Uí Briúin in 766 at Shrule must mark their coming under Uí Briúin control, eventually passing from that of Clann Choscraig to become demesne of the Uí Chonchobair kings who made Tuam their capital during the eleventh century. The genealogical linkages of all three Connacht Conmaicne groups are remote.[50]

C12: *Kilmaine* (1214); *Conmacnekuly* (1235); *Conewecnecoly* (13th cent.); *Conykcoul* (1347)[51]

Extents of the manors of Shrule and Lough Mask (Ballinchalla) in this cantred were made in 1348 and again five years later. While several of the places in these cannot now be identified those that can include lands in the parishes of Shrule, Ballinchalla, Kilcommon, Kilmainmore and Cong.[52] A third manor in this cantred was Rothba (Rodba: Ballinrobe).[53] A further useful indicator of the extent of this cantred is that of the rural deanery of Shrule which seems to have comprised the area of the cantreds of Conmacnekule and Conmacnemar.[54] The northern boundary of this deanery reflects the Irish boundary between Conmaicne Cúile Talad (**T12**) and Cera (**T16**): the River Robe.[55] It will be noticed that this excludes the parish of Robeen and that of 'Rodbad in Kera' – that part of Ballinrobe parish north of the Robe – from Conmacnekule. Conmacnekule thus contained all of Kilmaine Barony, Co. Mayo, apart from these lands. The parishes of Ballinrobe, Ballinchalla and Cong extended across Lough Mask to its western shore, indicating that the barony of Ross was also part of this cantred.[56]

T12: *Conmaicne Cúile Talad*

This *trícha* gives the cantred of Conmacnekule. This lineage slew the king of Uí Briúin Seóla in 682, when no doubt still independent. Their pedigree comes down to around 900 and it may have been after this that they fell under alien lordship,

49 AI, 1095; AFM, 1162. **50** O'Brien, *Corpus*, 317–21; BF, 383. **51** CDI, i, 84; MacNiocaill, *Red Book of Kildare*, 28; Curtis, 'Feudal charters', 288; GO 192, 27. **52** PRO SC/6/1239/30. These extents mention the lands of Killeenbrenan, Balston [?], Delgyn [in Shrule: BSDM, 16], Coryn [Carn in Ballinchalla?], Coleston [Ballinchalla], Manyfallaghty [Bunnafollistran in Shrule: BSDM, 17], Incheclon [?], Clontuskryt [in Kilcommon: see O'Sullivan, *Strafford Inquisition Mayo*, 65, 75], Cloncrawe [in Kilmainmore: *Staff. Inq.*, 53], Dirkenetig [?], Achirk [Athquark in Cong: BSDM, 47]. **53** CIPM, vi, 161. **54** CDI, v, 229–30. By the seventeenth century the ruridecanal structure in Tuam had changed completely. For the identifications of the parishes of *c.*1306 see Knox, *Tuam, Killaha and Achonry*, 197, 201–2. Knox is mistaken in his identifications of the last four parishes. Margos is Moyrus; Kilkemantuyn, from its position, must be Ballynakill; for Rossclaran read Rosflanayn *alias* Kilflannan in Ballinadoon (CPR, xv, 215); and for Innisclin read Inishbofin. **55** Ó Muraíle, *Mac Firbhishigh*, i, 611. **56** It has long been recognized that the Joyce fee in Ross originated under the Geraldine lords of Conmacnekule (Knox, *Mayo*, 324).

probably that of Uí Briúin Seóla. Cúl Talad is explicitly referred to as a *trícha* in 1225 (and, by implication, in 1235).[57]

C13: *Comacmar* (1333); *Conmacnemar* (1342)[58]

The extent of this cantred is preserved in that of the rural rectory of Conmacni Mara, the present barony of Ballynahinch, Co. Galway.[59] The name survives in the district name, Connemara, now unhistorically applied to a much larger area.

T13: *Conmaicne Mara*

This was the only one of the three adjacent Conmaicne kingdoms of Connacht to maintain internal autonomy, with kings recorded in 1016 and 1139. These occur as a dynasty in 660 and 923 and what must have been a *trícha* in 1154 (with a fleet), 1196 and 1235. Conmaicne Mara gives the cantred of Conmacnemar.[60]

C14: *Chorinn* (1195); *Corhin* (1204); *Korn* (1240); *Coran* (1289)[61]

The *caput* of this cantred was at Ballymote and its extent appears to be preserved in that of the rural rectory of Dachorand and Mota (that is, the two Corrans and Ballymote), which included all of the parishes of the present barony of Corran, Co. Sligo.[62]

T14: *Corann*

Corann occurs as a territory in 595. Gailenga Corann occur as a lineage in 651, 743 and 993 and the later deanery of An Dá Chorann suggests that the cantred of Coran may have had two divisions, one of which was Gailenga Corann. The other would have been the eastern Corcu Fir Trí *alias* Corcu Ráeda, who appear to have been distinct genealogically from the Luigne (for whom see **T18**). The first of their kings to be recorded, Dobalén mac Gormgusa, was also king of Luigne (d. 885). He is eponym to the Uí Dobailéin kings of Corcu Fir Trí and five kings of this line are recorded between 885 and 1032, one of whom was killed by Gailenga Corann. Three of these kings were also overkings of Luigne. By 1248 Uí Dobailéin were styling themselves *rí Corann*, which I take to be the area of the later cantred, surely the successor of an earlier *trícha cét*.[63]

C15: *Crigfertur* (1333); *Crysyrdire & Tyrneyn & Tyrnaghten* (1347)[64]

This cantred is ancestor to the barony of Clanmaurice, Co. Mayo. Tyrnaghtyn was the earliest name for Kilcolman parish (in 1306) while Kilvine bears the *alias* Cryfortyer in 1584, and this territory was still known as 'Clanmorris, Tirenene and Tirnaghton' in 1585. Ahena in Tagheen parish perhaps preserves the name of the

57 CS, 678; AT, 681; ALC, 1225, 1235. **58** GO 192, 27. **59** Knox, 'Connacht', i, 397; Hardiman, *Galway*, 61n.; Nicholls, 'Rectory, vicarage and parish', 71. **60** AI, 1016; ALC, 1235; AT, 1139; AFM, 923, 1154; CS, 660. **61** Mills, *Gormanston*, 143; CDI, i, 37; MacNiocaill, *Red Book of Kildare*, 74. **62** Nicholls, 'Rectory, vicarage and parish', 74–5; Orpen, *Ireland under the Normans* iii, 199–200. **63** O'Brien, *Corpus*, 168–70, 439; Ó Muraíle, *Mac Firbhishigh*, ii, 647–57; P. Walsh, *Irish leaders and learning*, 200; Byrne, *Kings and high kings*, 69; Ní Dhonnchadha, 'Cáin Adomnáin', 213; Pender, *Déssi genealogies*, 29; AC, 1248; AT, 595, 651; AFM, 885, 920, 984, 993, 1032; CS, 945; AU, 743. **64** GO 192, 27.

eponym of the *theodum* of Tirenene. Crigfertur thus contained the parishes of Kilcolman, Kilvine, Crossboyne, Tagheen and Mayo. The cantredal boundaries here are further shared by those of the diocese of Mayo on three sides.[65]

T15: *Crích Fer Tíre, Tír nÉnna & Tír Nechtain*
The cantred of Crigfertur, Tyrneyn & Tyrnaghtyn must derive from an earlier *trícha* which contained Crích Fer Tíre, Tír nÉnna and Tír Nechtain. These seem to have been three distinct *túatha* united into a single *trícha* but of their history virtually nothing is known. That Nechtan is made a son of Brión of the Connachta in the spurious pedigree of the latter suggests that the line claimed some antiquity here.[66]

C16: *Ker* (1333); *Kerre, Fertyr & Clancowan* (1347)[67]
C17: *Fertyr & Clancowan* (1333)
While the 1333 inquisition clearly distinguishes between the cantred of Kerre and the half-cantred of Fertyr & Clancowan, these are grouped together in the Connacht cantredal list of 1347. Again, the later barony of Carra includes both territories, all of which suggests that, for administrative purposes, the Anglo-Normans treated these as one cantred.[68]

   While no extent survives of the cantred of Kerre its likely form can be reconstructed from a number of sources. It is part ancestor to the barony of Carra, Co. Mayo, although Kerre constituted only the southern part of the modern barony, more or less. We know from notice of the de Stanton/McEvilly lords of this cantred that its *caput* was at Castlecarra and the lands of this family stretched northwards as far as Manulla, while the rectory of Manulla also included that of Balla. Again, the southern boundary is fixed by that of the cantred of Conmacnekule (**C12**) and that of the deaneries of Mayo and Shrule. A further useful source is the extent of the Irish *trícha cét* of Cera (**T16**), upon which the cantred must have been based. From all of this it would seem that Kerre contained the parishes of Burriscarra (*Buirghéis Ceara*: the borough of Cera), Ballyovey, Ballintober, Manulla, Balla, Drum, Ballyhean, Rosslee, Touaghty, Robeen and part of Ballinrobe.[69]

   The area of the half-cantred of Fertyr & Clancowan can be reconstructed from ecclesiastical sources. Clancuan was the original name of Aglish parish and the parish of Islandeady must also have been in it. The rectory of Fertyr contained the parishes of Turlough, Breaghwy ('the church of Brechnach in Fertire' of 1297) and Kildacommoge. It will be noticed that the northern and eastern bounds of this extent coincide with that of the diocese of Tuam.[70]

T16: *Cera*
Mac Firbisigh's Uí Fhiachrach tract describes the *trícha* of Cera which gives the cantred of Kerre. Cera was certainly a local kingdom, whose kings descend from

65 Knox, 'Connacht', i, 397, 403–4; idem, *Mayo*, 322; TCD MS 1066, 443. **66** Ó Muraíle, *Mac Firbhishigh*, i, 430. **67** GO 192, 27. **68** Knox, 'Connacht', i, 398, 404–5. **69** Idem, *Mayo*, 287; Ó Muraíle, *Mac Firbhishigh*, i, 610–14; Nicholls, 'Rectory, vicarage and parish', 72. **70** Knox, *Tuam, Killaha and Achonry*, 245; Idem, 'Connacht', i, 405.

Máel Cothaid, a king of Uí Fhiachrach and Connacht living in 603, whose line appears to have been driven southwards into Cera by Dúnchad Muirisci in the late seventh century. A king of Cera of this line is recorded in 1032, while Fir Chera are mentioned as a lineage in 1094.[71] Mac Firbisigh names the last indigenous king of Cera as Giolla an Ghoill Mac Néill whom he places in the late twelfth century. He appears to have been replaced by King Ruaidrí Ua Conchobair's sons Áed and Tairrdelbach in Cera, from which they were eventually driven by the Anglo-Normans. While one is tempted to dismiss the reference to a king of Partraige Cera in AFM 1207 and read *taísech* in its place, Mac Firbisigh has a similar reference while *Lebor na Cert* also has a king of Partraige, all suggesting that this *túath* in southern Cera was a kingdom![72] Therefore, **T16** appears to be one of a small number of *tríchas* which contained two local kingdoms.

T17: *Fir Tíre & Clann Chuáin*
Fir Tíre and Clann Chuáin were related lineages, probably originally part of Cera, and these give the half-cantred of Fertyr & Clancowan (**C17**), suggesting that this may have been a distinct *trícha*. Cuán probably lived in the early seventh century and represents a collateral line of Fir Chera. Mac Firbisigh has a story relating how the lordship of Clann Chuáin was transferred by its *taísech* from its Uí Dubda over-lord to Tomaltach Mac Diarmata, apparently around 1200, and this is confirmed by a reference of 1232 to Donnchad mac Tomaltaig as dying in Aicedacht, an *alias* for Fir Tíre and Clann Chúáin.[73]

C18: *Luine* (1195); *Luyne* (1235); *Lune* (1240); *Lowyn* (1333)[74]
This cantred was early divided into two fees, the manors of Esdar (Ballysadare) and Bannada on the one hand and that of Athleathan (Ballylahan). The rural rectory of Bannada contained all of the parishes of Leyny barony, Co. Sligo, apart from that of Ballysadare, while that of Athleathan contained most of the barony of Gallen, Co. Mayo (that is, all of those parishes in the diocese of Achonry). The parishes of Attymas and Kilgarvan, though in the modern barony of Gallen, are not in Achonry but in the diocese of Killala. While this suggests that these were not part of this cantred an early (*c.*1240) extent of the *theodum* of Moyntirlathnan proves otherwise. This large *theodum* appears to have contained the western half of the modern barony of Gallen. Among its villates was that of 'Lothbrothry', which we can identify with certainty with the seventeenth-century *baile* of Lough Brohly in Kilgarvan parish, illustrating that both Kilgarvan and Attymas lay in Moyntirlathnan. This *theodum* is elsewhere described as being 'a moiety of the half cantred of Luyna'. Therefore this cantred contained the entire modern baronies of Leyny in Sligo and Gallen in Mayo.[75]

71 AI, 1032; AT, 1094. **72** Ó Muraíle, *Mac Firbhishigh* i, 570, 610–14; idem, 'Connacht population groups', 174–5; Byrne, *Kings and high kings*, 238–9; Knox, *Mayo*, 83, 89; Dillon, *Lebor na Cert*, 60; ALC, 1227. **73** Ó Muraíle, *Mac Firbhishigh* i, 614–16; AFM, 1232. **74** Mills, *Gormanston*, 143; MacNiocaill, *Red Book of Kildare*, 28. **75** MacNiocaill, *Red Book of Kildare*, 28, 60, 69 (where Bennede is Bannada, Rathardkreth is Ardcree and Clarath is Claragh), 167; Nicholls, 'Rectory,

T18: *Luigne*

The Luigne and Gailenga are closely associated in Connacht as in Mide and indeed the terms, in both provinces, seem to have become interchangable. It is likely the Connacht group were ancestral to those of Mide and thus may have been here since perhaps the fifth century. Their genealogies are sparse and many of their kings do not appear therein. The term Luigne refers both to a regional and local kingdom. Its regional kingdom contained three *tríchas*, **T14, 18**, and **26**. The earliest king we can be sure of is Toicthech mac Cinnfhaeled who occurs as a guarantor of Cáin Adomnáin and who would thus have lived around 697. He seems to have had three sons, probably the ancestors to the later 'trí sloinnte' of Luigne Connacht, a title which first occurs in 790. The senior line cannot be traced beyond one Diarmait who may be the man of that name who died as *rí Luigne* in 892. The later kings come from a second line, descending from Flaithgius mac Toicthig. This produced both later ruling families, Uí Eagra and Uí Gadra, the former dominating the king-ship from 1024 onwards. When Duarcon Ua hEagra died in 1059 the style *rí na Trí Sloinnte* is again used, showing Uí Eagra to have been the overlords here. Their own immediate lordship must be represented by the *trícha* of Luigne, the cantred of Lune. This however has had two moieties since colonial times, reflected in the modern baronies of Leyny and Gallen (from Gailenga). The later Gailenga Corann are derived from the third son of Toicthech, Dúngalach, who died as king of Luigne in 766. Confusingly, however, this combines Corann, which gives the cantred of Coran (**C14**), with Gallen, two quite separate territories.[76]

C19: ***Momeniach*** (1206); ***Menevy*** (1227); *Mannach* (1308); ***Monewagh*** (1333)[77]

This cantred is ancestor to the later barony of Loughrea, Co. Galway. The extent of 1333 identifies lands in the parishes of Kilconierin, Kiltullagh (in 1407 'Kiltulagh Maonmaigh'), Killimordaly, Grange, Killeenadeema, Lickerrig and Loughrea. In addition the rural rectory of Loughrea, as well as containing the last three parishes above, also included the parishes of Kilconickny, Kilteskill and Kilcooly. We should also include those parishes not already mentioned which were included in the rural rectory of Monewagh ('Muynmac'): Killaan and Bullaun. Finally, Kilreekil and Kilmeen must also have been in this cantred, the latter being in Irish Máenmag (**T19**). The rural deanery of Loughrea was almost identical with the cantred.[78]

vicarage and parish', 74–5; Orpen, *Ireland under the Normans*, iii, 195–8.   **76** O'Brien, *Corpus*, 168–9, 439; Ó Muraíle, *Mac Firbhishigh*, ii, 647, 653, 657; Ní Dhonnchadha, 'Cáin Adomnáin', 213; ALC, 1023, 1059; AT, 1177; AU, 878; CS, 964; AFM, 766, 846, 891, 926, 931, 1155, 1183. **77** CDI, i, 46; McNeill, *Alen's Register*, 47; RC 7/7, 4. **78** Knox, 'Connacht', i, 133–6; Nicholls, 'Rectory, vicarage and parish', 59, 72; idem, 'Clonfert and Kilmacduagh', 139; AT, 1132; CS, 1132. The only list of the rural deaneries of Clonfert diocese is that of the '1306 Taxation' (CDI, v, 221–3). Of those vicarages difficult of identification here follows, where possible, the correct locations. Buellio = Bullaun; Benn = Benmore and Benbeg in Grange parish; Kyllyngenduna = Killeenadeema; Kilseskynn = Kilteskil; Killaspugmoylan in Kilconickny (Egan, 'Annates Clonfertenses', 56); Kilfrelan = Killilan in Kilconickny (?; CPR, xiii, 373); Athneg = the obsolete Athnagarra in Kilconickny; Kildagan = Kilaan.

T19: *Tricha Máenmaige*
The cantred of Monewagh derives from (Tricha) Máenmaige of the annals, the name of a territory a king of which is first recorded in 585. This area must then have been under Uí Fhiachrach Aidni control and this king is unknown in the Uí Maine pedigrees (see **T113**). Its first Uí Maine kings were of Clann Chommáin, a line which held the kingship of Uí Maine five times between 601 and 750. The last of these, Cathal *Máenmaige*, was perhaps the first of them to invest Máenmag. Later kings of this line metonymically styled themselves *rí Locha Riach* (825, 884) after the chief place of Máenmag (Loughrea). Clann Chommáin seem to disappear after 900 and, while no later kings are recorded – probably due to the arrival of Uí Chellaig here – *Nósa Ua Maine,* for what it is worth, records two ruling families of Máenmag, Uí Nechtain and Uí Máelalaid.[79]

C20: **Wintelmolmen** (1207); *Muntermolinan* (1242): **Montramolynan** (1333)[80]
As described in 1333, this cantred, ancestor of Leitrim Barony, Co. Galway, contained the parishes of Ballynakill, Tynagh, Lickmolassy, Leitrim, Kilmalinoge, Duniry, and Abbeygormican, and was nearly identical to the deanery of Duniry (which, however, lacked Abbeygormican).[81]

T20: *Muintir Máelfináin*
This gives the cantred of Montramolynan. This was a *tricha* comprised of four *túatha*, as described in 1207 ('a cantred in which are located Estyre, Wintelmolmen, Ulunan and Nyaki' for which read Áes Tíre, Muintir Máelfináin, Uí Lomáin, and ?). It was part of the regional kingdom of Uí Maine (see under **T113**). Its history is obscure. The reference to the ten *tricha céts* of Uí Maine in the extent of Clann Chuinn in the Lecan Miscellany is hyperbole, this tract uses the figure of ten for several *mórthúatha*.[82]

C21: **Wintermurhath** (1200); *Muntyrmurwyth* (1327); **Muntyrmurghyth** (1347)[83]
The situation here is complex.[84] The principal manor of the cantred was that of Admekin (Headford, Co. Galway). Detailed extents of this manor survive which show it to have contained lands in the parishes of Killursa, Kilkilvery, Killeany, Kilcoona, Cargin, a portion of Belclare, and probably part of Donaghpatrick as well.[85]

79 Russell, 'Nósa Ua Maine', 534; AC, 1315.16. For Uí Maine I rely on Kelleher's excellent 'Uí Maine'. For the source of the pedigrees used by Kelleher see O'Donovan, *Hy Many*, 25–59. **80** CDI, i, 54; PRC, 199. **81** Knox, 'Connacht', i, 395–6 (where Olamman is Uí Lomáin, the colonial manor of Duniry (Hogan, *Onomasticon*, 674)); CDI, v, 222–3. The following are the obscure identifications of this deanery. Dundoyri = Duniry; Lochr' = Leitrim; Kynnugi/Kynmunmugy = *alias* Kenvoy, was in Tynagh (Nicholls, 'Clonfert and Kilmacduagh', 147); Kynaleyn = Cenél Fhéchín or Ballynakill; Kylcarban = Kilcorban in Tynagh; Drummackyth = Drumkitt in Duniry (Nicholls, 'Clonfert and Kilmacduagh', 138). **82** CDI, i, 54; GT, 190–1. **83** Nicholls, 'charter of William de Burgh', 122; RC 8/15, 237; GO 192, 27. **84** Much of what follows is based on an unpublished MS history of Muntyrmorghyth kindly supplied by Mr Kenneth Nicholls. **85** Knox, 'Admekin (Headford)', passim. I comment on Knox's identifications as follows. *Karneferrachyn* and *Clongad*: these places occur under the forms Carnefarthir and Clongad in a pleading of 1299, when

That this was not the full extent of the cantred is shown by the extent of the rural rectory of Muntermurchuga, which adds the parish of Killower to those above which were also in this rectory.[86] A second manor here was that of Clancoskri, extents of which were made in 1347 and 1354, with lands in the parishes of Donaghpatrick, Kilkilvery, Killower, Belclare, and probably parts of southern Tuam, Kilbennan and the north-western quarter of Killererin.[87] Yet a third manor, that of Corofin, completes the picture. This manor is represented by the parish of Kilmacregan (now Cummer). The feudal history of these manors suggests that they were all in Muntyrmorghyth. The original de Ridelesford lord of Muntyrmorghyth, Walter, appears to have granted its benefices to his family foundation, the Crutched Friars of St John at Castledermot, Co. Kildare. At the Dissolution this house was possessed of the rectories of Muntermurchuga and Kilmacregan. Upon Walter de Ridelesford's death around 1239, Muntyrmorghyth was divided between his two daughters. One got Admekin and the other Corofin. So much is certain. However, upon the death, in 1276, of the daughter, Emeline, who inherited Corofin, this manor also appears to have been divided between heirs, resulting in the 'new' manors of Corofin and Clancoskri. It will be noted that the parishes of Donaghpatrick, Belclare and Tuam were ultimately church-land and it would seem that Clancoskri was largely composed of such.[88] Again, the lands of Clancoskri and Admekin were somewhat intermixed, suggesting a colonial rather than pre-Invasion division.

they are associated with a place called Ballylegan, which appears in the possession of one Stephen le Prout. In the same pleading Andrew Cor is named as tenant of Carnefarthir, both he and Prout holding as tenants of Geoffrey fitz Alan, named in the Admekin extent as mesne-lord of Karneferrachyn and Clongad. All of this serves to confirm in a general way Knox's tentative location of these places as 'lying in the middle of Kilkilvery', for le Prout was the eponym of Ballyfruit in that parish. (In 1347 John Prout was elected coroner for the cantred of Montyrmorghyth.) This suggests the present Cordarragh as the location of one or both of the above places (RC 7/6, 480; 7/10, 53; 7/13 (1 Ed. 11), 58, (2 Ed. 11), 9; GO MS 192, 27). *Kildarine*: Knox is perhaps being too literal in refusing to accept the obvious identification with Kildaree (Killursa parish) here. *Radmoy*: Knox is mistaken here: this is certainly Rafwee in Killeany. *Monimorgin/Mommorgan*: this is the Munmargyl of a plea of dower of 1316 of the Gaynard family, which Nicholls identifies with the Ballywonyworoghill of 1608, which he locates in probability with Cahernaheeny in Kilkilvery (RC 8/11, 148, 426). *Baillikyn/Balihechun*: this place occurs as Balyeghan in the Gaynard pleading of 1316 and must be the Ballahene of the BSDG, which Petty's map suggests lay in Ballycasey in Kilcoona. *Kinenaud*: this place occurs as Kanynard in the 1316 pleading, which Nicholls identifies with the Cahircanahard of 1617, which lay in or near Glennagarraun in Kilkilvery. *Kilcoruy*: this seems to be Kilgarriff in Killeany. *Fawer*: this is unlikely to represent Ower, where no significant medieval settlement is noted, but must represent the sixteenth-century territory of 'The Oure', still extant as the second element of Cloghanower, the location of a major tower house of the McRedmond Burke lords of Muntermoroghue.   **86** Fiant Eliz., 3370.   **87** PRO SC/6/1239/30 and 31. The lands and tenants were the Hakets of Knockmaa [the eponyms of Castle Hacket and Lough Hacket]; Beagh; an unnamed de Ridelesford tenement of three villates [probably in Donaghpatrick and Kilkilvery to judge by contemporary references to the family]; and the 7 villates of McEthe. These were the Meic Áeda or MacHugh family, the indigenous ruling family of Clann Choscraig. These seven villates would seem to correspond to much if not all of the 31 quarters of Moyntagh MacHugh as extended in the composition of 1585, which Nicholls (see fn. 84) shows to have lain in the parishes of Killower, Belclare, southern Tuam, north western Killererin and southern Kilbennan.   **88** Knox, *Tuam, Killaha and Achonry*, 243.

T21: *Muintir Murchada*

Deiscert Connacht was the area within the overlordship of Uí Briúin Seóla, whose linkage with the other Uí Briúin was remote and may be fabulous. Alternatively, Nicholls suggests that the Patrician legend involving Uí Briúin at *Mag Selce* may have been Tírechán's rewriting of an original reference to *Mag Seóla*, and thus that the original homeland of Uí Briúin was Mag Seóla, the plain between Loch Corrib and Tuam, a record perhaps already being written out of history in the ninth century. The first historically visible king of the ruling line of Uí Briúin Seóla, Cennfáelad mac Colgan, died in 682 as king of Connacht, leaving two sons from whom the rival lines of Muintir Murchada and Clann Choscraig descend.[89] The regional kingdom of Uí Briúin Seóla itself was one of those where the term *rí* was strictly reserved for the two senior segments, as illustrated by the tract on its chief families.[90] This shows the lordship with borders which do not agree with those of the diocese of Annaghdown, generally thought to represent the boundaries of Deiscert Connacht when established around 1179, indicating that the tract is older. It may be a later recension of an original dating to the reign of Flaithbertach Ua Flaithbertaig, king of Connacht (d. 1098).

The demense territory of the senior line, Muintir Murchada, as described in the Muintir Murchada tract, largely gives the area of the later cantred of Muntyrmorghyth (**C21**). Muintir Murchada occur as a lineage in 1061 and as a territory in 1238. Its eponym was a king of Deiscert Connacht who died in 896.[91] A Latin charter of the 1190s mentions a grant of land in 'Clonfergale' by an unnamed *comes* of 'Muntir Moroghow', no doubt the Ua Flaithbertaig of his day (see under **T9**). The situation of the rival Clann Choscraig is much less clear-cut. The eponym was the son of a king of Deiscert Connacht who died in 757 and this line held its own against Muintir Murchada until the death of its last king (of Deiscert Connacht) in 993. Clann Choscraig occur as a lineage in 1030 and 1063 but by 1124 their royal line had been replaced by a branch of Muintir Murchada, of whom were the kings of Clann Choscraig recorded in 1124 and 1170.[92] Clann Choscraig gives colonial Clancoskri. If the area of this manor and that of its associate, Corofin, accurately reflects the extent of Clann Choscraig, this would place the latter stretching from Killererin to Donaghpatrick. Significantly, there is evidence that Clann Choscraig originally extended further to the east (see p. 135). The problem with this suggest-

89 Ó Muraíle, *Mac Firbhisigh*, i, 442–8; Kelleher, 'Uí Maine', 112; Nicholls, 'Patrician Sites', 118 fn.12. **90** Hardiman, *Iar-Connaught*, 368–72. This tract does not include lands west of the Corrib yet extends eastwards to include Muintir Fhathaig (Killererin). A holding so far east suggests the early date. Hardiman's identifications are generally sound, although he is in error in the cases of *Cluain Ai* and *Baili Colu* – I cannot suggest an identification for the latter. To his identifications the following can be added. *Maighleaslaind* is Manuslynn in Kilcoona parish. *Cluain Ai* is Clonee in Kilkilvery. *Ardratha* is the Aerdray of the Admekin extent, which lay near Ardfintan in Killursa. *Ratha hIndile* – with its erenagh – must be Cargin. This parish occurs, under the corrupt form Rathmaolid, in the early Papal Taxation, and is 'Cargin *alias* Rahihilan' in CPR, xv, 154. *Muine inradain* occurs under the forms Monyonnran and Manumrechan in the Admekin extent and is now Bunanraun in Kilkilvery. **91** AT, 1061; AFM, 1238; Kelleher, 'Uí Maine', 112. **92** AU, 1030; AFM, 1063, 1170; CS, 991; AT, 1124; Kelleher, 'Uí Maine', 112.

ed location for Clann Choscraig is that only its western sections occur in the tract – which does not mention Clann Choscraig at all – as part of Muintir Murchada proper. This confused situation must owe much to Uí Chonchobair aggression here which meant that the area south of Tuam was a land of war with uncertain borders, something further reflected in the dual claims to the parishes of Cummer and Belclare by the dioceses of Tuam and Annaghdown.[93] In summary, there is insufficient evidence to show that Clann Choscraig was a *trícha cét* at the time of the Invasion. It remained a local kingdom at least until 1170, presumably much diminished in area, but its territory is subsequently found to be part of the cantred of Muntyrmorghyth.

C22–23: *The cantreds of Ofecherath*

Anglo-Norman records mention 'the two cantreds of Ofecherath', whose total area certainly agrees with that of the diocese of Kilmacduagh. The southern cantred is referred to as 'Keneloth' or 'Kinalethes', and seems to correspond to the manor of Ardrahan (**C22**). From Mac Firbisigh, clearly drawing on earlier material, we learn that this was the division of Cenél Áeda na hEchtge (**T22**), one of the two divisions of Uí Fhiachrach Aidni. In 1241 Maurice fitz Gerald had a grant of chase and free warren in Kinalethes and Kilcolgan, among others, from which it would appear that Kilcolgan, the second manor here, corresponds approximately to the second, unnamed cantred, which Mac Firbisigh calls Cenél Guaire. The rural rectory of Ardrahan *alias* Ofyerach contained the parishes of Ardrahan, Kilthomas, Killinny, Killeenavarra, and Kinvarradoorus, suggesting that Keneloth had two divisions, the second remaining in native hands to become the Uí Seachnusaigh lordship of Keneloth, consisting of the parishes of Beagh, Kilbeacanty, Kilmacduagh and Kiltartan. 'Kenealea' remained an alternative name for the Uí Seachnusaigh lordship here into the sixteenth century.[94] Kilcolgan/Cenél Guaire (**C23**) must have occupied the area of the remaining northern parishes here. It may have been represented by the deanery of Kinaelga, whose extent is, unfortunately, unknown. By 1585 the eighteen quarters of a much shrunken Kennalgory (Cenél Guaire) lay around the parishes of Kilcolgan and Drumacoo. The 'half-cantred of Ogehechie' of 1252, which contained lands in Kilcolgan parish, must have been a division of Cenél Guaire. Although this sounds like Echtge this cannot be and it is more likely to derive from Óic Bethra, an early *túath* here.[95]

T22: *Cenél Áeda na hEchtge*
T23: *Cenél Guaire*

Genealogically derived from Fiachra, one of the four sons of Echu Mugmedón, Uí Fhiachrach appear to have been the original ruling line of Connacht and to have split into the principal sections of Uí Fhiachrach Aidni and Uí Fhiachrach Muaide

93 O'Flaherty, *Ogygia*, 30; Knox, *Tuam, Killaha and Achonry*, 243; Hardiman, *Galway*, 335. **94** RC 9/14, no. 12; PRO State papers Ireland, vol. 134, no. 56. **95** MacNiocaill, *Red Book of Kildare*, 17, 27, 35, 53–61; Knox, 'Kilcolgan', passim; Nicholls, '*Red Book of Kildare*', 27–30; idem, 'Rectory, vicarage and parish', 59, 73; CIPM, vi, 160–1; PRO London SC/6/1239/30; Freeman, *Compossicion Booke*, 32, 34, 40, 50; Ó Muraíle, *Mac Firbhishigh*, i, 584; Fiant Eliz., 1465.

in the late fifth century, at least according to the genealogies. We can certainly pick up Uí Fhiachrach Aidni in the person of Goibniu, their king, in 538. Of this line were five kings of Connacht between *c*.610 and 696, after which their power faded quickly. Their overkingdom probably included much of Co. Clare and what later became southern Uí Maine (in east Galway). Their overlordship in Co. Clare appears to have collapsed after 721 as at the same time they were losing further ground in the north to Uí Maine. By around 800 Uí Fhiachrach Aidni had probably shrunk to its later, rather diminutive area, home to least three ruling lines which had been in existence since the mid-seventh century.[96] The continued domination of the monastery of Tuamgraney, Co. Clare, by Uí Fhiachrach clerics into the late eleventh century preserves some memory of their former power here.[97]

The two cantreds of this area (**C22–3**) give two *tríchas*. Cenél Guaire (**T23**) derives from the famous saga king who died in 663 while Cenél Áeda na hEchtge (**T22**) derives from Guaire's uncle. Both *cenéla* shared the kingship of Aidne until after 872 when Cenél Guaire came to monopolize it. Later, the Cenél Guaire ruling family, Uí Eidin, were demesne kings of Cenél Guaire while Cenél Áeda was divided into moieties respectively between Uí Chathail, descendants of the earlier Cenél Áeda kings of Aidne, and Uí Seachnusaigh, claiming descent from Murchad mac Áeda, cousin of Guaire Aidni. Both are described as kings of their respective moieties of Cenél Áeda na hEchtge between 1179 and 1224, a division probably preserved here by the later colonial division of the cantred. Earlier, in 1154, Uí Chathail appear as sole kings. A reference from a Co. Limerick pipe roll of 1260, which includes a cantred of Ohecherach among the lands held by Uí Briain in that county (that is, in Thomond), may indicate that by then, if not considerably earlier, Cenél Aeda had come under Uí Briain overlordship.[98]

C24: *Urres* (1195); **Orrus** (1333)[99]
The barony of Erris, Co. Mayo.

T24: *Iorrus*
The territory of Iorrus gives the cantred of Orrus. Two Uí Cathniad kings of Iorrus are recorded, in 1180 and 1206, of a family claiming Uí Amalgado descent (for which see **T29**).[1]

C25: *Owyl* (1333); *The two Omylly's* (1347)[2]
The toponym here, Umall, also occurs in that of the later barony of Burrishoole, Co. Mayo (Buirghéis Umhaill). The inquisition of 1333, apart from the cantredal rent itself, names only places in the parishes of Aghagower and Kilmeena. We can add to this the parishes of the rural rectory of Umhall Uachtarach: Kilgeever and Oughaval, while Burrishoole itself must have been the *caput* of the cantred. From

96 AT, 538; Kelleher, 'Uí Maine', 112. **97** Ó Corráin, 'Early Irish churches', 328. **98** O'Brien, *Corpus*, 174–5, 438; Ó Muraíle, *Mac Firbhishigh*, i, 584–90; Byrne, *Kings and high kings*, 241–3, 250; AU, 663; AFM, 1154, 1179, 1191, 1222, 1224; RIA MS 12 D 9, 205. **99** Mills, *Gormanston*, 143. **1** AFM, 1180, 1206. **2** GO 192, 27.

the reference to the Butler lords of this cantred as lords of 'Akkill and Owles' we may safely infer that it contained the present baronies of Murrisk and Burrishoole.[3]

T25: *Umall*

Umall gives the cantred of Owyl. Umall is first mentioned by Tírechán (seventh century) while a reference to Uí Briúin Umaill of 787 shows that by then the fiction of descent from Brión was already current. That the immediate Umall ancestor in the Connachta pedigree was Conall Oirisen suggests rather that Fir Umaill were of the Partraige, an old lineage here (see **T16**). Kings of Umall occur regularly in the annals from 774 onwards although after 1176 its Uí Máille ruling line was replaced by Muirchertach Muimhnech, son of King Tairrdelbach Ua Conchobair, or perhaps by his sons in turn, a family certainly established as kings of Umall by the 1230s.[4]

C26: *Scleslouweth* (1195); *Slefluueth* (1240); *Sleoflow* (1333); *Sleflowe & the two Kerry's* (1347)[5]

As described in 1333 this cantred consisted of Sleoflow proper and three additional *theoda*. The rural rectory of 'Sliabloga' contained the parishes of Castlemore, Kilcolman, Kilbeagh and Kilmovee, basically that portion of the barony of Costello (in both Mayo and Roscommon) within the diocese of Achonry. In addition, Sleoflow proper must have contained the barony of Coolavin, Co. Sligo, in later medieval times the territory of the O Gara lineage who had earlier been kings of Gaelic Sliabh Lugha. The 'two Kerrys' are named in the extent as Caryoghtragh and Keryloghnayrne, names which occur with variations into the sixteenth century. The eponymous Loch na nAirneada is now Mannin Lake, shared between the parishes of Bekan and Aghamore. The rural rectory of Kiarraiduchtaraidlochnanaireneada, which combines the names of both Kerrys, consisted of the parishes of Aghamore, Bekan and Annagh, Co. Mayo. In 1585 the territory of Keryoughter contained lands in the parishes of Aghamore and Knock. From these references it is clear that the shape of the two Kerrys is preserved in that of that portion of Costello barony in Tuam diocese. The final *theodum* was Artagh or Airtech, whose rural rectory consisted of Tibohine parish, Co. Roscommon. Kilnamanagh was probably also in this cantred.[6]

T26: *Sliab Luga & Ciarraige*

This *trícha* was part of the regional kingdom of Luigne, a branch of whose kings ruled Sliab Luga (see under **T18**). In 964 Taithlech Ua Gadra is described as king of Luigne Deiscirt and this must surely represent the later Sliab Luga, the cantred of Sleoflow. From here came at least one Ua Gadra overking of all Luigne, in 1128, and Uí Gadra kings of Sliab Luga are recorded in 1181, 1207 and 1227.[7] At some stage Uí Gadra

3 Knox, 'Connacht'. ii, 58; Nicholls, 'Rectory, vicarage and parish', 71; idem, 'Butlers of Aherlow', 126. **4** Stokes, *Tripartite Life*, 322; Walsh, *Irish leaders and learning*, 195–6; Ó Muraíle, *Mac Firbhishigh*, i, 432–6; Knox, *Mayo*, 84–6; AU, 786, 812; AFM, 773, 779; AT, 1123, 1176; AI, 1095; ALC, 1235. **5** Mills, *Gormanston*, 143; GO 192, 27. **6** Knox, 'Connacht', ii, 60; Nicholls, 'Rectory, vicarage and parish', 71, 75–6; AFM, 1227, 1237, 1256, 1285, 1461; Knox, *Tuam, Killaha and Achonry*, 244; idem, *Mayo*, 319; Ó Riain et al., *Historical dictionary of Gaelic place-names*, 1, 47. **7** CS, 964; AFM,

must have taken over Coolavin, which had originally lain in Grecraige (see **T117**), as the later Uí Gadra kingdom was confined to Coolavin. The full title of this cantred was Sleoflow & the Two Kerrys. In addition to Sliab Luga 'proper', it contained three *túatha* of Ciarraige, which, with the fourth, Ciarraige Maige Aí, must originally have constituted an independent Ciarraige polity here. Most of these Ciarraige territories are mentioned by Tírechán in the seventh century, a *leth-rí* of Ciarraige Connacht is recorded in 847, a probable king in 997, and a certain king in 1032–3. Kings of Ciarraige Locha na nAirnead are recorded in 1155 and 1224 and this probably refers to the two western *túatha* of Ciarraige Locha na nAirnead and Ciarraige Uachtarach.[8] Ciarraige Maige Aí had already come under Síl Muiredaig control around 800 (see **C28**, **T28**) while the situation with the remaining *túath*, Ciarraige Airtig, is unclear. This was part of the cantred under discussion. Interestingly, all four *túatha* were within the bounds the diocese of Cong as constituted in 1111, but after 1152 the eastern two were transferred to Elphin, although the exact significance of this is unclear, as is the general position with lordship here. Airtech came under Mac Diarmata rule in the years before 1186 yet a reference of 1228 links Airtech with Sliab Luga.[9]

C27: *Miloc* (1215); *Syllanwath* (1333).[10]
The ancestor to the later barony of Longford, Co. Galway, and for which 'Syllanmuighie' was still an *alias* in 1585, even though there had been significant boundary change in the interim. As described in 1333, Sylanwath contained the parishes of Clonfert, Donanaghta, Meelick (its *caput*), Kiltormer, and Kilquain east of the Shannon/Suck and those of Lusmagh, Co. Offaly, and Creagh and Taghmaconnell, in Co. Roscommon. The deanery of Clonfert was the ecclesiastical parallel to this cantred, even to containing the parishes across the Shannon and Suck. This deanery helps fill in the gaps caused by obsolete toponyms in the extent and enables us to add the parishes of Fahy, Tiranascragh and Killimorbologue to the cantred. (Abbeygormican, although in Clonfert deanery, was not in the cantred of Sylanwath.) However, this leaves the cantred in two discrete portions, and we must add the Roscommon parish of Moore to unite both. As a detached portion of the diocese of Tuam this is not part of the deanery of Clonfert.[11]

1128; ALC, 1207, 1227; AU, 1181. **8** ALC, 1032, 1224; AU, 847; AFM, 997, 1155. **9** Stokes, *Tripartite Life*, 300, 320; Walsh, *Irish leaders and learning*, 199–200; Ó Muraíle, 'Connacht population groups', 165–73 (where his tentative locations of the various Ciarraige should be reconsidered in light of my identifications above); McErlean, 'Ráith Breasail', 8; Knox, *Mayo*, 79; AB, 1159, 1186; AC, 1228.3. **10** Brooks, *Llanthony Prima and Secunda*, 98. **11** Knox, 'Connacht', i, 393–5 (where Moyfyn is the rural rectory of Muyfynne identified by Nicholls with the parishes of Creagh and Taghmaconnell ('Rectory, vicarage and parish', 72); CDI, v, 221 (the following are the parish identifications here. Bolgu = Killimorbologue; Spathu = read Fathy: Fahy; Kiltonan = Kilquane; Lussnach = Lusmagh; Moyntirkynich = Muintir Chionnaith in Clonfert (Nicholls, 'Clonfert and Kilmacduagh', 137); Sukyn = Creagh (CPR, xvi, 49. This is Suicín, an important Anglo-Norman manor held by the Rochelle lord of the adjacent cantred of Tirmany but not part of that cantred. This is confirmed by pleas of dower of the late 1290s in which a Rochelle widow was claiming dower in one instance from the manor of Sukyn and in a slightly later version of the same plea from two villates of land in Moyfynne and where the same holding is clearly intended (RC 7/4, 229; 7/7, 15, 150)); Fynnawyr = Finure in Abbeygormican (Egan, 'Annates Clonfertensis',

T27: *Síl Anmchada*
The cantred of Sylanwath derives from the Irish kingdom of Síl Anmchada. This occurs as a territory in 951 and its kings are recorded regularly between 999 and 1235. The annals recognize two of these as overkings of Uí Maine (in 1032 and 1135), while the traditional king list of Uí Maine recognizes a further four, three of whom would seem to have lived during the eighth century. The eponym, Anmchad, would seem to have lived during the seventh century.[12]

C28: ***Kermochy Cleon Molroni*** (1200); *Schylmolrony* (1305); **Sylmolron** (1333)
This cantred is first described as Kermochy Cleon Molroni, giving the names of both its constituent *theoda*, Ciarraige Maige Aí and Síl Máelruanaid. (There is an early reference to the '*teod* of Selmoroni'.) The extent of 1333 shows that it included boroughs at Toberbride and Rathfernan, the former now Ballintober, Co. Roscommon. Knox did not make the connection between Rathfernan and the parish of Rathfaranayn/Raydcurnayn, which he wrongly identified with that of Bekan. In 1428 this parish (Rathfaranayn) was given the *alias* Sylmulruayn and was associated with the O Flynn family, lords of that territory. The name survived, as Cloghrahernan (still in O Flynn possession), into the seventeenth century as a super-denomination for much of Kiltullagh parish, other parts of which can be identified in the 1333 inquisition. In addition to the parishes of Ballintober and Kiltullagh this cantred must have contained that of Kilkeevin, the location of the ancient Ciarraige Maige Aí (see also **T26**). In 1305 the recently deceased de Rochfort lord of this cantred was said to have held twenty four villates in 'Typirbride and Rathfarnan in Schylmolrony'.[13]

T28: *Ciarraige Maige Aí & Síl Máelruanaid*
The cantred of Kermochy Cleon Molroni must derive from a *trícha* composed of two distinct *túatha*. The second element in the cantred name, Síl (Clann) Máelruanaid, claimed descent from a sixth-century offshoot of Uí Briúin Aí, a claim which should be treated with caution although it does suggest that this line was of some antiquity. Of course, it does not follow that Síl Máelruanaid were established here from an early time. Its rulers are always called *taísig* even though an offshoot became kings of Cremthann in Tír Maine (**T114**) in 999. Síl Máelruanaid first occur

70)); TCD MS 1066, f. 458.   **12** O'Donovan, *Hy Many*, 75; Kelleher, 'Uí Maine', 79, 82–3, 85, 88, 93, 96, 99; ALC, 1235.   **13** Nicholls, 'Charter of William de Burgh', 122; Curtis, 'Feudal charters', 289; Knox, 'Connacht', ii, 59–60 (where Fichbary is the super-denomination of Coillte O'Barra (*Fidh = Coill*) in the extreme south-west of Kiltullagh as recorded by O'Donovan (OSNB, Kiltullagh parish) and Clanfadd is the nearby Cloonfad); Knox, *Tuam, Killaha and Achonry*, 196; CPR, viii, 8; CPR, x, 544; 'O'Doherty, 'Annates, Tuamensis', 63; RC 9/15, Jas I no. 24; CIPRJ, 264–5; BSDR, 21–2 (which shows that Cloghraharanan included at least the present townlands of Coolcam, Coolfineen, Milltown, Glanline, Ballybane, Rathleany and Clooncalgy. The actual location of Rathfernan itself remains uncertain, possibly Stonepark South where there is a burial ground or Milltown which had an old church marked in 1841); Hogan, *Onomasticon*, 232; RC 7/11, 133. The fifteenth-century Prendergast association with the rectory of Radcurnayn (Nicholls, 'Rectory, vicarage and parish', 72) must date back to the tenure of Gerald fitz David de Prendergast here in 1268, when he held the villates of Fythbarry and Faythoskirt of Henry de Rochfort, lord of the manor of 'Shilmalron' (RC 7/1, 441; 7/4, 30).

in the annals in 1130. The second *túath* here was Ciarraige Maige Aí. This must originally have formed part of the independent Ciarraige kingdom here (see **T26**). This
túath was wasted by Síl Muiredaig in 805 after its people had slain a Síl Muiredaig
dynast placed over it, and it cannot subsequently have had any independent history. While Baslick lay in this *túath* in Tírechán's time, it was later occupied by a branch
of Síl Muiredaig and, significantly, the border between the dioceses of Airther
Connacht and Cong as fixed at the synod of Ráith Breasail excluded Baslick from
Ciarraige Mag Aí. There is no record of any king of this *trícha*.[14]

C29: *Tirameli* (1195); *Tyramlyff* (1308); **Tyraulyf** (1333)[15]
This and the cantred of Bac & Glen (**C6**) taken together are ancestors to the present barony of Tirawley, Co. Mayo. While the 1333 inquisition names only a few
places in this cantred the extent of the rural rectories of 'Tyreaiwhaly' and Bredach
enable us to complete the extent. The former rectory contained the parishes of
Ballysakeery, Doonfeeny, Kilbride, Kilcummin, Lackan and Templemurry, and
Bredach those of Kilfian and Moygawnagh. Killala and Rathreagh must have lain
in this cantred as well. As the inquisition names places in both rectories we can be
sure that the *theodum* of Bredach was part of Tyraulyf despite the claims of the lords
of Bac & Glen to it. Further confirmation of this is to be found in the pattern of
impropriation here, where most of these rectories (including that of Bredach) were
either held or claimed by Mullingar priory.[16]

T29: *Tír Amalgado*
The eponym Amalgaid, if the genealogies of Uí Fhiachrach an Tuascirt are correct,
would have lived in the mid-fifth century (see **T30**). While numerous lineages are
derived from him it is clear that this territory (**T29**) had early come under the direct
sway of the mainline and did not maintain its own ruling line. Note, however, an
Ua Siblén king of Uí Echach Muaide in 1159 (of a lineage not mentioned by Mac
Firbisigh). This territory represented the eastern half of Tír Amalgado while na
Brétcha (Bredach), significantly described by Mac Firbisigh as a *leth trícha cét*, gives
the other moiety. The later ruling family of Uí Fhiachrach, Uí Dubda, retained sole
possession of the overkingdom and there is some evidence that one of the unsuc-
cessful discard segments of this lineage, Clann Domnaill, were compensated with
the kingship of Tír Amalgado during the second half of the twelfth century.[17]

C30: *Tirfichre Omohy* (1195); *Tireighrachbothe* (1200); **Tyromoy** (1333);
Tyryethrachmoye (1340); **Tyreragh** (1347)[18]
This is ancestor to the present barony of Tireragh, Co. Sligo. The inquisition of
1333 names two cantreds in this territory, those of Tyromoy and Castleconor, but

14 Ó Muraíle, *Mac Firbhishigh*, i, 452; Walsh, *Irish leaders and learning*, 199; Stokes, *Tripartite Life*,
320; McErlean, 'Ráith Breasail', 14. **15** Mills, *Gormanston*, 143 RC 7/7, 4. **16** Knox, 'Connacht',
ii, 59; idem, *Mayo*, 290; Nicholls, 'Rectory, vicarage and parish', 73. **17** Ó Muraíle, *Mac Firbhishigh*,
i, 594; Knox, *Mayo*, 46; AU, 1159. **18** Mills, *Gormanston*, 143; CDI, i, 22; BM Add. MS 4789,
220; GO 192, 27.

the remaining evidence relates solely to a single cantred here, and this reference is almost certainly corrupt or inaccurate. The de Lacy grants of 1195 and 1240 mention only one cantred here while the 'Irish' extent of Tír Fhiachrach (**T30**) is similarly undivided. Furthermore, the appendant fees in the 1333 inquisition are clearly confused. I can find no other reference to a cantred of Castleconor, as stated in the inquisition. In 1333 and again in 1340 the manor of Castleconor ('Castleconchowyr') was said to lie in Tyryethrachmoye/Tyrearachmoye. It may be that the de Bermingham manors of Castleconor and Culcnawa represented two half-cantreds here. The rural rectory of Castleconor contained the rectories of Castleconor, Easky and Kilglass while that of Culcnawa contained those of Dromard and Skreen, suggesting the likely division. This cantred must therefore have contained the present barony of Tireragh.[19]

T30: *Tír Fhiachrach Muaide*
This branch of Uí Fhiachrach an Tuascirt, which duly came to dominance, was one of several with a north Connacht base, all apparently of fifth-century provenance. Their first king of prominence was Dúnchad Muirisci, king of Connacht, who lived in the late seventh century, and who seems to have replaced a related ruling line here. Three further kings of Connacht were amongst his descendants (707–73). This line, Uí Fhiachrach Muaide *alias* Uí Fhiachrach Muirisc, took their titles from the eastern Moy valley and the coastal strip east of Kilalla Bay (Muiresc). By the mid-eighth century the title used by their kings was characteristically *rí Ua Fiachrach & Ua nAmalgada*, to indicate the regional kingdom. These names give Tír Fhiachrach Muaide (a territory in 1191) and Tír Amalgada, which in turn give the cantreds of Tyryethrachmoye (**C30**) and Tyraulyf (**C29**). Tír Fhiachrach Muaide is the original demesne *trícha* of this line.[20]

CORK[21]

Four lists of cantreds for Cork have come down to us, from 1301, 1346, 1358 and 1375.[22] In Cork, as in Limerick and Tipperary, some cantreds experienced periodic amalgamation, and their number is therefore not constant. In the fourteenth century, the colonized portion of the county was arranged into ten cantreds, two of which occasionally divided into four, giving a maximum number of twelve. By this time eight cantreds in western parts of the county had been lost to the land of peace, giving a maximum number for the county of twenty cantreds.

19 Knox, 'Connacht', ii, 59 (where his identification of Conegdunmore (see COD, ii, p. 333) with Castleconor is, of course, erroneous: this was the cantred of Conmakne Dunmor); idem, *Mayo*, 295; Ó Muraíle, *Mac Firbhishigh*, i, 618–24; Nicholls, 'Rectory, vicarage and parish', 73–4; BL Add. MS 4792, f. 157; NAI Lindsay MS, vol. 6. **20** Ó Muraíle, *Mac Firbhishigh*, i, 593, 598, 606; O'Brien, *Corpus*, 438; Ní Dhonnchadha, 'Cáin Adomnáin' 204; Byrne, *Kings and high kings*, 298; AU, 603, 815, 909, 938; ALC, 1128, 1192; AT, 1096, 1143; AFM, 1135, 1162, 1191. **21** What follows is largely based on my 'Cantreds of Desmond', with revision. **22** RC 7/8, 76–91; CCH, 52, 72; Richardson and Sayles, 60–2.

C31:Eastern section = ***Winterderich & Legarha*** (1207); ***Corkely*** (1282)
   Western section = ***Ubulc & Bere*** (1213)
   Entire cantred = ***Corkelye & Berre*** (1299)[23]

This cantred is divided into two discrete sections. The first section is the half-cantred of Winterderich & Legarha, later given as the half-cantred of Corkely. These names derive from Muintir Doirc and An Garrga, the two *túatha* which made up this section of the cantred. These territories occur in a pre-Invasion tract concerning Corcu Loígde which helps to locate them. Confirmation of this identification can be found in the parishes of the rural deanery of Corkygh Teragh (probably from Corca Laoighdhe Iartharach) of 1306 and its successor of 1615, Collymore & Collybeg. This section contained the parishes of Myross, Castlehaven, Tullagh, Creagh, Aghadown, Kilcoe, Abbeystrowry and Clear. The application of the regional-kingdom name, Corca Laoighdhe or Corkely, to just this section of cantred, after 1207, may perhaps be due to the displacement westwards of the ruling family of Uí Eterscéoil by the colonists. The second section is that of Ubulc & Bere, which comprised the greater portion of the Beara Peninsula. Its extent must have been similar to that of the deanery of Boerry of 1302, which contained the parishes of Kilcaskan, Killaconenagh, Kilnamanagh and Kilcatherine.[24]

T31: *Corcu Loígde & Bérre*

No evidence of the names of the original local kings survives for the regional kingdom of Corcu Loígde, far removed from the northern centres where the annals were compiled. Corcu Loígde was an important naval power in later centuries and preserved faint memories of having once ruled Munster. The cantredal stucture here was complex, with three divisions in the main section of the diocese of Ross and a fourth in the diocesan outlier of Beara (**C31, C43, C50**). The overall shape of the main section can be confirmed by a tract on this polity dated by Ó Corráin to post-1111 which lists many of its *túatha*. Again, a Meic Carthaig propaganda tract of the 1130s implies the existence of three *trícha* here.[25]

The Corcu Loígde tract shows that the *trícha cét* of 'Trícha Meadhónach' (**T50**) comprised seven *túatha*. Yet the later cantredal structure shows that the westernmost two of these, Dúthaig Uí Gilla Michíl *alias* Muintir Doirc and Túath Uí Chonneid (An Garrga), had later been detached from Trícha Meadhónach and added to Bérre, to form **T31**. This movement seems to echo the expulsion westwards from Trícha Meadhónach of the ruling family, Uí Eterscéoil. While this may have occurred under the colonists, as suggested above, it is just as likely that this event was as a result of Uí Echach Muman pressure on Corcu Loígde before the Invasion. Significantly, Uí Eterscéoil retained the entire area of **T31** after the Invasion. The western section of **C31/T31**, at least once styled Ubulc & Bere, preserves the name of Uí Builc, ancestors to Uí Eterscéoil.[26] This must represent the westernmost of the three original

23 Nicholls, '*Pontificia*', 96; CDI, iii, 492. **24** MacCotter, 'Sub-infeudation', ii, 98–9; idem, 'Cantreds of Desmond', 53. **25** Ó Corráin, 'Corcu Loígde', passim; Bugge, *Caithreim*, 29. **26** For the Corcu Loígde genealogies see O'Brien, *Corpus*, 256–63 and O'Donovan, 'Chorca Laidhe', 3–65.

*trícha*s of Corcu Loígde of *Caithréim Cellacháin Chaisil*. Although by the twelfth century the western border of this outlier corresponded closely to the modern county
border, mention of Áes Glinne Sibne as part of Corcu Loígde indicates that originally Uí Builc & Bérre may have extended as far north as the *glen* of the *Sheen* at
Kenmare.

C32: *Fermoy* (1228, 1301, 1358, 1366)[27]
See p. 31.

T32: *Fir Maige*
This is the best documented *trícha cét* in Ireland because of its contemporary extent,
Críchad an Chaoilli.[28] When this extent is compared with that of the later cantred of
Fermoy it will be seen that both units were virtually identical in area. The record
suggests the presence of two local kingdoms here, memory of which seems to be
echoed in the belief of the author of *Críchad* that the single *trícha cét* of his time is
the result of an earlier unification of two such distinct units, which are delineated
in the tract. By the time of *Críchad* the lords of Fir Maige were Uí Chaím, the successful ruling family of the kingdom of Eóganacht Glennamnach. This lineage were
certainly direct lords of the eastern moiety of Fir Maige and it would appear that Uí
Dubhagáin, a ruling family of original Fir Maige stock, were mesne lords, under Uí
Chaím, of the western moiety. Kings of the original Fir Maige are recorded in 638,
908, 1014 and 1016, and kings of Eóganacht Glennamnach in 891, 1046 and 1135.
However, at least one late seventh-century king of the royal line of Eóganacht
Glennamnach is actually described as king of Fir Maige (perhaps anachronistically).[29]
After 1135 Uí Chaím abandoned the style *rí Glennamnach* in favour of *rí Fir Maige*,
clearly demonstrating a consistent differentiation between the term Fir Maige in a
lineage and toponomastic sense. *Lebor na Cert* reflects the mesne lordship of
Eóganacht Glennamnach over the western polity. The existence of these two local
kingdoms is likely to be of considerable antiquity. Eóganacht Glennamnach were
certainly established at Glanworth by the mid-seventh century and perhaps as early
as around 580.[30]

C33: *Iflanlo* (1365); *Flanlow* (1439).[31]
This cantred appears to have been among those – including Kenalbek – held by
Richard, brother to Milo de Cogan, one of the first lords of Cork. By the time Cork
cantredal lists begin, in the early fourteenth century, much of Flanlow is in the power
of the Irish. This probably explains why the cantred is subsequently found united
with that of Kenalbek for administrative purposes, although one late and somewhat
uncertain cantredal ascription occurs. Another Cogan relative and namesake, Richard,
lord of Muscrimittine (**C42**), had been enfeoffed of Flanlow, which appears to have

27 MacCotter, 'Sub-infeudation', i, 90; RIA MS 12 D 10, 161.   **28** See Appendix 3.   **29**
MacCotter, *Colmán*, 54, 61n.   **30** Ibid., 61; AI, 629; CS, 641; Dillon, *Lebor na Cert*, 34.   **31** Armagh
PL MS KH II 46, 195.

been a distinct cantred.[32] The Cogan *caput* here was at Dundrinan (now Castlemore, Moviddy parish), and we know the manor of Dundrinan *alias* Flanlow[33] to have contained lands in the parishes of Moviddy, Kilmurry, Dunisky and Macloneigh at the height of colonial power here during the thirteenth century.[34] The parish of Inchigeelagh shows an interesting pattern of impropriation, with those lands north of the River Lee being impropriate to the Cogan foundation of Mourneabbey (*Mona*) and those south of the river being held by Gillabbey (*de Antro*).[35] This suggests that the cantredal border here followed the river and divided this parish in two, with its northern half being in Muscrimittine and its southern in Iflanlo. This also suggests, of course, that the cantredal border here was older than its parish formation. Kilmichael, erected in 1493 from parts of the parishes of Macloneigh and Inchigeelagh, must also have lain in this cantred, along with that of Cannaway, much of which was cross-land.[36]

T33: *Uí Flainn Lua*
The area of the regional kingdom of Uí Echach Muman is later occupied by six cantreds (**C33–8**), the names of which must indicate the local-kingdom structure here. This structure was grouped around the two principal divisions of Uí Echach, Cenél Áeda and Cenél Láegaire, each with three *tríchas*.[37] The cantred of Flanlow is derived from Uí Flainn Lua, a segment derived from a son of Láegaire, eponym of Cenél Láegaire.[38]

C34: *Foniertheragh* (1299); *Funerthrath* (1301)[39]
The extent of this cantred must be preserved in that of the 1615 rural deanery of Fonieragh, which consisted of the parishes of Kilmocomogue, Durrus, Kilcrohane, Caheragh (described as being 'in Funerthrath' in 1301), Skull and Kilmoe. The rectories of the first three of these parishes were impropriate to St Catherine's abbey, Waterford, the customary monastic beneficiary of the Carew lords of Cork, whose moiety of Cork included Foniertheragh. The rectories of the remaining three parishes are later found in the possession of the earls of Desmond, successors to the Carews as lords of Foniertheragh.[40]

T34: *In Fonn Iartharach*
In Fonn Iartharach: the western land, may have been relatively recent Uí Echach swordland. It first occurs as a territorial designation in 1283 but must be of pre-Invasion origin. Its southern peninsulas had originally been part of Corcu Loígde, some of whose aristocratic families remained here into the twelfth century, while Benntraige (Bantry) gave their name to the northern half.[41]

32 Jefferies, 'Anglo-Norman Cork', 35; PRC, 195. **33** Brewer and Bullen, *Cal. Carew MSS Misc.*, 362–3. **34** DKRI 36, pp 63–4 (where 'Clonehyt' represents Macloneigh); AI, 1261.11; Sheehy, *Pont. Hib.* i, 152; White, *Extents*, 105, 120. As late as 1317 the area under Cogan control here extended well into Kilmurry parish (AI, 1317.2). **35** *Civil Survey*, vi, 323. **36** CPR, xvi, 65–7. **37** O'Brien, *Corpus*, 210–12. **38** Ó Donnchadha, *An Leabhar Muimhneach*, 173. **39** MacCotter, 'Sub-infeudation', i, 75. **40** *Archivium Hibernicum* 2 (1913), 189; UCC MS U/83/8/69; MacCotter, 'Sub-infeudation', i, 75; Ó Murchadha, 'Dún Mic Oghmainn', 78–9. **41** AI, 1283; O'Donovan,

C35: *Glinshalewy* (1260); *Glynshalewy* (1298); *Glansaluy* (1299); *Glansallwy* (1372)[42]
The 1615 deanery of 'Glansalny' (read Glansaluy) contained the parishes of Kinneigh, Fanlobbus, Desertserges, Ballymoney, Murragh, Drinagh and Dromdaleague. By the mid-fourteenth century the 'paper' lordship of this cantred had passed from the Carews to their de Courcy equals, and it is noteworthy that the later de Courcy lords of Kinsale retained possession of the rectory of Garrinoe in Desertserges parish into the nineteenth century.[43]

T35: *Clann Selbaig*
This may have been the *trícha* of the Uí Donnchada kings of Cenél Láegaire, and sometimes of Uí Echach, whose power-base certainly lay hereabouts. Selbach was one of their direct ancestors and probably lived during the seventh century. Clann Selbaig occur as a lineage in 1283.[44]

C36: *Kinalbek* (1301); *Kenalbek* (1345); *Cenalbech* (1375); *Kinealbeky* (1456)[45]
The extent of this cantred can be reconstructed from the list of its vills amerced in the '1301 List', in addition to a detailed extent of that large segment of Kinalbek comprising the Barry Óg manor of Inishannon. The area given by these sources includes lands in the parishes of Inishannon, Brinny, Ballymodan, Killowen, Kilbrogan, Templemartin, Moviddy, Aglish, Kilbonane, Desertmore, Athnowen, Knockavilly, the adjacent detached segment of Dunderrow, Kilnaglory, Carrigrohane, and Inishkenny.[46]

T36: *Cenél mBéicce*
This polity had its own king in 1161, and so was a local kingdom. We may extrapolate from this that the other *tríchas* of Uí Echach (**T33–5, 37–8**) must also have been local kingdoms, whose records are denied us by the extremely meagre annalistic coverage of this region. The overking of Uí Echach is styled 'ardrí', further emphasizing this point. Bécce occurs in the main Cenél Áeda pedigree, and so is claimed to be a direct ancestor to the Uí Mathgamhna ruling family here. He appears to have lived in the mid-seventh century. The precise genealogical filiation of the king of 1161 is unclear.[47]

C37: *Kenalethe* (1301); *Kenelech* (1346); *Kenalle* (1358); *Kenneleth East* (1375)
C38: *Kynaleth Ytheragh* (1301); *Kynnaleth Ertragh* (1346); *Kenneleth West* (1375); *Kennale to West* (1406)[48]
The 1301 list of amerced vills for Kenaleth can be supplemented by an even more extensive extent (of the manor of Ringcurran, the *caput* of Kenaleth) from 1335.[49] Both sources agree well, and give the area included in the civil parishes of

---

'Chorca Laidhe', 42–3. **42** MacCotter, 'Sub-infeudation', i, 73–4. **43** LPL MS Carew 635, fos. 29–31; CIPRJ, 497. **44** O'Brien, *Corpus*, 210–12; AI, 1283. **45** Nicholls, 'Lordship, Co. Cork', n. 190; COD, iii, 370. **46** *Dinnseanchas* 2/1, 3–5; RC 7/9, p. 210; RC 8/20, p. 192. **47** AI, 1161; O'Brien, *Corpus*, 210–12. **48** NAI Fergusson MS xv, 21. **49** *Dinnseanchas* 2/1, 5–6; RC 8/20, 192.

Ringcurran, Ballyfeard, Ballymartle, Ballyfoyle, Clontead, Kinure, Kilmonoge, Templemichael, Nohaval, Tisaxon, southern Cullen, the main segment of Dunderrow and the greater portion of Ballinaboy as comprising Kenaleth. The 1301 list for Kenaleth Ytheragh[50] gives an area comprising the parishes of Ringrone, Kilbrittain, Kilroan, Ballinadee, Templetrine, Rathclaren, Leighmoney and Kinsale. This extent can be confirmed by records of the de Courcy manor of Ringrone, the *caput* of this cantred.[51] These include lands in all of the above parishes, in addition to that of Tisaxon.

T37: *Cenél Áeda*
T38: *Cenél Áeda Iartharach*
The cantred of Kenaleth (**C38**) derives from Cenél Áeda, which must have been the *trícha* of the Uí Mathgamna kings of Uí Echach. To west of this lay Kenaleth Ertragh (**C38**), whose affix (Iartharach), indicates its pre-Invasion origins.

C39: *Cantred of the Ostmen* (1177); *Kericuruhy* (1216); *Kerycurk* (1301); *Kery* (1375); *Kyarrai Churyhy* (1538)[52]
First attested as 'the cantred of the Ostmen' [of Cork], soon it is described as 'the cantred of Kericuruhy, namely that cantred which the Ostmen of Cork held'.[53] As indicated by its amerced vills in 1301, this cantred contained all of the present barony of Kerrycurrihy and the greater portion of that of Cork lying south of the north channel of the Lee.[54] Kericuruhy further included the northern part of Cullen parish. All of Kilpatrick must also have lain in Kericuruhy and, apparently, Tracton.[55] Its western boundary was marked by the Curraheen River, also the western boundary of the main portion of St Finbar's parish.[56] A further partial template for this cantred are those rectories impropriate to Gillabbey (*de Antro*), namely Carrigaline (*caput* of the feudal barony of Beauvoir *alias* Kericuruhy), Ballinaboy, Kilmoney and Barnahely.[57]

T39: *Ciarraige Cuirche*
A reference to Ciarraige Cuirce as a dynasty and kingdom occurs in 828.[58] Their genealogy ends with their king who died in battle in 908 just as a more permanent Norse settlement became established at Cork.[59] It is hardly coincidental, therefore, that the later cantred of Kericuruhy was first attested (in 1177) as 'the cantred of the Ostmen' and one suspects it also to have been a demesne territory of the Meic

---

50 *Dinnseanchas* 2/1, 7–9. **51** LPL MS Carew 635, f 4, is a copy of an extent of Ringrone manor of 1372, in which about two-thirds of the place-names can be identified. For other references see Brewer and Bullen, *Cal. Carew MSS Misc.*, 371; BL Add. MS 4790, f. 69v; RC 7/8, 477; 7/9, 94; 7/12, 289; 8/20, 17. **52** *Topographer & Genealogist* 1863, 455. **53** Ware, *History of Ireland*, 119–20; Nicholls, 'Inqs. 1224', 111. **54** *Dinnseanchas* 2/1, 9–11. **55** Jefferies, 'Anglo-Norman Cork', 34. **56** Nicholls, 'Lordship, Co. Cork', n. 190, quoting a deed of 1456 which describes the Curraheen ('Glassynysheanaghe') as dividing the cantreds of Kierychuryhi and Kinealbeky. **57** Fiant. Eliz., 3538. **58** FIA, p. 156. **59** Lec. 120rd30; BB 159a50; Ó Muraíle, *Mac Fhirbhishigh* ii, 468; AFM, 903.

Carthaig kings of Cork. This is a typical pattern involving several changes of dynasty where the lineage name of the original ruling line is retained.

C40: *Mackill* (1254); *Ymakille* (1301); *Mac Kyll* (1358); *Machyll* (1375); *Imchill* (1404)[60]
In its presentation in 1301 before the justices in eyre the cantred of Ymakille was described as including all the modern barony of Imokilly, the Barrymore parishes of Mogeesha, Inchinabacky, Clonmel and Templerobin, and the Co. Waterford parishes of Tallow, Kilwatermoy, Kilcockan and Templemichael.[61] Here, however, Ymakille includes the additional cantred of Oglassyn (**C48**), with which it was sometimes united for administrative purposes. For most of the fourteenth century these cantreds, each with its own chief-serjeant, were treated seperately, although again united in the list of 1375.[62] Ymakille comprised the Carew manor of Castlecorth (Ballynacurra near Midleton) and the episcopal manor of Cloyne.[63] The eastern border of Ymakille thus ran approximately from Danganodonovan in the north to Kilcredan on the coast. Oglassyn constituted the remainder of the area detailed in 1301.

T40: *Uí Meic Caille*
The regional kingdom of Uí Liatháin is well attested from 646 onwards. Ogam references to *Mucoi Liteni* suggests evidence of the lineage that ruled this kingdom from as early as the sixth (fifth?) century. In addition, we should note the probable reference to one of the royal line of this kingdom in a late sixth-century poem.[64] The territory of this kingdom comprised four cantreds under the Anglo-Normans (**C40, 44, 48, 49**), which must represent Irish local kingdoms. One of these was Ymakille, which derives from Uí Meic Caille.

Kings of Uí Meic Caille are recorded in 906 and several times during the twelfth century.[65] The political situation in the regional kingdom of Uí Liatháin is unclear after 1127 when record of its kings cease. Several ruling families of Uí Meic Caille follow one another after this date but these seem to have ruled an area greater than the local kingdom of Uí Meic Caille itself, and it may be that by Uí Meic Caille here we should understand the entire regional kingdom. There are some indications that the western section of Uí Meic Caille, Uí Thassaig, (from which may derive the parish name Mogeesha) had kings of its own around AD 900. The king of Uí Meic Caille of 906, Glassín, descended from a mid-eighth-century offshoot of the Uí Liatháin mainline.[66]

C41: *Musckiri onDunegan* (1207); *Muskeridon* (1301); *Muscridonegan* (1346); *Muscrydonygan* (1402)[67]
The 1301 list of amerced vills[68] describes its colonial portion, which included all but the very western section, over which, however, the Barry lords of the cantred claimed suzerainty as of their manor of Ardnacrothen or Athnacrothen

60 *Analecta Hibernica* 2 (1931), 221; PRC, 132. **61** *Dinnseanchas* 2/2, 44–50. **62** MacCotter, 'Cantreds of Desmond', n. 12. **63** Idem, 'The Carews of Cork', i, 66; ii, 68; PRC, 3–22. **64** CS, 646; Macalister, *Corpus*, 269; MacCotter, *Colmán*, 42. **65** FIA, 906; AFM, 1135, 1151, 1160. **66** O'Brien, *Corpus*, 225, 228–9; Ó Buachalla, 'Uí Liatháin', 31–3; LL, l. 6624. **67** Armagh PL MS KH II 24, f. 88v; PRC, 122. **68** *Dinnseanchas* 2/1, 11–12.

(Newmarket).[69] The extent of the entire cantred is confirmed by the area of the rural deanery and those parishes impropriate to the Barry foundation of Ballybeg (priory of St Thomas; *Bothon*), as well as by the lands of the episcopal manor of Kilmaclenine – 'in Muscridonegan' – which completes the picture by adding the cross-lands.[70] These three sources agree exactly. The core of the cantred descended into the present barony of Orrery & Kilmore, while Muscridonegan also included in the north-east the entire parishes of Ballyhay, Ardskeagh and Imphrick and part of the Co. Limerick parish of Colmanswell *alias* Cloncourth. Westwards, Muscridonegan included at least half of what is today the barony of Duhallow, namely the rest of Ballyclough and Tullylease, and Roskeen, Clonmeen, Castlemagner, Subulter, Kilroe, Knocktemple, Kilbrin, Kilcorcoran and Clonfert.

T41: *Múscraige Uí Áeda*

Múscraige Uí Áeda or Múscraige Trí Maige duly became the cantred of Muscridonegan, after its ruling family, the later O Donegans. Four kings of Múscraige Uí Áeda are recorded between 845 and 1045,[71] some of whom were of Uí Dondacáin, not to be confused with the unrelated Uí Donducáin of **T42**. The linkage between both ruling genealogies is remote.[72] Evidence from the early ninth century suggests that Orbraige was a polity in Iarmumu and this can only have been in Múscraige Trí Maige where a *theod* of Orrery lay in 1212 which has partly given its name to the modern barony of Orrery and Kilmore.[73] This unit may be the Orbraige referred to in *Lebor na Cert*. Did Múscraige supersede Orbraige in kingship here? The *Frithfholaid* texts imply the existence of an overking of Múscraige under Cashel and a late echo of this may be found in the person of Ronán mac Cuirc, joint king of Múscraige Breogain (near Cashel) and of Múscraige Mittíne, who died in 1025 (unless, of course, this is an error).[74]

C42: *Muscry Omittone* (1207); *Muscryemychene* (1254); *Muscrilyn* (1345); *Muscrimittyn* (1358); *Moyscrilyn* (1372)[75]

The 1301 amercement list[76] describes the colonial eastern half of the cantred although the high incidence of unidentified place-names has to be supplemented by records of the Cogan lordship here, which, fortunately, are plentiful, if mostly unpub-

---

69 In the 1290s the Barrys possessed three manors in Muscridonegan: Buttevant, Liscarroll and Ardnacrowan/ Ardnacrothen. A slightly later variant is Adnogrothen, suggesting an identification with the parish name Anathcrohan in Muscridonegan deanery. Later again an inquisition states that Diarmaid MacCarthy gave his son as hostage to the earl of Desmond at Athenacrogham. This place must be the later parish of Anacherochayn *alias* Clonferta, the modern Clonfert, where, in the sixteenth century, was located Kanturk castle, the chief place of MacCarthy's descendants, the lords of Duhallow. Therefore this manor is to be identified with Clonfert and other western parts of Muscridonegan. 'Killanaghcrohane' occurs as an *alias* for Newmarket in 1622. See RC 8/17, 89; BL Add. MS 4790, 165v; CCH, 68; *Analecta Hibernica* 23 (1966), 19; *Archivium Hibernica* 24 (1961), 10; CIPRJ, 553. **70** PRC, 30–4. For the rural deaneries of Cloyne in 1306 see CDI, v, 273–8, 310–13. **71** AI, 1010, 1029, 1045; AFM, 843. **72** O'Brien, *Corpus*, 371–2. **73** McNeill, *Reg. Kilmainham*, 140. **74** Meyer, 'Laud Genealogies', 315–17; Dillon, *Lebor na Cert*, 24, 28; AI, 1025. **75** Hardy, *Rot. Chart.*, 173; *Analecta Hibernica* 2 (1931), 221; CCH, 83; COD, iii, 370. **76** *Dinnseanchas* 2/3, 65–7.

lished.[77]The episcopal manor of Donoughmore, an extent of which survives, is explicitly stated to have lain in this cantred, while another useful source is the list of parishes impropriate to the Cogan foundation of Mourneabbey (*Mona*).[78] This foundation lay adjacent to the Cogan *caput* of Mona in Muscrimittine. The extent of the deanery of Muscrylyn confirms these sources, all showing that this cantred contained the parishes of Whitechurch *alias* Donoghanere, Grenagh, Mourneabbey, Kilshannig, Donoughmore, Garrycloyne, Matehy, Carrigrohane Beg, Inishcarra, Magourney, Aghabulloge, Clondrohid, Aghinagh, Macroom, Kilnamartery and Ballyvourney. Kilcorney cannot be identified in the early deanery list, and, while it lay in the seventeenth-century deanery of Muscridonegan, the possession of its rectory by Mourneabbey indicates it to have originally lain in Muscrimittine.

T42: *Múscraige Mittíne*
This gives the cantred of Muscrimittine. The corresponding deanery of Muscrilyn derives from what was an alternative name for the cantred, deriving from its Uí Fhlainn kings. Reference to **T42** as a territory occurs in 828 and references to at least three of its kings occur between 1025 and 1115.[79] These represented both ruling segments of Múscraige Mittíne, Uí Bercháin and Uí Blaithmeic, dividing perhaps during the seventh century, and giving respectively Ua Donducáin and Ua Flainn kings. As to the borders of Múscraige Mittíne, among its *túatha* as listed in a pre-Invasion source was Túath Uí Chiabaig, later represented by the parish of Drishane. Yet this was subsequently part of the cantred of Alla (**C46**) and lay across a diocesan border from Muscrimittine. From this it would seem that this *túath* was in conflict between these two *tríchas*.[80]

C43: *Obaddamnia* (1228); *Obathan* (1301); *Obaghann* (1346); *Obaon* (1375)[81]
The extent of the cantred of Obathan, as suggested by the vills amerced within it in 1301,[82] contained lands earlier included in the cantred of Rosselithir (**C50**), and it is apparent that the colonial remnant in the south-eastern portion of the latter cantred, having survived the McCarthy onslaught after Callann, was for utilitarian purposes thereafter included in Obathan. In order to gauge the actual extent of Obathan it is necessary to compare the probable extent of its three manors: Timoleague, Rynnanylan (Courtmacsherry) and Lislee, with the corresponding rural deanery of 'Obathumpna', while subtracting those parts of Obathan earlier described as lying in Rosselithir.[83] This indicates that Obathan consisted of the parishes of Kilmaloda, Lislee, Timoleague, Templequinlan, Abbeymahon, Donaghmore, Templeomalus and Desert.

77 Lands in the parishes of Kilshannig, Mourneabbey, Grenagh, Whitechurch, Garrycloyne, Carrigrohane Beg, Iniscarra, Matehy, Magourney, Clondrohid and Ballyvourney can be shown to have lain within the Cogan lordship of Muscrimittine *alias* Mona (CJRI, i, 65, 160; PRC, 64; DKRI 36, p. 63; RC 7/5, 395, 475; RC 7/8, 277; RC 7/13, 54; RC 8/6, 237–8; RC 8/29, 686, 716; GO MS 192, p. 96). Possible identifications with lands in Donoughmore and Aghinagh also occur (PRC, 58–62; RC 7/6, 47). **78** PRC, 58–62; White, *Extents*, 104–5; Fiant Eliz., 3121. **79** AI, 828, 1025, 1096; AFM, 1115. **80** Ó Muraíle, *Mac Firbhishigh*, iii, 277; O'Connell, 'Annatis Ardfertensis', 11, 19; Butler, *Gleanings*, 272.**81** Oxford MS Rawl. B 499, 125v. **82** *Dinnseanchas* 2/1, 6–7. **83** Nicholls, 'Barry charters', passim.

T43: *Uí Badamna*

This was the third *trícha* of the regional kingdom of Corcu Loígde (see **T31**), from which derives the cantred of Obathan. The pedigree of its dynasty fails to get as far as the tenth century and there is no later record of this line apart from the reference of *c.*900 to one Cobhtach as 'rí Ua Badamna'.[84] The *trícha* is not mentioned in the Corcu Loígde tract and the pattern of patronage of Abbeymahon (Mainistir Ua mBadhamhna: *Fons Vivus*) suggests that, at least by the 1160s, this *trícha* had been incorporated into the regional kingdom of Uí Echach Muman.[85]

C44: *Ocurblethan* (1271); *Courblyan* (1346); *Curiblethan* (1372); *I Correblehan* (1520)[86]

In the fourteenth century this cantred was often united with that of Olethan (**C49**) for administrative purposes, as, for instance, before the justices in eyre in 1301. However, the existence of a serjeanty of Ocurblethan and several other references to it as a distinct cantred survive.[87] While initially thought by the invaders to have been part of Olethan, its cantredal independence was soon recognized once proper cognisance was taken of indigenous pre-Invasion boundaries, no doubt once the military stage of the Invasion was over. Ecclesiastical confirmation of the independence of Ocurblethan is illustrated by the presence of its deanery in the diocese of Cork while that of Olethan lay in Cloyne. A partial ecclesiastical extent of 'Ucurp' from 1199 survives, showing it to have been similar in extent with the later deanery of Ocurblethan.[88] Records of the Prendergast manor of Shandon *alias* Ocurblethan agree with the area of the deanery.[89] Therefore Ocurblethan contained lands in the parishes of Ardnageehy, Dunbolloge, Kilshanahan, Kilquane, Killaspugmullane, Templeusque, St Michaels, Caherlag, Ballydeloher, Little Island, Rathcooney, SS Mary's and Ann's Shandon, Kilcully, and Currykippane.

T44: *Uí Chuirb Liatháin*

The diocesan border which divides this *trícha* from that of Uí Liatháin (**T49**) must have been in existence since at least the mid-twelfth century. Its eponym, Corb, is a remote figure somewhat removed from the mainline of Uí Liatháin. The recorded pedigree of his descendants ends in the mid-eighth century. The separation of this *trícha* from the remainder of the regional kingdom by its inclusion in another diocese is perhaps due to its having been taken over intact as demesne territory by the Meic Carthaig kings of Desmumu during the early twelfth century.[90]

C45: *Yoghenacht Lokhelen* (1200); *Ionath Edoneth* (1254); *Ogenathy Donechud* (1281); *Owenathydythontha* (1365)[91]

A detailed study of local lordship structure, ruridecanal structure and patterns of

84 O'Donovan, 'Chorca Laidhe', 23; LL, 6624. **85** AI, 1231.3; Gwynn and Hadcock, 125. **86** *Topographer & Genealogist* 1865, 449. **87** DKRI 36, p. 23; CCH, 52; MacNiocaill, *Red Book of Kildare*, 139; Caulfield, 'Early charters', 449. **88** Ó Murchadha, 'Decretal letter', 84, 87–92. **89** MacNiocaill, *Red Book of Kildare*, 139–43; PRONI MS D/3078/2/1/1; RC 7/1, 271, 294; 7/2, 252, 256, 320; 7/3, 275; 7/6, 220, 249, 267; 7/12, 114; 8/5, 53–4. **90** O'Brien, *Corpus*, 224–5, 229–30; Ó Buachalla, 'Uí Liatháin septlands', 35–6; MacCotter, *Colmán*, 115–16. **91** Armagh PL

monastic impropriation, suggest that this cantred contained the parishes of Killarney, Aghadoe, Killaha, western Kilcummin and Kilcredan. While this is usually treated as a single cantred an inquisition of 1281 mentions its 'three cantreds', and this is almost certainly to be understood as a reference to Ogenathy Donechud 'proper' and its two associated cantreds, described below (**C46** and **C47**).[92]

T45: *Eóganacht Locha Léin*
This was the name of an ancient regional kingdom, one of the most powerful in Munster in the early historical centuries. Its area of hegemony declined dramatically during the eighth century, becoming subject to its former subjects to the north, Ciarraige. It is likely that it contained three local kingdoms, one of which appears to have born the name of the overkingdom, but no direct evidence of this survives. Memory of this threefold division may be preserved in the early genealogies of this people, whose three main branches bear names ancestral to what appear to have been later colonial cantreds.[93]

C46: *Aylly* (1282), *Alle* (1299); *Allith* (1305); *Alla* (1365)[94]
This would appear to be the second of the three cantreds of Ogenathy Donechud. Records of the colonial lordship of Alla indicate it to have contained lands in the parishes of Cullen, Drishane, Drumtariff and eastern Kilcummin. The pattern of impropriation associated with its FitzElias lords adds Kilmeen to the above parish list. Nohoval Daly must also have lain in Alla. The name is preserved in the later barony name Duhallow (Dúithche Ealla), a significantly larger area. There is one somewhat uncertain cantredal ascription.[95]

T46: *Áes Aella*
Aella/Ealla and Iste (see **T47**) are toponyms rather than personal names and both lines are linked into the main stem of Eóganacht Locha Léin in the remote period. They may be of some antiquity as local kingdoms.[96]

C47: *Osyste/Glanorogtey*
The modern barony of Glanarought appears to represent the area of the third cantred of Ogenathy Donechud. This unit probably originates in the ancient local kingdom of Áes Iste (see **T46**). The MacCarthy entail of 1365 associates Osyste (Áes Iste) and 'Glanorogtey' together. Osyste occurs in the parish name Tuosist (from Túath Áesa Iste).[97] This toponym suggests the southwards relegation of the original ruling line by later kings or lords, as the lordship pattern here indicates that this unit was ruled from the main unit (Loch Léin). Note the association of Uí Muircheartaig, the last indigenous royal line of Eóganacht, with Áes Iste in the *Topographical Poems*,[98] an association confirmed by record of conflict between Uí Muircheartaig and the Carew lords of Glanarought, and the apparent rule of the Glanarought area by the Uí

MS KH II 46, 195. **92** MacCotter, 'Cantreds of Desmond', 55–7. **93** O'Brien, *Corpus*, 388–9. **94** CDI, ii, 492; CJRI, i, 228; RC 7/11, 38; Armagh PL MS KH II 46, 195. **95** MacCotter, 'Cantreds of Desmond', 55–6. **96** O'Brien, *Corpus*, 388–9. **97** MacCotter, 'Cantreds of Desmond', 55, 57. **98** TP, 49.

Donnchadha junior line of Glenflesk in the mid-thirteenth century.[99] These were descendants of an earlier line of kings of Eóganacht Locha Léin.

T47: *Áes Iste*
See **C47** and **T46**.

C48: *Oglassin* (1187); *Oglassin & Offergus* (1299); *Oglassyn* (1325, 1346)[1]
For the area of this cantred see **C40**. Offergus comprised the parishes of Oglassin which now lie in Co. Waterford.

T48: *Uí Glaisín*
The eponym, Glassín, was king of Uí Meic Caille (**T40**) in 906. This suggests that Uí Glaisín may not be as old a local kingdom as Uí Meic Caille, and perhaps was created when Uí Glaisín were superseded as kings of Uí Meic Caille at some time between the early tenth to mid-twelfth century. After 1177 the Anglo-Normans briefly relegated the kings of Uí Meic Caille to the position of kings of Uí Glaisín. The cantred of Oglassin (sometimes styled Oglassyn & Offergus) included at least four parishes in the diocese of Lismore, a territory known to the Anglo-Normans as Offergus (Uí Fhergusa). One would expect the diocesan and cantredal boundaries to be identical; is the explanation for this divergence the addition of Offergus to Uí Glaisín after the boundary of Lismore was set at Kells-Mellifont as some kind of royal demesne territory? At the centre of Uí Fhergusa was an important Meic Carthaig fortress, Oileán Mail Anfaid (Molana), which suggests that this territory may have become Meic Carthaig demesne, appendant to Lismore to the north.[2]

C49: *Olethan* (1177, 1207, 1301, 1346, 1358, 1375); *Oleghan* (1393)[3]
Usually amalgamated with Ocurblethan (**C44**) for administrative purposes, Olethan was in fact a distinct cantred. The combined area of both are given in the '1301 List'.[4] Olethan had a parallel rural deanery of the same name, whose extent agrees well with the few surviving records of the Barry lordship of Olethan, which comprised two manors, Castleolethan (now Castlelyons) and Carrigtohill.[5] Olethan contained the parishes of Castlelyons, Knockmourne, Mogeely, Ballynoe, Aghern, Coole, Britway, Rathcormack, Gortroe, Templebodan, Lisgoold, Ballycurrany, Carrigtohill, Templenacarriga, Ballyspillane, Dungourney, and Clonmult.

T49: *Uí Liatháin*
This name was shared by both regional kingdom (for which see **T40**) and local kingdom. This local kingdom was the home of the overkings of the regional kingdom,

---

99 MacCotter, 'The Carews of Cork', i, 66–8; AI, 1253; MIA, 1254. **1** MacNiocaill, *Red Book of Kildare*, 14; PRO SC 8/98/4889. **2** Ó Buachalla, 'Uí Liatháin septlands', 30; Scott and Martin, *Expugnatio Hibernica*, 237; MIA, 1182; AI, 1170.3. **3** Armagh PL MS KH II 24, 88v, 90; KH II 46, 237. **4** *Dinnseanchas* 2/3, 61–5. **5** MacCotter, 'Cantreds of Desmond', 51. For records of the Barry lordship of Olethan see Barry, *Barrymore*, 20, 27, 48; PRC, 76–8; RC 7/6, 350; 7/9, 200; 7/10, 76, 343; 8/17, 93–5; GO MS 192, pp 178, 211.

Uí Anmchada, who appear to have descended in an unbroken line of kings dating back to the late sixth century. This lineage fell from power early in the twelfth century. The western border of this *trícha* partially forms a diocesan border as well, proving its existence from at least the mid-twelfth century.[6]

C50: *Rosselithir* (1207), **Rosyletir** (1229), **Rossilider** (1254, 1261), *Rosselhir* (1355); *Tryuchamenach* (1527)[7]
A combination of lordship records and the extent of the rural deanery of Ross combine to enable us to delineate this cantred.[8] It contained the parishes of Ross, Kilgariff, Templebryan, Kilnagross, Island, Rathbarry, Castleventry, Kilkerranmore, Ardfield, Kilfaughnabeg, Kilmeen, and Kilmacabea.

T50: *An Trícha Meadhónach*
The chief place of this *trícha* was the episcopal seat of Ros Ailitihir (Rosscarbery), which gives the successor cantred its name. As its name implies, this was the middle *trícha* of the three into which the regional kingdom of Corcu Loígde was divided. As this *trícha* contained the chief church of the kingdom, it must represent the local kingdom of the original kings of Corcu Loígde, Uí Chonaill, who were replaced by rivals, Uí Builc, around 900. The last Irish kings of this *trícha*, Uí Chobthaig, claimed descent from the earlier Uí Chonaill kings.[9] There is evidence to suggest that the boundaries of this *trícha* were altered sometime after 1111 (see under **T31**).

DUBLIN

This county had four cantreds. Early records of these mostly occur in relation to their serjeanties which, as royal possessions, occur in exchequer pipe rolls. These records refer to the serjeanties of (1) the Vale of Dublin in the region of Newcastle Lyons and Taxsagard (**C51**), and (2) the Vale of Dublin in the region of Bree [Bray] and Newcastle McKynygan (**C52**), while north of the Liffey there were respectively the serjeanties of Fyngal to north (**C53**) and to south (**C54**) of the water of Gouere.[10] There was no cantred of Dublin as Dublin was earlier a regional kingdom rather than a local kingdom.

C51: *Lymhim* (1207); **Newcastle Lyons & Taxsagard** (1228 to 1344); *Clondalkin* (1377); **Newcastle by Lyons** (1407, 1413)
Those cantreds south of the Liffey can be described although the dividing line

6 O'Brien, *Corpus*, 225, 228–9; Ó Buachalla, 'Uí Meic Caille', 24; idem, 'Uí Liatháin septlands', 28–30. 7 Armagh PL KH II 46, 175; Nicholls, 'Lordship, Co. Cork', 179; idem, 'Some Barry Charters', 116; RIA MS 12 D 9, 85. 8 MacCotter, 'Cantreds of Desmond', 54. 9 Ó Corráin, 'Uí Chobthaigh', passim; for the Corcu Loígde genealogies, see O'Brien, *Corpus*, 256–63 and O'Donovan, 'Chorca Laidhe', 3–65. 10 DKRI 35, p. 31; 39, pp 21, 53, 69; 42, p. 52; 43, p. 32; 44, pp 18–19; 54, pp 21, 23.

between them is somewhat unclear. These were the two cantreds retained by Henry II in his own hand when he granted Leinster to Strongbow, and together formed the area of the pre-Invasion kingdom of Uí Dúnchada, ruled by its Meic Gilla Mo-Cholmóc kings. The western cantred certainly included Newcastle Lyons and Saggart, representing the pre-Invasion territory of Uí Dúnchada proper, and must have extended southwards to include those parts of the medieval county west of the watershed of the Wicklow Mountains, apparently described as being among the lands of Macgillamochalmoc 'on the other side of the mountains' (that is, the western side) in a grant of 1173, an area approximating to that of the rural deanery of Ballymore. This would have included the parishes of Ballybought, Ballymore and Tipperkevin, which today lie in Kildare, and the Wicklow parishes of Kilbride, Blessington, Burgage, Boystown, Hollywood, Crehelp, Tober, Dunlavin, Rathsallagh and part of Donard. This area would be the 'half-cantred of the abbey of Glendalough next to Ballymore' referred to in a grant of 1185, and the 'tenement of half a cantred within the diocese of Glendalough' of 1213, when given the *alias* Coillech (Hollywood). Presumably the remaining half-cantred here was the lands of Newcastle itself in south-west Dublin. This cantred is 'the cantred of Lymhim' granted by King John to Diarmait Mac Gilla Mo-Cholmóc in 1207, where Lymhim (later Lyons, as in Newcastle Lyons) represents a corruption of *Liamhain*. It occurs as the 'cantred of Clondalkin' in 1377. As late as 1413 a chief serjeant was appointed to 'the cantred of Newcastle by Lyons'.[11]

T51: *Uí Dúnchada*
The powerful lineage of Uí Dúnlainge, which had risen to dominance in Laigin Tuadgabair (see under **T65**), divided into three segments during the early eighth century, each of which in turn formed distinct kingdoms. These derived from various sons of Murchad, king of Uí Dúnlainge (d. 727). Each of these kingdoms expanded its territory at the expense of older local kingdoms which were absorbed and extinguished. The third brother, Dúnchad mac Murchada (d. 728), was ancestor to Uí Dúnchada, whose regional kingdom was later represented by two cantreds, Newcastle Lyons (**C51**) and Fercoulen (**C52**).

The cantred of Newcastle Lyons appears to derive from the *trícha* of Uí Dúnchada 'proper', as distinct from the regional kingdom of the same name. Uí Dúnchada may have moved into this area as early as the late eighth century, and were certainly here by the early tenth century, when one of their kings is styled Lorcán Liamna (from Liamhain or Newcastle Lyons, their later seat).[12] The Uí Dúnchada tract mentions two territorial units in the kingdom in addition to Fir Chualann: Uí Dúnchada 'proper' and Uí Gabla, both of which seem to have lain in **T51**. Uí Dúnchada itself certainly contained all of south Dublin west of the Dodder. Nicholls' tentative location

11 McNeill, *Alen's Register*, 2, 21, 210; Mills, 'Norman settlement in Leinster', 161; Nicholls, 'Land of the Leinstermen', 537–9; Gilbert, *Crede Mihi*, 33–4; Hardy, *Rot. Chart.*, 173; Hunter, *Rotuli selecti*, 68; Frame, 'Commissions of the Peace', 11; NAI Fergusson MS xv, p. 31; CDI, i, 77. 12 LL, 6625; Gilbert, *City of Dublin* i, 404 (for which see Nicholls, 'Land of the Leinstermen', 537); Byrne, *Kings and high kings*, 289.

of Uí Gabla (Fine) as somewhere around Ballymore and Hollywood seems accept-
able, for where else within the Uí Dúnchada overkingdom can it have lain?[13] Kings
of Uí Gabla are recorded around 900 and again in 1072.[14]

C52: ***Bree & Newcastle McKynygan*** (1228 to 1344); ***Fercoule[n]*** (1303); *Fercolyne*
(1482).
This eastern cantred certainly contained Bray and Newcastle (Makinegan). It was
based on that part of Mac Gilla Mo-Cholmóc's kingdom known as Fir Chualann,
as is clear from reference to the *cantred de Fercoule[n] in Valle Dublin*. The constituent
túatha of the *trícha* of Fir Chualann (**T52**): Uí Briúin, Uí Chellaig and Uí Théig, survived in truncated form as the manors of Obrun, Okelly and Othe. The lands of
these manors can be identified as including all of Co. Dublin south of the city from
Tallaght eastwards and that north-eastern part of modern Wicklow extending
south to include the royal manor of Newcastle Makinegan. The southern border
of this cantred (which was also that of the medieval county of Dublin), was formed
by the southern limits of both parishes of Newcastle. Further confirmation of this
may be had from the royal confirmation of 1173, where land is clearly arranged
under cantredal headings, and where Glendalough held lands stretching
from Templeogue southwards to Delgany in Wicklow, all said to lie 'in the land of
Macgillamochalmoc'.[15]

T52: *Fir Chualann*
The political history of the regional kingdom of Uí Dúnchada is complex.
Geographically this area was known as Cualu, essentially the Dublin and Wicklow
mountains and their littorals.[16] Here the earliest kings were Uí Théig of whom were
several kings of Leinster between the late sixth century and 715. The actual kingdom
name used by these dynasts was Cualu, and this may have represented an overkingdom covering much of the area, to west as well as to east of the mountains. The styles
Cualu and Uí Théig are used interchangeably by its last kings, whose line ends in 831.[17]

　　The next reference to descendants of these Uí Théig/Cualu kings occurs in 915,
when a collateral branch, descended from Eterscél, a son of Cellach Cualann (d.
715), now style themselves kings of Uí Chellaig Cualann. Eterscél is probably the
king of Brí (Bray) recorded in 726 and their territory now appears limited to the
east side of the mountains.[18] In the same general area we find Uí Briúin Cualann,
whose first king is recorded in 738, and who are linked politically with the early Uí
Dúnlainge. The subsequent transfer of the Bray area to Uí Briúin Cualann suggests
that they grew in power at the expense of Uí Chellaig Cualann whose last kings

13 Nicholls, 'Three topographical notes', 409–13; idem, 'Land of the Leinstermen', 537–9; Price,
Place-names of Wicklow v, 336–7; Dillon, *Lebor na Cert*, 104; Gilbert, *City of Dublin*, 406–7; Todd,
Cogad, 154. **14** LL, l. 6612; AU, 1072. **15** Nicholls, 'Land of the Leinstermen', 538, 552; idem,
'Three topographical notes', 409–13; McNeill, *Alen's Register*, 2, 21, 247; Cambridge University
Library MS Add. 3104, f. 59. **16** O'Brien, *Corpus*, 14; Price, *The place-names of Co. Wicklow* vii,
pp vi–vii. **17** Byrne, *Kings and high kings*, 288; Ó Muraíle, *Mac Firbhishigh*, ii, 245; AU, 777, 803,
831. **18** O'Brien, *Corpus*, 76–7; Mac Shamráin, *Glendalough*, 46–9, 92–3; AFM, 915; FIA, 726.

died in internecine strife during the 1030s.[19] It seems likely that the combined area of Uí Briúin and Uí Chellaig after about 900 included south Dublin east of the Dodder and north eastern Wicklow as far south as Newcastle, exactly the area of the later cantred of Fercoulen which is derived from Fir Chualann. In 894 an Uí Briúin dynast is styled king of Fir Chualann while a twelfth-century tract on Uí Dúnchada uses the term 'Fir Chualann' as referring to a concrete territory, which I believe to have been the *trícha cét* of Fir Chualann. Kings of Uí Briúin Cualann occur down to 1130, although its later pedigrees are confused. The undoubted Ostmen settler presence in parts of this area does not seem to have had any impact on the indigenous units of spatial organization here.[20]

C53–4: *The cantreds of Fyngal*
The Fyngal cantreds are easy enough to describe, consisting of that area of Co. Dublin north of the Liffey, divided by the River Gouere or Gowre, now known as the Broad Meadow Water.[21] Thus we have Fyngal north of Gouere (**C53**) and Fyngal south of Gouere (**C54**), cantreds which occur continuously in the record during the period 1228 to 1344.

T53: *Saithne (in Fine Gall)*
The Lecan Miscellany refers to Fine Gall as a *trícha*, apparently a reference to Túath Tuirbe.[22] What later became Fine Gall originally comprised two minimal polities, Saithne and Túath Tuirbe. The Uí Chathasaig kingdom of Saithne was part of the Gailenga/Luigne conglomerate which shook off the overlordship of Deiscert Breg before 1000 and subsequently challenged for the title *rí Breg*. Nine kings of Saithne are recorded between 1019 and 1179.[23] At the time of the Invasion the ecclesiastical benefices of this kingdom contained all of the barony of Balrothery West and much of Balrothery East, an area lacking evidence of significant Ostmen settlement ('Okadesi's land of Finegall').[24] Indeed, Saithne must have contained the great monastery of Lusk as well, whose abbacy had been held into the ninth century by a branch of Ciannachta Mide.[25] There is late and perhaps unreliable evidence to suggest that the Uí Chathasaig kingdom here included Kilsallaghan, south of the Gouere.[26] Saithne, therefore, was probably identical in area with the later cantred of Fyngal North (**C53**). The abbacy of Lusk in Saithne was outside of the diocese of Glendalough (= Dublin) as established in 1111 but had been absorbed by Dublin by 1148, a development which probably reflects the contemporary transfer of Saithne from Mide to the regional kingdom of Dublin or Dyflinarskiri. Thus Saithne was not originally in Fine Gall, a term which must initially have referred exclusively to

19 O'Brien, *Corpus*, 73, 342–3, 431; Nicholls, 'Three topographical notes', 409–13; AFM, 738; AT, 1030, 1037. **20** Gilbert, *City of Dublin*, i, 406–7; AFM, 783, 868, 955, 1061, 1130; AT, 1027, 1048; AU, 880; FIA, 908; Bradley, 'Scandinavian settlement', 56–7. **21** *Civil Survey*, vii, 223, 233. This river remained an important barony border until the revisions of the 1830s. **22** GT, 190. **23** ALC, 1019, 1045; AT, 1023, 1160; AU, 1021; AFM, 1086, 1153, 1179. **24** McNeill, *Alen's Register*, 14, 24; Gilbert, *Crede Mihi*, 57–8. **25** Ó Corráin, 'Early Irish churches', 328. **26** Bhreathnach, 'Tara', 6–7.

T54 below. Confusion regarding the overlordship of Saithne continued into the colonial period, when its status was contested between the lordship of Meath and the royal demesne of Dublin.[27]

T54: *Fine Gall*
The second polity here was the Gailenga-derived Túath Tuirbe, a toponym preserved as Turvey, near Swords. This territory included Glasnevin and Tuirbe must originally have contained all of southern Fine Gall. Reference to *Túath Tuirmhe* occurs in an annal of 603. The Gailenga pedigree of the ruling Uí Chormaic ends in one Cormac Tuirbe but the only king of Tuirbe recorded in the annals (in 902) does not feature in it.[28] This area experienced heavy Ostmen settlement, no doubt resulting in its new name, Fine Gall, which first occurs in the annals in 926 (AU). There is some evidence to suggest that, under the overlordship of Diarmait Mac Murchada, the lordship of T54 was granted to Meic Giolla Mócholmóg of Uí Dúnchada in the mid-twelfth century. The division of Fine Gall into two cantreds echoes the earlier Irish arrangement of two local kingdoms here.[29]

KERRY

Medieval Kerry was somewhat smaller than its modern equivalent, much of the south then being part of Cork. Two lists of Kerry cantreds survive (1346 and 1375), showing the medieval county to have contained at least seven cantreds.[30]

C55: *Hakemy* (1189); *Akunkery* (1200); *Acumkery* (1282); *Acmys* (1295); *Akomys* (1375); *Trughenackmye* (1584)[31]
An extent of 1298 of the manor of [Castle] Island, the *caput* of this cantred, survives. The place-names which can be identified in this refer to locations within the parishes of Castleisland, Tralee, Ballymacelligott, Dysert, Currans, and Brosna.[32] The 1306 rural deanery list of Acumys contains all of these parishes, as well as those of Ratass, Ballyseedy, Nohoval, Killeentierna, Ballincuslane, Kilbonane, Molahiffe and Aglish.[33] Further sources confirm this extent, in particular the 1584 extent of the 'cantred of Trughenackmye' and the impropriate rectories held by the lords of Acumys, the earls of Desmond (that is, Castleisland, Killeentierna, Aglish, Tralee, Ballymacelligott and Nohoval).[34]

T55: *In Trícha*
The thirteenth-century cantred of Acumys is given an indigenous parallel in the annals, In Trícha, from whence the later Triúcha an Aicme.[35] The early forms

27 Flanagan, *Irish royal charters*, 72; and see the following footnote. 28 AU, 603, 902. 29 GT, 191; Ó Muraíle, *Mac Firbhishigh*, ii, 657; Walsh, *Leaders and Learning*, 83–4; Ó Corráin, 'Early Irish churches, 328; Lec. 222va30; Flanagan, 'Historia Gruffud vab Kenan', passim; eadem, *Irish royal charters*, 276; Bradley, 'Scandinavian settlement', 58–9. 30 MacCotter, 'Cantreds of Desmond', 57. 31 Ibid., 58; Hardy, *Rot. Chart.*, 77; CJRI, i, 20; COD, ii, 429. 32 'Cantreds of Desmond', nn. 69, 70. 33 For the rural deaneries of Ardfert see CDI, v, 294–8. 34 MacCotter, 'Cantreds of Desmond', nn. 71, 72. 35 AI, 1275.3.

'Akunkerry' and 'Kery'[36] for this cantred indicate an original form *Aicme Ciarraige, which may perhaps suggest that this *trícha* originated as swordland of the Ciarraige in a (late?) southwards push against other polities, for which I cannot uncover direct evidence. The lower Laune lands of this cantred must surely have belonged at an earlier stage to Eóganacht Locha Léin. Here the River Maine, its southern bank a bog and dense forest zone into the seventeenth century, once formed a natural frontier. Despite this, however, it would seem that In Trícha did contain these southern lands at the time of the Invasion. This is suggested by various references to Uí Flaithim, a family who occur as *airchinnig* of Ardfert and give their names to *bailte* in the parishes of O'Dorney and Killiney, all of which securely locates them within Ciarraige. They are also eponyms of Molahiffe, a parish and plain lying south of the Maine and which links the Cois Leamhna parishes of Kilbonane and Aglish to the remainder of In Trícha. The impropriation of the tithes of Molahiffe by Abbeydorney, a pre-Invasion foundation, further strengthens the nexus.[37]

C56: *Listuthal* (1190); *Alterie* (1295); *Altry* (1301, 1346)[38]
Thirteenth-century lordship sources locate lands in the parishes of Listowel, Kilconly, Kilnaughtin, Finuge, Dysert and Aghavallen in Altry. Meiler fitz Henry, lord of Altry, endowed his foundation at Rattoo with all benefices in his possession around 1206, and Rattoo is later found holding the vicarages or rectories of Listowel (*caput* of Altry), Rattoo, Dysert, Murher, Knockanure, Kilnaughtin, Killehenny, Ballyconry, Aghavallen, Galey and Lisselton. An earlier lord of Altry, William de Burgh, appears to have endowed his foundation of Athassel with benefices in Killehenny, Kilconly and Aghavallen. All of the above parishes constituted the early rural deanery of Altry.[39]

T56: *Alltraige*
The cantred of Altry represents the older kingdom name Alltraige, which seems to have represented a distinct polity into the mid-seventh century, until eclipsed by Uí Ferba (**T59**). Ogam inscriptions indicate the existence of the Alltraige dynasty in fifth-century Kerry.[40]

C57: *Killorg[l]an* (1254); *Moconekyn* (1286); *Mayconcken* (1299); *Kilorglan* (1299); *Maghconkyn* (1365)[41]
Evidence for the cantredal structure of south Kerry is meagre and sometimes contradictory, yet it is possible to perceive its broad outline. Clearly Killorglin was the *caput* of Moconekyn, while Kilcolman and Kilgarrylander certainly lay in it. The pattern of impropriation and landownership of Killagha priory (*de Bello Loco*: Kilcolman parish), in addition to the ruridecanal structure here, further suggests the inclusion of Kiltallagh and Kilnanare in Moconekyn.[42] While Moconekyn is ances-

36 Hardy, *Rot. Chart.*, 77b; CDI, i, no. 2680. **37** AI, 1032; MIA, 1214.3. **38** MacCotter, 'Cantreds of Desmond', 57; CJRI, i, 44; DKRI 38, p. 97. **39** MacCotter, 'Cantreds of Desmond', 57; idem, 'Anglo-Norman Kerry', 41–3. **40** Macalister, *Corpus*, 240, 244; Ó Corráin, 'West Munster ii', passim. **41** Armagh PL MS KH II 46, 195. **42** MacCotter, 'Cantreds of Desmond', 60–1 (where the evidence presented is here re-interpreted).

tor to the later barony name, Magunihy, the territories represented by both bear little relation to each other due to name-drift.[43]

T57: *Áes Conchind*

The kingdom of Corcu Duibne is attested in ogam inscriptions of the fifth century
naming its female ancestor, Dovvinia, yet later sources are meagre.[44] At least three
cantredal names survive, Ossurys (**C60**), Moconekyn (**C57**) and Orathath (**C59**),
which can be related to the early history of this people. (It may be of some relevance to note that Ó hUidhrín mentions just these three also.) A tract of the 1130s
also implies the existence of three *trícha*s here.[45] The annals record only kings of
Corcu Duibne. Moconekyn derives from Mag Coinchinn, whose extent, at the
head of Dingle Bay, is clear. This takes its name from the Áes Conchind, an offshoot of the main stem.[46]

C58: *Hyerba* (1200); *Offarbe be West Stronde, Offarbe be Estronde* (1346); *Offarbe* (1375); *Offeorba* (1441); *Ofarriba alias Farbowe* (1584)[47]

This cantred was in three distinct parts, all bordering Tralee Bay. The northern two
are sometimes described as one half cantred, the remainder making up the other.
The 'stronde' dividing these was the *trá* of the River Lí (Tralee). The few medieval
lordship records here are supported both by the area of the early rural deanery of
Offerba and the late sixteenth-century extent of 'the cantred of Ofarriba'. The north-
ernmost section consisted of the parishes of Ballyheige and Killury. The central section contained the parishes of Ardfert (main portion and southern outlier),
Ballynahaglish (in which was located the *caput* of Offarbe, at Tawlaght), and
Clogherbrien. The western section, which lay entirely on the Corca Dhuibhne
peninsula, contained the parishes of Cloghane, Ballyduff, Stradbally, Killiney,
Kilgobban and Annagh, all fronting Tralee Bay, and the eastern portion of
Ballinvoher parish, fronting Dingle Bay. This latter half-cantred section is still known
in Irish as Leithtriúch: the half-cantred, and Lettragh in English. This very distinc-
tive tripartite shape is further confirmed by being exactly reproduced on a sixteenth-
century map.[48]

T58: *Uí Ferba*

Uí Ferba were the ruling family or lineage of the regional kingdom of Ciarraige
Luachra, the eponyms of Co. Kerry. Uí Ferba first emerge in the mid-seventh century and remain dominant. The later kings of Ciarraige, Uí Chonchobair, were of
Uí Ferba. Ogam inscriptions indicate the existence of Ciarraige as a dynastic name
in fifth-century Kerry.[49] The extent of the cantred of Offarbe may therefore represent the original area ruled by Ciarraige Luachra before their expansion eastwards
and northwards, which began in the seventh century.

43 Ibid., n. 86; idem, 'Anglo-Norman Kerry', 54, 60–1. **44** Macalister, *Corpus*, 146, 149, 152,
156, 168, 171. **45** Bugge, *Caithreim*, 29; TP, 48. **46** For the Corcu Duibne genealogies see
O'Brien, *Corpus*, 378–9; Ó Muraíle, *Mac Firbhisigh*, ii, 129–30. **47** *Kerry Magazine* 1854, 169.
48 MacCotter, 'Cantreds of Desmond', 59–60. **49** Ó Corráin, 'West Munster' ii, passim; O'Brien,
Corpus, 132, 287–8, 391; Ó Muraíle, *Mac Firbhishigh* ii, 434, 464.

C59: *Orathath* (1244); ***Dunloy*** (1254); ***Denloyth*** (1282); ***Orathoh*** (1283); *Irahath* (1365)[50]

I have changed my interpretation of the evidence since I last wrote about this cantred.[51] I now believe that the cantred of Orathath and that of Dunloe are one and the same, the latter being merely a metonym. This is clear from the grant of chase and free warren granted to John fitz Thomas of Shanid in 1244, which included Orathath but no other lands in south Kerry. Compare this with the comprehensive Geraldine inquisition of 1282, which solely lists the (half-) cantred of Dunloe in the same region. As one might expect for such a mountainous cantred, Orathath was usually united with that of Moconekyn (**C57**) for administrative purposes, although occurring independently on a couple of occasions. This cantred approximately comprised the Iveragh peninsula. Its northern and eastern boundaries can be deduced from those of its surrounding cantreds here. It certainly contained Dunloe – its probable *caput* – and Valencia 'and other islands'. Its first lord, Geoffrey de Mareis, appears to have endowed his foundation of Killagha with most of the rectories of Orathath. In summary, Orathath probably contained the parishes of Knockane, Templenoe, Kilcrohane, Dromod, Glanbehy, Killinane, Caher, Valencia, Killemlagh, and Prior.

T59: *Uíbh Ráthach*
This *trícha* derives from Ráthach, a remote offshoot of the Corcu Duibne mainline.
It seems to have been the home of Áes Irruis Deiscirt, perhaps 'the people of the southern peninsula', one of the two main groupings of Corcu Duibne.[52] The name survives in that of the peninsula name, Iveragh.

C60: *Ossuris* (1240, 1375); *Ossoris* (1254); *Ossur* (1295); *Ossurrys* (1346)[53]
Lordship references locate Dingle (its *caput*), Ballinacourty, Ventry, Dunquin and Kilmalkedar in Osurrys. Killagha priory, founded by the first lord of Osurrys, Geofffrey de Mareis, held the rectory of Dingle and the vicarages of Dingle and Garfinny. De Mareis also founded the preceptory of Any, Co. Limerick, which held the rectory of Minard. The early deanery list for Osurrys is rather damaged, but allows us to add Kildrum, Kilquane, Kinard, the obsolete parish of Inch (in Ballinvoher), and probably Dunurlin. This extent agrees well with that of the descendant of Osurrys, the sixteenth-century cantred of Corkaguiney.[54]

T60: *Áes Irruis*
The cantred of Osurrys derives from the first part of the population term, Áes Irruis Tuascirt, perhaps 'the people of the northern peninsula', one of the two major divisions of Corcu Duibne.[55]

50 LPL Carew MS 610, f. 49; Armagh PL MS KH II 46, 195.   **51** MacCotter, 'Cantreds of Desmond', 60–1; 'Anglo-Norman Kerry', 67–8; 'Sub-infeudation and descent', 101–3.   **52** Uí Ráthach is not, as MacNeill, thought, recorded on an early ogam. See Bergin, 'Varia 7. Uí Rethach', passim.   **53** *Analecta Hibernica* 2 (1931), 252; CJRI, i, 45.   **54** MacCotter, 'Cantreds of Desmond', 58–9; 'Anglo-Norman Kerry', 67–8.   **55** See **T57**.

C61: *Othorna & Oflannan* (1299); *Ottorne* (1346).

An early rental roll of the FitzMaurice lords of this cantred is our chief source for its extent. This refers to lands in the parishes of Kilmoyly, the adjacent and detached portion of Ardfert, Odorney, Killahan, O'Brennan, Kiltomy, Kilflyn, Kilfeighny, Kilshenane and Duagh. To this should be added the *caput*, Lixnaw, and its parish of Kilcaragh. This is confirmed by the pattern of impropriation here, with six of the above parishes being impropriate to Any, Co. Limerick, representing the ecclesiastical rights to 'one cantred in Kerry' of a grant of before 1212. All of this is confirmed by the area of the rural deanery of Othorna & Oflannan.[56]

T61: *Uí Thorna & Uí Fhlannáin*

The cantred of Othorna & Oflannan must represent a *trícha* called Uí Thorna & Uí Fhlannáin where the former indicates an ancient lineage division and the latter a much later ruling line. The linkage of this alleged ancestor, Torna Éces, with the Ciarraige genealogy is unhistorical and this *trícha* must represent a polity early eclipsed by Uí Ferba (**T58**).[57] The Ciarraige genealogy is patently artificial.

KILDARE

Medieval Kildare comprised five large cantreds, and was much bigger than the modern county and included, in addition, large parts of counties Leix, Offaly and Wicklow. Professor Otway-Ruthven has attempted an extent of the cantreds of Kildare but her work is unsatisfactory and requires revision. Otway-Ruthven's principal mistake was to use as her primary source the topographical details from the eyre of Kildare of 1297, where pleas were heard by juries chosen by cantred, to fashion what she thought was the extent of these cantreds based on the places mentioned in the pleas heard before each cantredal jury. Her assumption that all places mentioned before each jury lay in each relevant cantred does not bear up under scrutiny.[58] Had she sought other sources to confirm her findings she might have seen this. Her error led her to include Oboy and Obargy (which she called Slievemargy) in Kildare when these cantreds lay in Carlow, while she overestimated the size of the cantred of Leys and underestimated that of Omurthi and of Wykinglo & Arclo.

---

56 'Cantreds of Desmond', 57–8.   57 Ó Corráin, 'West Munster', i and ii, *passim*; GT, 183.   58 CJRI, i, 167–208. Close scrutiny of this source reveals that, while the majority of places mentioned in pleadings presented before these cantredal juries did indeed lie in the relevant cantred, this was not always so. To take just a few examples of many: Killybegs and Clonshanbo are mentioned before an Offaly jury but lay in Offelan; Bremoy, which lay in Tothmoy, is mentioned before a Leys jury; Littlerath, mentioned before a Leys jury, lay in Offelan; while Castelloboy, which did not even lie in the county, was also mentioned before a Leys jury (pp 174, 177, 199–200, 202). Often defendants were alleged to have committed separate crimes in several different places, sometimes clearly lying in different cantreds, and it is not clear if the principal of selection was the residence of the defendant or the location of the crime. Again, one has to take into account that these courts were medieval and would not have suffered from the modern plague of bureaucracy. A similar pattern may be observed in the Co. Limerick plea roll of 1290 (RC 7/2, 261 ff).

Finally, her suggested schema – which she used as further evidence for her cantredal extents – whereby each cantred was held by service of 12 knights, is quite without foundation.[59] Lists of Kildare cantreds date from 1297 and 1358.[60]

C62: *Wykinglow* (1176); *Wiginglo* (1234); *Arclo & Wykinglo* (1297); *Wykynlo* (1315). *Offineglas* (1270); *Offyneglas* (1311; both half-cantred references)[61]
This cantred was composed of two moieties represented by the manors of Arklow and Wicklow which in turn seem to have represented two half-cantreds, that of Arklow being more usually styled the half-cantred of Offyneglas (Uí Enechglais) from its Irish precursor. That such a similar alternative existed for Wicklow in the colonial period is not in doubt but this has not survived to my knowledge. The earliest source for these moieties is Earl Richard's grant of lands to Glendalough, from 1173, which is clearly arranged by cantred or lordship. Under 'the land of Wyglo' we can identify lands in the parishes of Glenealy, Rathdrum, Ennereilly and Killiskey while under that of Arclo we find lands in the parishes of Arklow, Castlemacadam and Killahurler.[62] While this might suggest that Wicklow and Arklow were originally distinct cantreds the grant of Naas and Wicklow to Maurice fitz Gerald in the 1170s unambiguously locates Arklow in the cantred of Wicklow. Additionally, land in the manor of Arklow is said to lie 'in the cantred of Wiginglo'. The *commote* of Arklow was retained by the crown, later to be granted to Theobald Walter.[63] This may explain why a branch of the Geraldines held the Wexford parishes of Inch and Kilgorman which lay in Offyneglas but were not subject to Butler overlordship.[64] Lands in the parishes of Arklow, Ballykine, Ballinacor, Ballintemple, Killahurler and Castlemacadam certainly lay in the Butler manor of Arklow, while lands in Dunganstown, Kilpoole, Killoughter and, of course, Wicklow itself lay in the other manor.[65] This rather skeletal extent, understandable in light of the mountainous nature of the terrain here, can be filled out to some extent by reference to the rural deaneries of Wicklow and Arklow, although early evidence concerning the parochial structure of the central mountainous area is obscure. The deanery of Arklow certainly contained the parishes above indicated (including those in modern Wexford), as well as Ennereilly and probably much if not all of Rathdrum and of Knockrath, stretching west to meet the eastern boundary of Omurthi as indicated thereunder (**C66**). The deanery of Wicklow certainly included the parishes of Rathnew, Killiskey, Glenealy, Kilcommon, Drumkay, Kilpoole, Dunganstown and Redcross. It also contained Glendalough priory and so the northern boundary of Wicklow here probably included all of the parish of Derrylossary.[66] Confirmation that the

59 Otway-Ruthven, 'Medieval Kildare', 181–3; eadem, 'Fees in Kildare, Leix and Offaly', 163–5, 182. For lists of the cantreds of Kildare see CJRI, i, 167; CCH, 75. **60** CJRI, i, 167–70; CCH, 75. **61** DKRI 39, p. 67; COD, i, 71, 168. **62** McNeill, *Alen's Register*, 2, 21. **63** Price, 'Place-names of Arklow', 265–6; Nicholls, 'Land of the Leinstermen', 539n; Orpen, *Ireland under the Normans* i, 379–80; COD, i, 8; Mills, *Gormanston*, 193. **64** Nicholls, 'Land of the Leinstermen', 539n; Brooks, *Knights' fees*, 159. In addition Offyneglas certainly included the parishes of Ballykine, Arklow and Castlemacadam (Brooks, *Knights' fees*, 170–1; COD, i, 71). **65** Brooks, *Knights' fees*, 25, 167–71; idem, *Llanthony Prima and Secunda*, p. xxv, 255; COD, i, 71, 168. **66** Early lists of

northern boundary of the deanery of Wicklow so described also represents the medieval county boundary between Kildare and Dublin is further indicated by Glendalough lying in medieval County Kildare.[67]

T62: *Fortúatha Laigen*

The cantred of Wykinglo & Arclo (**C62**) was based on the earlier Irish overkingdom of Fortúatha Laigen, in turn composed of the local kingdoms of Uí [F]enechglais (the later half-cantred of Offyneglas *alias* Arklow) and Uí Garrchon (Wicklow). The ruling lines of these kingdoms were unrelated. We should probably heed the cantredal status here and consider Fortúatha Laigen to have been a single *trícha cét*.

Uí Garrchon were of Dál Messin Corb (see **T65**). It seems that they were driven eastwards at some stage from the great plain of Liphi into Wicklow but the chronology of this is obscure.[68] This migration can hardly have occurred later than the early eighth century, however. *Vita Tripartita* makes a well-known reference to Ráith Inbir as a seat of a king of Uí Garrchon and this place has been variously located at Arklow, Rathnew and Dublin. The latter identification comes from Kenneth Nicholls who suggests that the migration of Uí Garrchon from the plains of Kildare was a clockwise one via the Dublin area. An additional reference in *Vita Tripartita* (datable perhaps to the mid-ninth century) to Inbir Dea (Arklow) as being in the lordship of Uí Garrchon indicates that the kingdom then included everything it later did. References to kings of Ráith Inbir occur in 781 and 953, and the first of these, to Cú Chongalt, is very probably to the man of that name in the Uí Garrchon pedigree.[69] A king of Uí Garrchon is recorded in 782 but Conall mac Con Congalt who died in 827 and who occurs in the Uí Garrchon genealogy is styled king of Fortúatha Laigin and this, together with the Inbir Dea reference, suggests that the situation of these kingdoms in 827 was very similar to that in the twelfth century, when the Uí Fergaile kings of Uí Garrchon were overlords of Uí Enechglais, although on occasion the rôles could be reversed.[70] As to Uí Enechglais, this lineage are attested in an ogam found near Duleek of perhaps the fifth century. The late eighth-century Timna shows Uí Enechglais already in their later homeland and several kings are

the deaneries of Wicklow may be found in CDI, v, 241–2 and in Gilbert, *Crede Mihi*, 143–4. Among the demesne lands of Glendalough was Fertir which gives its name to the Vartry River. **67** CJRI, i, 270.   **68** The location of an obsolete Cell Ugarrcon around Ballymore, west of the mountains, may mark a transitory stage in such a migration while the presence of a minor segment of Dál Messin Corb associated with Kilranelagh, near Baltinglass, and record of a king of a distinct line of Dál Messin Corb in 952 (when slain by Uí Muiredaig), perhaps suggests a continued and distinct kingship of Uí Garrchon west of the mountains. This is further suggested by evidence of Dál Messin Corb activity in northern Kildare in the late eighth century. (O'Rahilly, *Early Irish history and mythology*, 27–9; Price, *Place-names of Wicklow* iv, 240; O'Brien, *Corpus*, 42; Mac Shamráin, *Glendalough*, 73.)   **69** Stokes, *Tripartite Life*, 186; Price, 'Place-names of Arklow', 275–6, 285–6; Mac Shamráin, *Glendalough*, 46–7; Nicholls, 'Land of the Leinstermen', 543–5; O'Brien, *Corpus*, 35–40; Ó Muraíle, *Mac Firbhishigh* ii, 225; AU, 781; AFM, 953.   **70** AU, 782, 826, 846; ALC, 1014, 1022, 1043; AI, 1072; AT, 973, 1095; FIA, 908; AFM, 774, 972, 983, 1039, 1170. At least one king of Uí Enechglais is styled king of the Fortúatha, in 983, and his father is styled *flaith na Fortúath*, suggesting a reversal of the traditional rôle.

recorded in the period 916–1170.[71] There is evidence to suggest that their territory here originally stretched further south, well into the later county of Wexford (see under **T183**).

C63: *Leix* (1180, 1212); *Leiss* (1185); *Leys* (1297, 1331)[72]
See pp 33–4.

T63: *Loígis*
The cantred of Leys derives from the kingdom of Loígis. The dominant segment from whom the kings were drawn were Loígis Réta, named from Mag Réta, and kings of this line are recorded regularly from 799 until the Invasion.[73] At least one additional local kingdom existed here, Uí Crimthannáin, linked to the Laigin in Timna Catháir Máir. Kings of this polity are recorded between 921 and 1071 after which it may have been absorbed by Loígis.[74] Its territory lay around the barony of Maryborough East where the descendants of its ruling line, Uí Duibh (Deevy, Devoy), remained powerful into the sixteenth century. Ó Murchadha has suggested that these may have been one of the constituent lineages of the Three Commain (see **T3**). The cantred of Leys is described in a grant of 1200 as 'the land of Leis and Houkreuthenan' (Uí Crimthannáin).[75]

C64: *Offaly* (1297, 1358).
This cantred must have contained much of the feudal barony of Offaly, which certainly contained the *theoda* of Tothemoy and of Oregan and four fees in Geashill and Lea. Tothemoy, however, lay in the cantred of Offelan in 1297. Oregan is now the barony of Tinnahinch, Co. Leix, which lay in the rural deanery of Offaly.[76] The fees of Geashill (Co. Offaly) and Lea (Co. Leix) must be represented by the remainder of that rural deanery, covering the modern baronies of Upper Philipstown and Geashill in Offaly and Portnahinch in Leix. These fees probably had their origins in indigenous *túatha*, as suggested by the survival of 'Touogeishel' (< Geashill barony) into the sixteenth century.[77] Matters concerning lands in the parishes of Dunmurray, Ballysax, Duneany, Walterstown and Harristown were heard before a jury from the cantred of Offaly in 1297. Some of these presentments were made before a jury 'of the cantred of Offaly and the city of Kildare' suggesting that the latter was also included in this cantred, while the later baronies of Offaly within Co. Kildare and in which Kildare itself lies further confirm this. Again, there is evidence that the southern border of 'Offalie' in the early thirteenth century lay along the northern border of

---

71 Price, 'Place-names of Arklow' 283–5; Mac Shamráin, *Glendalough*, 44–51; Dillon, *Lebor na Cert*, 170; CS, 916, 1154, 1170; AT, 1103; Todd, *Cogad*, 34. **72** Scott and Martin, *Expugnatio Hibernica*, 194; MacNiocaill, *Red Book of Kildare*, 116; Oxford MS Rawl. B 499, f. 98v; Gilbert, *Reg. St Thomas*, 115. **73** O'Brien, *Corpus*, 89–91, 433–4. At least 21 kings are recorded in the annals, spanning the period 799 (AI) to 1153 (AFM). **74** AFM, 921, 1042, 1071. **75** Dillon, *Lebor na Cert*, 158; O'Brien, *Corpus*, 44, 55–6, 337; Ó Muraíle, *Mac Firbhishigh*, ii, 295, 303; Ó Murchadha, 'Laígis', 51; CDI, i, p. 22. **76** For the ruridecanal structure of the diocese of Kildare see fn. 4, p. 127, above. **77** Touogeishel occurs on the well-known map of Leix and Offaly of 1563.

Kilberry parish, just as does the southern border of West Offaly barony today. In 1297 the serjeant of the barony of Conal (Connell) presented before an Offaly jury, suggesting that we should also include this barony in the cantred of Offaly, but this does not appear to have been the original arrangement (see Offelan below).[78]

T64: *Uí Failge*

The cantred of Offaly descends from the kingdom of Uí Failge. This has ancient roots and some of its sixth-century kings may also have been kings of Leinster. Kings of Uí Failge are recorded very regularly in the annals from the earliest times down to the Invasion.[79] For such a large kingdom there seems little evidence for the existence of sub-kings apart from one reference to a king of *Léige ocus Rechet* (Lea and Morett), in 976.[80] He represents the Clann Máel Ugrai segment of Uí Failge in what is today north-eastern Leix. The last king of Irish Uí Failge, an Ua Dímmusaig, was also of this line. In genealogies of the late eleventh century the three main non-regnal segments of Uí Failge are all introduced as *flaithe*, mirroring the annals where kingship seems to be almost exclusively reserved for the traditional ruling line.[81]

C65: *Ofelan* (1176); *Offelan* (1297, 1322, 1358, 1378).[82]

The cantred of Offelan can be reconstructed from a number of sources. In 1297 it had two serjeanties, one for Carbry (Carbury), Tothemoy and Otymny, the second for the (unlisted) remainder of the cantred. From another source we learn that the right of appointment to the serjeanty of Otymny was held by the chief serjeant of Offelan. Matters dealt with by Offelan juries before the eyre of 1297 concerned lands in the parishes of Brideschurch, Carnalway, Balraheen, Cloncurry and Clane. These parishes and the barony of Otymny *alias* Clane all lay within the areas granted to Adam de Hereford and Maurice fitz Gerald in the early 1170s, both of which lay in Offelan. The descent of both grants can be followed and show that the total area of these included the modern baronies of Ikeathy & Oughterany, North and South Salt, Clane, and North and South Naas, Co. Kildare, excluding just three parishes which lay in medieval Dublin (Ballymore, Ballybought and Tipperkevin). Thus the cantred contained all of these along with the baronies of Carbury and Tothemoy. The rural deanery of Tothemoy (in Co. Offaly) contained the parishes of Kilclonfert, Killaderry, Croghan, Ballyburley, Ballynakill, Ballymacwilliam and Monasteroris, and a pleading of 1329 suggests that its secular lordship mirrored this extent.[83]

In Offelan (as with the Kilkenny cantreds), its boundaries as revealed in records of the period when the colony was fully developed do not appear to represent the original cantredal structure. This is clear from records of the sub-infeudation of

78 Otway-Ruthven, 'Fees in Kildare, Leix and Offaly', 178–9; CJRI, i, 173–7,188. For the evidence for the southern border of Offaly see fn. 97, p. 177, below.   **79** For earliest and latest within this span, see AFM, 600, ALC, 1193.   **80** CS, 976.   **81** Mac Shamráin, *Glendalough*, 48; Ó Murchadha, 'Laígis', 37; O'Brien, *Corpus*, 56–61, 432–3; Flanagan, *Irish royal charters*, 213–23.   **82** Orpen, *Song of Dermot*, l. 3092; DKRI 42, p. 41; *Analecta Hibernica* I (1930), 198.   **83** CJRI, i, 167, 195–202; DKRI 42, p. 41; Otway-Ruthven, 'Fees in Kildare, Leix and Offaly', 165–9; COD, i, 13, 19–20, 360; Nicholls, 'Land of the Leinstermen', 541; Orpen, *Ireland under the Normans*, i, 378–80.

Offelan, when the kingdom is described (by Cambrensis) as being divided into three cantreds. Flanagan has treated of this subject but a number of her conclusions need revision.[84] It is clear from the charter evidence, in addition to the comments of Giraldus, that three distinct grants were made in what had been the kingdom of Offelan. Adam de Hereford received 'the cantred of Offelan nearest to Dublin', Maurice fitz Gerald received 'a cantred which Makelan [Mac Fháeláin, king of Uí Fáeláin] had held, not that nearest to Dublin but the next one', while Meiler fitz Henry received 'the more remote cantred of Offelan'. The descent of each of these three grants can be traced, thus giving a fairly exact idea of the areas involved.[85] Giraldus's implied description of these as three distinct units is somewhat inaccurate. In the case of the de Hereford lands these were in two distinct portions, Clane, Ikeathy and Oughterany on the one hand and parts of the baronies of Salt on the other, the land in between being part of the (undivided) Geraldine grant which lay in Naas and the remainder of Salt (see Map 1, p. 17). When William fitz Gerald, son of Maurice, enfeoffed his brother in half of his grant he describes it as a half-cantred, yet when John confirmed the Hereford grant in 1202 it is described as 'the half-cantred of Offelan which is nearest Dublin', confirming the conclusion reached below that Offelan was originally a single cantred. What is most remarkable is that – with the exception of the 1234 and 1282 references to 'the cantred of Naas'[86] – at no stage are these individual cantreds given names of their own. Indeed the Hereford grant is described by *commote* with vill, one of which, the *commote* (= *túath*) of Ogurk, is evenly divided between the Hereford and Geraldine cantreds. Again, the Fitz Henry cantred is composed of two territories (divided by a great bog), as indicated by its description in 1212, when expenditure on it is referred to as 'for the cantred of Conal and for Karbri'. This somewhat ambiguous reference confirms what is suggested in other sources, namely that the baronies of Connell and Carbury made up 'the more remote cantred' of Offelan. When the approximate acreages of these three cantreds are compared they are seen to have been similar in size,[87] and the most reasonable conclusion here is that the threefold division of the Irish kingdom of Uí Fáeláin (**T65**) was not based on the Gaelic *trícha cét* system but on an imposed unit

84 Flanagan, 'Uí Fáeláin', passim. Flanagan's reading of the Irish pipe roll of 1212 takes Conal and Carbry to be distinct cantreds but I understand the reference to indicate that just one cantred was intended. Furthermore, such a conclusion makes more sense in the overall context. Cairpre had been conquered and incorporated into Uí Fáeláin by its Mac Fháeláin kings a few years before the Invasion (AFM, 1150; CDI, iv, p. 18). Her placement of Kildare in Offelan rather than Offaly is not consonant with the evidence (see **C64**). In addition, her use of the local ruridecanal structure to support her conclusions, while sound in its methodology, cannot be sustained in this instance. The deaneries of this part of Kildare bear only a very superficial resemblance to the area of the three primary grants in Offelan, and there exist very significant differences in the areas of the early cantreds as compared to the rural deaneries.   85 COD, i, 13, 19; Mills, *Gormanston*, 145; MacNiocaill, *Red Book of Kildare*, 14; Davies and Quinn, 'Pipe Roll of 14 John', 17; Otway-Ruthven, 'Fees in Kildare, Leix and Offaly', 165–9; Scott and Martin, *Expugnatio Hibernica*, 143; Orpen, *Ireland under the Normans*, i, 378–82; Nicholls, 'Land of the Leinstermen', 554–5; idem, 'Topographical Notes', 413–5; McNeill, *Alen's Register*, 293.   86 COD, i, 38; CDI, iii, 448.   87 Approximate acreages are: Hereford, 75K, Geraldine, 70K, Fitz Henry, 83K.

of infeudation, an Anglo-Norman cantred that, in this case at least, bears no resemblance to any indigenous precursor. Interestingly, the administrative structure here simply had one cantred of Offelan by 1297, as illustrated above, showing a reversion to the original situation. Further evidence of administrative evolution during the colonial period can be seen in the situation regarding the (sub-)serjeanties of Conal and Tothemoy in 1297, when Conal was in the cantred of Offaly and Tothemoy in that of Offelan.[88] All of the evidence clearly indicates that the reverse situation had prevailed originally, that is, Conal was then in Offelan and Tothemoy in Offaly, and clearly at some stage before 1297 a 'swap' had occurred here between the chief serjeants of these cantreds.

T65: *Uí Fáeláin*

The cantred of Offelan derives from the Irish kingdom of Uí Fáeláin. This area, with its royal centres at Naas and elsewhere, was the seat of royal power in Leinster from the earliest. The first known rulers here were Dál Messin Corb, believed to have provided two kings of Leinster during the late fifth century. The evidence has been interpreted as indicating that Dál Messin Corb maintained a local kingdom based at Naas until its overthrow during the early seventh century. They may have been displaced by Crimthann Cualann of Uí Théig, king of Leinster (d. 633), of a dynasty who would spend the next century competing for the kingship with the emerging Uí Dúnlainge whose first historically reliable king of Leinster was Fáelán mac Colmáin (d. 666). His reign marks the last possible date for the beginning of Uí Dúnlainge power here.[89] Gradually Uí Dúnlainge forced Uí Théig eastwards and extinguished the other petty kingdoms of Cenél Ucha (around Feighcullen), whose only king is recorded in 776, and Fothairt Airthir Liphi (or Fothairt Náis), whose last kings are recorded around 900.[90] Most of the locations associated with Uí Dúnlainge in the earlier genealogies (800 or earlier) are located in the area later known as Uí Fáeláin.[91] Its eponym was Fáelán mac Murchada (d. 738). Following this expansionary period the Uí Néill kings of Mide, during the early ninth century, made several efforts to divide Uí Dúnlainge between its ruling lines, resulting in the creation of the new kingdoms of Airthir Liphi (**T65**) and Iarthar Liphi (**T66**).[92] (Liphe originally refers to the plain and not the river.) During the tenth century the first of these adopted the new style Uí Fáeláin, and kings of this polity continue to be recorded down to the Invasion.[93]

The only area of uncertainty regarding the borders of Uí Fáeláin concern the territory held by the descendants of Ailill Céthech, made one of the sons of Catháir Már in Timna Catháir Máir, which suggests that before 800 or so this was a distinct polity though no kings appear in the annals. Its pedigree does not run beyond the ninth century. Both the territories of Uí Chéthig and possibly Crích na Cétach are associated with this lineage, suggesting that its original extent may have ran from

88 CJRI, i, 167, 188. **89** Mac Shamráin, *Glendalough*, 45–6, 71; Byrne, *Kings and high kings*, 131–2, 288–9. **90** AFM, 776, 897; LL, 6610. **91** Mac Shamráin, *Glendalough*, 235; O'Brien, *Corpus*, 73–5, 83, 339, 341–2. **92** AU, 815, 831, 845, 862, 883, 916; FIA, 871. **93** AFM, 970, 973, 1141, 1161; AT, 1044; AU, 1127; MIA, 1134; ALC, 1024, 1039.

Cloncurry westwards to Castlejordan and thus included all of Carbury.[94] The incorporation of Crích na Cétach into Mide may be associated with the migration of the Uí Chiarda kings of Uí Chairpre (**T103**), in north western Mide, to Carbury in Kildare – to which they gave their name. This migration probably happened during the period when the Uí Máel Sechnaill kings of Mide were overlords of Uí Fáeláin, a suzerainty exercised from 1136 into the 1150s. By the date of the Invasion, the Mac Fháeláin kings of Uí Fáeláin had re-incorporated Carbury into Uí Fáeláin.[95]

C66: *O Morethi* (1176); *Omuredhi* (1188); **Omurthy** (1297); **Omurthi** (1331, 1358).[96] This cantred contained the southernmost parts of modern Kildare, a large area of Wicklow adjoining to the east as well as a portion of Carlow. It was divided into at least four units of sub-infeudation, three of which, the feudal baronies of Kilkea, Dunlost and Reban, are specifically said to have lain in this cantred.[97]

To take Kilkea first, a confirmation of its original grant and an extent of 1311 survive. These indicate that this feudal barony included lands in the parishes of Kilkea, Castledermot, Graney and Killelan in Kildare, part of Baltinglass in Wicklow, Kineagh, shared by Kildare and Carlow, and Kiltegan and Hacketstown, shared between Wicklow and Carlow. In addition, Kilkea included half of the territory of Omayl (Uí Máil: Imaal), the other half being church-land, and all of which lay in Omurthi.[98] An extent of Kilkea's moiety of Omayl shows it to have contained lands in the Wicklow parishes of Donaghmore and Donard. Places in the parishes of Donaghmore, Baltinglass (which lay in medieval Kildare) and Freynestown can be identified as lying within the church's moiety of Omayl.[99] A final confirmation of much of this extent can be had from the rectories impropriate to the nunnery of Graney, founded by the first de Ridelesford lord of Kilkea, namely (*inter alia*) Kilkea,

94 *Per contra*, Diarmuid Ó Murchadha (pers. comm.) suggests that Crích na Cétach may perhaps derive from *céitech*: flat-topped hill. (DIL s. vv. céite, céitech.) **95** O'Brien, *Corpus*, 13, 44, 69; Dillon, *Lebor na Cert*, 173; Mac Shamráin, *Glendalough*, 76; Byrne, *Kings and high kings*, p. xvi; AFM, 1055, 1117, 1124, 1128, 1150; Flanagan, 'Uí Fáeláin', 230–1; CDI, iv, p. 18. **96** Orpen, *Song of Dermot*, l. 3097; Scott and Martin, *Expugnatio Hibernica*, 194; MacNiocaill, *Red Book of Kildare*, 116. **97** Kilkea is said to have lain in 'Omurethi'; Ardree, the original *caput* of Dunlost, is similarly described; while an early grant of the obsolete parish of Cluain Andobair in the barony of Reban, (now Cloney in northern Kilberry parish: see White, *Dignitas Decani*, 5, 106, 112), makes it clear that the boundary between Omurthi and Offaly lay along the northern border of Kilberry. (Orpen, *Song of Dermot*, lines 3096–9; Scott and Martin, *Expugnatio Hibernica*, 195; Gilbert, *St Mary's, Dublin*, i , 117 (where Roger Waspail was then lord of Reban in right of his wife, see Orpen, *Ireland under the Normans*, i, 383n).) **98** Brooks, 'de Ridelesfords, i', 123–4; White, *Book of Ormond*, 12–17. (This extent is chiefly distinguished by its large numbers of obsolete place-names. Some of the more obscure identifications are Ballycullane in Kineigh and Woodfield in Baltinglass (?), while Kilgelan is, of course, Killelan. For further identifications here see Nicholls, 'Carlow and Wexford', 35–7). **99** An extent of that moiety of Omayl which lay in Kilkea is given in White, *Book of Ormond*, 19–21. In this we can identify Donaghmore itself and Kilbreffy, Leitrim, Brittas and Eadestown (Nicholls, 'Baltinglass charter', 193) in its parish, as well as Ballylion in Donard and Keadeen on the border with Kilranelagh. A list of places in the other moiety is given in McNeill, *Alen's Register*, 2, 21, where again Donaghmore features, as well as Raheen in its parish and Loch Leig, which lay in Baltinglass (Nicholls, 'Baltinglass charter', 192–3). Freynestown also lay in this moiety of Omayl (Otway-Ruthven, 'Fees in Kildare, Leix and Offaly', 171).

Killelan, Castledermot, Graney, Kineagh, Hacketstown, and Kiltegan.[1] The barony of Dunlost contained lands in the parishes of Ardree, Dunmanoge and Tankardstown (part of which lies across the Barrow in Leix) while the barony of Reban is more difficult to describe, but certainly contained lands in the parishes of Churchtown and Kilberry, thus forming a western bridgehead of Omurthi across the Barrow just as it does of Kildare today.[2] Reban must also have included the Wolfe fee of Kilcolyn (*sic*) mis-identified by Otway-Ruthven.[3] This establishes the western, southern and eastern bounds of Omurthi. Our primary source for its northern border must be the rather loose one of those places mentioned in pleadings heard before Omurthi juries in 1297. These include several places already identified as lying in this cantred, such as Kilkea, Athy, Graney, Reban, Omayl, Dunmanoge, and Tankardstown. The inclusion of places such as Moone, Narragh, and Castlemartin in Kilcullen parish in this source would tend to confirm the obvious conclusion that the seignorial manor of Moone and the baronies of Narragh and Kilcullen must also have lain in Omurthi.[4]

The extent of the rural deanery of Omurthi confirms very much the cantredal extent above with one exception. This concerns that part of the deanery of Ofelmyth which extended northwards to include Baltinglass and its asssociated parishes: Rathtoole, Rathbran and Ballynure, thus cutting in two the deanery of Omurthi.[5] These lands, of course, lay in the cantred of Omurthi.[6] This exception apart, the deanery follows exactly the boundaries as set out above, with its northern borders formed by that of the parishes of Kilberry, Fontstown, Davidstown, Kilcullen and Usk. In the south the deanery of Omurthi included the parish of Kineagh, confirming exactly the sinuous line of the southern border of the cantred here. Finally, in the east the detached section of the deanery contained the parishes of Hacketstown, Kiltegan, Moyne, Donaghmore, and Freynestown, giving the eastern and northern borders of the cantred of Omurthi here, which, as adduced above, also included parts of Donard.

T66: *Uí Muiredaig*
The kingdom of Iarthar Liphi was the kingdom of Muiredach mac Murchada (d. 760), the eponym of its later form, Uí Muiredaig, from which derives the cantred of Omurthi. During the early eighth-century Uí Dúnlainge expansion had overrun the Uí Gabla Roíreann kingdom around Athy, and it was this modest portion of swordland, the area from the Curragh of Kildare southwards to the stronghold of

---

1 White, *Extents*, 124.   2 See fn. 97, p. 177, above. Otway-Ruthven ('Fees in Kildare, Leix and Offaly', 165; 'Med. Co. Kildare', 182) located Reban within Leys on the basis of its being mentioned in pleas heard before Leys juries. However, even here she ignored other pleas where Reban was featured before Omurthi and Offaly juries (CJRI, i, 178, 181–3, 191).   3 Otway-Ruthven, 'Fees in Kildare, Leix and Offaly', 169–70, 174. Kilcolyn in the feodaries is certainly an error for Kilcolman, now Tomard, Barrowford and Paudeenourstown in Kilberry parish, in the heart of 'Woulfes Country' north of Athy.   4 CJRI, i, 170–3, 182–6, 196.   5 Baltinglass itself, of course, does not appear in the Papal Taxation but Tinoran (Tachnotheran) in Ballynure does, while both Ballynure (*alias* Ballitaxi) and Baltinglass occur in the deanery lists from 1589 onwards. (See fn. 4, p. 127, above.)   6 Baltinglass was part of medieval Co. Kildare (CCH, 84).

Maistiu (Mullaghmast near Athy), that comprised the original area of Iarthar Liphi. Later, pushing southwards and eastwards, Uí Muiredaig expanded at the expense of Uí (or Dál) Chormaic Loisc and Uí Máil. The territory of the former had stretched as far north as Kildare itself in the mid-seventh century but by 800 only the Athy-Castledermot area was left to them, centred on their fortress of Roíriu. Around 900 an Uí Muiredaig dynast is described as 'lord of Maistiu and Roíriu' and the last king of Uí Chormaic is recorded in 932. As for Uí Máil, their first king is recorded in 736. No doubt the decline in the fortunes of Uí Théig to their north weakened Uí Máil and their territory along the upper Slaney was duly incorporated into Uí Muiredaig. The last king of Uí Máil is recorded in 848.[7] Kings of Uí Muiredaig continue to be recorded down to the Invasion.[8]

KILKENNY

The cantreds of medieval Kilkenny have been described and mapped by C.A. Empey.[9] Unfortunately he did not grasp the nature of the administrative system in operation here and this, in addition to his failure to differentiate between cantred, manor and feudal barony, has led to the need to revisit the subject in some detail.[10] It is necessary to describe what I will call the administrative cantreds established some time after the original settlement before working backwards to establish the outline of the original cantreds. In Kilkenny these administrative cantreds, certainly amalgamations of the original cantreds, had a chief serjeant who held his office in fee of the lords of the liberty. A document dealing with the division of the liberty between the sisters and heiresses of Gilbert de Clare after 1317 deals with these chief serjeanties and lists all knights' fees under the relevant cantred. This enables us to describe the four administrative cantreds of Kilkenny in detail as follows.[11] These administrative cantreds appear to have been made up of at least seven and probably nine original cantreds.

7 O'Brien, *Corpus*, 12–13; Mac Shamráin, *Glendalough*, 72, 81–4; Ó Riain, *Corpus*, 117; AU, 813, 876; AFM, 932; AT, 736, AU, 848.   8 AT, 1103, 1112, 1176, 1178; AFM, 1124, 1154, 1164; FIA, 908.   9 'Cantreds of Kilkenny'; and see his 'County Kilkenny', passim.   10 There are four main lists of administrative units in medieval Kilkenny, the 1317 partition (see following note), and lists of 1358 (CCH, 74), 1375 and 1420 (Richardson and Sayles, 59, 161). Three of these differentiate between cantred and feudal barony in a consistent manner while that of 1375 lumps everything together under the convenient title of 'cantred'. It is clear from a comparison with the other lists and other evidence that the list of 1375 includes both feudal baronies (Erley, Kells, Knocktopher) and even simple manors (Callan, Kilkenny) in addition to genuine cantreds. Empey has viewed this list uncritically. In addition he has made only selective use of the important 1317 list (which he describes as containing 'a number of blatant inaccuracies' (Empey, 'Cantreds of Kilkenny', 128)) and ignored this source where it contradicts the list of 1375. Had he proceeded in reverse order he might have arrived at a more realistic number of cantreds for Kilkenny. It will be further noted that the few references to Kilkenny cantreds to be found outside of these lists (CJRI, i, 218, 471; CCH, 24) corroborate my findings. This criticism aside, Empey's works are most valuable for extending the various feudal baronies and manors of Anglo-Norman Kilkenny.   11 McNeill, *Liber Primus Kilkenniensis*, 54–7. While most of the fees in this document can be identified with the help

1: *Overk*

This included the feudal baronies of Kells, Erley, Knocktopher and Overk in addition to a few other minor fees (and, of course, cross-lands). If we translate this area into its modern equivalent, it contained the modern baronies of Ida, Iverk, Knocktopher, Kells, the parish of Earlstown and probably the parishes of Ennisnag and Stonecarthy.[12]

2: *Ogenti*

This cantred contained the feudal baronies of Ogenti and Oskellan *alias* Gowran and a few other fees and cross-lands. It contained all of the modern barony of Gowran excluding the parishes of Shankill, Kilmacahill, Grangesilvia, Powerstown and Ullard, which lay in medieval Carlow, and also contained the parishes of Kilmademoge and Kilmadum.[13]

3: *Shillyrhir*

The manors of Kilkenny (= the modern barony of Kilkenny) and of Callan (= the parishes of Callan and Killaloe) certainly lay in this administrative cantred and, apparently, everything in between. In addition to lands in these manors we can identify fees in the parishes of Kilmanagh, Tullaroan, Ballycallan, Castleinch, Kilferagh, and Tullaghanbrogue as lying in this cantred. It must also have included the parishes of Outrath, Grange, Ballybur, Burnchurch, Tullamaine, Grangekilree and Danesfort which lay in its descendant, the modern barony of Shillelogher.

4: *Odogh*

This cantred contained the remainder of the medieval county. The northern borders of the cantreds to its south are clear as are most of the southernmost fees of Odogh. It contained all of the modern barony of Fassadinin apart from Kilmademogue and Kilmadum, all of Galmoy, and certainly the northern Crannagh parishes of Tubbridbrittain, Clomentagh, Ballylarkin, Clashnacrow, Odagh and Ballinamara. This cantred also contained that part of modern Leix which lay in medieval Kilkenny, that is, the baronies of Upper Woods, Clarmallagh and Clandonagh.

So much for the administrative cantreds of Kilkenny. What of the original cantredal structure here? Some of this can be reconstructed from colonial sources while a study of pre-Norman Osraige offers indications of the form of the remainder.

C67: *Ogenti* (1317, 1326); **Ognenoy** (1358); *Ogenty* (1420)
C68: *Oscallan* (1299); **Oskelan** (1317); **Oscall'** (1326); **Osquellan** (1358); *Oscalle'* (1420)[14]
The 1317 division of the lordship glosses the four knights' fees of Ballygaueran

of Brooks' *Knights' fees*, there are a few obscure ones. Kilcranyn (p. 55) is Kilcreen in St Patrick's parish while Grottengros (55) is associated with Ballybeagh in Tullaroan parish (Brooks, *Knights' fees*, 271) and Aghnyrle (56) is, of course, Urlingford. I am unable to identify Lesdonnchy (54, this cannot be Lisdowney) and Tiryskeffe.   **12** For the extents of the various feudal baronies of Kilkenny see Empey, 'Cantreds of Kilkenny', passim, and idem, 'County Kilkenny', 85.   **13** Shankill and Powerstown were still considered to be in the county of 'Catherlogh' in 1509 (PRONI MS 3078/1/1/3/156).   **14** White, *Book of Ormond*, 89; COD, i, 243–4.

(Gowran) as being in Oskelan, the only exception to the standard pattern of gloss-
ing in this document which otherwise confines itself to the four administrative
cantreds above. In the cantredal list of 1358 Ogenti is 'Osquellan & Ognenoy [*sic*]'
which seems to further indicate that Ogenti and Oskelan were the original constituent cantreds of the administrative cantred of Ogenti, and both appear, in rather
mutilated form, as distinct cantreds in the list of 1375. The original extent of Oskelan
would therefore have comprised all of Ogenti from Gowran northwards while 'true'
Ogenti would have been the remainder of the administrative cantred.

T67: *Tír Ua nGentich*
T68: *Uí Scelláin*
The regional kingdom of Osraige may have contained perhaps nine *tríchas*, but even
its cantredal structure is somewhat unclear, rendering the following conclusions tentative. Osraige threw off the rule of their Corcu Loígde overlords in the 640s and
thereafter were ruled by a few closely related lines of their own kings. Both Gentech
and Scellán represent remote lineages which did not leave pedigrees. Remarkably,
an ogam commemorating a member of Uí Geintig was found on the northern border of the cantred of Ogenti.[15]

C69: **Shillyrhir** (1317); **Sileyrther** (1358); *Shillelogher* (1420); **Shillelogher** (1441)[16]
I can find no evidence that this was ever anything more than a cantred whose borders remained immobile. The 1375 list from which Empey infers the existence of
the additional cantreds of Callan and of Kilkenny is certainly untrustworthy and, in
the complete absence of any further reference to Callan and Kilkenny as cantreds
and given the unrealistically small size of these units, I believe that there was only
one cantred here, Shillyrhir. The ruridecanal structure in Ossory diverges significantly from the cantredal and the existence of the small deanery of Kilkenny is proof
of nothing, although it may be noted that the deanery of Shillelogher comprises
those parts of the cantred not in the manors of Callan (in the deanery of Kells) and
Kilkenny. Callan and Kilkenny originated as seignorial manors.[17]

T69: *Síl Faelchair*
The cantred of Shillyrhir derives from Síl Faelchair, the eponym being a king of
Osraige who died in 688, belonging to a close collateral line of the later kings.[18]

C70: *Odoch* (1250); **Odogh** (1317, 1326, 1334, 1375); **Odoth** (1358)
C71: *Cavalmuy* (1212); *Kankillich* (1305); **Galmoy** (1358)[19]
The ruridecanal structure of Odogh may be of some help in reconstructing the orig-
inal cantredal structure here. The extent of the administrative cantred of Odogh

---

15 O'Brien, *Corpus*, 103, 114; Ó Riain, *Corpus*, 12; Ó Floinn, 'Freestone Hill', 28. Dr Catherine
Swift kindly drew my attention to the latter reference. **16** COD, iii, 128. **17** For the ruridecanal
structure of the diocese of Ossory see the list of 1318 in Lawlor, 'Calendar of the *Liber Ruber*',
175–9 and, for 1615, TCD MS 1066. **18** O'Brien, *Corpus*, 111; Ó Riain, *Corpus*, 58; A Clon,
688; AU, 693. **19** COD, i, 47, 152, 243; DKRI 44, p. 40; Sheehy, *Pont. Hib.*, i, 72; CCH, 24.

agrees closely with that of three deaneries, Odagh (Odogh), Aghour and Aghaboe. The southern border here gives merely an approximate agreement as the parish of Dunmore in the administrative cantred is not in the deanery of Odagh and that of Ballinamara, again in the administrative cantred, is rather in the deanery of Shillelogher. The 1358 reference to the cantred of Odoth & Galmoy suggests that these may originally have been two cantreds, with the deanery of Odagh giving an approximate outline of Odogh (**C70**) and Aghour that of Galmoy (**C71**). The deanery of Odagh contained all the parishes of the barony of Fassadinin apart from Kilmadum, Kilmademoge and Dunmore, and in addition the parishes of Aharney, Rathbeagh, Clashnacrow and Odagh (some partly in Leix; these included the greater share of Durrow and the detached southern portion of Abbeyleix, originally a distinct parish). All the places known from Irish sources to have lain in Uí Duach (**T70**) also lay in the deanery.[20] The deanery of Aghour contained the remainder of Galmoy (some of whose parishes run over the border into Leix) and the parishes of Tubbridbritain, Killahy, Clomentagh, Ballylarkin, and Freshford, in addition to the Leix parish of Aghmacart. 'Cavalmuy' occurs as a territorial designation in 1212, while a reference from around 1305 to the territory of 'Kankillich' gives an alternative name for this cantred. This certainly derives from Cinn Caille (see **T71**).

T70: *Uí Duach Argatrois*
The cantred of Odogh is the Irish kingdom of Uí Duach Argatrois. Uí Duach were the Corcu Loígde (see **T31**) dynasty who originally ruled Osraige until overthrown in the 640s. Duach is placed in the mid-sixth century by the genealogists. Their genealogy comes down to 743, and ends in one Laidgnén mac Doineannaig, bishop of Saigher (Seir Kieran). Its later ruling family, Uí Bergda, were of Clann Dubthaig of Osraige. Kings are recorded in 851, 951 and 1026 and as a territory Uí Duach is again noted in 1156. The *Topographical Poems* appear to refer to this as the *trícha cét* of An Comair (cf. Castlecomer).[21]

T71: *Áes Cinn Caille*
The cantred of Galmoy (**C71**) seems to correspond to the earlier Áes Cinn Caille whose king, Ua Broigte of uncertain lineage, was killed in 1165.[22]

C72: *Hatebo* (1201); *Haphebo* (1210); *Les Glannys* (1297); *Clannys* (1326); *na Clanna* (1370)[23]
Aghaboe was certainly the *caput* of a distinct cantred in the early thirteenth century and its outline is probably preserved in that of the corresponding deanery.[24] This cantred occurs, under an alternate name, Clannys, along with several other known cantreds, in a 1326 list of estreats. References from the 1290s, locating Rathdowney and Skirk in Clannys, make the identification certain, while Bordwell is associated

20 Carrigan, *Ossory*, i, 11. **21** Ó Buachalla, 'History of Munster', 70, 85; O'Brien, *Corpus*, 105, 107, 191, 222–3; AFM, 951, 1026, 1156; AU, 851; TP, 34. **22** Ó Riain, *Corpus*, 109, 111; Carrigan, *Ossory*, i, 12; AU, 1165. **23** CDI, i, 27; COD, i, 20, 135–6, 244, 248; TP, 78. **24** Empey ('Cantreds of Kilkenny', 128) missed two further references to this cantred (CDI, i, 27; PRIA C 27 (1908), 118).

with the Hereford lords of part of this cantred.[25] Clannys again occurs in 1339, when described as a barony 'now waste and in the march of the Irish' in a source which styles several cantreds as baronies.[26] The deanery of Aghaboe lay entirely in Leix, and consisted of the barony of Upper Woods, the barony of Clandonagh apart from the parishes of Erke and Kyle, and the northern half of the barony of Clarmallagh.

T72: *na Clandaibh*
This is the *trícha cét* referred to as 'na Clandaibh' in the *Topographical Poems*, whose king (*rí na Cland*) died in Lismore in 1096.[27] During much of the twelfth century until the Invasion this kingdom appears to have been ruled by its Uí Caellaide kings, perhaps, as Carrigan suggests, as one of the three divisions of Osraige.[28] Its early history is murky. Ó Murchadha has shown that Carrigan was quite mistaken in locating the kingdom of Ráith Tamnaig here and has suggested that most of this area was part of Loígis Réta. While some Loígis segments are found in this area, such as Uí Chuillín, whose king is recorded in 1033,[29] the presence here of the chief ecclesiastical seat of the Osraige indicates that part at least of na Clandaibh must have been in Osraige from quite early on. The northern moiety of Aghaboe, Uí Fairchelláin, represents a polity whose king is recorded in 899 while in 950 this polity was recorded acting independently of the Osraige.[30] This lineage was associated with the Loígis and their sub-kings, the Three Commain – of whom they may have been a constituent, until eventually incorporated into Osraige.[31]

C73: **Overk** (1305, 1317, 1326, 1330, 1334, 1358, 1375)[32]
*C74: *Obercon*
The area of the modern baronies of Iverk and Ida and the Knocktopher parishes of Killahy and Rossinan was largely occupied by the great feudal barony of Overk, in addition to one or two smaller fees and church and seignorial lands. Overk had one significant sub-manor, Obercon, and the names of both of these echo those of pre-Invasion polities (**T73, 74**), suggesting two original cantreds here, Overk and Obercon, probably approximately similar in extent to their modern descendants, Iverk and Ida. This is indicated by fourteenth-century references, seventeenth-century manorial extents, and even the ruridecanal structure here.[33]

T73: *Uí Eirc*
T74: *Uí Berchon*
The cantred of Overk derives from Uí Eirc but there are several possible persons of this name in the Uí Eirc pedigree, one remote, the others of the seventh and eighth centuries. The *Topographical Poems* refer to Uí Eirc as a *trícha*.[34] Ibercon derives from Uí Berchon, an acephalic line of the Osraige. The death of a king of Uí Berchon, Óengus mac Néill, who features in its pedigree, occurred in 851.[35]

25 COD, i, 130, 136, 243–8. **26** DKRI 53, p. 40. **27** TP, 34, 43; AI, 1096.4. **28** AFM, 1036, 1152, 1170, 1172; Carrigan, *Ossory*, i, 3, 6–7, 52–3. **29** AFM, 1033. **30** AFM, 899, 950. **31** O'Brien, *Corpus*, 116; Ó Riain, *Corpus*, 115, 167; AFM, 950; Ó Murchadha, 'Laígis', 38–42, 52. **32** CJRI, ii, 471; COD, i, 248, 260; DKRI 44, p. 40. **33** Carrigan, *Ossory*, i, 19–20. **34** O'Brien, *Corpus*, 107; TP, 34. **35** O'Brien, *Corpus*, 109; Ó Riain, *Corpus*, 57; AFM, 851.

*C75, T75: *name unknown*
What has gone before leaves the remainder of 'administrative' Overk, basically the
feudal baronies of Kells, Erley and Knocktopher, unaccounted for. These constituted, more or less, the large deanery of Kells. This area seems to have comprised another cantred, whose name has not come down to us. This name is perhaps preserved
in the 1205 reference to Kells as 'Kenlis in Offathith'. The *Topographical Poems* have
two references to a *tricha* here, said to lie along the Callan or Kings River. This *tricha*
is certainly our unnamed cantred here.[36]

LIMERICK

The medieval county of Limerick contained, more or less, the present counties of
Limerick and Clare. The cantreds south of the Shannon have been described and
mapped by Empey[37] and I have also described and mapped three of these cantreds
in my 'Cantreds of Desmond'. In a number of cases Empey's conclusions merit revision.[38] My revised list of Co. Limerick cantreds gives a total of twelve as against
Empey's fifteen.

C76: *Karebry Wuh'trah* (1206); *Adlekath* (1237); *Ocarbry* (1288, 1346, 1377);
Ocarbre (1297); *Athlakach* (1303)
I have shown in my 'Cantreds of Desmond' (61–2) that this cantred was significantly larger than its extent as given by Empey. Furthermore, both Empey and I appear
to have given insufficient consideration to the nomenclature here. It is important
to distinguish clearly between **C76** and **C77** given the similarity of nomenclature
shared by both. To further confuse matters the lists of 1375 and 1377 distinguish
between the cantreds of Adare and of Croom (**C77**: where the term 'cantred' is
clearly being misused for that of 'manor').[39] Athlacca was the *caput* of **C76**.

C77: *Kenry Heutred* (1195); *Carbry Othrath* (1230); *Ocarbry Otherach* (1290); *Adare
& Cromith* (1346); *Adaar* (1358)
The manors of Croom and Adare together constituted the cantred (**C77**) described
as Kenry Heutred in an early grant which goes on to name its four constituent *theoda*. One of these has the same name as the cantred, whose proper name, Carbry
Othrath (*Uí Cairbre Íochtarach*), occurs later.[40] Empey offers no evidence for his suggested area of **C77**. While no early description of Ocarbry Othrath appears to survive its outline can be reconstructed from a number of sources. The manors of Adare
and Croom descended in the same family for five centuries which suggests that we

---

36 COD, i, 15; TP, 43. **37** Empey, 'Limerick'. **38** For lists of the cantreds of Limerick see BL
Add. MS 4790, f. 169v; RC 7/2, 260 ff; CCH, 52, 72, 102; Richardson and Sayles, 61–2. **39**
MacNiocaill, *Red Book of Kildare*, 19, 61 (the latter reference locating Kilgobban, in Adare parish,
in the cantred of Ocarbry Othrath); 'Cantreds of Desmond', 61 (where my comments regarding
Uí Cairbre Uachtarach and Íochtarach should be revised in light of the above). See also my 'Sub-
infeudation and descent', 95–6. **40** MacNiocaill, *Red Book of Kildare*, 19, 61.

may place some confidence in the belief that their earliest extents (of 1559) may be close enough in area to that of the original cantred. These extents include lands in the parishes of Adare, Croom, Drehidtarsna, Kildimo, Chapelrussell, Anhid, Killonahan, Killeenoghty and Ardcanny. Dysert must also have lain in this cantred while one of its original *theoda*, Clanethe, can be identified with the parish of Kilcornan.[41] Finally it should be noted that the parish of Iveruss was originally part of that of Askeaton and so must have lain in the cantred of Inyskysty (**C78**) rather than in Ocarbry Othrath.[42]

T76: *Uí Chairpre Uachtarach*
T77: *Uí Chairpre Íochtarach*
These lay in the regional kingdom of Uí Fhidgente, which is attested in the earliest records. The area of this kingdom was later represented by six cantreds (**C76–81**). The customary two-fold sub-division was an east-west one between Uí Chairpre and Uí Chonaill, the linkage between both eponyms being prehistoric, if not fabulous.[43]

The two *trícha*s of Uí Chairpre were Uí Chairpre Uachtarach and Uí Chairpre Íochtarach, from which derive the cantreds of Ocarbry Wuhtrah (**C76**) and Ocarbry Othrath (**C77**). Uí Chairpre, like Uí Chonaill (see below) was divided between the semi-provincial kingdoms of Desmumu and Tuadmumu, with **T76** lying in Desmumu and **T77** lying in Tuadmumu. An *alias* for cantred **C77** was Kenry Heutred, after one of its four constituent *theoda*. Kenry derives from Caenraige, which survives into modern times as the barony name Kenry. Another of these *theoda* was Kinellerc, perhaps from *Cenél *Eirc*, which lay around Adare. This may have been the native *túath* of the Uí Donnabháin ruling family, who are associated with Croom in *Caithréim Cellacháin Chaisil*, written in the 1130s. Uí Mac Eirc were an early division of Uí Chairpre while another Eirc lies in direct ancestry to Uí Donnabháin.[44] It may be that *trícha* **T77** comprised Kinellerc and three other *túatha*, some of the latter perhaps associated with the Caenraige polity whose king is recorded in 1031. Upon his death, the eponymous Donnubán, in 980, is styled *Rígh Ressad*, apparently an archaic name for Uí Chairpre or one of its divisions. Earlier, in 975, Donnubán is described as king of all Uí Fhidgente, while his son died as king of Uí Chairpre. Clearly, Uí Donnabháin must have been local kings of **T77**.[45]

As inveterate enemies of Dál Cais Uí Donnabháin must have been relegated under Brian Boraime, who advanced their cousins (?), Uí Chléirchín, to the kingship of Uí Chairpre and even the overkingship of all Uí Fhidgente, the last such on record. Under Uí Briain patronage Uí Chléircín may have retained the kingship of Uí Chairpre into the twelfth century. Whatever of this, they were certainly local

41 PRONI MS 3078/1/1/3 fos. 165–182 (these extents can be partly supplemented by the *Civil Survey* iv (121–149) which records various chief rents due to the manors of Adare and Croom). For Clanethe see my forthcoming monograph on the early Knights of Glin. **42** Begley, *Limerick ancient and medieval*, 277. **43** O'Brien, *Corpus* 230–4, 365, 388. **44** Nicholls, 'Red Book of Kildare', 25; Bugge, *Caithreim*, 15; O'Brien, *Corpus*, 231–2. **45** AI, 980, 982, 1031; AT, 975; MacCotter, *Colmán*, 38.

kings of Uí Chairpre Uachtarach (**T76**).[46] Given the presence of **T76** in Desmumu, and the close connection between Uí Donnabháin and the Meic Carthaig kings, it would appear that, sometime after the 1130s, Uí Donnabháin were relegated solely to **T76**, from where they were eventually driven into Carbery, Co. Cork.

C78: *Inskyfty & Rathgele* (1290); *Inyskysty* (1346); *Inskysty* (1375)
This is a metonym and the older form of the present toponym, Askeaton. See Empey, 'Limerick', 9, 19.

C79: *Bronry* (1290); *Brouury* (1328)[47]
The modern Bruree. This was united with Inyskysty sometime after 1290. No extent survives. See Empey, 'Limerick', 10–12.

C80: *Scenede* (1260); *Shennede* (1282); *Scened* (1299)
Later united with Ardagh. See Empey, 'Limerick', 6, 8, 20, then see MacCotter, 'Cantreds of Desmond', 61.

C81: *Killede* (1207, 1299); *Corkoyhe* (1251); *New Castle* (1260); *Killyde* (1282); *Ardach* (1290); *Corckoy* (1299); *Ardagh* (1346, 1375)[48]
See Empey, 'Limerick', 8, then see MacCotter, 'Cantreds of Desmond', 61 and 'Subinfeudation and descent', 76–7.

T78 to T81 (*in Uí Chonaill*)
An interesting feature of the four cantreds of Uí Chonaill (**C78–81**) is that they were named metonymically from their chief centres and not from a lineage name. The early Norman lordships of Cork/Desmond and Limerick shared Uí Chonaill between them: Shanid and Killeedy lay in Desmond and the remaining two in Limerick. Given that both provincial lordships derive directly from the pre-Invasion division of Munster into Desmumu and Tuadmumu it would appear that these Irish kingdoms also shared Uí Chonaill between them, further suggesting that these four cantreds must preserve the outline of earlier *tríchas*. Elsewhere[49] I have suggested that this division reflected the rival spheres of the competing Uí Chonaill dynasts, Uí Chuiléin – whose chief place was certainly at Clenlish near Killeedy – and Uí Chinn Fháelad, with Uí Chuiléin holding Killeedy and Shanid and Uí Chinn Fháelad Askeaton (Inis Géibtine) and Bruree (Brug Ríg). These were related families, descending from brothers who had lived in the early eleventh century.[50] These four *tríchas* are likely to be much older than this, however, as suggested by the occasional usage in thirteenth-century sources of derivatives of the name Corcu Óche (Corkoyhe, etc.) as an alternative for Killeedy (**T81**). Íta, the eponym of Killeedy, belonged to this earlier lineage who, in the semi-historical tales of sixth-century Munster, are credited with political importance and who continued to be regarded

46 AFM, 1013; ALC, 1045; AT, 1088; AU, 1108. **47** DKRI 43, p. 15. **48** Hardy, *Rot. Chart.*, 172. **49** MacCotter, 'Rise of Meic Carthaig', 71. **50** AFM, 1027; AT, 1156; AI, 1000.

as a significant kingdom in *frithfholaid* and other texts datable, in probability, to the late eighth or early ninth century.[51] Shanid derives from *seanad*: assembly place, and this place bore this function during the 830s when it was the site of an important victory over the Vikings by Uí Chonaill.[52] Seanad was certainly an important *óenaig* site, certainly of the *trícha cét* of Seanad (**T80**) if not of all of Uí Chonaill.

C82: *Yolethor* (1295); *Ocholochor* (1300); *Esclon* (1346, 1358, 1375, 1377).
Empey believes that both Esclon and Ioleger were distinct cantreds.[53] It is clear, how-ever, both from the references cited by Empey and its small size that Ioleger was a *theodum* rather than a cantred. Admittedly, there is a reference to the serjeanty of the cantred of 'Yolethor', but the evidence suggests that we are here dealing with a cantred comprised of two *theoda*, Esclon and Ioleger, either of which could represent the name of this cantred. In 1237 Esclon is described as a *theodum*. It must be significant that Ioleger follows immediately upon Esclon in a list of 1290 where cantreds and half-cantreds were presenting in eyre before the justices itinerant in Limerick, suggesting that the full name for this cantred may have been Esclon & Ioleger.[54]

T82: *Áes Cluana*
C82 is the first of the six cantreds based on Dál Cais minimal polities of which we must treat (**C82, 83, 88–91**). Dál Cais were originally the Déis Tuascirt or northern Déis, whose king, Andelaith, was present at the proclamation of *Cáin Fuithirbe* around 680, and who is also associated with another such proclamation about twenty years later.[55] From this period onwards this people are associated with an extensive expan-sion into Co. Clare from their original settlement area in Limerick, culminating in their assumption of a new identity as Dál Cais during the tenth century, when they succeed to the kingship of Munster.[56]

    The original area of this people appears to have been on both sides of the lower Shannon, around Limerick itself. The later cantreds of Limerick (**C83**) and Esclon (**C82**) must have formed this area as well as parts of southern Uí Blait (**C89**), a part of which lay south of the Shannon to east of Limerick City. Esclon derives from *Áes Cluana*, a lineage descending from Conall mac Echach who may have lived around 800.[57]

C83: *Cantred of the Ostmen* (1200); *Limerick* (1234, 1237)[58]
See Empey, 'Limerick', 9, 19–20. While he locates Kilmurry in Estremoy (in **C89**) I would rather place it in Limerick, in whose diocese it lay.

T83: *Luimneac*
Limerick, once settled by the Vikings, became a kingdom in its own right from the tenth century onwards and had Irish governors (*airríg*) appointed by Uí Briain from

51 MacCotter, 'Cantreds of Desmond', 76; Meyer, 'Laud Genealogies', 315; Fraser et al., *Irish Texts*, i, 19–22. **52** Todd, *Cogad*, 8. **53** Empey, 'Limerick', nn. 18, 40. **54** CJRI, i, 18; RC 7/2, 278; BL Add., 4790, f. 169v. **55** Ní Dhonnchadha, 'Cáin Adomnáin', 180, 200. **56** MacNeill, 'Vita Tripartita', *passim*. **57** Ó Corráin, 'Dál Cais – church and dynasty', 53, Table I. **58** CDI, i, 24; BL Add. Charter 13598, f 169v.

the 1050s. A reference in *Vita Tripartita* clearly associates Singland, just outside of Limerick, with Dál Cais while Carn Feradaig (Cahernarry) in the same cantred was an important centre of Déis Tuascirt in the eighth century.[59]

C84: *Fontimel* (1199); *Fontymkyll* (1237); *Fontymychyl* (1290); *Fontymshyll* (1346); *Fontymghill* (1377)[60]

Empey considers Natherlach (Aherlow) to have been a distinct cantred but adduces no evidence in support of this view, which is not surprising, as none appears to exist. In the absence of such evidence, to deduce the existence of a distinct cantred of Natherlach based solely on the existence of a rural deanery of that name (and, by implication, the division of Fontymkill between two dioceses) is unsound.[61] Natherlach was in the cantred of Fontymkill during all of the colonial period from which records survive and the evidence for the political situation in this region in the pre-Invasion period, when the area of the entire cantred of Fontymkill appears as one polity, would suggest that this situation has its roots in that period.[62] Furthermore, the contemporary topographical tract, *Crichad an Chaoilli*, indicates that the territory to north of the entire *trícha cét* of Fir Maige (**T32**), was then all called Fonn Timchill.[63] It is made quite clear in the 1199 grant of Ardpatrick with three knights' fees to William de Burgh by John, that the de Burgh grant was the residue of the cantred of Fontymkill following upon earlier grants of the remainder to others, namely five fees 'in the *theodum* of Eleuri' to Thomas fitz Maurice and another five fees to Maurice fitz Philip.[64] De Burgh's three fees passed by marriage and descent to its de Cogan and de Rochfort co-heirs, and records of this fee, the manor of Tobernea, show it to have contained lands in the parishes of Effin, Ballingaddy, Ardpatrick, Kilbreedy Minor, Kilquane, and a large part of the parish of Doneraile (in modern Co. Cork).[65] The five fees in Eleuri are to be identified with the later Roche (of Fernegenel, Co. Wexford) barony of Garthgriffin (Ballingarry) which was said to lie 'in Olethere/Olehere', certainly the earlier Eleuri. From the records of this barony we know it to have contained lands in Ballingarry, Kilfinnane, and Kilflyn but it must have been more extensive than this.[66] Allowing for the cross-lands in Fontymkill and those of Monasteranenagh, the only place one could possible locate the remaining five fees here, those granted to fitz Philip, is in Natherlach, and indeed it is probable that the grant to fitz Philip later descended in

59 Ó Corráin, 'Nationality and kingship', 26–7; Stokes, *Tripartite Life*, 206; AT, 711. **60** Hardy, *Rot. Chart.*, 19. **61** While, in general, diocesan boundaries agree with cantredal there are enough exceptions to show that such convergence is far from absolute. To take just those negative examples where the evidence is unambiguous: the cantred of Wetheny in the dioceses of Cashel and of Emly, Moyeuen in Cashel and Lismore, Ymakille in Cloyne and Lismore, Offelan in Dublin/Glendalough and Kildare, Omurthi in Dublin/Glendalough and Leighlin, Ogenti in Ossory and Leighlin, Sylmolron in Elphin and Tuam, and Sleoflow and the two Kerrys in Achonry and Tuam. **62** Empey, 'Limerick', n. 27. For pre-Invasion Fonn Timchell see my 'Rise of Meic Carthaig', 69–70. **63** Power, *Crichad*, 47, 49. **64** Hardy, *Rot. Chart.*, 19; CDI, i, p. 14; Empey, 'Limerick', 13. **65** Empey, 'Limerick', 6; MacNiocaill, *Red Book of Kildare*, 138–40; CDI, i, p. 478; RC 7/2, 168, 185–6; 7/6, 393; Nicholls, '*Red Book of Kildare*', 35, 62. **66** RC 7/1, 351; 7/2, 185; 7/5, 62, 353; NLI D.3331.

some fashion to the Butler lords of the barony of Natherlach. Five knights' fees was, of course, the traditional size of the feudal barony. Finally, for proof positive that Natherlach lay in Fontymkill, note the plea roll references from the Limerick eyre of 1290 concerning pleas heard before a Fontymkill jury, where, *inter alia*, Natherlach itself and its member, Duntryleague, are mentioned.[67] The cantred of Fontymkill comprised the area of Fontymkill and Natherlach as mapped by Empey, with the addition of western Doneraile parish, Co. Cork.[68]

T84: *Fonn Timchill*
This gives the cantred of Fontymkill, and there seems to have been two polities here. The western, Déis Becc, gave most of its southern and eastern borders to those of the diocese of Limerick here, which date from at least 1111. The ruling family of Déis Becc claimed descent from the remote Rosa who occurs in the main Déisi pedigree and kings of Déis Becc are recorded in 982 and 1058, and the kingdom is mentioned in *Vita Tripartita*. (In 638 and 734 Uí Rosa kings ruled all of Déisi.)[69] The place-names Brug na nDéise (Bruff) and Áth na nDéise (Athneasy), both of which lay outside of Fontymkill, suggest that Déis Becc must once have extended further to the north and west. I have argued elsewhere[70] that the second polity here was represented by a branch of Uí Briain who became established in the Duntryleague/Aherlow area of eastern Fonn Timchill on swordland taken from Eóganacht Glennamnach during the eleventh century. A remarkable feature of the area was the string of Uí Briain fortresses built on the southern borders of Fonn Timchill, apparently during the second half of the eleventh century.[71] All of this suggests that, by perhaps 1100, Déis Becc, earlier firm allies of Uí Briain, had become incorporated into a single *trícha* of Fonn Timchill just as later there was a single cantred here. The term Fonn Timchill appears to mean 'boundary land'. Its history suggests that this meaning likely arose in light of the position of Fonn Timchill as a salient of Tuadmumu protruding into Desmumu.[72] For the continuing border dispute between Fonn Timchill and Fir Maige, see Appendix 3.

C85: *Huhene* (1199); *Any* (1237, 1290, 1346, 1358, 1377)
C86: *Grene* (1290, 1346, 1358)[73]
In 1199 John made a number of grants of lands 'in the cantred of Huhene', some of which mention individual *theoda*. These included the fees of Knocklong 'in the *theodum* of Otothel' and Carrickittle 'in the *theodum* of Syachmedth' as well as lands which certainly lay in the later manor of Any[74] and a grant of five fees at Radhoger. Orpen is certainly correct in identifying this Radhoger grant with the lands subse-

---

67 Westropp, 'On certain typical earthworks', 37–8. **68** Empey, 'Limerick', 9. **69** MacCotter, 'Rise of Meic Carthaig', 69–70; Hogan, *Onomasticon*, 67, 130; Stokes, *Tripartite Life*, 208–9; Pender, *Déssi Genealogies*, 9–10, 178; AI, 982, 1058. **70** MacCotter, 'Rise of Meic Carthaig', 69–70; idem, *Colmán*, 56–8. **71** Todd, *Cogad*, 141. **72** DIL s.v. timchell. **73** Hardy, *Rot. Chart.*, 19. **74** These were Corballi and Kildeyn. The former must be Corballydaly in Any, now Ballydaly in Knockainy parish (CDI, iii, p. 205), while Kildeyn is now obsolete but was in the manor of Any in 1305 (CJRI, ii, 189).

quently known as the manor of Grene & Asgrene. Huhene is very probably a partial Normanization of Uí Énna Áine (*alias* Eóganacht Áine), a pre-Invasion polity here (**T85**) which also gives the term 'Any'. After 1199 we find just three principal manors here, Any, also a cantred (**C85**), Carrickittle, and Grean & Asgrean, both comprising the cantred of Grean (**C86**). While the distinct cantreds of Any and Grene are noted in 1290, each with its own coroner, by 1346 we find reference to 'the cantred of Grene & Any'. In 1358 we again find reference to two cantreds while the lists of 1375 and 1377 mention only the cantred of Any. The ruridecanal structure here echoes this, with a single deanery of Grene containing both Grene and Any (in 1306: later each had its own deanery).[75] Therefore, what was considered to have been a single cantred – and unit of sub-infeudation – at the begining of the colony is later treated as two. This is not a unique situation (see **C44, C49**). One suspects that, once the violence and turmoil of the conquest had passed, better clarity prevailed regarding pre-existing spatial divisions. In this case what was thought to have been one cantred was later found to comprise two, subsequently periodically united for administrative purposes. Empey has mapped these cantreds.[76]

T85: *Uí Énna*
These are, of course, Eóganacht Áine, whose kingdom 'proper' is no doubt preserved in the extent of the cantred of Any. This lineage succeeded in providing two or three kings to Munster in the early historical period and at least five kings of Uí Énna are recorded in the period 999–1123.[77]

T86: *An Sechtmad/Tídell*
The Dál Coirpre people had three major branches, Dál Coirpre Arad Cliach, Dál Coirpre Arad Tíre, and Uí Chuanach. The linkages are remote and very uncertain.[78] The genealogically senior line, as revealed in the earliest pedigrees, were those of Araid Cliach and it is this kingdom which seems to be meant in *Vita Tripartita* where references to Araid Cliach occur. These references show that this kingdom then included Grean, Kilteely and the territory of Uí Chuanach. In addition we know that An Sechtmad, a sub-division of Dál Coirpre Arad Cliach, lay around Kilteely. Where *Lebor na Cert* refers to the kingdom of Sechtmad it seems to mean this Araid Cliach overkingdom. A king of Tídell (Kilteely) occurs in the late 900s, at a time when we also first note reference to kings of Uí Chuanach.[79] This suggests that the (over)kingdom of Araid Cliach may have had two constituent local kingdoms. Clearly, the western one of these, containing An Sechtmad, Kilteely, and Grean, is the template for the cantred of Grean & Asgrean. An earlier polity or ruling lineage here may have been Áes Gréne, who give 'Asgrene' to the barony title. These claimed to be of Eóganacht Locha Léin, a claim which must be older than *c*.AD 800,

75 Hardy, *Rot. Chart.*, 19, 20, 28; CDI, i, pp 14–16; Orpen, *Ireland under the Normans*, ii, 170; RC 7/2, 260. For the ruridecanal structure of Emly see CDI, v, 278–80, 287–9. **76** Empey, 'Limerick', 9. **77** Byrne, *Kings and high kings*, pp xxvi, 293; AI, 999, 1012; AU, 1109, 1115; ALC, 1123. **78** O'Brien, *Corpus*, 26–7, 96, 386–8; Ó Muraíle, *Mac Firbhishigh*, ii, 205–17. **79** Stokes, *Tripartite Life*, 198–203; MacCotter, *Colmán*, 27; Dillon, *Lebor na Cert*, 14, 24; Todd, *Cogad*, 72–3.

given the political context. They may have been displaced northwards by Dál
Coirpre, to their eponymous parish of Tough(esigreny).[80]

C87: *Wetheny*
Mapped by Empey, see 'Limerick', 9. This cantred was later enlarged by the addition of part of the cantred of Arech & Wetheny to the north as a direct result of the
division of the county of Munster into the new counties of Limerick and Tipperary
(see **C87a,** pp 212–3).

T87: *Uaithne Cliach*
See pp 213–14.

(THOMOND)

Empey[81] confines himself to a superficial treatment of the cantredal structure here,
but he does present a useful map of its seventeenth-century ruridecanal structure.
Ó hÓgáin[82] describes the *trícha*s of Thomond in a useful manner but inadequate use
of colonial sources necessitates caution when using his work. It is possible to reconstruct the cantredal structure of Thomond using the relatively abundant contemporary evidence preserved by the competing colonial and Irish lordships here, as well
as the ruridecanal structure of the diocese of Killaloe, which closely parallels that of
its cantreds. In 1287 Toirdelbach Ua Briain held seven cantreds in Thomond as of
the de Clare manor of Bunratty. We should add to this the de Clare demesne cantred
of Tradery and the neighbouring cantred known to the colonists as Islands, both of
which were colonized, to give a total of nine cantreds here.

C88: *Traderi* (1199); ***Tradery*** (1252, 1263, 1276)[83]
This cantred became the basis for the colonial manor of Bunratty, extents of which
survive from 1287 and 1320, and which show it to have agreed exactly with the area
of both the rural deanery and rural rectory of Tradry, giving a triple confirmation.
This cantred contained the parishes of Bunratty, Drumline, Clonloghan, Kilconry,
Kilmaleery, Kilnasoolagh, Tomfinlough, and Feenagh.[84]

T88: *Tratraige*
The cantred of Tradery derives from the *trícha* of Tratraige. This is recorded as a territorial name in 1054 and retrospectively in *Cogad* in a tenth-century context, when
apparently in the possession of the Limerick Ostmen (and in the *Bansenchas* in a
much earlier context which puts it on a par as a division with Uí Blait: **T89**). As a

---

80 O'Brien, *Corpus*, 389; MacCotter, *Colmán*, 50–6; Empey, 'Limerick', 20. **81** Empey, 'Limerick',
3, 4. **82** Ó hÓgáin, *Chláir*. **83** CDI, i, 16; CDI, ii, 1, 218; RC 7/1, 404. **84** For the extents of
Tradery see CDI, iii, p. 207ff; CIPM, vi, 160; Westropp, 'Wars of Turlough', 191–3; Gwynn and
Gleeson, *Diocese of Killaloe*, 283. For the ruridecanal structure of Killaloe see Dwyer, *Diocese of
Killaloe*, 89ff.

name in *−rige* this clearly represents the remnant territory of a pre-Dalcassian lineage here.[85]

C89: *Truohekedmalech* (1201); **Drochedoblic** (1279); **Oblyc** (1279); **Omilid** (1282); **Triucha Céad Ó mBloid** (1400)[86]

This cantred derives from *Trícha Cét Ua mBlait*, the 'trícha cét of Ua mBloid' of the mid-fourteenth-century saga *Caithréim Thoirdhealbhaigh*, and which contained Killaloe. It is described as a 'half cantred' in its original grant, a usage which echoes that of the *Papal Registers* of 1419 and 1443 ('the half cantred of Yblayd'). This may, in fact, refer to Uí Blait proper as being merely the southern half of the entire cantred, as the rural rectory of Yblayd contained only the parishes of Clonlea, Killokennedy, Kilseily and Kilfinaghta. Further evidence of a north-south division here is found in the existence of another rural rectory, that of Ogonnelloe and Oronayle, which contained the parishes of Ogonnelloe, Kilnoe, Feakle, and Killuran. All of the above parishes are contained in the rural deanery of Omulled (= Ó mBloid), which adds those of O'Briensbridge, Tomgraney, Moynoe (stated in *Caithréim* to have lain in Uí Blait), Iniscaltra, Clonrush (in Galway), Kiltenanlea, and, in Co. Limerick, Killeenagarriff and Stradbally.[87] The latter three parishes formed the colonial *theodum* of Estremoy (Áes Trí Muige, a branch of Dál Cais). Empey believes Estremoy to have been a cantred in its own right, but in this he is mistaken, as the single reference cited clearly shows it to have been a *theodum*. This is confirmed by the wording of its original grant of 1201, to William de Burgh, which describes it as 'the five knights' fees called Toth [= *Túath*] in which is sited Castle Conyn [Castleconnell]'. It was certainly part of the original cantred of Uí Blait as its three parishes were part of the later deanery of Omulled, and must have been attached to one of the surrounding Limerick cantreds for administrative purposes after the collapse of the de Clare lordship of Thomond.[88]

T89: *Trícha Cét Ua mBlait*

Trícha Cét Ua mBlait bears the name of Blat, a remote ancestor whose descendants included both chief ruling lines of Dál Cais: Uí Thairdelbaig and Uí Óengusa. That part of Uí Blait lay south of the Shannon suggests that this may have been its original area and that it later expanded northwards along the west bank of the river during the Dalcassian expansion.[89] No kings are recorded. This is because from the mid-tenth century onwards the kings of Uí Blait were also kings of all Dál Cais.

C90: *Ocassin* (1215, 1234, 1279); **Okassyn** (1277, 1292); **Truchlidocassyn** (1282); **Triucha Céad Clann Caisín** (1400)[90]

This Anglo-Norman cantred derives from the Irish *trícha cét* of Uí Chaissíne, which certainly contained Quin. The rural rectory of Quin *alias* Ocassyn contained land

85 Todd, *Cogad*, 8, 61; Dobbs, 'Ban-Shenchas', 184. **86** COD, i, 12; CDI, ii, 327, 492; TP, 58. **87** COD, i, 11; O'Grady, *Caithréim*, 4, 5; CPR, vii, 124; viii, 471, 475; Nicholls, 'Rectory, vicarage and parish', 78. **88** LPL Carew MS 619, f. 200. **89** For the Dál Cais pedigrees see O'Brien, *Corpus*, 235–245. **90** CDI, i, 94, 325; CDI, ii, 327, 492, 549; DKRI 38, p. 74; TP, 58.

in the parishes of Quin, Clooney, Doora, Inchicronan, Kilmurrynagall, Kilraghtis, Templemaley, and Tulla. Yet further confirmation of this extent may be had from that of the rural deanery of Ogassin, which is identical.[91]

T90: *Uí Chaissíne*
Its eponym, Caisséne, brother of Blat, was again remote. At least five kings of Uí Chaissíne are recorded between 1014 and 1151.[92]

C91: *Kilnaverik* (1260); *Kilnaruerik* (1261); *Clare* (1292, 1303); *Triucha Uachtarach* (1400)[93]
The first forms above derive from Cenél Fermaic, a style also found in *Caithréim*. When referring to its northern moiety *Caithréim* uses the style *leth-trícha céd uachtarach*, and this is translated as the 'upper half-cantred' in which Killinaboy and Rath parishes were located in 1445 (the rural rectory of 'Clandyfernon and Yflathrigy': *Clann Ifearnáin, Uí Flaithrig*). The core of the Uí Dedaig patrimony of Cenél Fermaic consisted of the parishes of Ruan, Kilnamona and Dysert. As late as 1574 we note the corrupt form 'Troghkyed Kylveroge'. The extent of this cantred appears to be largely preserved in that of the deanery of Drumcliff, which contained all of Inchiquin barony and the parishes of Drumcliff, Killone and Kilmaley.[94] For the style 'Clare' see **C93** below.

T91: *Cenél Fermaic*
The *trícha*/cantred of Cenél Fermaic probably grew out of the local kingdom of Uí Flaithrig which Ó Murchadha has identified with the kingdom of Ráith Tamnaig, three kings of which are recorded between 874 and 1069. The first of these was the eponym, Flaithrí, followed by his son: a stock of uncertain origin. By 1069 these had been replaced by Meic Bruaideda, a discard segment of Corcu Modruad, who in turn had been replaced here by Uí Dedaig of Cenél Fermaic by 1114. Interestingly, this line is joined to the main Dál Cais stem in a most artificial manner and Gibson has suggested that Cenél Fermaic may have been originally Corcu Bascind.[95]
   A second local kingdom had once existed in the south of this *trícha*. This was Uí Chormaic, a branch of Uí Fhidgente of Limerick (see under **C93** and **T76**). The creation of this territory must pre-date the slaying of Célechar mac Commáin at the hands of Corcu Modruad in 705, showing as it does Uí Fhidgente expansion across the Shannon. This king occurs in the Uí Chormaic pedigree which derives this line from a remote link with Uí Fhidgente. The later ruling family of Uí Chormaic, Uí Aichir, descend from Donnchad mac Aichir, described as king of Uí Chonaill and Uí Chormaic upon his death in 1071, suggesting that even as late as this Uí Fhidgente

91 CIPM, vi, 160; CDI, i, 94; O'Grady, *Caithréim*, 85; Nicholls, 'Rectory, vicarage and parish', 78; Ó hÓgáin, *Chláir*, 49. **92** AFM, 1099, 1142, 1151; AI, 1014; ALC, 1135. **93** RIA MS 12 D 9, 205; 12 D 10, 2; DKRI 37, p. 51; 38, p. 74; TP, 57. **94** O'Grady, *Caithréim*, 87, 134; Nicholls, 'Rectory, vicarage and parish', 79; Ó hÓgáin, *Chláir*, 116; TP, 57. **95** O'Brien, *Corpus*, 235–8, 242–5; Stokes, *Tripartite Life*, 206; AFM, 737, AT, 711, AI, 713; Ó hÓgáin, *Chláir*, 61–5; Ó Murchadha, 'Clann Bhruaideadha', passim; Gibson, 'Chiefdoms, confederacies', 123.

power sometimes spanned the Shannon. By the colonial period 'Ocormuck' was regarded as merely a *theodum*, indicating that, probably long before the Invasion, Uí Chormaic had diminished significantly in stature.⁹⁶

C92: *Corkobasky[n] Ethragh* (1217); 'the cantreds of **Corcumbaskyn**' (1260)⁹⁷
'Three cantreds in Corkinbaskin' are attested from early-colonial sources, one of which was Corkobasky[n] Ethragh, which seems to have included Kilkee. This style survived into the sixteenth century and was clearly derived from Corca Baiscinn Iartharach. In 1574 the new barony name Moyarta was given to 'West Corkewasten' and included, unlike its modern successor, the parish of Killard.⁹⁸

C93: *Eastern Corca Baiscinn/**Islands***
The sixteenth-century form East Corkewasten, in addition to the style Corkobasky Ethragh above (**C92**), indicates the form Corca Baiscinn Oirthearach for this cantred. Its descendant, the barony of Clonderalaw, was formed in 1574. This cantred contained all of Clonderalaw and the parish of Clondagad in Islands barony. The deanery of Corkavaskin also contained Clondagad.⁹⁹

This cantred must be that known to the colonists as Islands (*cantredum Insularum*), a usage spanning the period 1252 to 1299.¹ This is usually equated with the later barony of the same name, but, while both names are probably related, they cannot refer to the same territory. The explanation for this situation is complex.

The cantred of Islands was granted to the justiciar, John fitz Geoffrey, in 1253, to hold by a fee farm grant directly of the king. This rent appears to have been paid until around 1262, after which it ceased, probably due to the resurgence of Uí Briain in Thomond. In 1299 fitz Geoffrey's son, Richard, died seized of Islands, upon which an extent was made prior to its division among his sisters and heirs.² This found the cantred to contain forty villates of land and to be worth twenty marks as against a potential value of eighty marks. (Such a large number of villates may suggest that this 'cantred' in fact contained two or even three of the cantreds of Corca Baiscinn.) The problem with the identification of this cantred with the area of the later barony of Islands is that the latter territory has a distinct feudal history. Shortly before the grant of Islands was made to fitz Geoffrey, John de Muchegros received a similar grant of the cantred of Tradery (**C88**), to hold of a near identical rent. While the original grant speaks only of Tradery, shortly after we hear of Muchegros' lands 'in Traderi and Ocormuck', where he had a grant of free warren and license to encastellate. Muchegros duly built castles at Bunratty in Tradery and Clare(castle) in Ocormuck. In a charter of 1263 Muchegros speaks of 'the castle of Bunrath with the cantred of Traderye and Okormuck'. In 1276 however, when Muchegros exchanged these lands with Thomas de Clare, they are more precisely described as 'the cantred of Tradery and the *theodum* of Ocormok'.³ The latter reference, with

96 CS, 701; AT, 704; O'Brien, *Corpus*, 231; Ó Donnchadha, *Leabhar Muimhneach*, 308; Ó hÓgáin, *Chláir*, 66; UM, 28rd47; AI, 1070. **97** RIA MS 12 D 9, 205. **98** Empey, 'Limerick', 4; CDI, i, 16, 117; Hogan, 'The tricha cét', 232–3. **99** Ó hÓgáin, *Chláir*, 96. **1** DKRI 37, p. 51; COD, i, 50; CDI, ii, 549; CDI, iv, 308. **2** CDI, ii, 43; iv, 308; DKRI 37, pp 30, 51; 38, p. 74. **3** CDI,

its precision, indicates that Ocormuck was a *theodum* and thus cannot have been a cantred. It also shows that Ocormuck cannot have been part of Tradery. It must therefore have lain in another cantred.

The area of Ocormuck is easily discerned. It contained the castle of Clare while the later rural rectory of *Ocormayc contained the parishes of Kilmaley and Drumcliff.[4] Ocormuck thus contained the parishes of Clareabbey and Killone in addition to the above. The cantred of Islands has a separate feudal history and so cannot have contained Ocormuck. The ruridecanal structure places Ocormuck in the deanery of Drumcliff, the ecclesiastical template for the cantred of Cenél Fermaic (**C91**). Colonial references to a cantred called Clare, in Thomond, occur in 1292 and 1303, when its rent is long overdue.[5] This can only refer to the cantred of Cenél Fermaic, title to which had passed from Muchegros to de Clare in 1276. This is proven by the other cantreds listed in the same rental: Islands, Tradery and Ocassin.

It is clear that the colonized portion of Thomond was limited to the lands along the Shannon estuary, from Limerick west to sea.[6] Therefore the cantred of Islands must be located here. It cannot be equated with either Tradery or Ocormuck, and so must have lain further to the west. The greatest concentration of islands in the estuary lies off the shore of Eastern Corca Baiscinn, and this must account for the name 'Islands'. That the area was colonized is apparent from a series of pleadings concerning lands and rents in the parishes of Clondagad and Killofin, datable to between 1252 and 1290, concerning men with Anglo-Norman surnames.[7] As we have seen, some income was still issuing from Islands as late as 1299. A barony, bearing the original title of 'Clonroad and the Islands', was erected in 1574 grouped around the demesne lands of Clarecastle.[8] This is the ancestor to the present barony of Islands. The islands in question were largely those of the parish of 'Clondagad and the islands'. It is unclear if this name has anything to do with the earlier cantred of Islands. It may be suspected that some memory of the earlier name had survived and so contributed to the later usage. The large parish of Clondagad was the only area in common between the earlier and later 'Islands'.

C94: *Tricha na nAicmed*

Hogan is certainly correct in identifying the third cantred of Corca Baiscinn with the *Tricha na nAicmed* of *Caithréim*, ancestor to the present barony of Ibrickan. The rural rectory of Obrikayn/Obrakan, first attested in 1347, contained lands in the parishes of Kilfarboy and Kilmurry-Ibrickan, exactly the area of the late sixteenth-century barony. Uí Brecáin also occurs in *Caithréim*. The combined area of these three cantreds (**C92–4**) is certainly represented in that of the rural deanery of Corkavaskin, which comprised all of these baronies as well as the parish of Clondagad which must have lain originally in eastern Corkobasky.[9]

i, 465; ii, 1, 23, 217–8; RC 7/1, 404. **4** Nicholls, 'Rectory, vicarage and parish', 78. **5** DKRI 37, p. 51; 38, p. 74. **6** Empey, 'Limerick', 4. **7** RC 7/1, 191, 348, 378, 448; 7/2, 387. **8** Ó hÓgáin, *Chláir*, 96; Fiant Eliz., 4761. **9** Hogan, 'The tricha cét', 232–3; Nicholls, 'Rectory, vicarage and parish', 78; Ó hÓgáin, *Chláir*, 74, 76, 81–2, 123–4; Armagh PL MS KH II 46, 116; O'Grady, *Caithréim*, 134.

T92–4: *Corcu Baiscind*

If the later tales are of any real value for the so-called 'proto-historical' period, Corcu Baiscind owe their early dominance of what is today Co. Clare to Eóganacht associations during the sixth century. Developments during the eighth century relegated them to their later area as demarcated by three *tríchas*, named in Irish sources as Corca Baiscinn Iartharach (**T92**) and Oirthearach (**T93**) and Triúcha na nAicmedh (**T94**). By the early twelfth century they were further relegated to the former two, described as *tríchas* in *Caithreim Cellachain Caisil*. All three gave corresponding cantreds. In a later *inspeximus* of a grant of 1189 Domnall Ua Briain granted Clare abbey (*de Forgio*) 'the rectories of two cantreds in lay fee from the bounds of Athdacara [Clare] to Saltum Congoluni [Loop Head]' and these would represent **T92** and **T93** above.[10] Flanagan, however, regards this charter as a probable forgery.[11] Only kings of the regional kingdom are recorded.

C95: *Trícha Cét Fir Arda/Corcu Modruad Iartharach*

In 1268–9 Brian Ruadh, king of Thomond, accounted for £135 rent for 'two cantreds in Corcumroth'. Earlier, in 1260, reference to 'the cantreds of Corcumroch' occurs. The first of these is **C95**, given the first title above by Ó hUidhrín, while the second title occurs as a territorial name in *Caithréim*. The area of both combined is represented by that of the diocese of Kilfenora. **C95** is the exact ancestor to the barony of Corcomroe.[12]

C96: *Crích Bóirne*

This is the second of the cantreds of 1268, given the above title in *Caithréim*.[13] It is the direct ancestor to the barony of Burren.

T95–6: *The tríchas of Corcu Modruad*

The ancient kingdom of Corcu Modruad was subject from the early tenth century onwards to various efforts to replace its ruling families by members of Dál Cais. The division of the area of this kingdom into two cantreds must reflect an earlier division into two *tríchas*. This probably reflects a political division of the kingdom into two sections, ruled by rival lines who descend from brothers who were both dead by 1002. This division would seem to have been in place by the 1040s at latest.[14]

MEATH

In the lordship of Meath alone in colonial Ireland the cantred was not the preferred unit of local government and, accordingly, the original cantreds into which it was divided have left little direct trace. For the existence of the cantred in Meath in gen-

10 Hull, 'Conall Corc and the Corco Luigde', 900; Bugge, *Caithreim*, 29; BL Add. MS 4793, f. 122. 11 Flanagan, *Irish royal charters*, 163–74. 12 DKRI 36, pp 25, 39; TP, 52; O'Grady, *Caithréim*, 134; RIA MS 12 D 9, 205. 13 O'Grady, *Caithréim*, 10, 53. 14 Gibson, 'Chiefdoms, confederacies', 122; Ó hÓgáin, *Chláir*, 83–4, 88; AFM, 983, 1002; O'Brien, *Corpus*, 315.

eral we should note the reference from 1204 to a grant of cantreds in Connacht 'nearest to those of Walter de Lacy in Meath'.[15] The unit of local government in Meath was the administrative barony, which operated in a similar manner to the cantred but which was based on the feudal baronies and seignorial manors into which Meath was divided at the time of its sub-infeudation, rather than the original cantreds.[16] Unfortunately, the ruridecanal structure of Meath shows little agreement with that of the Irish *trícha céts* here, whose names are known, and so is of little value in attempting to reconstruct the lost cantreds of Meath. Just two Meath cantreds are known with certainty, and both had corresponding *tríchas*. For the likely outline of the others one should look to the extents of the *trícha céts* of Mide and Brega. Cantred enumeration (*C) is continued on the assumption that the *tríchas* of Mide and Brega had corresponding cantreds when first colonized.

The territory of Mide proper is unique in having a list of its thirteen *trícha céts* which appears to be a genuine record and whose contents suggest it perhaps to represent the situation in the early twelfth century. The two cantreds which can be identified with certainty in Meath occur as *tríchas* in this list.[17] Most of these *tríchas* can be described, at least approximately. It should be noted that the usual correlation between Irish *trícha* and colonial cantred in relation to sub-infeudation does not hold good for the rich de Lacy lordship of Meath, where smaller units, of uncertain origin but perhaps deriving from the extremely fragmented and disturbed state of pre-Invasion Mide, were the template for settlement.

C97: *Hadhnorkur* (1190); *Kinaleagh* (1209); *Athnurcher* (1260)

Athnurcher or Ardnurcher (now Horseleap) was the *caput* of the cantred. References to this as a cantred continue into the mid-thirteenth century.[18] Its extent can be gauged from such references, from the extent of the rural deanery of Ardnurcher, and in particular from the extent of the rural rectory of Firkyl (this cantred is the successor of the Irish *trícha cét* of *Fir Chell ⁊ Cenél Fiachach*: T97).[19] It consisted of the Westmeath barony of Moycashel except for the parishes of Castletownkindalen and Newtown, and the Co. Offaly baronies of Kilcoursey, Ballycowan, Ballyboy, Eglish and all of Kilmanaghan parish.

T97: *Fir Chell & Cenél Fiachach*

This *trícha* contains two names which appear to refer to the same dynasty. These derive from Fiachu son of Niall Noígiallach, placed in the early sixth century in the annals, and this kingdom is noted by Tírechán in the late seventh century. The kingdom is first described as Cenél Fiachach, in 740.[20] The usual style was simply Fir Chell, as evidenced from 918 onwards, and about twenty kings in total are recorded, the last in 1175.[21] The kingdom bears the name of the *trícha* as given above in 1139 and 1165, and in 1207 is simply the *trícha* of Cenél Fiachach.[22] Its bounds

15 CDI, i, p. 37.   **16** For lists of the medieval baronies of Meath see CCH, 115b, 141b, 161b. **17** Walsh, *Irish leaders and learning*, 62–8.   **18** Orpen, *Song of Dermot*, l.3138; A Clon, 1207; RC 7/1, 316–20.   **19** Elrington, *James Ussher* i, App C, p. cxv.   **20** AT, 739.   **21** For the first and last of the series see CS, 921 and AT, 1175.   **22** AFM, 1139, 1165; A Clon, 1207.

correspond with those of the cantred of Athnurcher *alias* Kinaleagh (**C97**: from Cenél Fiachach).[23]

C98: *Curkenie* (1190); *Corkenii* (1216); *Logseuthy* (1216)

The existence of a cantred here is signified by the reference from 1216 to 'the four cantreds in the fee of Logseuthy'.[24] The other three must be among the *trícha céts* identified in this area below. Ballymore Lough Sewdy was the *caput* of the demesne manor of Loxeudi of the lords of Meath, and there was also a rural deanery of Loxeudi. An early charter mentions lands in Meath *juxta Loccsouedi in cantredo de Curkenie* which suggests that Curkenie was the original name of the cantred of Loxeudi. The benefices in question and those of a neighbouring grant are again located in the cantred of 'Corkenii' in 1216 and these have been identified with the parishes of Piercetown and Ballymorin, lying north of Lough Sewdy.[25] The barony of Kilkenny West was known as Magheraquirk in the sixteenth century, which derives from Machaire Cuircne, while Gaelic sources include Dromraney and Forgney in Cuircne (**T98**). At a minimum, therefore, Curkenie/Loxeudi contained Kilkenny West, those parts of Meath diocese in southern Longford and the parishes of Ballymore (Lough Sewdy), Ballymorin, Piercetown and Templepatrick. Taking into account the known extent of the surrounding territorities, we should also probably include the parishes of Killare and Rathconrath in Curkenie. This gives the combined area of the seignorial manor of Loxeudi and the feudal barony of Fiehengall *alias* Kilkenny.[26] From this it would seem that, when cantreds were abandoned in Meath, the new system of baronies was based on a sub-division of the cantreds.

T98: *Cuircne*

Cuircne gives the later cantred of Curkenie *alias* Loxeudi. Cuircne were not of the Southern Uí Néill and were said to have early come under the domination of Uí Garbáin, a segment of Síl nÁedo Sláine who ruled over them, a situation reflected in an annal of 821. A *flaith* of Cuircne is recorded in 953 whose descendants are later styled *taísig* (of Cuircne). These are Uí Tolairg, of the southern Brega dynasty of Lagore.[27] These may have been planted in Cuircne by Congalach Cnogba (944–56), who restored the high-kingship to Brega. Much of Cuircne appears to have been ruled by lineages of Fir Thethba from the tenth century onwards and thus to have become part of that kingdom, notwithstanding which the earlier extent of the polity of Cuircne appears to have been preserved in that of the *trícha* (see **T102**). Cuircne occur as a people in 1082.[28]

23 Walsh, *Irish leaders and learning*, 75; idem, *Leaves of history*, 17–32. **24** CDI, i, 107. **25** Gilbert, *Reg. St Thomas*, 37; Sheehy, *Pont. Hib.*, i, 174; ii, 320n; Nicholls, '*Pontificia*', 94. For Cuircne see Dillon, *Lebor na Cert*, 96, 102; AFM, 1171; Hogan, *Onomasticon*, 316. **26** Walsh, *Westmeath*, 8, 9, 86–7; Otway-Ruthven, 'Verdon partition', 422–3, 426–7, 429–30, 435; Mills, *Gormanston*, 12; Armagh PL MS KH II 46, 90. **27** AU, 821; AFM, 952; Ó Muraíle, *Mac Firbhisigh* i, 373; Walsh, *Irish leaders and learning*, 78–9; idem, *Westmeath*, pp xvi–xviii, 86–7; idem, *Leaves of history*, 33–4; Doherty, 'Vikings in Ireland', 328. **28** AFM, 1082.

T99: (***C99***): *Delbna Ethra*
The Delbna pedigrees are confused but all genealogical linkages are remote. While
the kingdom of Delbna Ethra is clearly ancient, with the ecclesiastical *civitas* of
Clonmacnoise at its centre, its kings are only recorded from 829 onwards, at least
six down to 1130.[29] Its extent certainly included all of Garrycastle barony apart from
Lusmagh parish. This area made up the bulk of the diocese of Clonmacnoise but it
is unclear whether the remainder of the diocese, which lies in Westmeath, was part
of this *trícha*. In this context we may note the colonial evidence. Abbeylara is found
at its suppression to have possessed most of the rectories of Clonmacnoise. This must
have been as the result of a single grant made to this abbey by its founder, Richard
de Tuit, in 1210. One of his principal manors in Meath was at Ballyloughloe in
Clonmacnoise, consisting of that part of Clonmacnoise diocese in Westmeath. This
manor represented the earlier kingdom of Bregmaine, whose Uí Bráein kings are
recorded from 923 onwards.[30] Tuit seems to have received a grant of the entire *trícha*
of Delbna Ethra which probably included both Delbna and Bregmaine (and thus =
the diocese of Clonmacnoise).[31]

T100: (***C100***): *Uí Moccu Uais & Uí Thigernáin & Cenél Énda & Delbna Becc*
This *trícha* was composed of four *túatha*, at least one of which had earlier been a
kingdom. *Taísig* are recorded for both Uí Moccu Uais (1152) and Delbna Becc
(1011)[32] while the former is called a *theodum* in colonial sources and treated as a kingdom in the *Topographical Poems*. The lineages concerned are of various origins; Uí
Moccu Uais were Airgialla, Tigernán was a son of Áed Sláne (d. 604) and Énda a
son of Niall Naígiallach. Uí Moccu Uais contained the parishes of Kilbixy,
Kilmacnevan, Templeoran, Lackan, and Leny. Uí Thigernáin, a name preserved in
Magheradernon (Machaire Ua dTigernáin), consisted of the parish of Mullingar and
probably that of Portloman. Cenél Énda became the colonial manor of Kenalean,
which contained lands in the parishes of Castletownkindalan ('the castletown of
Cenél Énda'), Dysert, Conry and Churchtown. I cannot locate Delbna Becc. Both
Uí Thigernáin and Cenél Énda were demesne lands of the Uí Máelsechnaill kings
of Mide at the time of the Invasion.[33] Earlier, at the time *Betha Colmáin maic Lúacháin*
was written (? 1120s), Uí Thigernáin was a kingdom, whose area is perhaps represented by this *trícha cét*.[34]

T101: (***C101***): *Brédach & Fir Bile & Fir Thulach*
The genealogists derive Fir Thulach from Cináed son of Brandub of Uí Chennselaig,
a powerful king of Leinster who lived around 600 and who appears to have temporarily re-established Laigin control over parts of Mide. Tírechán refers to *Campus*

29 CS, 829, 896; AT, 1001, 1053, 1130; AFM, 1089. **30** ALC, 1188; AT, 1101, 1146; CS, 923;
AFM, 1040. **31** O'Brien, *Corpus*, 170–1; Ó Muraíle, *Mac Firbhishigh* ii, 637–45; Walsh, *Irish lead-
ers and learning*, 79–80; idem, *Westmeath*, 107–8; Otway-Ruthven, *A history of medieval Ireland*, 121.
32 AFM, 1012; AT, 1152. **33** TP, 2; Brooks, *Llanthony Prima and Secunda*, 90, 103; Walsh,
Westmeath, 201–3, 292–7; idem, *Irish leaders and learning*, 68–72, 89, 95–6, 101, 271; Orpen, 'Le
Wastyn', pa sim. **34** Meyer, *Betha Colmáin*, 64.

Teloch and to *Campus Bili*. Kings of Fir Thulach are recorded at least five times between 828 and 1143 and a king of Fir Bile is recorded in 1095.[35] The latter were said to be 'outlanders' of Clann Chuinn. Newtown ('of Fartullagh'), Carrick, Clonfad, Kilbride and Lynn all lay in Fir Thulach 'proper', which therefore consisted of Newtown parish and the barony of Fartullagh. Fir Bile consisted of the barony of Farbill. Brédach – ruled by *taisíg* and so a late-*túath* – was located around Kinnegad and so also lay in Farbill.[36]

T102: (*C102): *Tethba & Bregmaine*
T103: (*C103): *Cairpre Gabra*

Identification of the first of these *trícha*s presents many difficulties. Tethba originally referred to an area north of the River Inny approximating to Co. Longford, as is clear from Tírechán and other early sources. This was the kingdom of Cenél Maine or Fir Thethba, descendants of Maine son of Niall Naígiallach. There is some evidence to suggest that all of Tethba was comprised in this kingdom, which clearly has sixth-century origins, and that a southwards expansion by the rival Cenél Cairpre, probably during the seventh century, drove Cenél Maine out of northern Tethba. This reflects the *status quo* in Tírechán's time, when Granard was a significant centre in Cairpre Gabra and similarly Ardagh in Cenél Maine. In addition to Ardagh a number of other places are identified with segments of Fir Thethba in early sources, principally Frémann, an obsolete toponym located somewhere west of Ardagh, Lissardowlan, a residence of Diarmait mac Béicce, king of Tethba (d. 791), Moydow, and Mag Brecraige (= Westmeath west of the Inny and Mostrim in Longford). All of this suggests that until perhaps the tenth century the kingdom of Tethba lay mostly north of the Inny. Then, perhaps due to pressure from Cairpre and especially Conmaicne and Uí Briúin Bréifne, Tethba is driven southwards. (The suggested linkage between Durrow and the sixth-century king of Tethba, Áed mac Brénainn, seems dubious.) By the 940s the Tethba mainline, Síl Rónáin, originally associated with Frémann, are found on the Loch Ree shore north of Athlone, when described as kings of Fir Cúl Tethba, while a related line, Meic Carrgamna, are found adjacent on the southern Inny upstream, both located in Cuircne (**T98**). At least two other segments, Muintir Tlamáin and Uí Chonfhiacla, appear to have relocated into the same general area. These appear to have been proceded southwards by Síl Cremthainn, who are ancestors of Meic Amlaib in Callraige Bregmaine (Ballyloughloe) and Uí Bráein in Bregmaine proper. These latter were the ruling lineage of Bregmaine from at least 923, a kingdom in extent approximating to the baronies of Brawny and Clonlonan. This southward movement is also reflected in the politics of Fir Thethba. The older ruling line, Tellach Congaile, from which descend the lineages of Uí Lachtnáin, Uí Fhócarta and the associated Uí Airt, were located in Mag Brecraige. Associated with this 'Eastern Tethba' were the territories of northern Bregmaine (around Shrule) and Moydow. Kings of Bregmaine recorded in 822 and 840 of the line of Muintir Shercacháin probably belong to this

35 AFM, 828, 1095; AT, 1021, 1040; CS, 978; MIA, 1143. **36** Walsh, *Westmeath*, 94–5, 161–4, 371; idem, *Irish leaders and learning*, 78, 247, 264, 267–8; Meyer, *Betha Colmáin*, 94.

northern Bregmaine rather than the other. Uí Raduibh *alias* Muintir Máelfhinna (not to be confused with Muintir Maelshinna), are associated with Moydow. The first king of the nascent Muintir Thadgáin of 'West Tethba' to gain the throne was Ágda (d. 972). Uí Ágda, and probably the associated Uí Chathernaig and Uí Muirigéin, are first found around Drumraney and Loch Sewdy and I suspect were only driven into their later home in Kilcoursey Barony at the time of the Norman invasion. While the men of 'east' and 'west' Tethba would continue to struggle for the kingship, the latter gradually gained the upper hand.[37]

By 1100 at least western Tethba, as we have seen, lay largely in the *trícha* of Cuircne (**T98**). The eclipsed territory of eastern Tethba comprised land within what later became the rural deanery of Granard, which seems to have included both Cairpre Gabra and what remained of Cenél Maine territory. Here the ruridecanal structure appears to preserve the outline of the older *trícha* structure, perhaps because, unlike lands to the east, these lands were not heavily colonized. Therefore the *trícha* of Tethba & [northern] Bregmaine (**T102**) must have lain north of Cuircne, and I take it to have comprised the southern parts of the deanery of Granard, that is, the Longford parishes of Shrule, Abbeyshrule, Kilcommock, Taghshinny, Agharra, Taghsheenod, Kilglass, Rathreagh and Moydow and the Westmeath parishes of Rathaspick, Russagh and Street.

As to the *trícha* of Cairpre Gabra (**T103**), this must have comprised the remainder of Granard deanery, that is, Abbeylara, Granard, Clonbroney and Columbkille in Longford and Ballymachugh, Drumlumman and Scrabby in Cavan (the former two originally being part of Granard parish). The incorporation of both of these *trícha*s into the Uí Ruairc overkingdom of Bréifne accounts for their presence in the diocese of Ardagh.[38] For aspects of the early history of Cairpre Gabra not addressed here, see under **T8**. As to its later history, this involves continual and sometimes successful conflict with Uí Ruairc. The Uí Chiarda kings of Cairpre Gabra are usually considered to have been expelled to Carbury, Co. Kildare, named from them. The annals do not bear this out, however. These record continued conflict between Uí Chiarda and Uí Ruairc Bréifne in a context which suggests the 'migration' may have been temporary – around 1150 – and subsequently reversed, and this is further confirmed by the re-incorporation into Uí Fáeláin of Carbury before 1170 (see under **T65**), and by annals showing a joint rebellion against Ruaidrí Ua Conchobair by Uí Chiarda and Fir Thethba in 1158. It may be that the situation can be interpreted in light of pro- and anti-Bréifne factions here. In 1161 the same Kells charter was attested by (*inter alia*) an Ua Ciarda 'rí Cairpre' and a Mac Rónáin 'rí Cairpre Gabra'. In the same year, we have mention of Matudán Ua Rónáin, 'rí Cairpre Gabra'. The continued existence of a *trícha*/cantred of Cairpre Gabra is indicated by the thirteenth-century ruridecanal structure here.[39]

37 Dobbs, 'Southern Uí Néill', 5–20; eadem, 'Tethba', vol. 68, 241–59; vol. 71, 101–10; vol. 72, 136–48; Pender, 'O Cleary genealogies', 67–71; Ó Muraíle, *Mac Firbhishigh*, i, 395–403, iii, 453; Walsh, *Irish leaders and learning*, 75–7, 85–90, 257–60; idem, *Leaves of history*, 33–47; AFM, 822, 960; CS, 840, 949. **38** *Inq. in officio rot. canc. Hib.*, ii, App No. 7. For the deaneries of Ardagh see TCD MS 1067, 127 ff. **39** AFM, 1128, 1138, 1150, 1158, 1162, 1165; ALC, 1024, 1046; AT,

T104: (***C104***): *Corcu Raíde & Uí Beccon & Uí Fhiachrach & Grecraige*
This was another *trícha* composed of several large *túatha*. All names are clearly ancient. The genealogists derive Uí Beccon and Uí Fhiachrach from early offshoots of Uí Fhiachrach of Connacht while Grecraige were another trans-provincial people, if we may believe the genealogies. Tírechán mentions Patrick's journey through *regiones Roide*. An *ard dux* of Corcu Raíde is mentioned in an annal of 1185 while the *Topographical Poems* treat it as a kingdom. Uí Beccon appear as a lineage in 1066, echoing *Lebor na Cert*'s kingdom of Uí Beccon, perhaps the present *trícha*. Another reference to this *trícha* is probably to be found in one of 1159 to *inter alia* Tír Beccon and Tír Fhiachrach.[40] Both the Uí Áeda lords of Uí Beccon and the Uí Fhiachrach were said to be of Clann Cholmáin, showing these to have replaced the earlier rulers while retaining the names of their *túatha*. Corcu Raíde gave the colonial fee of Corkry which included Taghmon and Stonehall and must be represented by much of the present barony of Corkaree. Uí Fhiachrach was located around Mayne while Grecraige was situated on the south side of Lough Sheelin. The priory of Fore was, before 1186, endowed with the benefices of *Tyrebegan et totum Tyrefeihred*, a term I think here to mean Tír Beccon, Tír Fhiachrach and Grecraige. In 1541 Fore was possessed of the rectories of Faughalstown, Mayne, Foyran, Lickbla, Rathgarve and Oldcastle. From all of this it is certain that this *trícha* contained much of the present barony of Corkaree, all of Fore (Westmeath) and probably the Meath parishes of Killeagh, Oldcastle and Kilbride.[41]

T105: (***C105***): *Mag Assail*
T106: (***C106***): *Delbna Mór & na Sogain*
The name Mag Assail is preserved in that of the half barony of Moyashel (= Rathconnell parish). This was thus a very small *trícha*. Assal was a territory of greater extent than this; Delbna Mór is called Delbna Assail in *Vita Tripartita* (which also mentions *Assaliorum populos*). In the *trícha* of Mag Assail was located Ruba Conaill (now Rathconnell), a residence of the Uí Máelsechnaill kings of Mide, and perhaps Mide's capital. This may explain why this was such a relatively small *trícha*. The Delbna Mór pedigree links in with the others remotely and at least eight kings are recorded between 1030 and *c*.1230. On one occasion the metonym Telach Caíl (now Castletown Delvin) is used. It is clear from the original grant to the Nugents that the kingdom of Delbna Mór equals the barony of Delvin. As to the segment of Sogain here, the location of this *túath* is uncertain. It may originally have been a significant polity: Írgalach mac Máel Umai, a dynast of neighbouring Caílle Follamain, died as *rex Corcu Sogain* in 816, while an Uí Labhrata *flaith* of Sogain witnessed a Kells charter around 1115.[42]

1174; AU, 953, 992, 1001, 1012, 1077, 1087, 1115; CDI, iv, p. 18; Mac Niocaill, 'Irish "charters"', 159. **40** ALC, 1185; AFM, 1159; TP, 2. **41** Walsh, *Westmeath*, 96–7, 125, 372–4; idem, *Irish leaders and learning*, 241, 244–5, 247–8, 255–6; idem, *Mac Firbhishigh* i, 362; Mac Síthigh, 'Mhainistir Fhobhair', 174; Dillon, *Lebor na Cert*, 96, 102. **42** Doherty, 'Vikings in Ireland', 318, 328–9; O'Brien, *Corpus*, 170–1; Ó Muraíle, *Mac Firbhishigh* ii, 637–645; Walsh, *Westmeath*, 199–201, 367–9; Mac Niocaill, 'Irish "charters"', 157, 159; Flanagan, 'Telach Cail', passim; AT, 1144, 1168,

T107: (*C107): *Caílle Follamain*
T108: (*C108): *Crích na Cétach*

The ruling line of Caílle Follamain represents the third main branch of Southern Uí Néill, descending from Colmán Becc (d. 587), perhaps a doublet of Colmán Mór. While the family were presumably established here from this time the earliest evidence locating one of them (Tuathal mac Máel Tuile) in the general area, in this case Kells, dates from 718. The eponym is Tuathal's nephew, Follaman mac Cú Chongalt, who died as king of Mide in 766. Five kings of Caílle Follamain (**T107**) are recorded between 851 and 1017 while, around 1090, Áengus mac Meic Rancáin, *lántaisech Síl Tuathal ocus Caílle Follamain* is noted.[43] The latter entry suggests a weakening of the polity in the face of Uí Ruairc expansion and it is telling that the ruling line, Uí Fallamhain, has relocated to Crích na Cétach (**T108**) on the Leinster borders by 1124. Uí Fallamhain kings of this newly conquered swordland (?) are recorded in 1124 and 1142.[44] As to the extent of Caílle Follamain, its name is preserved in the parish of Killallon while the parishes of Diamor and Kilskeer also lay in it. A land dispute among Síl Tuathail – whose eponym has been noted above – around 1130, was settled with sureties from the abbots of Kilskeer and Girley, suggesting the latter also to have lain in this *trícha*. As Caílle Follamain was clearly adjacent to the *trícha* of Gailenga (**T109**), its borders must have run eastwards as far as the area of Kells, which, given its Southern Uí Néill associations, probably lay in Caílle Follamain. Therefore **T107** seems to have comprised approximately the bulk of the barony of Fore (Meath) and much if not most of Upper Kells. The normal correlation between Irish and colonial borders does not seem to exist in this instance, perhaps due to the late conquest of this part of Mide by Uí Ruairc – who made Kells their capital – and the expulsion of its kings. As to Crích na Cétach (**T108**), presumably this corresponds to the colonial fee of Crinagedach, the parish of Castlejordan (shared by Meath and Offaly) and probably parts of Ballyburley. The small size of this *trícha* is perhaps due to its probable status as late swordland.[45]

T109: (*C109): *Gailenga & Luigne & Saitni*

In Mide as in Connacht, the first two terms are interchangeable, leading to a very confused situation. Indeed all three peoples above claimed remote relationships. The earliest reference to a king of Luigne, apart from an ogam reading *Luguni*, occurs around 700, but the king, Bodbchad, was a brother to the ruling Clann Cholmáin king of Mide and certainly imposed. Indeed, it seems likely that early dominance over Gailenga and Luigne by Southern Uí Néill was relatively shortlived. An important weapon in this control was the kingdom of Fir Chúl Breg, ruled by various descendants of Áed Sláine since its establishment in the early 600s. The chief seat of this polity was Ráith Airthir (near Donaghpatrick), and its last certain Síl nÁedo Sláine king died in 876 (Cathalán mac Cernaig).[46] After this, Fir Chúl, which also

---

1174; AU, 815, 1096; AFM, 1085. **43** AT, 1017; AU, 765, 850, 884, 920; AFM, 890. **44** AFM, 1124, 1142. **45** Walsh, *Leaves of history*, 47–51; idem, *Irish leaders and learning*, 77, 238–9; Mac Niocaill, 'Irish "charters"', 156. **46** AU, 877; Byrne, 'Cnogba', Table 1; O'Brien, *Corpus*, 161.

included Emlagh, declined until absorbed by Gailenga in the early eleventh century. Meanwhile, kings of Gailenga/Luigne begin to be recorded from 848. Many such – around thirty in total – are noted in the annals and Kells charters, most seemingly members of closely related lines who use the above terms as well as that of Túath Luigne interchangeably. Complications increase after the 1078 imposition of a Munster Ua Briain dynast by Uí Ruairc as king of Gailenga. Another Ua Briain occurs as king of Luigne in a Kells charter of around 1150 in company with an indigenous king of Gailenga. Shortly after this an Ua Ragallaig 'tributary king' of Machaire [Gaileng] occurs, yet another symptom of Bréifne dominance.[47] Yet another polity here was Uí Moccu Uais Brega, around Kilshine, several kings of which are recorded between 783 and 1017.[48] It is not surprising that such a confused kingship picture in pre-Invasion times renders useless the search for an imprint of the indigenous structure in the post-Invasion divisions here. Some idea can, nonetheless, be gained of the extent of this *trícha*. The barony of Morgallion, from Machaire Gaileng, must have lain in it as must have Fir Chúl to the west. The occurrence of several Gailenga and Luigne kings as witnesses of Kells charters suggests that the western border must have extended to near Kells. We know that Gailenga/Luigne extended northwards to Lough Ramor, while it also included Sliab Guaire, a territory similar in extent to the barony of Clankee (Clann Chaích) in Co. Cavan. In this context it is useful to note the existence of a *túath* called *Fidh na Saithni* in Clann Chaích in 1314, which gives the Saitne of the title above, as well as a reference to a river, *Abaind Saitni* in a Kells charter. In summary, then, this *trícha* included approximately the baronies of Morgallion, Lower Kells, the eastern tip of Upper Kells, Clankee, parts of Castlerahan, and probably parts of Slane. It will be noted that the size of this *trícha* is similar to its fellows in the Uí Ruairc lordship of Tír Briúin, and is bigger that the other *trícha*s of the Mide list, which largely remained outside of Uí Ruairc control.[49]

T110: (*C110): (*Tuascirt*) *Breg(a)*

The Irish computation of *trícha*s, including that appendant to the list of Mide *trícha*s described above, gives Brega five such, unfortunately not named. Unsurprisingly, this figure agrees with the number of local kingdoms found here in the twelfth century, while the names of some of these *trícha*s can be supplied from other sources. In this work one of these five units (**T/C53**) is treated of under Dublin, another (**T/C159**) under Uriel.

The Southern Uí Néill dynasts of Brega descend from Áed Sláne (d. 604), overlord of most of Mide. He himself is associated with Brug na Bóinne and this suggests his power-centre lay around Slane. Several dynasties, some of which held the high-kingship, descend from him, including two in the area under discussion. Firstly we have Uí Chonaing, who used three royal titles alternatively: Brega, Cnogba

47 Mac Niocaill, 'Irish "charters"', 155, 159, 162. 48 AU, 782, 838, 910; AFM, 1017. 49 O'Brien, *Corpus*, 161, 168; Ó Muraíle, *Mac Firbhishigh* ii, 647; Walsh, *Irish leaders and learning*, 81–4; Byrne, 'Cnogba', 394–5; idem, *Kings and high kings*, p. xvi; Walsh, *Leaves of history*, 94–5; Hogan, *Onomasticon*, 369; Mac Niocaill, 'Irish "charters"', 163; AC, 1314.11.

(Knowth) and Ciannachta, and who descend from Congal mac Áeda (d. 634). From an original base around Slane this dynasty, *c.*700, absorbed the territory of its subsidiary kingdom, Ciannachta Breg. This accounts for one of its titles. The centre of Ciannachta Breg lay around Duleek and its first king is recorded in 572. After the 950s the title *rí Breg* is used almost exclusively by Uí Chonaing. Once again differentiation must be made between Brega as a local kingdom and regional kingdom. As early as 987 we find an underking of 'Tuascirt Breg' under the senior kings of the regional kingdom, and this must indicate the existence of **T110** already.[50] As to the extent of this local kingdom in the twelfth century, our evidence is patchy. It certainly contained both baronies of Duleek and probably Upper Slane. By this time its royal centre may have come to lie around Duleek where, post-Invasion, its Uí Chellaig kings retained some lands. These had come to dominance in Brega after the collapse of Uí Chongalaig power after 1017, but, once again, it is not clear if references to Brega after this refer to the regional kingdom or the local kingdom. The evidence suggests both.[51] Congalach mac Flainn of this dynasty (d. 978) bore the title *rí Gaileng* but it is unclear whether this relates to Gailenga settlement around Knowth or to the Gailenga kingdom of Uí Áeda Odba which seems to have been located somewhere in Skreen barony, perhaps including Navan itself, and whose eponym, Áed Odba (d. 700), was among the royal guarantors of Cáin Adomnáin. The Skreen/Tara area was royal demesne (of Uí Máelsechnaill) and was probably part of Tuascirt Breg.[52]

The existence of an Uí Néill kingdom of Cremthann, located in the baronies of Slane, as suggested by four centuries of historiography stretching from Colgan to the present, appears to be without foundation and seems to have arisen through confusion with the Cremthann of Mugdorna and of Uí Maine. The actual Cremthann of Brega, a king of whom is noted in the early tenth century, appear to have been one of the *saer-aicmi* of Mugdorna (see **T163**), suggesting that it is in Slane barony that we should locate the earlier kingdom of Mugdorna Breg.[53] The absorption of Slane by the Uí Ruairc kingdom of Bréifne by 1150 may explain the lack of evidence regarding the indigenous political status of this barony.

T111: (*****C111**): *Deiscert Breg*
The second Uí Néill dynasty of Brega was Uí Chernaig, who descend from Diarmait son of Áed Sláne. They used the titles *rí Locha Gabor* (Lagore) and *rí Deiscirt Breg* and

---

50 AU, 987. 51 Bhreathnach, 'Tara', 7–8; AI, 1129; ALC, 1025, 1028, 1046, 1053, 1060, 1073, 1086; AU, 1093, 1160. 52 O'Brien, *Corpus*, 159–162; Byrne, 'Cnogba', 392–3, 395–8, Table 3; idem, *Kings and high kings*, 115; Walsh, *Leaves of history*, 7–13; idem, *Irish leaders and learning*, 81; Byrne, 'Ciannachta Breg', passim; Ní Dhonnchadha, 'Cáin Adomnáin', 207–8; BB, 196a19; Clinton, 'Kingdom of Lóegaire', 384–6; AFM, 978; Ó Murchadha, 'Odhbha', passim; Bhreathnach, 'Tara', 8–9. 53 Todd, *Cogad*, 37; Swift, 'Óenach Tailten', 111, and the references she quotes. Of the four kings of Cremthann proposed by Swift three were rather kings of Cremthann in Uí Maine in Connacht, while the fourth is of uncertain origin, while Byrne's reference ('Two lives of St Patrick', 14) seems to be an error. Again, the annal in AFM, 1029, used by Hogan (*Onomasticon*, 302), which seems to locate Cremthann in Meath, is erroneous, the correct reference being in AT. See Ó Fiaich's 'Airgialla', 104–6, and Ó Mórdha's 'Mugdorna', 438–9.

their demense territory lay around Dunshaughlin, Ratoath and perhaps Dunboyne. Originally their overkingdom included the polity of Déisi Temro/Breg to the west and all of north County Dublin but they lost overlordship of the latter to the kingdom of Dublin. Déisi Breg gives the later barony of Deece. Kings of Déisi Breg are recorded in 757, 1034, and 841 (Galtrim: a metonym),[54] but it is clear from the grant of sub-infeudation here that Déisi lay in the Meic Gilla Shechlainn kingdom of Deiscert Breg at the time of the Invasion, along, no doubt, with Ratoath and Dunboyne.[55]

T112: (*C112): *Laegaire*

The dynasty of Laegaire claimed a somewhat questionable descent from Laegaire son of Niall Naígiallach. Its kings are recorded regularly in the annals from 641 down to the Invasion, sometimes bearing the metonym Telach Aird.[56] Clinton has attempted to reconstruct the bounds of this kingdom and has shown that, at a minimum, it contained most of the baronies of Navan and parts of Lune and northern Lower Moyfenrath. There are reasons for thinking that this reconstruction is too minimalist. Immediately west of Laegaire lay the Uí Néill kingdom of Ardgal, three kings of which are recorded between 746 and 836.[57] This occupied approximately the area of the later barony of Lune and vanishes from history following warfare with Laegaire. As Tlachtga lay in Laegaire, but earlier seems to have been in Ardgal, one suspects that this area was absorbed in Laegaire during the ninth century. While Ardgal survived as a territorial designation into the twelfth century it may be significant that its area came to be known by the colonists as Lune, probably derived from Luaigne (rather than Luigne), an old *túath* name here. It is clear from twelfth-century annals that the only significant polity lying immediately east of the Clann Cholmáin area of dominance, as indicated by the *trícha cét* list for Mide, was Laegaire, and Ardgal/Luaigne does not feature in the Mide *trícha* list. Furthermore, to the south of Laegaire 'proper' lay Mag Lacha, a king of whom is recorded in a Kells charter of *c.*1040, although this 'kingdom' does not feature in any other record. Fir Maige Lacha are said to be of Clann Cholmáin in the genealogies and it seems probable that their small kingdom, which certainly contained lands in Rathmolyon parish and may have included Clonard, was eclipsed during the eleventh century by the growing power of Laegaire. Probable evidence for this is found in the lands in Rathcore parish, south of Rathmolyon, in which the Uí Chaíndelbáin kings of Laegaire were enfeoffed by Hugh de Lacy after the Invasion. Surely these lands had formed part of the Uí Chaíndelbáin kingdom of Laegaire! A final confirmation that Laegaire was bigger than its core territory is found in a reference to Clann Laegaire themselves as occupying a *leth-trícha cét*.[58] This implies that the full *trícha* of Laegaire was greater than Laegaire 'proper'.

---

54 AU, 757, 841, 1034. **55** Byrne, 'Cnogba', 391, 394, 397, Table 2; Orpen, *Ireland under the Normans* ii, 85; Walsh, *Irish leaders and learning*, 80–1; Bhreathnach, 'Tara', 3–5; AT, 1053, 1160; 1171; AFM, 1121. **56** AI, 1104; ALC, 1018; MIA, 1129; AT, 1033, 1136, 1157; AU, 1085, 1116; CS, 926; AFM, 639, 1160. **57** AU, 746, 811, 836; Mac Niocaill, 'Irish "charters"', 157, 159.

ROSCOMMON

Five cantreds of the Irish kingdom of Connacht were retained by the crown as demesne and duly shired as the county of Roscommon.

C113: *Omany* (1258, 1280, 1298, 1305, 1309)[59]
See p. 35.

T113: *Uí Maine/Sogain*
Uí Maine refers to both a local and regional kingdom. The area of the latter was occupied by five cantreds (**C19, 20, 27, 113–4**). The earliest king of Uí Maine, the regional kingdom, of which we can be certain was Brénainn Dall, whose death is recorded in 601 and who was sixth in descent from the eponym, Maine Mór. Rathbrennan in Roscommon parish appears to bear his name while *Vita Tripartita* (mid-ninth century) indicates that neighbouring Fuerty was also originally in Uí Maine. Pressure from Uí Briúin Aí would drive Uí Maine southwards over several centuries. Its ecclesiastical echo by the early twelfth century is the diocese of Clonfert. By this time the northern Uí Maine lands had been largely overrun by Uí Briúin Aí, yet memory of their origins was preserved in the name of the *trícha* of Tír Maine (**T114**) which gives the cantred of Tirmany.[60]

The cantred of Omany (**C113**) must derive from Uí Maine but seems rather to correspond to the *trícha* of the Sogain, although this is only attested in a late (*c.*1400) tract. A king of Sogain is recorded in 1135. Sogain were an ancient *daer-thúath* in Connacht. The name change may derive from the occupation of the Aughrim area by Uí Chellaig, kings of Uí Maine. However, the style 'Omany' may have been purely colonial, as we find reference to Sogain as a territory as late as 1224.[61] Note that the rural deanery here is styled Aughrim in the early fourteenth century but Sogain in 1615.

C114: *Tirmane* (1201); *Tyrmany* (1233, 1314); *Tirmany* (1261, 1291); *Tyrmani* (1309)[62]
As the only one of the 'king's cantreds' to be extensively settled significant records survive pertaining to lands in this cantred, which lay along both sides of the Suck in counties Roscommon and Galway. It contained the royal castles of Athlone and Rindown (St John's parish) and grants to settlers were made in the parishes of Killian, Killeroran, Taghboy, Athleague, Kilmeane, Killinvoy, Cam, Dysert, Tisraha and Kiltoom.[63] Two ecclesiastical sources can be used to fill in the remainder of this

58 Clinton, 'Kingdom of Lóegaire', passim; Walsh, *Leaves of History*, 10, 13–17; idem, *Irish leaders and learning*, 74–5, 77–8, 89; Byrne, 'Trim and Sletty', 318; Mac Niocaill, 'Irish "charters"', 157; Nicholls, 'Anglo-French Ireland', 381. **59** COD, i, 55, 97, 172; CJRI, ii, 134. **60** Stokes, *Tripartite Life*, 104, 350. For much of what follows see Kelleher's excellent 'Uí Maine'. For the source of the pedigrees used by Kelleher see O'Donovan, *Hy Many*, 25–59. **61** O'Donovan, *Hy Many*, 71–4; AT, 1135; ALC, 1224. **62** CDI, i, 24, 297; DKRI 35, p. 44; 37, p. 45; 39, p. 54. **63** CDI, i, 81, 92; ii, 132, 143, 323, 489–90; iv, 356–7; Knox, 'Connacht' ii, 286–92; COD, i, 102; DKRI

extent. Firstly there is the rural deanery of Tyrmane in the diocese of Elphin and secondly, the rectories impropriate to the abbey of Athlone (*de Innocenta*), sources which are near identical in area. The extent of Tirmany as revealed by these sources add the parishes of Ahascragh, Killosolan, and Raharra. In the south our ecclesiastical templates fail us in the case of the parishes of Drum and Moore, as these were a detached portion of the diocese of Tuam. While Moore certainly lay in the cantred of Syllanwath, Drum probably lay in Tirmany, especially given the lay of the line of the parish boundaries here and those of Athlone parish.[64]

T114: *Tír Maine*
Tír Maine contained a number of minimal polities. Delbna Nuadat lay around Rahara between the Suck and Shannon. Two kings are recorded in 756, and the territory is again noticed in 818.[65] *Lebor na Cert* mentions its king, but this may be an anachronism. Cremthann was a territory derived from the Clann Chremthainn of Uí Maine, the eponym being remote. By the sixteenth century this territory was confined to the barony of Killian west of the Suck but originally must have included lands across the river in Roscommon. Cremthann succeeded to the kingship of Uí Maine at least five times between 749 and 938, after which they were replaced here by a branch of the Uí Briúin Aí segment of Muintir Máelruanaid, who held the kingship of Cremthann several times between 999 and 1048. Another polity here must have been Cenél Coirpre Chruim, whose kings are recorded around 722 and again in 785. The eponym was father to King Brénainn Dall above (**T113**). These were the principal ruling line of Uí Maine, subsequently Uí Chellaig, who came to dominate the kingship almost entirely after 938. Their original territory can only have lain in Tír Maine, probably east of the Suck. Just when Uí Briúin pushed them southwards is unclear. Their lands were probably taken by Clann Chonnmaig, Clann Murchada and Clann Uatach, the eponyms being princes of Uí Briúin who had lived in the eighth century.[66] Epithets given to Uí Chellaig kings in a poem of 1268 suggests that they were certainly established around Aughrim and Loughrea by the early eleventh century.[67] Tír Maine first occurs as a territorial term in 1163, and this *trícha*, rather than a local kingdom, seems to represent memory of Uí Maine territory which had passed under Uí Briúin Aí control.[68] (Yet all may not be as simple as this for see the *Annals of Tigernach* s.a. 1163, which suggests that Uí Chellaig still exercised some lordship here.)

C115: *Moyhee* (1204, 1305); ***Roscoman*** (1215); ***Roscuman*** (1232); ***Mackny*** (1261); *Le Maghery* (1314); *Moyhe* (1329)[69]
The principal templates for this cantred are the rural deanery of Syllmurigh and the rectories impropriate to Roscommon priory. Our ecclesiastical templates fail us on the western border with the cantred of Sylmolron and cause some confusion in the

39, p. 27. **64** TCD MS 566, f. 170; 1066, 489 ff. **65** Kelleher, 'Uí Maine', 70, 75. **66** Dillon, *Lebor na Cert*, 52, 58; Jaski, *Irish kingship*, 314–15; Kelleher, 'Uí Maine',69, 73, 81–2, Plates I–II. **67** O'Donovan, *Hy Many*, 100. **68** AT, 1163. **69** CDI, i, 37, 97, 297, 299; DKRI 35, p. 44; 39, p. 54; CJRI, ii, 134; *Analecta Hibernica* I (1930), 214.

south west. What can be said with certainty to have lain in this cantred are the parishes of Roscommon, Kilteevan, Kilbride, Fuerty, Cloonycormican, Kilcorky, Killukin, Ogulla, Kilcooly, Elphin, Shankill, Kilcolagh, Kilmacumsy, Creeve, Baslick, Ballynakill, Drumatemple and Kilcroan. The *theodum* of Clanconway exhibits some signs of an older claim from Tirmany. Its parishes of Kilcroan, Dunamon and Kilbegnet were part of the deanery of Tyrmane, but the first two were impropriate to Roscommon. Dunamon certainly lay in Mag Aí (**T115**), and I think these parishes, along with Oran, must also have lain in Moyhee.[70]

T115: *Mag Aí*

The Uí Briúin Aí dynasty and their close relatives, the proto-Uí Neill, are said to have originated around Crúachan in Mag Aí. When we take into account the borders of the surrounding polities the area originally available to Uí Briúin here cannot have consisted of more than the area of a few civil parishes, which must throw doubt on the received wisdom here, and which makes Nicholls's suggestion of Mag Seóla as the true font of the Connachta more attractive, if still uncertain (see under **T21**).

Byrne suggests that Rogallach mac Uatach (d. 649) is the first historically reliable king of Uí Briúin Aí. By Tírechán's time (*c.*690) their territory was still hemmed in to the north and east by Uí Ailello, to the west by Ciarraige and to south by Uí Maine. After the reign of Muiredach Muillethan (d. 702) his descendants, Síl Muiredaig, begin to expand in several directions, although the exact chronology of these expansions is unclear. The principal directions are north against Uí Ailello, whose kingdom collapsed around 800, and southwards against Uí Maine. Over time various *túatha* are created (or taken over) by segments of Síl Muiredaig and, based on their eponyms, one might suggest that the southern extent of the later cantred of Maghery *alias* Moyhee (**C115**: from Machaire Connacht and Mag Aí) must have been reached not long after 800. Mag Aí was the original name for the local kingdom whose kings came to dominate all Connacht and whose name continued as the name for this *trícha* as recorded between 1030 and the Invasion.[71]

C116: *Trasthueod* (1195); *Trithweth* (1214, 1229); *Trichta* (1233); *Tothes* (1284, 1305, 1309, 1314)[72]

Hogan has described this cantred based on the extents of its individual three *túatha* from which its name is taken (*na Trí Túatha*). Cenél Dobtha contained the parishes of Kilglass, Termonbarry, Clontuskert and eastern Lissonuffy, Corcu Achlann contained Bumlin, Kiltrustan, Cloonfinlough and western Lissonuffy, while Tír Briúin na Sinna contained Aughrim, Clooncraff and Kilmore. The first and last of these had corresponding rural rectories (Corcachlyn and Tyrbryun) which help con-

70 TCD MS 1066, 489 ff; AFM, 1154. For the territorial implications of the terms Maghery and Moyhee see Hogan, *Onomasticon*, 509. For an extent of Clanconway see CDI, ii, 489–90. **71** Byrne, *Kings and high kings*, 239; Stokes, *Tripartite Life*, 314, 318–20; AT, 1030; ALC, 1225, 1227. **72** Mills, *Gormanston*, 143; CDI, i, 92, 257, 299; CJRI, ii, 134; DKRI 39, pp 27, 54; BL Add. MS 4787, f. 312.

firm Hogan's extents. In addition we should probably add the parish of Kilgefin which, in company with several of the above parishes, was impropriate to the priory of St Mary, Clontuskert. This extent is further confirmed by that of the deanery of Tuatibh/Tughanligh, of which only a partial listing survives, all the parishes of which agree with the above.[73]

T116: *(na Trí) Túatha*

The Irish usages Trí Túatha and na Túatha give the colonial correspondents Trithweth and Tothes here. This *trícha* is more usually referred to by its parts, Corcu Achlann, Cenél Dobtha and Tír Briúin na Sinna. The first two are related and are of the same stock as Cenél Mac nEircc, and thus Uí Ailello (see **T117**). Uí Briúin na Sinna take their name from a fictitious descent from Brión of the Connachta, their true origins being obscure. The original kings of this shared polity may have been Corcu Achlann, mentioned in *Vita Tripartita* in the ninth century. Meic Branáin kings of Corcu Achlann are mentioned in 1159 and 1224 and Uí Manacháin kings of Uí Briúin in the same entry in 1159 and in 1208. Perhaps significantly, the AU entry in 1159 for Corcu Achlann has *rí*, while the same entry in *Tigernach* has *taísech*, which may indicate that the kingship of na Túatha rotated between both *túatha*. *Taísig* of Corcu Achlann are noted in five entries between 1088 and 1295, one for Tír Briúin na Sinna, in 1196, and three for Cenél Dobtha between 1136 and 1297. Na Trí Túatha is used in a territorial sense in 1225 and as a polity in 1233.[74]

C117: *Moilurc-Thirelele* (1195); *Moylurc-Tirlele* (1204); *Moylurg & Tyrelele* (1305); *Maglurg & Tyrelele* (1329)[75]

This cantred, whose name is always given as above, was composed of two half-cantreds. Moylurg was ancestor to the present barony of Boyle, Co. Roscommon, all of which must have lain in Moylurg apart from the parish of Kilronan which lay in the diocese of Ardagh. Tyrelele was ancestor to the barony of Tirerrill, Co. Sligo, and contained those ten parishes in that barony which lie in the diocese of Elphin. Confirmation is again available from ecclesiastical sources. The deanery of Tyrerrell agrees exactly with the extent of Tyrelele as given above. In the case of the deanery of Mullorg, this contained all of Moylurg as given above but in addition contained the parishes of Tibohine and Kilnamanagh which we know to have lain in the colonial county of Connacht rather than Roscommon, and so cannot have lain in this cantred.[76]

T117: *Mag Luirg & Tír Ailello*

The cantred of Moylurg & Tyrelele derives from the *trícha* of Mag Luirg and Tír Ailello. This must originally have been part of Uí Ailello, whose eponym was one of the sons of Echu Mugmedón, and thus an important and powerful lineage. Uí

---

73 Hogan, *Onomasticon*, 218, 292, 635; Nicholls, 'Rectory, vicarage and parish', 76; TCD MS 1066, 489 ff.   **74** Ó Muraíle, *Mac Firbhishigh*, i, 430, 547–53; Stokes, *Tripartite Life*, 95; AU, 1159, 1295, 1297; ALC, 1120, 1182, 1208, 1224–5, 1233; AT, 1088, 1136, 1159; AFM, 1150, 1196.   **75** Mills, *Gormanston*, 143; CDI, i, 37; DKRI 35, p. 44; CJRI, ii, 134; *Analecta Hibernica* 1 (1930), 214. **76** TCD MS 1066, 489 ff.

Ailello are usually thought to have collapsed around 800 after major defeats, yet a branch, Cenél Mac nEircc, occur as kings of Mag Luirg in *Vita Tripartita*, which seems to place them here as late as perhaps the mid-ninth century. (Kings of Cenél Mac nEircc recorded between 774 and 830 may have been of this polity or of its unconnected namesake in Ulster.)[77] Cenél Mac nEircc did not last here, and the indications are that Grecraige of Loch Teget, originally a subject lineage of Uí Ailello, subsequently became the only polity here. Their territory certainly included Mag Luirg and Coolavin and may also have included Uí Ailello. This is suggested by their presence in *Lebor na Cert* here. Later again, Grecraige were taken over by Uí Máelruanaid of Síl Muiredaig whose first king of Mag Luirg is recorded in 1124. (An earlier king was styled *rí Muintire Máelruanid* in 1014.) In the early thirteenth century their title changes to *comites* of 'Magluirg' in contemporary charters.[78]

TIPPERARY

The cantreds of Tipperary have been described and mapped by Empey.[79] While he is largely correct in his conclusions a re-evaluation of the evidence suggests a number of revisions.[80]

CII8: *Euermun* (1201); *Ermon* (1293, 1296, 1305); *Oremon* (1315); *Ermonia* (1337)[81] See Empey, 'Tipperary', 25, and 'Limerick', 18, where he anachronistically calls the cantred 'Ormond', the name of its descendant barony.

TII8: *Múscraige Tíre/Urmuma(n)*
Múscraige Tíre is typically linked remotely to the other Múscraige dynasties. The first annalistic record of a king occurs in 745. It appears to have had rival ruling families, one of whom, Uí Dúngalaig, first emerge in 914 and represent the main stem of the genealogies. Their kings are interspersed with others who may represent the rival segment of Uí Farga (a rivalry noted in the ninth-century *Vita Tripartita*).[82] Uí Farga divide from the main stem in the remote period and their territory lay in northern Múscraige Tíre. Separate annal entries for Domnall mac Lorcáin in 988 style him 'rí Múscraige Tíre ocus Ua Forga' and simply 'rí Ua Forga'. He occurs in the Uí Farga pedigree. A clearly corrupt entry in AFM for 1131 notes the slaying of a king of Uí Fuirg (*sic*) and another such king is recorded in 1060.[83] The situation is further complicated by the arrival of Uí Chennétig of Dál Cais from across the Shannon, who had certainly replaced any indigenous kings by 1159, if not earlier.

77 AU, 762, 796, 829; AFM, 769. **78** O'Brien, *Corpus*, 133; Walsh, *Irish leaders and learning*, 177–8, 196–8; Stokes, *Tripartite Life*, 94, 144; Dillon, *Lebor na Cert*, 48, 58; O'Flaherty, *Ogygia*, 30; Orpen, 'Irish Cistercian documents', 306–7; Hogan, *Onomasticon*, 222; Todd, *Cogad*, 168; Flanagan, *Irish royal charters*, 350; ALC, 1187, 1197, 1200, 1207–8, 1210, 1215, 1218; MIA, 1124; AT, 1159. **79** Empey, 'Tipperary', passim, and again, with some revision, in his 'Limerick'. **80** The principal lists of Tipperary cantreds can be found in DKRI 37, pp 50–1; 38, p. 29; NAI MS Cal. JI 33–4 Edward I, 4–8; RC 8/12, 798–9; COD, iii, 92–6. **81** COD, i, 12, 206, 298. **82** Stokes, *Tripartite Life*, 211; O'Brien, *Corpus*, 367. **83** AI, 1033, 1037, 1068, 1078; AU, 814, 990; CS, 988; AFM, 745, 898, 921, 990, 1060, 1131.

Untypically, these did not try to assume the mantle of those they had replaced but rather changed the name of the *trícha* to Urmuma, originally a term for a much larger area, and which gives the cantredal name Euermun (later Ermon and then Ormond). It may be that this name-change reflects a stewardship of the large region of Urmuma by Uí Chennétig, the name duly coming to apply to Múscraige Tíre as the *trícha* of which Uí Chennétig were direct lords.[84] Originally the border between Araid Tíre (**T121**) and Múscraige Tíre was the Gaethach (Nenagh) River. However, the style Óenach Urmuman for Nenagh suggests that Uí Chennétig may have expanded south of the river and incorporated some of Araid Tíre into Múscraige Tíre in the decades before the Invasion. Nenagh later became the *caput* of both successor cantreds (**C118, C121a**).[85]

C119: *Elykaruel* (1201); *Helyocaruel* (1210); *Elycarwyl* (1293, 1305); *Ely O Karwyl* (1315)
C120: *Elyhohogarthy* (1201); *Elyogrit* (1296); *Elyogryd* (1305); *Ely* (1432); *Elliogirth* (1486)[86]
See Empey, 'Tipperary', 25–6.

T119: *Éile Uí Cherbaill*
T120: *Éile Uí Fhócarta*
The cantreds of Elyocarwyl and Elyogryd together comprised the area of the ancient kingdom of Éli, whose kings occur in the annals regularly from 670. Éli feature in the Eóganacht origin tales in a context which suggests that they were originally lords of the Cashel area before the rise of Eóganacht, an event which occurred perhaps in the years around AD 500. These cantreds derive from Éile Uí Cherbaill and Éile Uí Fhócarta respectively. Certainly by the mid-eleventh century, in the annals and genealogies, we can trace a division between the ruling families of what are styled Éile Tuaiscirt (Uí Cherbaill) and Éile Deiscirt (Uí Fhócarta). The genealogies of both families do not converge and we are dealing, it appears, with unrelated segments who contested the overkingship of Éli until the Invasion, each local kings of their own *tríchas*.[87] Just one annalistic reference occurs to a king of Cenél Mechair, in 1012, and this is repeated in *Cogad* where it is associated with Uí Chérín (Ikerrin) in Éli and Uí Mechair (whose line is unclear).[88]

C121: *Arech & Wetheni* (1201)
C121a: *Arech* (1293)
C87: *Owethenihokathelan & Owethenihoiffernan* (1201); *Wodeny O Cathelan & Wodeny O Flian* (1204); *Wethenye* (1237)
C87a: *Wetheney* (1358, 1377)[89]
Between 1970 and 1981[90] Empey changed his position with regard to these cantreds but neither position appears to be wholly satisfactory. It is clear from the original

84 AT, 1164, 1168; AFM, 1159; AU, 1181. **85** O'Brien, *Corpus*, 206; *Civil Survey* ii, 210. **86** COD, i, 9, 12, 206; iii, 96, 258. **87** Byrne, *Kings and high kings*, 187–9; O'Brien, *Corpus*, 248–9, 384; AI, 670, 744, 1022, 1028, 1033, 1058, 1071; ALC, 1050, 1057; AT, 761, 1152, 1171, 1174; AU, 1115; AFM, 847, 900, 903, 975, 1163. **88** AFM, 1012; Todd, *Cogad*, 148. **89** COD, i, 12; BL Add. MS 4790, 169v. **90** Empey, 'Tipperary', 25; idem, 'Limerick', 3.

grant of 1185 made to Theobald Walter that his two cantreds of Arech & Wetheni (**C121**) and of Owethenihokathelan & Owethenihoiffernan (**C87**) were distinct. The second appears again as a distinct cantred slightly later when lands within it were donated by Walter to his foundation of Abbeyowney. This grant shows that the cantred contained lands in the parishes of Abington and Clonkeen. The location of the cantred of Arech [= Arra] & Wetheni (**C121**) must have conjoined this cantred to the north. As Empey has shown, the Wetheni section of this cantred must be represented by the de Burgh manor of Castle Amory or Wethentire (*Uaithne Tíre*), the lordship of which the Butlers lost early in the thirteenth century, while the Arra section had a distinct feudal history, remaining under Butler lordship for considerably longer. To further confuse the situation, this area, originally part of the county of Munster, was riven by a new shire border when Munster was divided into the new counties of Limerick and Tipperary around the middle of the thirteenth century. It is certain that in this reorganization the cantred of the two Wodenis (**C87**) was united with Wethentire to become the single cantred of Wetheney, in Co. Limerick (**C87a**), while the Arech (**C121a**) or northern portion of the original cantred of Arech & Wetheni remained inside Co. Tipperary as a distinct cantred which was, however, united for administrative purposes with the cantred of Muscriquirk (**C123**). Clearly, however, this division was based on older borders as reflected in the coincidence of these 'new' borders with the diocesan structure here.[91] Furthermore, Empey completely underestimates the size of the reduced cantred of Arech (**C121a**), merely using the modern barony boundary which was based on the sixteenth-century holdings of Mac Í Briain here. Arech certainly included at minimum the additional parishes of Kilmore and Dolla, and was probably more extensive still. Therefore Arech almost adjoined Muscriquirk, making their association easier to understand.[92]

T121: *Araid Tíre & Uaithne Tíre*
T87: *Uaithne Cliach*
The cantred of Wetheni (**C87**) gives a rare example of a cantred not based entirely on pre-Invasion polities, as we have seen above. It represents all of the Irish kingdom of Uaithne, which was, however, divided into two local kingdoms, Uaithne Tíre and Uaithne Cliach. Again this is an ancient kingdom: it has been suggested that it is represented on Ptolemy's second-century map of Ireland as Auteini.[93] Its two-fold division is at least as early as 915 when we find mention of the kings of Uaithne Cliach *alias* Uaithne Fidbaide (**T87**). Another king of Uaithne Cliach, Ua Catháláin, occurs in 1107, while kings of Uaithne Tíre occur in 949 and 1080.[94] While it is difficult to

91 COD, i, 12; BL Add. MS. 4787, f. 40; Empey, 'Limerick', 3; idem, 'Tipperary', 23; DKRI 37, p. 50–51. **92** The Assic family held a fief in Arech of at least five knights' fees extent which was ruled from their *caput* at Kilmore (CDI, iii, 511), while I would identify the 'teod' in Arech held by Robert Travers, in 1338, with the parish of Dolla, much of which was, in the *Civil Survey*, occupied by the three ploughlands of Traverstown, part ancestor to the present Traverston (CIPM, viii, 121). Kilmore was, of course, Cell Mór Arad Tíre (Hogan, *Onomasticon*, 203). **93** O'Rahilly, *Early Irish history and mythology*, 10–11. **94** AT, 1089; AFM, 949, 1080, 1107; AU, 915.

anchor in time the pedigrees of both families, their linkage is certainly no later than the early seventh century, and both local kingdoms must be of considerable antiquity.[95] The first reference to the successor of Uaithne Cliach describes it as the cantred of Owethenihokathelan & Owethenihoiffernan (**C87**). This indicates that this local kingdom had been further divided by the arrival of a new family of Dál Cais origin, Uí Iffernáin, whose presence here as co-rulers with Uí Chathaláin can be confirmed by an annal of 1158.[96] Strangely, Uaithne Tíre was joined to Araid Tíre by the invaders to make a single cantred of Arech & Wetheni (**C121**). Given the general rule that cantreds are based on earlier *trícha céts*, we must assume that this arrangement has pre-Invasion origins, and thus posit the existence of a *trícha* called Araid Tíre & Uaithne Tíre (**T121**). We may speculate that these had indeed been united in the pre-Invasion period, possibly by some newly-arrived Dál Cais segment. As against this hypothesis, we should note that indigenous kings of Araid Tíre are recorded as late as 1174, which may suggest that these had absorbed Uaithne Tíre during the twelfth century. As to the origins of Araid Tíre, this represents one of three local kingdoms of the Dál Coirpre group, with a typical remote linkage to the others (**T86, T124**). Its Uí Donnocáin kings are recorded regularly from 1013 onwards.[97]

C122: *Heyghanacassel* (1206); *Ardmull* (1207); *Ioganach Cassel* (1225); *Ounachcassell* (1296); *Ouenaghcassel* (1305); *Ouen[agh]* (1432)[98]
See Empey, 'Tipperary', 27 (where he modernizes the name form).

T122: *Eóganacht Chaisil*
The regional kingdom of Eóganacht Chaisil, at least as it existed during the mid-eleventh century, extended as far west as Emly and beyond, and contained an area represented by six or seven later cantreds. The largest of these was Ounachcassell, derived from Eóganacht Chaisil itself, the *trícha* which contained the seat of the Eóganacht kings of Munster (Cashel) until it was taken over by Uí Briain. *Caithréim Cellacháin Chaisil* states that they were seventeen *túatha* here, but it is not clear whether the local or regional kingdom is meant.[99] While most of the ruling aristocracy of Eóganacht Chaisil were expelled by Uí Briain around 1100 this did not alter the nomenclature of the *tríchas*/cantreds here, which therefore must have assumed their final form before the expulsions. A number of kings are recorded during the eleventh century, but these probably relate to the regional kingdom.[1]

C123: *Muskeriquirc* (1215); *Muscriquirk* (1225); *Muscri* (1293, 1305); *Muskry* (1335)[2]
See Empey, 'Tipperary', 28.

T123: *Múscraige Breogain/Múscraige Uí Chuirc*
The cantred of Muscri derives from Múscraige Uí Chuirc, and this is a late name formulation taken from the ruling family of Múscraige Breogain *alias* Múscraige

95 O'Brien, *Corpus*, 267–8; Ó Muraíle, *Mac Firbhishigh*, ii, 680–4. **96** MIA, 1158. **97** AI, 1031, 1043, 1094, 1122; ALC, 1014; AT, 1174; CS, 1125. **98** CDI, i, 44, 54, 192. **99** Bugge, *Caithreim*, 4. **1** MacCotter, 'Meic Carthaig', 62–3. **2** CDI, i, 94, 192; DKRI 45, p. 34.

Trethirne, whose kings are recorded in 853, 904, 1043 and 1100.[3] In addition, this kingdom is mentioned as such in ninth-century literature while, of course, its genealogical link with the other Múscraige ruling families is remote.[4] An earlier polity in this area was Eóganacht Airthir Cliach, one of whose dynasty was king of Munster in the late sixth century. An eighth-century text locates them around Donohill but they disappear after this.[5]

C124: *Okonegh* (1215); *Oconaghe* (1251); *Okonach* (1293, 1296); *Okonagh* (1305); *Oconagh* (1333)[6]
For its extent see Empey, 'Tipperary', 28–9; 'Limerick', 19. His derivation of Okonagh is erroneous.

T124: *Uí Chuanach*
The cantred of Okonagh derives from Uí Chuanach, a lineage noted in the ninth-century *Vita Tripartita* and whose king is recorded in 989. See **T86** for the early origins of this lineage. Uí Chuanach occur in the annals as a lineage in 1014 and 1124, and appear to have had kings in the twelfth century.[7]

C125: *Slefardacht* (1200); *Slevardah* (1206); *Slefardach* (1293); *Sleff* (1305, 1432)[8]
See Empey, 'Tipperary', 26.

T125: *Sliab Ardachaid*
The cantred of Slieveardagh derives from Sliab Ardachaid, described as lying in Eóganacht (Chaisil) in 1063. The kings of this *trí(ha* as given by Ó hUidhrín were Uí Dedaid, and there may be some basis for this, since a family of this name, to judge by their (tenth-century?) genealogy, were clearly of importance *i n-airthiur Eóganachta Chaisil* and claimed a remote Eóganacht ancestry.[9]

C126: *Moyeven* (1231); *Moyeuen* (1293, 1305); *Moyeuyn* (1296); *Moien* (1374, 1432); *Motheyn* (1514)[10]
This cantred was described in 1305 in union with Slefardach (**C125**) but Empey has not identified all the vills in this list. Moyeuen as described in this source contained the parishes of Magorban, Railstown, Brickendown, Kilconnell, Tullamain, Kilbragh, Mora, Outeragh, and Knockgraffon.[11] Moyeuen and Slefardagh were treated as a

---

3 AFM, 852, 899; ALC, 1043; AI, 1100. **4** O'Brien, *Corpus*, 373–4; Stokes, *Tripartite Life*, 196–8. **5** Fraser et al., *Irish Texts* i, 19–22; MacCotter, *Colmán*, 57. Significantly, the parish of Donohill in the cantred of Muskeriquirc was earlier the *theodum* of Yonachbeg or Eóganacht Becc which, I suggest, must preserve some memory of this dynasty (O'Grady, *Caithréim*, 25). **6** McNeill, *Alen's Register*, 38, 74; Oxford, Bodliean Laud MS 611, f. 79. **7** Stokes, *Tripartite Life*, 198–9; AU, 989; AFM, 1014; ALC, 1124. The later kings of Uí Chuanach would appear to have been Uí Dubchróin, also an ecclesiastical family of Emly (AI, 989.6; Ó Muraíle, *Mac Firbhishigh* ii, 217; MacCotter, *Colmán*, 89, 113). **8** Brooks, *Reg. St John Baptist*, 322; CDI, i, 44. **9** AT, 1063; TP, 44; O'Brien, *Corpus*, 195, 223. **10** Brooks, *Reg. St John Baptist*, 279; COD, ii, 132; iv, 15. **11** In Knockgraffon parish Rockwell ('Carrygtobyr'), Knockanaveigh, Knockgraffon and Donegal lay in Moyeuen while Woodinstown and Lough Kent lay in Offath, suggesting, given that Outeragh

single cantred for much of the Anglo-Norman period but from 1432 onwards are again treated separately. Empey's name for this cantred, Moyenen, is erroneous.[12]

T126: *Múscraige Airthir Femin*
The cantred of Moyeuen derives from Mag Femin, a territorial name regularly record-ed in the annals from 864, but which is considerably older.[13] The underlying *trícha* here appears to have been Múscraige Airthir Femin. This is one of the *túatha* (= min-imal polity, local kingdom) named in the ninth- or tenth-century literature about the semi-mythical Mór Muman, while its ruling line has a contemporary king, Carthach, eponym of Ráith Meic Carthaig, now Rathmacarthy in Kilbragh parish (in central Moyeuen).[14] In addition, note Ó hUidhrín's Ó Carthaig kings of Múscraige *Iarthar* Femin, for which we should probably read Múscraige *Airthir* Femin.[15]

C127: *Moytalyn* (1293, 1296, 1305); *Moct(alyn)* (1432); *Mothalyn* (1514)
C128: *Chumesi* (1200); *Cumsy* (1206); *Le Cungsy* (1215); *Comsi* (1230)[16]
For the extent of Moytalyn see Empey, 'Tipperary', 26–7. His usage of Moctalyn as the name for this cantred is anachronistic, as this usage begins only in the fifteenth century, incidentally suggesting that the toponym had become extinct in popular usage and was only known from the written record. Sometime after 1230 Comsey was united with Moytalyn for administrative purposes, and its extent is difficult to uncover. Comsey certainly contained the parishes of Kilvemnon, Modeshil and Isertkieran.[17] Empey additionally locates Grangemockler and Templemichael here, but both churches are listed amongst those in the half-cantred of Iffowyn in 1260.[18] However, for some reservations concerning the accuracy of this church list see under **C129** below. Both parishes were within the later barony of Slievardagh, so perhaps Empey is correct.

T127: *Moytalyn*
T128: *Comsey* (both indigenous etymologies uncertain)
These cantreds appear to derive from toponyms of uncertain origin, although the element *Mag* is indicated in the former. The location of these *tríchas* in the kingdom of Déisi Muman (see **T168**), based on their presence in the original area of the dio-cese of Lismore, is certainly correct. Donoghmore, which seems to have lain in Moytalyn (see **C129** below), is the Domnach Mór Maige Femin of the late seventh-century Forannán who was of the main stem of the Déisi.[19] Comsey is given the Irish form *na Cuimsionach* in late sources, the derivation of which is unclear.

---

was also in Moyeuen, a rather tortuous border here. (But see my comments under **C129** regard-ing quadruple vill units.) **12** Empey, 'Tipperary', 27. While both forms occur Moyenen is cer-tainly a scribal error for Moyeuen, which agrees perfectly with its Irish original, Magh Fheimhin. **13** FIA, 864; ALC, 1121; MacCotter, *Colmán*, 36. **14** Byrne, *Kings and high kings*, 167, 200; Mac Cana, 'King and goddess', 94–8; O'Brien, *Corpus*, 375; O'Nolan, 'Mór of Munster', passim. **15** TP, 50. **16** Brooks, *Reg. St John Baptist*, 274, 290; CDI, i, 44, 94; COD, iv, 15. **17** White, *Irish monastic and episcopal deeds*, 303. **18** Sheehy, *Pont. Hib.* ii, 299–300. **19** TP, 45; Ó Riain, *Corpus*, 15.

C129: *Ywoghyn* (1260); *Yfweyn* (1286); *Ivoyn* (1296); *Iffowyn* (1305, 1381); *Ivewyn* (1335); *I Eogain* (1444); *Iffa* (1358, 1374, 1432, 1457)[20]

Empey's treatment of the cantred of Iffowyn ignores that portion of the cantred which remained in Co. Waterford after the revision of the country boundary here during the thirteenth century. Again, his equation of this cantred with the Lismore deanery of Kilsheelan is merely approximate as there were significant differences. The Waterford parish of Kilronan was certainly not in the cantred of Iffowyn although in the deanery, while those of Dysert, Fenoagh and Kilmoleran were in the cantred but not the deanery.

The original border between the counties of Waterford and Munster (later Tipperary) corresponded to the northern border of the diocese of Lismore here. Therefore, the cantreds of Offath (**C130**) and Iffowyn originally lay in Co. Waterford before being transferred to Tipperary, probably some time in the mid-thirteenth century, when the River Suir was made the new border. While this realignment must have separated that lesser portion of Iffowyn which was left undisturbed in Waterford from the remainder of this cantred (and which was then presumably united with one of the Waterford cantreds for the purposes of civil administration, as happened elsewhere), it does not alter the fact that a significant portion of post-realignment Co. Waterford continued to lie in the cantred of Iffowyn for purposes non-administrative, and would thus have remained technically, at least on some levels, distinct from the other cantreds of Waterford.[21] It is not difficult to reconstruct the extent of this segment of Iffowyn remaining in Waterford. This can be done most obviously by reference to those parishes which spanned both sides of the Suir: Inishlounaght, Clonmel, Killaloan, and Kilsheelan. These were also part of the rural deanery of Kilsheelan, which rather loosely corresponds to the cantred of Iffowyn.[22] All of these parishes were certainly in Iffowyn. The evidence goes beyond this, however, and the area of Iffowyn remaining in Waterford was even greater. The Waterford parish of Dysert was a member of the manor of Kilsheelan, the capital manor of Iffowyn, while those of Fenoagh, Kilmoleran and a small part of Mothel were part of the Tipperary manor of Carrickmagriffin (Carrick-on-Suir), and so must also have lain in Iffowyn.[23]

Two significant sources for cantredal extents in Iffowyn and surrounding cantreds should not be ignored. These are the list of vills amerced in Iffowyn, Offath (**C130**), Slefardagh (**C125**) and Moyeuen (**C126**) in 1305 and a list from 1260 of the churches in the cantred of Offath and the 'half-cantred' of Iffowyn.[24] The latter source is

---

20 Sheehy, *Pont. Hib.* ii, 298; CDI, iii, 285; COD, ii, 38, 131, 187; iii, 180; DKRI 45, p. 34; *Misc. of the Irish Arch. Soc.*, i (Dublin, 1846), 205. 21 Empey, 'Limerick', 1–2; idem, 'Tipperary', 29. One suspects that the ecclesiastical claims to the churches of the cantreds of Offath and Iffowyn by the diocese of Cashel around 1260 were sparked by the secular realignment under discussion here. (Sheehy, *Pont. Hib.* i, nos. 475, 481.) 22 For the rural deaneries of Waterford and Lismore see TCD MS 1066, 279 ff; MS 1067, 448 ff; Rennison, 'Bishoprick of Waterford', vol. 35, pp 26–33; vol. 36, pp 20–2. While in the seventeenth century the parish of Inishlounaght was included in the deanery of Ardfinnan, it occurs ('Inchelafnach') among places amerced in the cantred of Iffowyn in 1305 (NAI MS Cal. Roll Justices Itinerant 33–34 Edward I, p. 89). 23 MacCotter, 'The Carews of Cork' (thesis), 26–7, 29; NLI MS 2509, 25–9; White, *Book of Ormond*, 118–22. 24 NAI MS Cal. Roll Justices Itinerant 33–34 Edward I, 28–81 for Offath, 82–139 for Iffowyn, 140–82 for the cantred of Slefardach & Moyeuen

rendered somewhat less valuable in view of the original possession of what appears to have been the entire area of the cantreds of Moytalyn (**C127**) and Comsey (**C128**) by the diocese of Lismore.[25] When these lands were transferred to the diocese of Cashel during the 1220s or 1230s, it would appear that some parishes in these cantreds were retained by Lismore thus rendering the 1260 list less trustworthy as an indicator of cantredal borders here. Additionally, the list of vills uses the system of grouping by fours into quadruple vill units, a kind of frankpledge of vills, and this may have brought some outlying vills in neighbouring cantreds into the amercement, thus weakening the value of this list. The 1305 list for Iffowyn certainly includes places in Inishlounaght, Rathronan, Ballyclerahan, Kiltegan, Newchapel, Lisronagh, Kilgrant, Killaloan, Temple-etney, Kilmurry and Carrick while Clonmel and Tibberaghny were also certainly in this cantred.[26] It must also have contained Kilsheelan, Kilcash, Garrangibbon and Newtownlennon. The case of the parish of Donoghmore may be instructive. This forms a salient of Lismore diocese protruding into Cashel. Around AD 1200 it was the seat of a rural dean, although it is later found in the deanery of Kilsheelan. Again, lands in the parish are associated with others to its north, in the cantred of Moytalyn, in grants made to the Hospital of St John in Dublin during the early thirteenth century, all of which suggests that Donoghmore was originally part of Moytalyn (and probably remained so in secular jurisdiction). The sources clash regarding Mora; its church is listed in Iffowyn, but its vills are in Moyeuen, and I think it must have belonged to the latter. Similarly, the church of Outeragh is placed in Offath while its vills are located in Moyeuen.

T129: *Uíbh Eóghain Fhinn*
This is the derivation of the cantred of Iffowyn, although our sources, including the *Topographical Poems*, are late. This *trícha* was also part of the regional kingdom of Déisi Muman.

C130: *Harfinan* (1206); *Ardfinnan* (1215); *Yffathiatha* (1260), *Hifathayhather* (1260); *Offathe* (1293, 1296, 1432); *Offa* (1374); *Offe* (1457)[27]
See Empey, 'Tipperary', 29.

T130: *Uí Fothaid Aiched*
See **T171**.

TÍR BRIÚIN

The extent of the Irish kingdom of Tír Briúin, the lordship of Uí Briúin Bréifne and their subsidiary allies, Conmaicne Réin, is preserved in that of the area of the

(in these lists Chancellerstown, Newchapel, Woodinstown and Lough Kent are located in Offath); Sheehy, *Pont. Hib.* ii, 299–300. **25** Nicholls, 'Matthew Ua Hénni', 268; Brooks, *Reg. St John Baptist*, 280–2, 289–90, 299 (where the bishop of Waterford has usurped the see of Lismore). **26** RC 7/7, 11. **27** CDI, i, 44, 94; Sheehy, *Pont. Hib.* ii, 298, 305; COD, ii, 131; iii, 180.

dioceses of Kilmore *alias* Tirbrun, and Ardagh, respectively. While there are no direct cantredal ascriptions here, the indirect evidence provided by the ruridecanal and rurirectoral structures, in addition to the Irish structures of lordship here, combine impressively to illustrate the almost certain existence of six cantreds in this territory whose extents can be arrived at. One of these (**T103**), a late conquest by Uí Briúin, has already been dealt with in a more appropriate location. The attribution of ten *trícha*s to Bréifne in the extent of Clann Chuinn is formulaic.

T131: (*C131): *Bréifne*
This leads to consideration of Uí Briúin Bréifne themselves. Both their early genealogies and the early annalistic record may be suspect. It is clear from Tírechán (who makes Connacht begin at the Shannon) that either no such polity existed in his time or it was insignificant. Reliable record of kings of Bréifne occur from 791 onwards but these early kings cannot be placed in the Uí Briúin Bréifne genealogies until Tigernán (d. 892). Toponomy does, however, provide clues to the expansion of Uí Briúin here. The baronies of Tullyhaw (Tellach Echach) and Tullyhunco (Tellach Dúnchada) derive from eponyms represented as sons of Máenach mac Baíthín (d. 653), apparently king of all Uí Briúin. This would seem to suggest that the initial Uí Briúin expansion (from Roscommon) into Bréifne occurred sometime between 650 and 700. It is hardly coincidental that the first record of kings of Bréifne in the annals coincides with the fragmentation of the Cenél Cairpre overkingdom here (see under **T8**). The pedigree of the senior line of Bréifne becomes reliable around the early 800s and a marked expansion of lineages of the main stem occurs around 900, in particular that of Máel Mórda and his sons Cerball, *a quo* Tellach Cerbaill (Upper Loughtee), and Garbíth, *a quo* Tellach Garbítha (Tullygarvey). This must represent a significant eastwards expansion of Bréifne into much of modern Cavan, whose earlier history is obscure. It is again not coincidental that both areas of expansion identified here are represented by thirteenth-century rural deaneries.[28]

What appears to have been the original Bréifne, with the Uí Ruairc homeland (around Drumlane?), as well as Tullyhaw and Tullyhunco and the 'outsiders' of Cenél Luacháin, became the deanery of Drumlane, which contained the parishes of Drumlane, Killashandra, Kildallan, Tomregan, Templeport, Killinagh, Carrigallen, Drumreilly, Oughteragh, Killesher and Kinawley. This deanery probably preserves the extent of **T131**.[29]

T132: (*C132): *Dartraige*
The subject lordships within the ambit of both Cairpres (see under **T8**) mostly belonged to Callraige. Tírechán, around 700 or earlier, locates this people (and, by implication, the associated Dartraige) in the area of the later baronies of Rosclogher and Drumahaire. The death of their king, Cathmug, in 791, seems to bring to an end their existence as a semi-independent kingdom.[30] While Callraige lordships are

---

28 Ó Duíbhgeannáin, 'Bréifne', 114–128; Ó Mórdha, 'Uí Briúin Bréifne', passim. 29 For the rural deaneries of Kilmore see TCD MS 1067, 117 ff. 30 AU, 791.

later found scattered throughout the area and to the west in Connacht proper, it is
Dartraige who maintained some political power in the area. From this line of
Callraige descend both the *comarbai* of Killarga and, more importantly, the *taísig* of
Dartraige, Meic Fhlannchada. An Ua Ruairc king of Dartraige is recorded in 1029,
indicating that this area passed from Cenél Cairpre control to become a local king-
dom within the overkingdom of Bréifne.[31] I suggest that the territorial integrity of
this ancient polity (**T132**) was maintained in the rural deanery and rural rectory of
Dartry, both identical in area, which contained the parishes of Inishmagrath, Killarga,
Cloonlogher, Cloonclare, Drumlease, Killasnet and Rossinver. The rural rectory (of
'Dartragie and Brefnithiar': *Dartraighe & Bréifne thiar*), was impropriate to St Mary's
abbey in Kells, Co. Meath. A coincidence of both deanery and rectory leads firmly to the existence of a *trícha*/cantred here, which formed the westernmost part of
the Uí Ruairc kingdom of Bréifne around 1200. Dartraige occurs as a territory within Bréifne in 1146.[32]

T133: (*C133): *Muintir Máel Mórda*

Further to the east, the deanery of Kilmore must represent, at core, the territory of
Muintir Máel Mórda and its satellites. The first Uí Ragallaig king of Muintir Máel
Mórda is recorded in 1161, although his father, during the 1130s, bears the interesting title *flaith Muintir Máel Mórda & ur-rí na Macaire* (i.e. Machaire Gaileng:
Morgallion).[33] While this must have began life as a local kingdom under the kings
of Bréifne it soon established its independence. The deanery of Kilmore consisted
of the baronies of Tullygarvey and Upper Loughtee, all of those of Castlerahan and
Clankee apart from the parishes of Enniskeen and Loughan, and probably the parish
of Ballintemple. It also contained Moybolgue, most of which lies in Meath. The
original *trícha* (**T133**) would have been somewhat smaller as the border between the
dioceses of Meath and Kilmore here was an arbitrary one resulting from the ecclesiastical dispute between colonial Meath and native Kilmore during the early thirteenth century. Clankee and parts of Castlerahan must have lain outside Muintir
Máel Mórda. Some confirmation of this may be had from the pattern of impropriation here, where the priory of Fore held most of the lands above suggested as lying
in Muintir Máel Mórda, no doubt granted by Hugh de Lacy when he attempted to
settle the area.[34] In relation to my use of the ruridecanal structure to suggest an underlying *trícha*/cantred structure here, it should be noted that the extent of the Uí Ruairc
kingdom as defined in a colonial grant of 1221 included exactly the area of the
deaneries of Dartry, Drumlane and Muintir Eolais.[35]

31 AFM, 1029. 32 Ó Duíbhgeannáin, 'Bréifne', 135–9; O'Donovan, 'Chorca Laidhe', 27ff; Ó
Muraíle, *Mac Firbhishigh*, ii, 671–5; Nicholls, 'Rectory, vicarage and parish', 77. 33 AFM, 1162;
Mac Niocaill, 'Irish "charters"', 155. 34 Masterson, 'Priory of Fore', 5–6. 35 Morrin, *Cal. Pat.
& Close Rolls, Ireland, Henry VIII–Eliz.*, 259 (better in BL Add. MS 4792, f. 157). The bounds of
this territory are given as from Lough Oughter to the Shannon, and from Sliabh Chairpre (in
northern Longford) to Lough Erne. The named territories in the grant are: Clenarwich (Clann
Fhermaige), Monterales (Muintir Eolais), Moniss (Mag Nissi), Mointerkinet (Muintir Chinaíth),
Kinolochan (Cenél Luacháin), Tellachdoneket (Tullyhunco), Calvach (in Tullyhaw, see *Analecta*

T134: (*C134): *Muintir Eolais*
The early history of Conmaicne Réin is quite obscure. Byrne believes that they may have crossed the Shannon with Uí Briúin, a not unreasonable supposition since there are several Conmaicne of Connacht. No trace of such a migration is preserved in the genealogies, which show the customary artificial schema whereby most branches divide in the remote period. Conmaicne Réin were subject to the kings of Bréifne in title from at least the mid-eleventh century onwards.[36] These latter sometimes styled themselves simply *rí Conmaicne* and at other times *rí Bréifne & Conmaicne*.[37] Perhaps significantly, Conmaicne do not seem to have been allowed kings of their own under Uí Briúin, echoing the situation regarding Conmaicne elsewhere in Connacht. The annals merely record *taísig* of the various *túatha* of Conmaicne, beginning in the 1080s.[38]

The original Conmaicne homeland here is probably represented by the deanery of Monterolis (Muintir Eolais). These were one of the principal lines of Conmaicne and their territory lay around the eponymous Mag Réin. This deanery, in addition, contained the discrete territory of Clann Fhermaige, an isolated Conmaicne *túath*. Muintir Eolais proper consisted of the Co. Leitrim baronies of Leitrim and Mohill (and all of Cloone parish) and the parish of Kilronan in Co. Roscommon, while Clann Fhermaige contained the parishes of Killanummery in Leitrim and Killerry in Sligo. These discrete territories probably represent a single *trícha*/cantred, similar to the cantred of Corkely and Berre (**C31**). Both parts of Muinter Eolais are mentioned in the de Lacy grant of 1221 and have corresponding rural rectories ('Munter Eolays' and 'Clanarwye'), further confirming the cantredal template for the deanery here.[39]

T135: (*C135): *Muintir Angaile*
It seems likely that a southwards movement by Conmaicne into Longford was related to the south-eastwards movement into Cavan by Uí Briúin, events probably contemporary. I suggest that the territory of the second major Conmaicne group, Muintir Angaile, is represented by the rural deanery of that name. This contained places, such as Lissardowlan and Ardagh, known to have earlier been in the Cenél Maine kingdom of Fir Thethba, suggesting that Conmaicne expansion here resulted in the shrinkage of the kingdom of Tethba, probably during the tenth and eleventh centuries (see under **T102**). Interestingly, the overkingdom of Bréifne as ruled by Ualgarg Ua Ruairc in the early 1200s did not include Muintir Angaile (de Lacy grant of 1221). Thus, Muintir Angaile would appear to have gained its independence as a result of the fragmentation of Uí Ruairc power in the face of the Invasion. Despite this the Uí Fhergail rulers of Muintir Angaile continue to be referred to in the annals by the inferior titles of *rí-thaísech* and *ard-taísech*.[40] This deanery contained the parishes of Ardagh, Cashel, Rathcline, Killashee, Ballymacormick,

---

Hibernica 3, p. 212), and Culkenvikedin (?). **36** O'Brien, *Corpus*, 317–21; BF, 383–7; Byrne, *Kings and high kings*, 236. **37** AT, 1078, 1152; AU, 1087, 1102, 1122. **38** Six *taísig* of Muintir Eolais are recorded in the pre-Invasion period, the first in 1085 (AFM), and one of Muintir Angaile (AT, 1150). **39** Ó Duíbhgeannáin, 'Bréifne', 133–4. **40** AU, 1172; ALC, 1207.

Templemichael, Clongesh, Killoe, and Mostrim. This was obviously a *trícha*/cantred: 'Munterhawyl' paid a single cash rent to the lords of Meath in the thirteenth century. The term is again used in a cantredal context in 1308. A rural rectory of Munterangaly, whose exact extent, unfortunately, is unclear, further confirms the existence of a cantred here.[41]

We should note in passing the Uí Cheallaigh claims to part of this territory in their fourteenth-century semi-fictitious propaganda tract, *Nósa Ua Maine*. This mentions a kingdom and *trícha cét* of In Chalaidh, whose lords (*flaith*) are named as Ó Laedhóg. Despite O'Donovan's (mis-)identification here, it is clear from the bounds given that the area in question lay around the 'Callows' located in the parishes of Rathcline and Cashel. Uí Laedóg occur as *taísig* of Síl Rónáin in annals between 1100 and 1106, when they may well have occupied this territory. These were, of course, men of Fir Thethba rather than of Uí Maine (see **T102**). Deriving from a late propaganda tract, this claim should be met with suspicion, and nothing additional can be found to support it, while all other indicators run contrary. This reference to an almost certainly fictitious *trícha cét* probably has at root the ancient tradition of a relationship between Uí Maine of Connacht and Cenél Maine of Mide.[42]

TÍR CONAILL

In Tír Conaill, as in western Tuadmuman (Co. Clare), large areas remained unsettled by the colonists but were subject to a cash rent, resulting in the cantredal structure being recorded contemporaneously in both Irish and colonial sources. In 1289 'the four cantreds of Tirconyll' were described as lying 'two near the sea from Roscule [the Roscuill peninsula] as far as Thethnegall [probably Donegal] and two cantreds between Locherne [Lough Erne] and Kynalmogn [Cenél Móen] and in the direction of Dery'. This rather general description can be supplemented by a contemporary description of the four named *trícha céts* of Tír Conaill from a Gaelic source (the *Book of Fenagh*) which agrees with the colonial record. The area of all four together, of course, was coextensive with that of the diocese of Raphoe.[43]

C136: *Tír Énna*
Lying from the head of Lough Swilly in the north to the Barnesmore Gap and Sruell in the south, this cantred is ancestor to the later baronies of Raphoe, but did not, of course, contain the parishes of Donaghmore, Clonleigh and Urney in the diocese of Derry (which lay in **T145**).

C137: *Tír Lugdach*
The boundaries of this cantred are given as the Swilly and Gweedore rivers, which show it to be ancestor to the later barony of Kilmacrenan.

41 Nicholls, 'Rectory, vicarage and parish', 77; Otway-Ruthven, 'Verdon partition', 411–13, 422–3, 427, 430, 435.   **42** O'Donovan, *Hy Many*, 74–5; Russell, 'Nósa Ua Maine', 537; Ní Mhaonaigh, 'Nósa Ua Maine', 381; AFM, 1100, 1102, 1106; Byrne, *Kings and high kings*, 92.   **43** Mac Giolla Easpaig, 'Co. Donegal', 152–6; MacNiocaill, *Red Book of Kildare*, 113–15.

C138: *Trícha Esa Ruaid*

From Assaroe (Esa Ruaid) on the Erne in the south to the Enny Water in the north are its bounds, which therefore show this cantred to have consisted of the parishes of Kilbarron, Drumhome, Donegal, Killymard and the eastern half of Inver. While this is certainly the ancestor to the later barony of Tirhugh its boundaries were not identical. If Esruaid had the boundaries as suggested by Mac Giolla Easpaig, who appears unaware that the large parish of Templecarn (in Clogher) cannot have lain in this cantred, it would have been just too small and it seems clear that the bounds as given in the *Book of Fenagh* are correct here.[44]

C139: *Tír Bóguine*

The bounds of this cantred are from the Gweedore River in the north to the Enny Water in the south-east, which show it to have comprised the later barony of Boylagh and that of Banagh west of the Enny Water.

T136 to T139: (*Cenél Conaill*)

This regional kingdom had four well attested *tríchas*/cantreds. Tír Énna (**T136**) was the patrimony of Cenél Énna, the eponym being a son of Niall Naígiallach. Six kings are recorded between 1011 and 1177, most of whom would seem to have been indigenous. By 1177 the kingdom 'of Cenél Énna & Mag Ítha' was ruled by an Ua Gairmledaig of the latter, suggesting that Cenél Énna had temporarily come under Cenél Eógain rule.[45] Tír Lugdach (**T137**) was the kingdom of Cenél Luigdech of Cenél Conaill. The eponym was a first cousin of Colm Cille and thus lived around the mid-sixth century. Uí Domnaill kings of Cenél Luigdech are recorded in 1009 and 1100, but earlier (868 and 905) this line held the overkingship of all of Cenél Conaill. A metonymic alternative, used in 1004, was Loch Beithach (Lough Veagh) from a seat of the kings of Cenél Luigdech.[46] The third *trícha* here was Tír Bóguine of Cenél Bóguine (**T139**). The eponym, Énna Bóguine, was a son of Conall Gulban and so traditionally believed to have belonged to the fifth century. At least seven kings of Cenél Bóguine are recorded between 609 and 1035.[47] Finally we have the *trícha* of Esa Ruaid *alias* Tír Áeda (**T138**). Its kings were Cenél Áeda whose eponym died as overking of Cenél Conaill in 598. No kings of this polity are recorded as its ruling line held the overkingship of Cenél Conaill almost exclusively from the sixth century down to 1250.[48]

TÍR EÓGAIN

At least four cantreds can be identified with certainty in this territory, while another three probable cantreds can also be identified.

---

44 For additional confirmation that Esa Ruaid was indeed both the capital and southern border of this *trícha cét*, see Ó Canann, 'Trí Saorthuatha', 24–6.   **45** ALC, 1036, 1057, 1078; AU, 1010, 1083, 1177.   **46** ALC, 1100; AU, 1004, 1009.   **47** ALC, 1035; AU, 785, 846; CS, 609, 668, 718; AT, 625.   **48** O'Brien, *Corpus*, 163–5, 435; Byrne, *Kings and high kings*, 283; Ó Canann, 'Trí Saorthuatha', *passim* (where, however, he exaggerates the extent of Tír Áeda to the south).

C140: *Tulacoch* (1199); ***Talachot*** (1213: *Tulloghoge*).[49]

Reference to the cantred of 'Talachot', associated with 'Kenlion' [Cenél Eógain] occurs in 1213. This cantred must have been conterminous with the rural deanery of the same name – in the diocese of Armagh – which includes the Tyrone parishes of Ballyclog, Carnteel, Clonoe, Desertcreat, Donaghmore, Drumglass, Errigal Keerogue, Kildress, Killeeshill, Pomeroy, Clogherny, Termonmaguirk and Tullyniskan, the Derry parishes of Desertlyn and Magherafelt, and the shared parishes of Arboe, Artrea, Ballinderry, Derryloran, Lissan, and Tamlaght.

T140: *Cenél Eógain Telcha Óic*

The kingdom of Cenél Eógain Telcha Óic was established gradually, over a period of perhaps a century from the 870s onwards, on the foundations of the fading Airgiallan kingdom of Uí Thuirtre, and the extent of both appear to have been similar. This area is reflected in that of the cantred/deanery of Tullaghoge (**C140**). (All early sites associated with Uí Thuirtre lay within this area.)[50] Uí Thuirtre were of Uí Moccu Uais and the eponym is once again remote. The history of this kingdom is complicated by the gradual migration of its aristocracy north-eastwards to Fir Lí and across the Bann, rather than by a clean break, and it is clear that for a period both Cenél Eógain and Uí Thuirtre co-existed side by side here. Kings of Uí Thuirtre appear regularly after 669, most of whom can be identified in the genealogies.[51] In addition this lineage held the overkingship of Airgialla five times between 598 and 919. *Derlas* is used (reliably) as a metonym for Uí Thuirtre on several occasions between 894 and 1215.[52] Warner has identified this place with Doorless (Ardtrea parish), an attractive identification. This usage begins just as Uí Thuirtre begin to come under pressure of expulsion from Cenél Eógain and, if correct, would appear to represent a rare example of a dynasty continuing to use the name of an old capital after expulsion from the area (another example would seem to be that of Eóganacht Chaisil, **T122**). The arrival of Cenél Eógain here was not just a matter of one royal line replacing another but of an extensive migration of segments, probably originating in Inis Eógain, who took over the *túatha* of the indigenous Airgiallan lineages. Genealogically, some of these Cenél Eógain segments diverge from their parent stem around 900, further confirming the chronology here. One of the Airgiallan lineages which survived longer was Uí Briúin Archaill, who maintained some independence around Errigal Keerogue in the very south of Uí Thuirtre until the death of their last king, in 1107.[53] Several kings of (Cenél Eógain) Telcha Óic appear in the annals between 1054 and 1078,[54] indicating that Telach Óc (Tullyhogue or Tulloghoge, Desertcreat parish) had by now become both the inauguration site of Cenél Eógain as well as the centre of an important sub-kingdom, sometimes held in demesne or direct lordship by its overkings.[55]

49 CDI, i, pp 17, 76. **50** The Moyola River formed the northern border of Uí Thuirtre, which certainly included Donoghmore, Ballyclog, Donaghenry and Lissan. (Hamlin, 'Tyrone', 90; Lacey, 'Derry', 141.) **51** AU, 668, 733, 742, 834. **52** AU, 932, 963, 983, 999; AFM, 1215. **53** AU, 1107. **54** ALC, 1054, 1064, 1068, 1078. **55** Ó Fiaich, 'Airgialla', 94, 142–3, 168–81, 209–10; Hogan, 'Telach Óc', 406–44; Warner, 'Clogher: archaeological window', 50; Lacey, 'Derry',

C141: *Kunnoche* (1212); **Kennacht** (1213); *Fernecreu & Kanack* (1272); *Le Kenauth* (1296); *Kenath* (1305)

C142: *Tirkerin* (1213); *Tirketine* (1215)[56]
Both cantreds are mentioned in a grant which further indicates that Kennacht began just west of the River Bann while Tirkerin lay still further west. From another source we learn that Kennacht included the manor of Roo (the Limavady area). From this it would seem that Kennacht must have included all of the present baronies of Keenaght and Coleraine in Derry. Tirkerin would seem to be ancestor to the present barony of Tirkeeran. The combined area of both cantreds would thus seem to correspond to that of the sixteenth-century rural deanery of Bynnagh.[57]

T141: *Ciannachta*
The *trícha cét* Ciannachta of 1197,[58] which gives the cantred of Kennacht, seems to represent the older kingdom of Ciannachta Glinne Geimin in addition to the territory of Fir na Craíbe (the colonial Fernecreu) and the northern section of Fir Lí as conquered by Uí Chatháin during the early twelfth century. The kingdom of Ciannachta Glinne Geimin (now Keenaght barony) derives from a branch of the Ciannachta who divide remotely from the others and who seem to be connected here as in Mide with Uí Néill from the earliest (see under **T110**). Traditionally this lineage arrived here in the early fifth century. Kings are recorded regularly in the annals from 616 onwards (around eighteen in all) and this kingdom continued to be ruled by indigenous kings until the death of the last of them, in 1121.[59]

T142: *Tír Meic Cáirthinn*
The cantred of Tirkerin must derive from Tír Meic Cáirthinn, the land of Uí Meic Cáirthinn, a kingdom allegedly derived from a remote member of Uí Moccu Uais of northern Airgialla. The slaying of its king at the hands of the king of Cenél Eógain in 677 marks the end of its independence. It appears to have been the territory referred to as Mag Dula in *Vita Tripartita* (mid-ninth century), clearly within the Cenél Eógain overkingdom, and which seems, in addition to Tirkeeran barony, to have included parts of northern Tyrone. These Tyrone lands must have been lost subsequently. Just as the Uí Meic Cáirthinn pedigrees end, around 800, we find a branch of Cenél Eógain, Clann Chonchobair, becoming established here from Mag Ítha. The only later king of Uí Meic Cáirthinn recorded was killed in 1096 but his origins are unclear. This *trícha* must have been the home of Uí Chatháin of Clann Chonchobair before they extended their territory eastwards during the eleventh and early twelfth centuries.[60]

*C143: *Rathlowry*
The sixteenth-century rural deanery of Rathlowry does not occur in the earliest listing of Derry deaneries, of 1397, when it was included in Bynnagh. However, it may

138–42; Mac Shamhráin, 'Tír nEógain', 76–80. **56** Orpen, 'Earldom of Ulster' i, 44; CDI, ii, 158; iv, 157; Bain, *Cal. Docs. Scotland* i, nos. 573, 625. **57** Reeves, *Ecclesiastical antiquities*, 323–4; Orpen, *Ireland under the Normans* iv, 142; COD, ii, p. 328; Jefferies, 'Derry diocese', 194–5. **58** AU, 1197. **59** Lacey, 'Derry', 126–33. For the first and last of these kings see AU, 615, 1121. **60** Lacey, 'Derry', 123–6; O'Brien, *Corpus*, 179; Ó Fiaich, 'Airgialla', 163–4; ALC, 1096.

be that it was simply united to Bynnagh on this occasion for the area in question clearly represents a much older territorial division while Ráith Lúraig itself was briefly the see of Derry during the twelfth century. This deanery agrees almost exactly with the territory held by Clann Aodha Buidhe Uí Néill in the diocese of Derry, first acquired during the fourteenth century, which in turn seems to be based on an even older polity here, the Uí Fhloinn kingdom of Fir Lí from which the later baronial name Loch Inse Uí Fhloinn (Loughinsholin), is taken. It was very probably a cantred, perhaps called Glen Oconcahil (Glenconkeen).[61]

T143: (Fir Lí?)

The kingdom of Fir Lí presents a complex picture. Fir Lí derive their name from Mag Lí, the west bank of the Bann from Camus to the Moyola river. These were a branch of Uí Moccu Uais and close relatives to Uí Thuirtre (see under **T140**). However no pedigree survives. Seven kings of Fir Lí are recorded in the annals between 893 and 1194, three of which are of uncertain genealogical filiation.[62] Two kings (1036, 1081) were of Cenél Binnig. These were a segment of Cenél Eógain who came to occupy three *túatha* in Fir Lí. Each *túath* had its own lineage and all three ramify from the main stem around 900, giving a likely date for their arrival here, just as other Cenél Eógain segments were investing Uí Thuirtre to the south. The early connections between Uí Thuirtre and Fir Lí appear to have continued after Uí Thuirtre had abandoned their original homeland, at least in the case of one of the ruling families of Uí Thuirtre, Uí Fhlainn. The eponym lived around the middle of the ninth century so the usage Ua Flainn must date to the early tenth century. The place-names Loch Inse Uí Fhlainn and the adjacent *Mainistir Uí Fhlainn (Loughinsholin and Moneysterlin, Desertmartin parish), the former, significantly, the origin of the barony name here, can hardly derive from so early a period and suggest continued Uí Fhlainn presence here into the twelfth century, as suggested by the title *rí Uí Thuirtre & Fir Lí* borne by members of this family in 1176 and 1194, as well as an earlier annal of 1081 (AU) which shows Uí Fhlainn in conflict with Cenél Binnig. The rival title to (*inter alia*) Fir Lí claimed by Uí Chatháin in 1138 is, I suggest, a reflection of the division of Fir Lí into two sections, the northern one under Ua Chatháin and the southern one under Ua Fhlainn.[63] The area of the Uí Fhlainn segment of Fir Lí is, I would further suggest, preserved in that of the later deanery of Rathlowry in Derry. This must reflect a *trícha* (**T143**) whose origins date to a carve up which had happened before 1138.[64]

C144: Inysowyn

While there is no direct attestation to the cantredal status of this division, such is implied in records of the Anglo-Norman period.[65] In addition, note the deanery of the same name which included the present baronies of Inishowen in Co. Donegal

61 Jefferies, 'Derry diocese', 195; Nicholls, 'Anglo-French Ireland', 384–5. 62 ALC, 1036, 1063, 1135, 1176; MIA, 1193; AU, 1003, 1081; AFM, 893. 63 AFM, 1138. 64 Ó Ceallaigh, *Gleanings*, passim; Ó Fiaich, 'Airgialla', 167–8, 170; Lacey, 'Derry', 136–8, 142. 65 BL Add. MS 6041, f. 49; Orpen, 'Earldom of Ulster' i, 44.

and the parish of Templemore (Derry), and which must preserve the outline of what was certainly a cantred.

T144: *Inis Eógain*

The *trícha cét* of (Inis) Eógain[66] was the original homeland of Cenél Eógain whence they spread over so much of Ulster. The original capital of the Northern Uí Néill, Ailech, lay just within its southern boundaries near the borders with Cenél Conaill. This *trícha* contained two local kingdoms. Southern Inis Eógain must have formed royal demesne attached to Ailech and so it does not appear as a kingdom except on a few occasions. After the centre of gravity of Cenél Eógain had moved southwards, we find reference from the early eleventh century onwards to the now relegated northern section as Cenél Eógain na hInnse.[67] A distinct Cenél Eógain polity, Muintir Donngaile, existed in the northern part of the peninsula, giving the kingdom of Carraig Brachaide (Carrickabraghy, Clonamany parish), whose kings are recorded regularly from 834 onwards.[68] The extent of the *trícha* of Inis Eógain must be reflected in that of the later deanery of Inishowen/Derry. The *civitas* of Derry, originally part of Tír Énna (**T136**), can only have been included in Inis Eógain after it came under Cenél Eógain control around 1100.[69]

*C145: *Mahya*
*C146: *Ardstraw*

No direct evidence survives for the cantredal structure in what remains of Tír Eógain. The ruridecanal evidence is of interest however, and suggests that, if the normal correlation between cantred and deanery applied here, there were at least two cantreds in this area. By 1397 there was just one deanery here, called Mahya, which included the Lagan in Donegal and the western half of Co. Tyrone (that part of the county not in the cantreds of Tulloghoge (**C140**) and Clogher (**C167**)). This deanery takes its name from an important segment of Cenél Eógain, Fir Maige Ítha (**T145**), the plain in question being that in the parishes of Donaghmore, Clonleigh and Urney in the western-most part of Mahya deanery. A second important lineage group occupied a territory in the deanery, Uí Fhiachrach, whose chief church was at Ardstraw, Co. Tyrone (**T146**).[70] At the synod of Ráith Breasail Ardstraw was selected as see for the Derry-Tyrone area and, at the same time, the northern boundary of the diocese of Clogher here was as it is today. This arrangement did not last however, and Simms[71] has suggested that Uí Fhiachrach may have been joined to Clogher during the 1160s. Whatever of this, it is certain that, at the time the ruridecanal structure was being organized here (probably during the early thirteenth century), Uí Fhiachrach/Ardstraw (***C146**) formed a distinct deanery in Clogher while at the same

66 BF, 398.   **67** AI, 1022; AT, 1023.   **68** AI, 1102; ALC, 1053, 1065, 1082; AU, 858, 880, 966, 1166, 1199; CS, 916; AFM, 834, 907.   **69** Hogan, 'The tricha cét', 203; Ó Muraíle, *Mac Firbhisigh* i, 339; Ó Ceallaigh, *Gleanings*, 6; Hogan, 'Telach Óc', 422–3; Lacey, 'Derry', 120.   **70** In the eleventh century the style of the local Cenél Eógain kingdom here was 'Inis Eógain & Mag Ítha', to which Uí Fhiachrach were a subservient though autonomous part. (Simms, 'Tír Eógain north of the mountain', passim.)   **71** Simms, 'diocese of Clogher', 190–1, 195–8.

time Mahya must have formed a separate deanery in Derry (**C145**). A few years later, during the 1240s, Derry, no doubt aided by the local secular power, subsumed Ardstraw into Mahya, which suggests that there were probably two distinct cantreds here at the time of the Invasion.[72] As to the area of these, we can again gain some idea by reference to ecclesiastical structures. Churches in the parishes of Longfield, Cappagh and Drumragh certainly have associations with that of Ardstraw and its patron, which gives a likely extent. The original deanery of Mahya certainly comprised Mag Ítha, but in addition probably also the parishes of Camus, Leckpatrick, Bodoney and Donaghedy, the latter two being included in Cenél Eógain in *Vita Tripartita*.[73] Geography suggests that Termonamongan also lay in Mahya.

T145: *Mag Ítha*
The plain of Mag Ítha must early have formed part of Cenél Eógain, and three of its kings are recorded between 812 and 1016, while kings of Inis Eógain & Mag Ítha (1023) and Cenél Énna & Mag Ítha (1177) also occur.[74] Two of these can be identified as princelings of the Clann Domnaill royal house of Cenél Eógain, and the remainder were probably of the same stock apart from an Ua Gairmledaig of Cenél Móen (1177), then mounting an attempt to capture the kingship. The extent of this *trícha* must be reflected in that of the original deanery of Mahya.[75]

T146: *Uí Fhiachrach Árda Srátha*
The kings of Uí Fhiachrach Árda Srátha belonged to Uí Moccu Uais of Airgialla. The eponym is remote, and kings of Uí Fhiachrach occur regularly from 787 to 1201, most of whom can be identified in the Uí Fhiachrach genealogies.[76] In addition, this dynasty held the overkingship of Uí Moccu Uais in 719 and 872 and that of all of Airgialla in 885. This kingdom long withstood Cenél Eógain pressure and it is only in the mid-twelfth century that Uí Chellaig of Clann Echdach an Chodaig, who must have settled in Uí Fhiachrach from the north, began to compete for the kingship with the indigenous lines, not entirely successfully. The extent of this *trícha* must be reflected in that of the deanery of Ardstraw.[77]

ULSTER

In the Anglo-Norman lordship of Ulster the best lands were colonized and the rest remained in the hands of Irish kings who paid rent to its lords. A reference of 1253 to 'all Ulster, Kynilyun, Oueth and Turtery'[78] neatly summarizes the situation as revealed in the sources, where 'Ulster' refers solely to the colonized and semi-colonized portions of the old native kingdom of Ulaid while the semi-independent

72 Sheehy, *Pont. Hib.* ii, p. 284; Nicholls, 'Reg. of Clogher', 409.   **73** Hamlin, 'Tyrone', 107–12; Stokes, *Tripartite Life*, 154.   **74** AT, 993, 1023; AU, 1016, 1177; AFM, 812.   **75** Ó Muraíle, *Mac Firbhishigh* i, 331; iii, 427.   **76** ALC, 1039, 1069, 1076, 1102, 1129; AT, 1044; AU, 1201; AFM, 787, 937, 1150, 1164.   **77** Ó Fiaich, 'Airgialla', 164–6, 208; Ó Muraíle, *Mac Firbhishigh*, i, 345. **78** CDI, ii, 38.

Irish polities of Uí Echach Cobo and Uí Thuirtri – the former, at least, also part of Ulaid – had come to be recognized as distinct territories. It was Ulster in this narrow sense, the actual area conquered and invested by John de Courcy, and which was granted by King John to Walter and Hugh de Lacy in 1204, which must have comprised the eight cantreds of this grant .[79] In addition, there is evidence to show that the Anglo-Normans regarded Oveh/Oueth, Turtery and Dalrede as additional cantreds, giving a total of eleven cantreds in this area. The extents of all of these can be arrived at with comfort given the relatively rich documentation surviving from the period, both secular and ecclesiastical. By at least 1226 and probably as early as 1212 those cantreds in secular lordship had been organized into six administrative units styled 'counties', extents of which survive, while the remaining two cantreds, as cross-land, do not feature in these extents. The term 'cantred' continued in use in Ulster as an alternative to that of 'county' into the mid-thirteenth century.[80] There are detailed early lists of the rural deaneries of the dioceses of Down and Connor which agree well with the extents of the counties, and both were clearly based on the same Irish pre-Invasion templates.[81] A further useful source is the series of early grants of lands to the church by the de Courcy and de Lacy lords of Ulster, in which the lands donated are all located within their respective cantreds.[82]

C147: *Cragfergus* (1226, 1326, 1333); *Cracfergus* (1276); *Maghelmourne* (1330); *Latherne* (1212)[83]

We have an extent of this county from 1333. Although it is usually styled from its chief place, Carrickfergus, there is a reference to the county as Maghelmourne or Mauchrimorne, the name of the corresponding rural deanery, and an early cantredal reference to it as 'Latherne'. The county contained, in addition to the entire area of the deanery, the parish of Belfast and parts of those of Shankill and Carnmoney, which must have been attached to the county as the only secular (and colonized?) portions of the cantred of Clandermod (**C156**). It would appear, therefore, that the deanery of Mauchrimorne represents the area of the original cantred. This contained the parishes of Carrickfergus, Kilroot, Templecorran, Island Magee, Glynn, Raloo, Inver, Larne, Grange of Killyglen, Kilwaughter, Carncastle, and the southern half of Tickmacrevan.[84]

T147: *Machaire Damhairne/Latharna*

Dál nAraide are a group of dynasties, also known as Cruithni, united in an artificial pedigree and who seem to have been driven eastwards across the Bann into their

---

79 Hardy, *Rot. Chart.*, 139b; Flanagan, *Irish royal charters*, 119–20. In fact, the area in question seems to have contained nine cantreds (**C147–50, 152–6**), a close enough figure given the occassional lack of clarity as to the exact number of cantreds that we find in colonial sources. **80** CDI, i, 222; Orpen, 'Earldom of Ulster', i–iii. The date of 1212 is suggested by a reference of that year to churches as lying in Carrickfergus and Moylinny (Sheehy, *Pont. Hib.* i, 149). **81** For the original extents see CDI, v, pp 203–211. These have been expertly identified by Reeves in his *Ecclesiastical antiquities*. **82** Reeves, *Ecclesiastical antiquities*, 164–6, 191; *Cal. Patent Rolls 1334–38*, 304–5. **83** CDI, i, 222; DKRI 43, p. 27; Orpen, 'Earldom of Ulster' i, 41; CCH, 33; Bain, *Cal. Docs. Scotland*, no. 573. **84** Orpen, 'Earldom of Ulster' i, 136–41; DKRI 43, p. 27; Reeves, *Ecclesiastical antiquities*, 51–63, 323–5.

later territories by the Northern Uí Néill during the mid-sixth century. The tale of Suibne Gelt mentions 'the five *trícha céts* of Dál nAraide', which is exactly the number of cantreds here (**C147–151**).[85]

The cantred of Machrimorne is derived from Machaire Damhairne, earlier Mag Damórna, a territory attested in *Vita Tripartita*. An older territorial name here was Latharna. The Lecan genealogies give a line of kings of Latharna of Uí (D)erca Céin ending during the first half of the seventh century, although a spur continues down to around 900, suggesting that Latherna may have survived as a kingdom much later. An alternative line of kings here may be those of Síl Fingín of Uí Erca Céin. This latter territory, made a kingdom by *Lebor na Cert*, has not been identified and the pedigrees of its dynasty are confused. While a lordly family using this title are found in Co. Down in the fourteenth century, these may have migrated from somewhere else during the intense local conflicts of that century. Síl Fingín were an early offshoot of the line of kings of Latharna and held the overkingship of Dál nAraide at least twice (645, 698). When we add to all of this the *Vita Tripartita* account (midninth century) which seems to locate Uí Erca Céin near Semne (Island Magee) in Mag Damórna, we must suspect, though not with certainty, that the Síl Fingín royal line resided around Carrickfergus.[86]

C148: *Antrum* (1226, 1326); *Maulin* (1272); *Auntrum* (1330); *Antrim* (1276, 1333); *Maulyn* (1333)[87]
This county was co-extensive with its namesake, the deanery of Maulyne. It contained the parishes of Antrim, Donegore, Grange of Nilteen, northern Templepatrick, Ballymartin, Kilbride, Rashee, Grange of Doagh, Ballylinny, Ballynure, Ballycor, and must also have contained Muckamore (in pre-Invasion Dál nAraide), Grange of Shilvodan and Glenwhirry.[88]

T148: *Mag Line*
The cantred of Maulyn is derived from the Irish territory of Mag Line, recorded as such in 1003. This was the indigenous local-kingdom of the royal mainline of Dál nAraide from 565, if the saga literature is to be believed, and certainly from 682, and so did not record kings of its own.[89]

C149: *Chueskert* (1180); *Tweskarde* (1212); *Toscharte* (1215); *Twescard* (1262, 1276); *Coulrath* (1330, 1333); *Dwyskard* (1353)
C150: *Dalrod* (1200); *Dalrethe* (1212); *Dalrede* (1215)[90]
Extents of this county (**C149**) survive from 1262 and 1333, and there are early cantredal ascriptions showing it to have been composed of two original cantreds,

85 Byrne, *Kings and high kings*, 108–9; O'Keeffe, *Buile Suibhne*, 62. **86** Reeves, *Ecclesiastical antiquities*, 269, 339; Dobbs, 'Descendants of Ir', 89–95, 108–9; eadem, 'Dál Fiatach', passim; Dillon, *Lebor na Cert*, 84, 88; O'Brien, *Corpus*, 155, 425–6; Stokes, *Tripartite Life*, 164; Morton, 'Tuathdivisions', passim; Flanagan, 'Latharna', 23. **87** CDI, i, 222; DKRI 43, p. 27; CDI, ii, 158, 477; CCH, 33. **88** Orpen, 'Earldom of Ulster' i, 141–3; Reeves, *Ecclesiastical antiquities*, 63–71; Orpen, *Ireland under the Normans* iv, 137. **89** Byrne, 'Clann Ollaman', 83; O'Brien, *Corpus*, 323; AU, 682; AI, 1003; ALC, 1198. **90** DKRI 43, p. 27; 44 p. 35; CDI, ii, 477; CCH, 33; McNeill, *Anglo-*

Twescard and Dalrede. Grants of the same period name a *theod* 'in Dalrod' and mention *totam terram inter Inverarma* [Glenarm] *et divisas de Dalrede*, indicating that its southern boundaries on the eastern coast agree with those between the deaneries of Twescard (north) and Turtery (south) here. Another such grant shows that Rathlin Island lay in Dalrede. Clearly then, the cantred of Dalrede was absorbed by Twescard sometime after 1215. Gaelic sources give the bounds of Dál Riata (**T150**) as extending from the River Bush to the Ravel Water and this general description is confirmed by ecclesiastical sources listing various churches in Dál Riata as well as by the deanery boundary referred to above, which also runs along the Ravel Water for part of its length. Therefore the rural deanery of Twescard gives the area of both cantreds. It can be said with certainty that Dalrede contained all of Cary barony and the parishes of Derrykeighan, Loughguile, Newton Crommlin, Dunaghy and probably Inispollen and Layd. Therefore Twescard must have contained the Liberties of Coleraine, all lands west of the lower Bush in Antrim, and at least the parishes of Ballymoney, Finvoy and Kilraghts. The parishes of Dundermot and Killagan were in the county and deanery of Twescard but which of its component cantreds they belonged to is unclear. Note that a few fees west of the Bann were included in the county of Twescard, but, as has been noted above (see under **C141**), these did not form part of the original cantred here, whose western border was the River Bann.[91]

T149: *An Tuaiscert*
The cantred of Twescard is derived from An Tuaiscert, a shortened version of Dál nAraidi an Tuaiscirt, from the northern branch of this kingdom. This is the territory of Mag Eilni as recorded by Tírechán, the plain east and south of Coleraine. Its ruling dynasty branched off from the southern Dál nAraidi mainline in the person of Fiachra Cáech (d. 608), brother of King Fiachnae Lurgan. This family must have been based around Eilne since at least the time of Fiachra's great-grandson, Dúngal Eilni (d. 681), if not earlier. This line held the overkingship of Dál nAraide at least seven times between 646 and 792, two of whom were also overkings of all of Ulaid. By 824 we begin to get kings of Dál nAraidi an Tuaiscirt, the last of whom occurs in 883, after which this line disappears from the record.[92] For the later history of this *trícha* see **T151**.

T150: *Dál Riata*
The polity of Dál Riata can certainly be traced back to the fifth century in light of its well-documented settlement in Scotland. Its history is obscure, and the Scots may have lost control of it by the eighth century, if not earlier.[93] Its territory continued to form a *trícha* into the twelfth century (see **T151**).

Norman Ulster, 142; Bain, *Cal. Docs. Scotland* nos. 573, 625.   **91** Reeves, *Ecclesiastical antiquities*, 71–81, 322–5; Otway-Ruthven, 'Dower charter', 79; Orpen, 'Earldom of Ulster' iii, 124–9, 138–9; idem, *Ireland under the Normans* iii, 288–90; CDI, i, p. 70; BL Add. MS 6041, f. 19; Ó Riain, *Corpus*, 131.   **92** Stokes, *Tripartite Life*, 329; Byrne, *Kings and high kings*, 287; Dobbs, 'Descendants of Ir', 113; AU, 824, 849, 883.   **93** Bannerman, *Dalriada*, 8, 51 fn. 9.

C151: *Kynilanmerach* (1215); *Crihenelanmerache* (1215); *Turtery* (1253); *Turtrie* (1272); *Turtry* (1305); *Turtreia* (1375)[94]

The Co. Antrim deanery of Turtery gives a precise extent of what must have been the cantred which remained in the hands of the Uí Fhlainn kings of Uí Thuirtre after the de Courcy conquest. This cantred is very probably that meant by the 1215 references to the cantred of (*Crích*) Kynilanmerach, which lay in the same area. That the boundaries of Turtery were early is shown by the grant above, which mentions 'all the lands between Inverarma and the bounds of Dalrede' (see **C150**). This describes exactly the strip of coastal land where Turtery reaches the North Channel. This deanery included most of the baronies of Toome, Lower Antrim, and Lower Glenarm apart from southern Tickmacrevan parish, and the parish of Rasharkin.[95]

T151: *Uí Thuirtri*

For the origins of Uí Thuirtri see **T140**. By the mid-twelfth century we find Uí Fhlainn of Uí Thuirtri describing themselves as kings of Uí Thuirtri (**T151**), Dál nAraide (i.e. an Tuaiscert: **T149**) and Dál Riata (**T150**), indicating the extent of their regional kingdom in northern Antrim.[96] Uí Thuirtri were active east of the Bann as early as 776 and were certainly fully established in the barony of Toome by the eleventh century. The deanery of Turtery must give the initial extent of their kingdom here (**T151**) before the conquests of an Tuaiscert and Dál Riata. An alternative name for Turtery seems to be (the cantred of) Kynilanmerach, which derives from Cenél Ainmirech. This appears to refer to an older pre-Uí Thuirtri Dál nAraidi lineage here, the most likely eponym being Ainmire, brother to King Eochaid (d. 553).[97]

C152: *Duffren* (1180); *Duffrian* (1207); *Blathewic* (1226); *Blachewyk* (1260); *Nova Villa* (1276, 1326); *Blathewyc* (1333); *Blawyk* (1334)[98]

All of the earliest references were to Dufferin, as for example to the grant of the cantred of 'Duffrian' by Hugh de Lacy to Roger Pipard in 1207, and those contemporary grants of lands 'in Duffren' to the church by both de Lacy and de Courcy. By 1226 we find reference to the county of Blathewyc, and in 1260 to the cantred of Blachewyk. The extent of 1333 reveals that by this time Blathewyc had absorbed the earlier county of Arde (**C153**) so we must rely on the extent of the deanery of Blathewyc to give the original area of the cantred. (The terms Arde and Newtonarde are also used to describe this enlarged county.) This deanery – which included those lands said to have lain in Dufferin above – consisted of the entire baronies of Lower Castlereagh and Dufferin excluding Inch, and the parishes of Bangor, Newtownards, Knockbreda, Killinchy, and probably Saintfield and Killaney. Onomastically Duibthrian 'the black third' suggests it was part of a greater area, almost certainly in

94 CDI, ii, 38, 158; Orpen, *Ireland under the Normans* iv, 146; Armagh PL MS KH II 46, 209; Bain, *Cal. Docs. Scotland* i, nos. 573, 625.   **95** Reeves, *Ecclesiastical antiquities*, 83–9, 323–4, 340n; CDI, i, p. 70.   **96** O'Brien, *Corpus*, 325–6; Dobbs, 'Descendants of Ir', 113; Stokes, *Tripartite Life*, 329; Byrne, 'Clann Ollaman', pedigrees.   **97** Reeves, *Ecclesiastical antiquities*, 323–5; O'Keeffe, *Buile Suibhne*, 44, 164 (n. 17); Dobbs, 'Descendants of Ir', 117.   **98** CDI, ii, 477; CCH, 33; DKRI 44, p. 35.

this case of that of Uí Blaithmeic (**T152**), even though the terms seem to have been interchangeable in the colonial period.[99]

T152: *Uí Blaithmeic*
Dál Fiatach were descendants of the Ulaid kings whose dominance of the province of Ulster collapsed at an early period, relegating them gradually to an eastern remnant of their former overlordship. These people can, of course, be identified on Ptolemy's second-century map of Ireland.[1]

The cantred of Blathewyc is derived from Uí Blaithmeic, a segment of Dál Fiatach descending from Blathmac, son of Áed Rón, king of Ulaid (d. 735). While no kings are recorded, Uí Blaithmeic appear as a polity in 1065 in the Lecan genealogies and as a kingdom in *Lebor na Cert*.[2]

C153: *Arde* (1200); ***del Arte*** (1226); *Ardo* (1305).[3]
The earliest references to this cantred occur in the early de Courcy and de Lacy grants alluded to above. By 1333 the original county of Arde (of 1226) had been united with that of Blathewyc as described above, and we must therefore rely on the extent of the deanery of Arde to give the area of the original cantred. This consisted of most of the Ards peninsula up to a line formed by the northern border of the parish of Grey Abbey, the continuation of which is given by the inclusion in Arde of the southern two-thirds of the parish of Donaghadee.[4]

T153: *Uí Echach Arda*
The cantred of Arde is derived from the Irish local kingdom of Uí Echach Arda. These were an early lineage whose link with Ulaid is probably artificial. They are mentioned as a polity in 557 but their pedigrees do not descend beyond 700 at latest. The Ulaid genealogies mention a proto-historic king of theirs residing in Dún Eathlaig, which Dobbs identifies with Dunevly in Ardkeen parish, while the literature on the battle of Mag Roth (642) also names a king of 'Ard Uladh'. The mainline were still in existence in 950 when, described as *Uib Echoch, i. o maccaibh Broin* (Bran was the ancestor of the earlier main segment), they slew the king of Ulaid. In 1086 they were associated with Uí Blaithmaic in another regicide, and these late references suggest that the apparently dubious manuscript reference to another king of this polity, in 1034, may well be accurate. Na hArda occurs as a kingdom in *Lebor na Cert* and as a territory several times in the annals from 823.[5]

C154: *Lechayel* (1180); ***Ladcathel*** (1226); *Leth Cathel* (1305); ***Down*** (1276, 1334); ***Dun*** (1333); ***Lecale*** (1427).[6]
This cantred is usually referred to as Lechayel, but as Dun (Down) in the extent of

99 COD, i, 365; Reeves, *Ecclesiastical antiquities*, 9–17, 166; RIA MS 12 D 9, 167; CDI, i, p. 222; Orpen, 'Earldom of Ulster' ii, 63–6; BL Add. MS 6041, f. 101. **1** Byrne, *Kings and high kings*, 50–1, 108; O'Brien, *Corpus*, 322. **2** Dobbs, 'Descendants of Ir', 85–6; Dillon, *Lebor na Cert*, 84, 88. **3** CJRI, ii, 135. **4** Reeves, *Ecclesiastical antiquities*, 17–27, 166; CDI, i, 222; Orpen, 'Earldom of Ulster' ii, 63–6; CCH, 144, 155b, 237. **5** Dobbs, 'Descendants of Ir', 349–59; Byrne, 'Clann Ollaman', 84, 89; Reeves, *Ecclesiastical antiquities*, 16n; Dillon, *Lebor na Cert*, 84, 88; AU, 823, 949, 1011; ALC, 1130. **6** CJRI,

1333, which agrees exactly in area with that of the rural deanery of Lechayl. The cantred included the entire baronies of Lecale and Mourne, and the parishes of Inch, Kilcoo, Maghera, Kilmegan, Loughinisland, and Kilmore.[7]

T154: *Leth Cathail*

The cantred of Lechayl is derived from Leth Cathail, 'Cathal's half'. As a political unit it seems to have been granted to Tommaltach mac Cathail of Cenél nÓengus-so (d. 789) as compensation for his failure to win the kingship of Ulaid from his cousins in the mainline. Among his descendants was at least one king of Ulaid and six kings of Leth Cathail (between 850 and 1147).[8] The cantred included Boirche (Mourne), ceded to Ua Cerbaill, king of Airgialla, by Eochaid Mac Duinnsléibe, king of Ulaid, in 1165. This shows that the boundaries of the cantred are older than 1165. A second polity here was Uachtar Tíre, on the southern shores of Dundrum Bay, which certainly operated as a kingdom for at least a few decades of the mid-eleventh century.[9] Two genealogies of this lineage survive, one claiming descent from a discard segment of Uí Echach Coba while another, more improbably, links them with Ind Airthir of Airgialla.[10]

C155: *Dalebingu* (1200); *Dalboing* (1204).[11]

This term occurs as an apparent cantredal designation in the early de Courcy/de Lacy deeds — when all of it was granted to the church — but it attracted little colonial settlement and did not subsequently form a county. The extent of this cantred must be identical with that of the rural deanery of Dalboyn, which included the Antrim parishes of Glenavy, Derryaghy, Ballinderry, Magheragall, Aghagallon, Aghalee, and Magheramesk; the parishes of Drumbeg, Lambeg and Blaris shared both by Antrim and Down; and the Down parishes of Hillsborough and Drumbo.[12]

T155: *Dál Buinne*

Having ceded Downpatrick, the ancient capital, to Cenél nÓengusso (see under T154), the mainline of Dál Fiatach soon moved north-westwards to Dál Buinne, a territory which included both the royal *dún* of Duneight and the *óenach* site of Cráeb Tulcha. From this *trícha* derives the cantred of Dalboyn. Dál Buinne were not Dál Fiatach, but the genealogical affinity of the only king so styled (1130) is unclear. In 1176 Dál Buinne were described as a lineage and may perhaps have retained a king of their own stock under the kings of Ulaid. Dál Buinne occurs as a kingdom in *Lebor na Cert*.[13]

ii, 135; CCH, 242; CDI, ii, 477; DKRI 44, p. 35. 7 Reeves, *Ecclesiastical antiquities*, 27–44, 165; CDI, i, 222; Orpen, 'Earldom of Ulster' ii, 60–3; Otway-Ruthven, 'Dower Charter', 79. 8 AT, 1022; AU, 896, 1006; AFM, 850, 927, 1147. 9 ALC, 1046, 1054, 1061. 10 O'Brien, *Corpus*, 184, 326–7, 412; Byrne, 'Clann Ollaman', 93–4, pedigrees; idem, *Kings and high kings*, 119; Dobbs, 'Descendants of Ir', 79. 11 JRSAI 50 (1921), 168. 12 Reeves, *Ecclesiastical antiquities*, 44–9, 166; BL Add. MS 6041, f. 101. 13 Byrne, *Kings and high kings*, 27, 119, 124; idem, 'Clann Ollaman', 88, pedigrees; Dobbs, 'Descendants of Ir', 77; Dillon, *Lebor na Cert*, 84, 88; ALC, 1130; AT, 1176.

C156: *Clandermod*

Reference to insignificant colonial settlement in 'Clanderemod' occurs in 1219, but this seems to have been confined to the eastern third of this cantred, most of the remainder of which appears to have been cross-land and was apparently not settled, which must account for its subsequent failure to become a county. Its extent must be preserved in that of the deanery of Clandermod, which contained the parishes of Killead, Camlin, Tullyrusk, the greater – southern – portion of Templepatrick, Shankill, Belfast and perhaps parts of Carnmoney.[14]

T156: *Clann Diarmata*

The cantred of Clandermod is derived from Clann Diarmata, a line descended from Dúnchad, son of King Eochaid mac Fiachna of Dál Fiatach (d. 810). Another segment in this polity was Clann Gormlaithe, associated with lands in what is now the northern suburbs of Belfast (Glengormley). These descend from a brother of Dúnchad's, Muiredach, whose son, Matudán (d. 857), was king of Ulaid. It would appear that this area was settled by these royal segments shortly after the mainline moved into Dál Buinne to the south, suggesting that both *trícha*s originate around 800 in an expansion of Dál Fiatach here, probably into what had been Dál nAraide territory.[15]

C157: *Oveh* (1180, 1200); *Oueth* (1253).

This term is used in an apparently cantredal context in early grants, suggesting the Anglo-Normans considered it to be a distinct cantred. Notwithstanding this it is clear that no significant settlement occurred in Uí Echach Cobo (**T157**), which remained a semi-independent Irish polity as evidenced by the ecclesiastical independence it achieved in the 1190s when the diocese of Dromore was detached from that of Down. The area of this cantred therefore would seem to be represented by the original extent of the diocese of Dromore, which included in Down the lordship of Newry, all of the various baronies of Iveagh excepting the parishes of Kilcoo, Maghera, Kilmegan, Blaris, and Hillsborough, and (included) the Kinelarty parishes of Magheradrool and Magherahamlet, and finally the Co. Armagh barony of Oneilland East.[16]

T157: *Uí Echach Cobo*

This kingdom gives the cantred of Oveh (from Uíbh Echach). Its kings are recorded regularly in the annals from 553 until the Invasion, around two dozen in all.[17] Its royal line held the overkingship of Ulaid in 692, 825 and 898.[18]

URIEL

In the kingdom of Airgialla (Uriel), as in some other parts of Ireland, its constituent cantreds were sub-infeudated long before they were settled, and our principal source

---

14 Reeves, *Ecclesiastical antiquities*, 1–9, 180. **15** Dobbs, 'Descendants of Ir', 83–5; Byrne, 'Clann Ollaman', 86, pedigrees. **16** Reeves, *Ecclesiastical antiquities*, 103–19, 164; Otway-Ruthven, 'Dower charter', 79; McNeill, *Anglo-Norman Ulster*, 12. **17** AU, AFM, ALC, passim. **18** O'Brien, *Corpus*, 324–6; Byrne, 'Clann Ollaman', pedigrees.

for its cantreds are these initial grants to its tenants-in-chief, the Verdons and Pipards. These early cantredal references are well supplemented by the ruridecanal pattern here, at least partly in existence since the 1230s, which once again closely parallels that of the cantreds.[19] In Uriel *inter anglicos* (now Co. Louth), by the fourteenth century the original cantreds with shape unchanged had come to be termed baronies, perhaps through the influence of the practice in neighbouring Meath. Again, as with Meath, there appears to have been little or no change in the boundaries of these medieval cantreds/baronies over the centuries. Uriel contained ten cantreds.

C158: *Luva* (1190, 1210); *Louedhe* (1221); *Louethe* (1375).
The eastern half of 'the cantred of Luva' was part of the original Verdon enfeoffment here while the western half remained in royal possession for some decades after. It is clear from the evidence that this cantred is now represented by the barony of Louth, Co. Louth. We find mention of a (cantredal) serjeant of 'Louethe' in 1260.[20]

T158: *Lugmad*
The cantred of Louth or Lugmad would seem to have been based on the demesneland of the Uí Cherbaill kings of Airgialla (see under **T165**), as conquered by them during the 1130s. Was it considered a *trícha*? It would appear so. It seems to have been originally part of the kingdom of Conaille (**T161**).[21]

C159: *Ferrardi* (1217: better Ferrard).
This is described as 'the cantred of the bridge of Ferrardi' in 1217, and this should be understood as a reference to the bridge over the Boyne at Drogheda. Its cantredal coroner is described as 'the coroner of Drogheda on the side of Uriel' in 1260. Its shape is largely preserved in that of the present barony of Ferrard, Co. Louth, and entirely so in that of the rural deanery of Ferrard, which has the same boundaries as the barony but with the addition of the parishes of Collon and Tullyallen.[22]

T159: *Fir Arda Ciannachta*
This local kingdom lay in Brega until absorbed by the Uí Cherbaill overkingdom of Airgialla (see under **T165**) in the middle of the twelfth century. Fir Arda was a remnant territory retained by the royal line of Ciannachta Breg after much of their territory was taken over by Uí Chonaing of Síl nÁedo Sláine around 700. A dozen or so kings are recorded between the late seventh century and 955.[23] After this the position here is unclear. Fir Arda may have continued as a local kingdom, as it gives

---

19 For the ruridecanal boundaries of the diocese of Armagh, see Murray, 'Primate George Dowdall', vol. 6, pp 217–28, vol. 7, pp 78–95. For Clogher, the only list of its rural deaneries that I can locate is that of the Taxation of 1306 (CDI, v, p. 212). All of the churches in this can be identified; see Duffy, *Landscapes of South Ulster*, 2–4. **20** Otway-Ruthven, 'Verdon partition', 402; MacIomhair, 'Fir Rois', 173; CDI, i, 155; RIA MS 12 D 9, 19. **21** MacIomhair, 'Fir Rois', 178; MIA, 1178. **22** CDI, i, p. 118; RIA MS 12 D 9, 25. **23** AU, 778, 821, 827, 838, 849, 883, 895; CS, 658, 684, 955; FIA, 688; AFM, 732, 812, 876.

the later cantred of Ferrard. Its chief church, Monasterboice, continued in the hands of a line descended from the earlier kings of Fir Arda down to around 1100.[24]

C160: *Ferros* (1190).
The original Pipard grant included 'two and a half cantreds of Ferrors [read Ferros] with the castle of Ardee' and this fee is now represented by the barony of Ardee, Co. Louth. The sum of two and a half cantreds is hard to understand and the text of the grant may have become corrupted in transmission. Ardee is unlikely to have constituted more than a single cantred and the rural deanery of Ardee was even bigger, containing in addition to that of Ardee the parishes of the barony of Louth.[25]

T160: *Fir Rois*
Kings of Fir Rois are recorded regularly from 739 to 1096 and it is recorded as a territory in 1131.[26] Where these kings can be identified, they belong to various segments of the Airthir section of Airgialla. The bounds of Fir Rois as given in *Vita Tripartita* (mid-ninth century), in addition to later references, indicate it to correspond to the later cantred of Ferros *alias* Ardee. (Ó Fiaich's derivation of Fir Rois from Ros in Mugdorna appears to be without foundation.)[27]

C161: *Dundalk* (1190); ***Machwercunuille*** (1204); *Dondalk* (1300)
C162: *Karlyngford* (1229); *Cole* (1240); *Coly* (1280, 1300)[28]
The early reference to the Verdon cantred of Machwercunuille probably refers only to the barony of Upper Dundalk. An early extent of the Verdon 'land of Dundalk' does not include Cooley (now the barony of Lower Dundalk), certainly part of the Verdon estate here. Although Coly is usually absent from the barony lists of Louth, there is a reference of 1300 to the baronies of 'Coly' and of 'Dondalk', and a further reference of 1370 to Coly as a barony, which indicates that Coly must have been a distinct cantred, given its omission from the extent of Dundalk and its status as a barony, for all the Louth baronies appear to have been simply the original cantreds under a new title.[29]

T161: *Machaire Conailli*
The royal line of the kingdom of Conaille Muirthemne is derived from an offshoot of Dál nAraide of perhaps mid-sixth-century date. At least twenty three kings are recorded in the annals between 740 and 1107.[30] The name of this kingdom last occurs in a territorial context in 1128, after which we find only reference to the territory of Machaire Conailli, which gives the cantred of Machwercunuille, an area signif-

24 O'Brien, *Corpus*, 168–71, 246–8; Ó Muraíle, *Mac Fhirbhisigh* iii, 703; Walsh, *Irish leaders and learning*, 81–3; Byrne, 'Cnogba', 396–7, 399; Byrnes, 'Árd Ciannachta', 127–31. **25** COD, i, p. 364; MacIomhair, 'Fir Rois', 172. **26** ALC, 1028; MIA, 1131; AU, 850, 936, 1052, 1073; AFM, 811, 892, 948, 953. **27** MacIomhair, 'Fir Rois', 144–79; Stokes, *Tripartite Life*, 184; Ó Fiaich, 'Airgialla', 155–9, 187, 197, 207. **28** Mills, *Gormanston*, 195–6. **29** Cambridge University Library Add. MS 3104, f. 59; Otway-Ruthven, 'Verdon partition', 403–5; Richardson and Sayles, 34, 135, 152; CCH, 158b. **30** Earliest and latest annals: AT, 740; AFM, 1107.

icantly smaller than the original kingdom.[31] This kingdom had stretched from parts of Louth barony into Upper Fews in Armagh (*Fid Conaille*). Thus Conaille was largely dismembered during the eleventh and early twelfth centuries by the Airgiallan Uí Cherbaill and Ind Airthir (**T164**). Muirthemne is described as a *trícha cét* in *Táin*.[32]

T162: *Cúailnge*

Cúailnge gives the barony of Coly, originally a cantred. There is one reference to a king of Cúailnge, in 968.[33] Sometime after, as part of a general eastwards extension of authority by Fir Fhernmaige, the kings of Uí Méith Macha (**T165**: in Co. Monaghan) extended their authority into Cúailnge (in the process giving their name to Omeath in Cooley). While Flanagan suggests that this annexation may date to the mid-twelfth century the association of Cúailnge and Uí Méith in annals of 1044 and 1131 may indicate an earlier date. It may be that the secondary Uí Méith kingdom, Uí Méith Mara, was merely the older kingdom of Cúailnge renamed. Certainly, Uí Innrechtaig, who had earlier been kings of Uí Méith Macha, continued to rule 'Coly' under the de Verdons into the thirteenth century. Cúailnge is described as a *trícha cét* in *Táin Bó Cúailnge* and in *Lebor Gabála*.[34]

C163: *Muderne* (1190); *Macherne* (1193)

'Half of the cantred of Muderne' was among the original Pipard grant in Uriel but a few years later Roger Pipard appears to have been seized of 'the whole cantred of Macherne'. While the Verdons were later seized of a rent from the MacMahons (for which see under **T165**) this may have derived from western Monaghan and not from the area of the cantred of Muderne where the Pipards certainly appear as sole feudal lords of the MacMahons. It is quite clear that this cantred was early divided into a southern half which saw significant colonial settlement and a northern section left in Irish hands. The chief Pipard manor in the colonized portion was Donaghmoyne which contained four knights' fees while a second important manor was that of Ros (now represented by the parish of Magheross), containing one fee, while there were also significant church-lands which had been colonized. The fourteenth-century rural deanery of Donaghmoyne ('Donaghoyagen': *Domnach Maighean*) was certainly the ruridecanal equivalent of the cantred of Muderne. This deanery was only fully emparished in that section corresponding to the colonized part of Muderne while that left unsettled contained just one parish, the remainder being described as the *túath* ('plebs') of Crích Mugdorn, whose church seems to have been that of Aghnamullen, and whose rural rectory was impropriate to the Augustinian abbey of St Mary, Louth. In a contemporary charter a MacMahon is enfeoffed of the 'regality of Crichnagarum' (*sic*) by Ralph Pipard, which contained the villate of Lowegus (Lough Egish). From all of this it is clear that the colonized portion of Muderne corresponds to the later barony of Farney, while the northern section, Crích Mugdorn,

31 AI, 1128; MIA, 1179. **32** O'Brien, *Corpus*, 327; Ó Fiaich, 'Airgialla', 58–60, 147–9; Murray, 'Conaille Muirthemne', passim; Hogan, 'The tricha cét', 210. **33** CS, 968. **34** Mac Ivor, 'Knights Templars', 74; LL 1541; Hogan, 'The tricha cét', 210; Ó Corráin, 'Hogan', 91–2; Flanagan, *Irish royal charters*, 295 (n. 7); ALC, 1044, 1131.

is ancestor to the present barony of Cremorne, both together constituting the area of the original cantred of Muderne (along, of course, with those portions of the parishes of Inishkeen and Killanny in Co. Louth).[35]

T163: *Mugdorna Maigen*

Mugdorna Maigen are given a doubtful Airgialla descent but were probably associates of Ulaid, and may have held lordships here before the rise of Airgialla. Mugdorna Maigen was originally quite large. Adomnán (seventh century) locates Ros (Carrickmacross) in Mugdorna while it seems to have stretched northwards to include much of Monaghan barony and southwards to include Mugdorna Breg in modern Meath. Kings of Mugdorna are recorded regularly between 611 and 1110, at least two being explicitly noted as kings of both Mugdorna Maigen and Mugdorna Breg, while many others undoubtedly were so.[36] The Monaghan (town) area was lost to the expanding Uí Méith around 700 and Mugdorna Breg incorporated into Mide after 954, leaving the area henceforth known as Mugdorna Maigen. Further developments during the second half of the eleventh century saw Fir Fhernmaige overrun southern Mugdorna, to give the core of the kingdom of Fernmag, the later barony of Farney, and it appears that the indigenous Uí Machainén kings of Mugdorna were confined to northern Mugdorna or Crích Mugdorn, which gives the barony of Cremorne. By the mid-twelfth century Uí Machainén had been replaced here by the kings of neighbouring Uí Méith (see **T165**) who, in turn, had been replaced by a cadet branch of the MacMahons by around 1200. Interestingly, the area of the cantred of Muderne agrees with that of the eleventh-century kingdom of Mugdorna before it experienced contraction. The latter is no doubt the *trícha* of Mugdorna of the Lecan Miscellany.[37]

C164: **Erthyr** (1190); *Ardmacha* (1205)

The cantred of E(r)thyr was one of the original Pipard cantreds but would seem to have been subsequently granted to the Verdons, probably in exchange for Fermanagh (see under **C166**). 'The lands of Ohanlon in Erthir' (doubtless the later baronies of Orior) were charged with a cash rent to the Verdon heirs in 1333 as were the lands of Othegan and two other lords (*duces*: read *taísig tuaithe?*) 'in the woods'. Part of this latter territory would seem to correspond with the *túath* ('plebs') of Othedigan as taxed in the Papal Taxation in the deanery of Erthyr, and must, along with the lands of the others, have lain in the Fews in Co. Armagh. As early as 1205 Nicholas de Verdon had granted Theobald Walter twenty knights' fees 'in my land of Honectath in the south part of Ardmacha', which seems to represent the territory of Uí Echach in the same area. The Ua hAnluain lordship in Armagh certainly

35 COD, i, 4–5, 106–7, 364; Mac Iomhair, 'Fir Rois', 173; Otway-Ruthven, 'Verdon partition', 406; CPR, xi, 674; White, *Extents*, 231–2; Fiant Eliz., nos. 568, 1312; CDI, v, p. 212 (where the difficult identifications are: Deynisdega = Inishkeen; Collenayth = Killanny; Mytynam = Muckno). 36 ALC, 1019; AU, 610, 749, 758, 778, 803, 815, 848, 936, 954, 1009, 1062, 1110; AFM, 773, 833, 997, 1053; MIA, 1179. 37 Ó Fiaich, 'Airgialla', 149–55, 187, 206; Ó Mórdha, 'Mugdorna', 432–445; GT, 146; MacIomhair, 'Fir Rois', 157; Arthurs, 'Mourne', passim.

extended much further north at this time than it did in the sixteenth century, and so the cantred of Erthyr would seem to correspond to the rural deanery of the same name, which included all of Co. Armagh except the barony of Oneilland East, those parts of Newry in the deanery, and the Co. Tyrone parishes of Aghaloo, Clonfeacle and Killyman. Erthyr must also have included the Co. Louth sections of those parishes the bulk of which lie in Co. Armagh.[38]

T164: *Ind Airthir*

Ind Airthir means the Easterners or the people of eastern Airgialla. Ind Airthir first appears in the annals s.a. 520. Its early kings were drawn from the Uí Nialláin, Uí Bresail and Uí Cruinn segments of Ind Airthir, whose eponyms were linked remotely and who, if indeed they were historic personages, may belong to the beginning of the sixth century. *Vita Tripartita* portrays Ind Airthir as a single kingdom with its capital at Armagh and this is reflected in the annals, where kings of Ind Airthir are recorded regularly between 520 and the early ninth century.[39] During the ninth century kings of the various segments of Ind Airthir begin to be recorded, and what are now clearly overkings of Ind Airthir only feature occasionally. The first king of Uí Nialláin is recorded in 803, using the metonym Loch Cal, after their capital at Lough Gall, and this kingdom occupied the area of the later barony of Oneilland West. The first king of Uí Bresail or Mag Duma occurs in 914, and this lineage occupied the barony of Armagh and parts of Tiranny and of the corresponding parts of Tyrone across the Blackwater, as reflected in the extent of the deanery of Erthyr. Mag Duma may, perhaps, be the early form of the name of the village of Moy near Clonfeacle, the latter being a monastery with Airthir connections. These royal lines were joined by Uí Echach, kings of whom are recorded from 993 onwards, and whose territory lay in southern County Armagh. After this the record is mixed, and kings of all three segments are recorded as well as occasional kings of all Ind Airthir.[40] The polity came under increasing pressure from Cenél Eógain from the 1150s onwards, resulting in the expulsion of the Uí Anluain kings of Uí Nialláin southwards to what is today the baronies of Orior and the imposition of a Cenél Eógain dynast over Uí Echach. In a charter of 1157, Donnchad Ua Cerbaill (see under **T165**) is described as king of Trícha Cét Airthir ('Tricaded Erthyr') while in 1184 'Triúcha Cead Oirigh' (*sic*) were attacked by another Ua Cerbaill, who camped against them at Armagh. Given that the thirteenth-century rural deanery of Erthyr contained all of Ind Airthir at its fullest extent, the early twelfth-century *trícha* of Ind Airthir must have been of similar extent.[41]

C165: *Clonoys (Clones)*

The cantred of Clonoys was among the original Pipard cantreds and must correspond to the rural deanery of the same name. This contained the modern baronies

38 COD, i, 364, 367; Otway-Ruthven, 'Verdon partition', 422; Simms, 'O'Hanlons and O'Neills', passim. **39** AU, 519, 609, 624, 640, 721, 742, 862; CS, 694. **40** AFM, 910; CS, 913; AU, 932, 1077, 1078, 1159. **41** Ó Fiaich, 'Airgialla', 56–103, 187–97, 211; Stokes, *Tripartite Life*, 228, 290; Flanagan, *Irish royal charters*, 292.

of Monaghan and Dartree, Co. Monaghan, and Clankelly and Coole in Co. Fermanagh.[42]

T165: *Clones*
In view of the general correlation between cantred and *trícha* in Airgialla the cantred of Clonoys (Clones) would seem to represent an earlier *trícha*. At its centre lay the ecclesiastical *civitas* of Clones and the nearby Loch Uaithne, centre of the Fir Fhernmaige branch of Airgialla. This *trícha* contained no less than four prominent ruling lines, each of which must have constituted a local kingdom at various times. These were Fir Fhernmaige, Uí Méith, Dartraige Coninse and Clann Chellaig.[43]

Fir Fhernmaige claimed descent from Nad Slúaig, son of Cairpre Dam Aircit (d. 514), and it was from him and his brother, Daimíne, that the chief ruling lines of Uí Chremthainn (see under **T167**) claimed descent. Uí Chremthainn was an overkingdom which seems to have included western and central Airgialla. Its competing regnal families must, however, have been kings of their own local kingdoms, one of which was certainly Fir Fhernmaige. Fernmag is a plain located in western Monaghan barony bordering Clones. Its ruling line provided a king of Airgialla in 697 and others were kings of Uí Chremthainn in 742, 833, 850 and 879. Following the collapse of Uí Chremthainn local kings of Fernmag occur, beginning in 850 with a king of Loch Uaithne, a metonym which changes to Fernmag in 892.[44] The line again succeeded to the kingship of Airgialla from 949 onwards, and these kings would include the later ruling lineages of Uí Cherbaill and Meic Mathgamhna. Fir Fhernmaige were based at Loch Uaithne (Lough Oony, Clones parish) at least from 719 to 1025, when they began to expand eastwards at the expense of their neighbours, in particular Uí Méith.

Kings of Uí Méith are recorded regularly from 673,[45] and this kingdom, an early offshoot of Uí Chremthainn, seems to have expanded southwards from the area of Trough barony into eastern Monaghan barony, where we can locate the historical kingdom of Uí Méith. Allocation of the later kings of Uí Méith is difficult because of the existence of two kingdoms of the name, the principal Uí Méith Macha, and the secondary Uí Méith Mara, in Cúailnge (**T162**). Most kings of Uí Méith recorded in the annals seem to have been of the principal kingdom, and references of 1161 and 1179 indicate that these kings were kings of both Uí Méith Macha and Crích Mugdorn at this time. A king of South Airgialla of the Uí Méith is recorded in 1092.[46]

The third line were the kings of Dartraige Coninse, three of whom occur between 946 and 1179.[47] Two of these were Uí Baígelláin, a lineage claiming descent from Baetáin mac Tuatháin, great-grandson of Daimíne, who may therefore have lived in the mid-seventh century. Uí Baígelláin were probably allies of Fir

42 COD, i, 364; CDI, v, p. 212 (where the identifications are: Gabalynan = Galloon; Droymseuta = Drumsnat; Thechalbi = Tyholland). **43** For much of what follows see Ó Fiaich, 'Airgialla', 124–33, 140–1, 146–9, 187, 202–5. **44** AU, 850, 886, 987; CS, 913; AFM, 901. **45** ALC, 1017, 1020, 1027, 1043, 1049, 1107, 1131, 1170; AU, 673, 710, 746, 754, 825, 1076, 1108, 1161; AFM, 893; MIA, 1179. **46** Duffy, 'Medieval Monaghan', passim; Flanagan, *Irish royal charters*, 294–5 (n. 7). **47** AU, 946, 1006; MIA, 1179.

Fhernmaige; one of them was king of Fernmag in 1093 and another had been king of Airgialla a few years before. Dartraige were an older stratum here who may have been taken over by branches of Airgialla quite early, though we have no record of this. The kingdom of Dartraige certainly included the barony of Coole in Fermanagh as well as the adjacent border country with Monaghan, but may not have included all of the later barony of Dartree. Fourthly we have Clann Chellaig who gave their name to Clankelly barony in Fermanagh. The eponym was fifth in descent from Daimíne and kings of Uí Chremthainn in 732 and 781 and of Airgialla in 875 were of this line. They fade into relative obscurity after this.

Thus the posited *trícha* of Clones (**T165**) appears to have consisted of the four westernmost local kingdoms subject to the overlordship of Fir Fhernmaige as it had become by the late eleventh century, a *status quo* which was maintained into the fifteenth century as Clankelly and Coole remained subject to the MacMahons until then. The location of the principal demesne and mensal (*lucht tighe*) lands of the Meic Mathgamna kings was also here (around Leck and Monaghan a few miles east of Loch Uaithne) in the thirteenth century, no doubt a continuation from the earlier period.[48]

C166: *Fermanach* (1239); *Locherna* (1290); *Locherny and the seven theods of Fermanath* (1293)[49]

In 1193 Peter Pipard had a grant from John of 'the three cantreds of the land of Uhegeni' in exchange for 'the nearer land of Uriel'. Here Uhegeni certainly represents Uí Éignig, the contemporary ruling dynasty of Fir Manach, and this exchange must account for the early loss of the cantred of Erthyr (**C164**) by the Pipards, as well, perhaps, of lordship of lands in parts of modern Co. Monaghan. While it might appear at first sight that these three cantreds were all within the kingdom of Fir Manach *alias* Lough Erne the reference is more likely to apply to the area of over-lordship of Uí Éignig at this time. In addition to the title 'king of Fir Manach' this dynasty also on occasion aspired to that of overlordship of all of western Airgialla, and it would appear that the same Ua hÉignig dynast, at the time of his demise a few years later, bore the title *Airdríg Airgiall* in the annals. Fir Manach/Lough Erne can hardly have comprised more than one cantred/*trícha cét* (**T166**), and the others were probably the adjoining cantreds of Clogher and Clonoys, together forming the western half of the overkingdom of Airgialla. As to the extent of the cantred of Fermanach, this is certainly to be found in that of the rural deanery of Lough Erne, which consisted of all of Fermanagh apart from the baronies of Clankelly, Coole and Knockninny, and the parish of Killesher, and also included the parishes of Inishmacsaint and Templecarn, part of which lie in modern Donegal, as well as Aghalurcher, partly in Tyrone, and Kilskeery, completely so. Early in the thirteenth century Uí Éignig were superseded by Meic Uidhir (Maguire) here, whose kingdom bore the title of Lough Erne *alias* the seven *theoda* of Fermanagh. This was the very time that rural deaneries were being formed, and it can be no coincidence that the deanery here bore the same name as its corresponding secular kingdom.[50]

48 Nicholls, 'Reg. of Clogher', 413; Simms, 'Lough Erne', 130; Livingstone, *Monaghan story*, 46–9.
49 COD, i, 37; MacNiocaill, *Red Book of Kildare*, 33, 69.   **50** COD, i, 6, 366; AU, 1127, 1201;

T166: *Lough Erne/Fir Manach*

In the case of Lough Erne once again we have a coincidence of deanery, cantred and doubtless *trícha*, although this contained two local kingdoms. The lake of Lough Erne itself originally formed the southern borders of Uí Chremthainn (see under **T167**). The subsequent Airgiallan kingdom here, more usually known as Fir Manach, grew around a section, Clann Lugán, claiming descent from Cormac, brother of Daimíne, although, suspiciously, the earliest annalistic reference to this line does not occur until four centuries later. The genealogies suggest that this line began to ramify around 900, and it is probably to this period that we should attribute the foundation of the kingdom of Fir Manach just as, significantly, the overkingdom of Uí Chremthainn collapses. Fir Manach originally referred to a distinct lineage (and local kingdom?) of alleged Laigin origins settled in Magherastephana barony whose land was taken over by Clann Lugán. This area, along with Tirkennedy and Muintir Pheodacháin across the Erne (northern Clanawley and southern Magheraboy) formed the original Lough Erne kingdom, which subsequently pushed further westwards to include Túath Rátha which reached the Atlantic. Clann Lugán held the kingship of Airgialla five times between 963 and 1201 and that of Fir Manach at least twelve times in the period from 1010 to 1200.[51] From 1234 onwards the term Lough Erne becomes interchangable with that of Fir Manach for the kingdom.[52] The second kingdom here was that of Fir Luirg, containing the barony of Lurg and adjacent parts of Co. Donegal. Its kings were of the northern Airgialla, Uí Moccu Uais, which may account for its being briefly united with Uí Fhiachrach Arda Srátha (**T146**) during the 1030s. Four kings of Lurg occur between 925 and 1082.[53] After this the polity and its Uí Máel Dúin kings became subservient to the Meic Uidhir kings of Fir Manach, and was duly absorbed completely. Thus once again this Airgiallan *trícha* assumed its form during the latter eleventh century.

C167: *Clogher*

Among the original Pipard cantreds in Uriel was half of the cantred of Cloghkerin (or Cloghkerim), and there is evidence to suggest that this is a corruption of the name Clogher, perhaps derived from the longer version, *Clochar mac nDaimhíne*.[54] After taking account of the rural deaneries of the diocese of Clogher in the early Taxation what remains of the diocese is the episcopal mensal lands which appear to have been largely unparished and were clearly, from the sum given, extensive. This area certainly corresponded to that part of Clogher diocese outside of the deaneries already enumerated and included, in addition to Clogher itself, the parish of Donagh

AFM, 1369; Nicholls, 'Reg. of Clogher', 422; Simms, 'Lough Erne', 129–30; CDI, v, p. 212 (where the identifications are: Termundabeog = Templecarn; Kulmany = Magheraculmoney; Deismysinagusam = Inishmacsaint; Dunymis = Devenish; Delbota = Boho; Lisnagabail = Lisnagole in Aghalurcher (?); Deymsk = Inishkeen in Enniskillen; Deyridmelan = Derryvullen; Deridbrogusa = Derrybrusk; Akadynbeychi = Aghavea). For the formation of rural deaneries see my 'Irish rural deaneries'. **51** ALC, 1057, 1076, 1095, 1118, 1189, 1200; AT, 1053, 1160; AU, 1009, 1022. **52** Ó Fiaich, 'Airgialla', 134–9, 198–200; Simms, 'Lough Erne', 126–33. **53** ALC, 1039, 1082; AT, 1000, 1053; AU, 925. **54** COD, i, 364; Gwynn, *The Medieval province of armagh*, 167 (for evidence of a fifteenth-century reference to Clogher as 'Cloocornan').

in Co. Monaghan, which then seems to have included all of Trough barony. It is therefore clear that this ecclesiastical division consisted of the Tyrone parishes of Clogher, Donacavey, Dromore, Errigal Trough, and the Monaghan barony of Trough. I would suggest that the original area of the cantred of Clogher was the same and that the Pipard half-cantred here is represented by the present barony of Trough, Co. Monaghan (and that portion of Errigal Trough parish in Co. Tyrone), which must have been secular land while Clogher was largely cross-land.

T167: *Clogher*
Again, as with Clones, the area of the cantred/deanery of Clogher very probably represents that of an earlier *tricha*. This was clearly based around Clogher itself, the capital of the great kingdom of Airgialla from a very early period. More immediately, this had been the capital of the lesser overkingdom of Uí Chremthainn which disintegrated in the face of Cenél Eógain aggression after 827. Clogher itself was certainly home to several segments of Síl Daimíni, the senior line of descendants of Daimíne (d. 565). Of these, Síl Tuathail were dominant until replaced by Síl Duibthíre whose first king of Uí Chremthainn died in 791. Dubthíre's father, Eochaid Lemna (d. 703), took his epithet from Mag Lemna, the plain stretching from Clogher eastwards down the Blackwater to Trough, an area which was certainly in Uí Chremthainn in the ninth century. Further Síl Duibthíre kings of Airgialla (827) and Uí Chremthainn (867, 878) followed until Clogher was reduced to a local kingdom by Cenél Eógain aggression. Three kings of Síl Duibthíre are recorded between 914 and 1089 and it would seem probable that this polity corresponded in area to the posited *tricha* of Clogher. In addition, a king of Fir Lemna is recorded in 951 but the evidence suggests that this was merely an alternative name for this polity.[55] *Lebor na Cert* places Uí Chremthainn, Síl Duibthíre and Fir Lemna under a single king, and it would seem that Fir Lemna is an *alias* for the northern branch of Síl Tuathail. During the twelfth century the polity under discussion was overrun and dismembered by the Cenél Eógain lineages of Cenél Feradaig, who took Clogher itself, and Muintir Birn, who took Trough. Thus, once again in Airgialla we see that the *tricha* structure seems to date from the late eleventh century.[56]

By 1261 Meic Cionaith (MacKenna) occur as *taísig* of An Tríocha Céad (Trough). Significantly, these claimed to be of Cenél Fiachach (Southern Uí Néill) origin. While this is probably not historical its significance lies in similar claims made for Síl Daimíne/Fir Lemna/Síl Tuathail by the genealogists. This claimed ancestry by Meic Cionaith rather shows that they were claiming descent from the older Airgiallan lords of Trough, Fir Lemna. The name Trough, derived from Tríucha, a *tricha cét*, merits comment. The suggestion that its use as a proper name represents a local singularity does not bear scrutiny. Annalistic and other Irish sources also show the term in use for the neighbouring *tricha*s of Mugdorna and Ind Airthir, while even to the present day in the spoken Irish of Kerry *An Leith-triúch* is the term used for the half-cantred of Offerba. Hogan has pointed out that the later barony of Trough

55 AU, 914, 950, 1062, 1086, 1089. **56** Warner, 'Clogher', 39–43; Ó Fiaich, 'Airgialla', 104–43, 198, 201–2, 212; Livingstone, *Monaghan story*, 68; Dillon, *Lebor na Cert*, 78, 82.

appears to have contained only half the area of a theoretical standard *tricha cét*. It may be that the term refers to that portion of the original *tricha cét* of Clogher (**T167**) recovered from Cenél Eógain by Airgialla, as An Tríucha formed part of the later MacMahon kingdom of Airgialla. Again, Trough, unlike the remainder of Clogher, was not cross-land, so would represent the secular portion of the original *tricha*.[57]

WATERFORD

Empey has attempted to describe and map the cantreds of Anglo-Norman Waterford.[58] This is an especially difficult task as the sources for uncovering the cantredal structure of Waterford are meagre and a major indicator in the case of other Munster counties, the nature of the cantred as primary unit of sub-infeudation, does not apply to Waterford.

C168: *Owathath* (1287); *Owath* (1299); *Oveagh* (1298, 1375)[59]
See Empey, 'Waterford', 142.

T168: *Uíbh Echach*
The regional kingdom of Déisi Muman must have existed in roughly its present location from a very early period. Ogams dating perhaps from the fifth century record unique first names associated with its kings. In all, twelve cantreds can be located within the area of this polity as evidenced by the original borders of the dioceses of Waterford and Lismore. These display a very high proportion of locative or metonymic as distinct from lineage nomenclature. Gaelic sources ascribe ten *trichas* to Déisi.[60]

   The cantred of Oveagh derives from Uíbh Echach, apparently the ancestral name for the ruling line of Déisi which became dominant from the early tenth century onwards and from which both later ruling families derive. The pedigrees as they survive, however, do not record this Eochu. The cantreds of Oveagh and Dungarvan (**C170**) may perhaps represent the demesne *tricha*s of the rival and related ruling lines of Uí Bric and Uí Fáeláin.

C169: *Ohenegus* (1250); *Ohengus* (1287); *Ohynnys* (1299); *Ohenwys* (1358); *Ohenuis* (1375)[61]
See Empey, 'Waterford', 142–3.

T169: *Uí Óengusa*
The eponym of Uí Óengusa occurs in the early section of the Déisi genealogy, while it occurs as a territorial designation in 864. An interesting reference occurs in the

57 Ó Dufaigh, 'McKennas of Truagh', 221–3; AU, 1181, 1185, 1261; TCD MS 1366, f. 71; Nicholls, 'Reg. of Clogher', 413; Hogan, 'The tricha cét', 206. **58** 'Waterford', 141–6. Three principal cantred lists survive, for which see DKRI 38, p. 64, CCH, 72, and Richardson and Sayles, 59–60. **59** NLI MS 760, p. 125; CDI, iv, 261. **60** Hogan, 'The tricha cét', 223. For the Déisi genealogies with commentary, see Pender, *Déssi Genealogies*, passim. **61** COD, i, 46; NLI MS 760, 125.

Recensio Maior of the *Corpus Genealogiarum Sanctorum*, material datable to the tenth or eleventh centuries, which locates Druim Luchan in (the *túath* of) Uí Lucháin, in turn ascribed to Uí Brigte. This is Drumlohan which lay in the cantred of Ohynws rather than that of Obride (**C172**), and the saint in question was in fact of Uí Óengusa.[62]

C170: *Dungarvan* (1204, 1299); *Dungaruan* (1358); *Doungaruan* (1375)[63]
See Empey, 'Waterford', 142.

T170: *Dún Garbháin*
See **T168**.

C171: *Ofathe* (1282); *Offathe* (1287); *Offath* (1299, 1358, 1375); *Ofath* (1589)[64]
Empey is correct in his very tentative correlation of the area of the diocese of Waterford with that of the cantred of Offath. He was unable to find any significant evidence for this apart from the inclusion of Killure in Offath. Offath also contained the parishes of Reisk and Kilmeadan, while a deed of 1453 adds that of Kilmacomb (all in Waterford diocese). That Offath was ancestor to its rather shrunken descendant, Gaultier, is evident from deeds of 1589 ('the cantred commonly called Ofath *alias* le Galtier') and 1618 ('the Galtire *alias* Offath').[65]

T171: *Uí Fothaid Tíre*
Two cantreds bore the name Offath(e), from Uí Fothaid, located at either end of Déisi. Three kings of Uí Fothaid Tíre occur between 813 and 937, and this lineage are associated with Loch Dá Caoch (Waterford Harbour) in 896.[66] The evidence suggests that these were the Uí Fothaid from whom the Waterford cantred (**C171**) is derived. Uí Fothaid Aiched, who slew the king of Déisi in 920,[67] were certainly eponyms of the Tipperary cantred of Offathe (**C130**), as illustrated by its earliest forms, Yffathiatha and Hifathayhather. Fothad, if indeed he was an historical personage, occurs in the pedigrees in the late sixth-century period in a rather artificial context. The Waterford Uí Fothaid must have been submerged in the Ostmen kingdom of Waterford or Port Láirge, several of whose kings are recorded in the annals during the eleventh century, and who seem to have merely taken over the pre-existing local kingdom here.[68]

C172: *Obrid* (1212); *Obride* (1299); *Obryde* (1298, 1358); *Obredy* (1375)[69]
The area of this cantred as estimated by Empey is based on a short and certainly not comprehensive late-thirteenth century extent.[70] It is fine as far as it goes, but I would suggest that, bearing in mind my comments on the location of Tarmun below (**C174**), Obride would seem to have extended much farther to the north.

---

62 Pender, *Déssi Genealogies*, 7–8, 13; Ó Riain, *Corpus*, 15; FIA, 864. **63** CDI, i, 34. **64** CDI, ii, 426; NLI MS 760, 125. **65** CJRI, ii, 248; NAI KB 2/5, 122; Original deeds, Curraghmore MSS; NAI Catalogue of Wadding deeds, no. 59. **66** CS, 896; AFM, 813, 849, 937. **67** AI, 920. **68** Todd, *Cogad*, 27; Pender, *Déssi Genealogies*, 12, 176; AI, 1018; ALC, 1022, 1035, 1037; B. Ó Cíobháin, 'Cammas hUa Fathaid Tíre and the Vikings: significance and location', save@viking-waterford.com (2005). **69** Sheehy, *Pont. Hib.* i, 72; CDI, iv, 261. **70** Empey, 'Waterford', 142.

Much of the certain area of Obride was part of the le Poher feudal barony of Dunhill or Dunohill, and there are links on several levels between this area and that of Oughtirtyr to the north which suggest that Oughtirtyr may also have been part of Obride, although it should be borne in mind that Dunhill, somewhat unusually, was extra-cantredal.[71] Oughtirtyr, probably a *theodum*, certainly included the manor (and parish) of Rathgormuck.[72] Ó hUidhrín ascribed the lordship of Uachtar Tíre to the O Flanagan dynasty in pre-Invasion times. These retained lands in the Fews, as tenants of the honour of Dungarvan, well into the thirteenth century.[73] The Fews occur as part of Obride in the extent noted above. If, as seems likely, the O Flanagan lands were a remnant of their original lordship, it follows that Uachtar Tíre must have included the combined area of the parishes of Rathgormuck, Mothel and the Fews. During the thirteenth century the barony of Dunhill claimed the manor of Rathgormuck as a member.[74] Furthermore, we should note the pattern of monastic appropriation here. The Augustinian abbey of Mothel possessed the rectories of Mothel and Rathgormuck and several rectories in the parish of Ballylaneen in Obride, which was, significantly, another member of Dunhill.[75] In light of the above, therefore, I would suggest the addition of the parishes of Rathgormuck and Mothel to the area of Obride as suggested by Empey, along with Guilcagh – yet another member of Dunhill – and Clonagam. It is significant that this suggested extent of Obride, when added to the area of the cantred of Ohenwys (**C169**), agrees well with that of the rural deanery of Kilbarrymeadan.

T172: *Uí Brigte*
The eponym occurs in the early section of the Déisi genealogy, the female Brigit being made a wife of a prince.[76]

C173: *Slesco* (1298); **Slef** (1299); ***Slestro*** (1358); ***Slefko*** (1375)[77]
In addition to the area of this cantred as described by Empey I believe, in light of what I have said above concerning Iffowyn (**C129**) and Obride (**C172**), that Slefgo must also have included the area of the parish of Kilronan, which was, like everything to its south, part of the honour of Dungarvan.[78]

T173: *Sliab gCua*
Slefgo derives from Sliab gCua, indicating the upland nature of the terrain.[79]

C174: *Tarmun* (1299); *Tarumn* (1358); *Tarmod* (1375)
Empey, who was unable to find any evidence as to its location, placed the cantred of Tarmun in the northernmost portion of Waterford as he believed there was no room for it elsewhere.[80] I have shown above that much of this area was, however,

---

A second list of lands in Obride may be found in CDI, i, 327. **71** For an extent of Dunhill see BL Add. Charter 13598, f. 159v. **72** RC 7/9, 384. **73** TP, 46; Curtis, 'Sheriff's accounts', 3. **74** RC 8/6, 367. **75** White, *Extents*, 348 ff; Fiant Eliz., 2938. **76** Pender, *Déssi Genealogies*, 7–8, 13; Ó Riain, *Corpus*, 15. **77** CDI, iv, 261. **78** The parish of Kilronan corresponds to the *theodum* of Glennother, the later Glenahiry, a member of Dungarvan ('Sheriff's accounts', 2; CDI, iv, p. 262). **79** Fr Colmcille, 'Where was Sliabh gCua?', *Decies* 46 (1992), passim. **80** Empey, 'Waterford', 143.

part of the cantred of Iffowyn (**C129**), and I have adduced evidence which suggests that the remainder of this area was very probably part of the cantred of Obride (**C172**). Where, therefore, was Tarmun?

Evidence from a number of sources indicates that Tarmun contained Lismore and its hinterland. Tarmun must derive from *tearmann*: 'church-land', and the episcopal manor of Lismore represents the largest area of cross-land in the diocese of Waterford and Lismore. The Power or le Poher family of Shanagarry, Co. Cork, held extensive lands throughout Co. Waterford from an early period. In 1320 John le Poher of Shanagarry had a grant of free warren in (*inter alia*) his lands of Tyrnebruyghisse and Tarmoun in Co. Waterford. The former place is now Ballybrusa in Lisgenan parish. 'Tyrnebroyhe' again occurs in a pleading of 1329 in company with (*inter alia*) 'Balynglanye', in a list of all of the Poher lands in Waterford. This place is the 'Balyglan *alias* Tarmon' of an undated but certainly fifteenth-century rental of the diocese of Lismore, in which this fee (in the manor of Lismore), paid £4 and must thus have represented a large area of land. This Balyglan *alias* Tarmon is now represented by the present Ballygalane near Lismore, although originally it must have been much larger.[81] Additionally, we find secondary evidence for locating Tarmun in and around Lismore. A survey of the few references to office holders in this cantred reveals, among surnames with a widespread distribution within the county, just one unusual surname, le Lunt.[82] The only family of this name subsequently found in Waterford occur in the sixteenth century, when they were landholders and burgesses of some importance in the town and manor of Lismore, and clearly of long standing there.[83] These were very probably the descendants of the earlier family of the name. It would seem, therefore, that the cantred of Tarmun was largely or entirely composed of the ecclesiastical manor of Lismore, containing the parishes of Lismore (partly in Co. Cork), Kilmolash and part of Whitechurch, an area certainly large enough to merit cantredal status.[84]

T174: *Tearmann*

Tarmun derives from *tearmann*, land owned by the church, which seems to have been the case with most of this cantred. Nevertheless one suspects that the preceding *tricha* here represented demesne territory of the Meic Carthaig kings of Desmumu, Lismore being one of their capitals.[85]

C175: *Athmethen* (1299); *Athmean* (1358, 1375)

If I am correct regarding the extent of Tarmun (**C174**), then the cantred of Athmean (from its *caput*, Affane) must have been confined to the area of its feudal barony, which Empey has described.[86]

---

81 PRC, 145–6 (where the identifications advanced for Ballynglanye are erroneous). For further evidence indicating that Balyglan was originally a super-denomination, see NAI MS 2550, f. 70v, and RC 7/9, 339. **82** CCH, 72b; Richardson and Sayles, 59. **83** 'Mansfield Papers', *Analecta Hibernica* 20 (1958), 92; *Civil Survey* vi, 10. **84** For an extent of the manor of Lismore around 1600 see Rennison, 'Bishoprick of Waterford', vol. 32, pp 47–9. For cartographic reasons the map shows only Lismore in Tarmun. **85** MacCotter, 'Rise of Meic Carthaig', 70. **86** Empey,

T175: *Áth Meadhain*
A simple metonym gives the cantred of Athmethan, from Áth Meadhain.

WEXFORD

The early loss of much of this county to the Gaelic Resurgence makes the task of reconstructing the cantredal structure in the north of the county difficult, although a loose reconstruction can be attempted with the help of the ruridecanal structure. Again, in the south, the primary pattern of sub-infeudation was generally of quite small fees, depriving us of such useful indicators of cantredal extent as baronial extents and patterns of monastic appropriation. We have just two lists of the cantreds of Wexford *inter Anglicos*, from 1375 and 1412.[87] These lists correspond closely with those of the rural deaneries as first recorded for this part of Wexford in 1591, and we may be sure that there was close correspondence between both entities. The original area of Co. Wexford, of course, corresponds to that of the diocese of Ferns.

C176: *Shylmalyr* (1375); *Shirmalyr* (1412)
C177: *Keyr* (1375)
Keyr must correspond to the feudal barony of the same name, which contained, at a minimum, the parishes of Clonmore (in which Keyr itself lay), Ballyhoge, Killurin, Whitechurchglynn, Ardcandrisk, Kilbrideglynn, Doonooney and, perhaps, Rossdroit, that is, approximately the eastern parts of the modern baronies of Bantry and Shelmaliere West.[88] Kilcowanmore probably also lay in this barony. While Shylmalyr occurs in both cantredal lists Keyr only appears in that of 1375, suggesting that these cantreds were sometimes amalgamated for administrative purposes, as happened elsewhere. Some confirmation of this may be had from the extent of the deanery of 'Shilmalere', which included all of Keyr. As to the true cantred of Shylmalyr (**C176**), there is no indication of its extent apart from that of the area of the remainder of the deanery of the same name, west of Keyr, which included the parishes of Templeudigan, Ballyanne, Clonleigh, Killegney, Chapel, Adamstown, Newbawn, Kilgarvan, Clongeen, Inch, Horetown, Taghmon, Coolstuff, Ballylannan, Ballymitty, and Ballingly.

T176: *Síl Máeluidir*
In 1167 Diarmait Mac Murchada's 'native territory' seems to have consisted of ten *trícha céts*.[89] This figure does not appear to refer to all of Uí Chennselaig. The medieval county of Wexford contained nine or ten cantreds and its ecclesiastical counterpart, Ferns, nine deaneries, but the regional kingdom certainly contained in addition at least three territories in what became Carlow, giving a total of twelve or thirteen cantreds. It may be that the 1167 reference relates simply to the area of the diocese of Ferns as the immediate Mac Murchada kingdom – having over time extin-

'Waterford', 142. **87** CCH, 98, 201. **88** Brooks, *Knights' fees*, 43–5. **89** AFM, 1167.

guished what had originally been its component local kingdoms – and the western territories remained discrete, still having kings as suggested by the annalistic record, and so representing associates rather than components of Uí Chennselaig.

Several lines of Uí Chennselaig descend from Eógan Caech, a king who may have lived around the middle of the sixth century.[90] The first of these to rise to prominence was that of Guaire mac Eógain, whose son, the seventh-century Máelodor, is eponym of Síl Máeluidir. This *trícha* gives its name to the cantred of Shylmalyr. Eight members of this segment were kings of Uí Chennselaig between the late sixth century and 858. Its pedigrees do not extend beyond the early tenth century.[91]

T177: *Síl Forannáin*
Forannán, brother of Élóthach, a king of Uí Chennselaig (d. 732), is eponym of Síl Forannáin, whose territory lay around Clonmore. It is hardly coincidental that the *caput* of the cantred of Keyr – a toponym from Keyer (obsolete), in Clonmore – was located here, and it is likely that this cantred (**C177**) preserves the outline of the *trícha* of Síl Forannáin.[92]

C178: *Fothard* (1375); *Fotherte* (1412)
C179: *Obarthy* (1176); *Bargy* (1375, 1412)[93]
This area was marked by conservatism to the extent of preserving its own dialect of Anglo-Norman English into the nineteenth century, which may suggest that the administrative boundaries here are unlikely to have changed significantly in eight centuries, an observation given further strength by the almost identical area of both the rural deaneries of Forth and Bargy with the corresponding modern baronies. The area of the cantred of Fothard must be preserved in that of the rural deanery, giving all of the present barony of Forth plus the parish of Carrick; and that of the cantred of Bargy in the area of its rural deanery, giving all of the barony of Bargy apart from the portion of Taghmon parish in it.

T178: *Fothairt in Chairn*
A second Fotharta *trícha* was Fothairt in Chairn *alias* Fotharta Mara, from which is derived the cantred of Fothard in Co. Wexford (see also **T1**). Little is recorded about this Fothairt, perhaps due to the activities of the Wexford Ostmen, who must have ruled it for a significant period. The townland of Ting (Rathmacknee parish) may mark the site of the Ostmen *thing* or meeting mound of Fothart. If so, this would have played a similar rôle in the governance of the *trícha* to the indigenous *óenach* elsewhere. This Fothairt is that referred to as the *Fotherth juxta Wexford* of a charter of 1160 × 1162, when Ballycushlane (Lady's Island parish) was located within it.[94] Mac Shamhráin, following Ó hUidhrín, suggests that Diarmait Mac Murchada plant-

---

90 For the kings of Uí Chennselaig I have relied upon Ó Corráin's 'Irish regnal succession', pas-sim. **91** O'Brien, *Corpus*, 343–6, 348. **92** Ibid., 348; Ó Riain, *Corpus*, 179. **93** Orpen, *Song of Dermot*, l. 3070. **94** Flanagan, *Irish royal charters*, 284, 286 (n. 5).

ed a branch of Uí Lorcáin (of Uí Muiredaig) here as rulers under him in the twelfth century.[95] Flanagan offers evidence that these Uí Lorcáin may have ruled both Fothairt in Chairn and the adjoining Uí Bairrche (**T179**).[96] There were, however, two Mac Lorcáin kings of Uí Chennselaig in the early eleventh century, otherwise unexplained, so the association between Fothairt in Chairn and Uí Lorcáin of Uí Muiredaig is far from certain.[97]

T179: *Uí Bairrche*
The cantred of Bargy is derived from a branch of Uí Bairrche, whose origins are discussed under **T2**. The earliest genealogies of this people, no later than the early ninth century in date, make mention of one Robertach mac Elgusa *princeps Banba Móre*. This is Bannow in Bargy, and this Robertach would have lived during the seventh century. The same section of pedigree mentions various lineages, including one from Tech Mo Shacro, now Tomhaggard. These places mark the western and eastern bounds respectively of the later cantred of Bargy, no doubt the successor of a *trícha* of Uí Bairrche here.[98]

C180: *Fergenal* (1176); Fernegenan (1316); *Farnygeneale* (1412)[99]
This cantred must equate with that of the feudal barony of the same name, of which, unfortunately, no extent appears to survive. The area of the sixteenth-century descendant of this feudal barony, the Roche and Synnott lands here, is represented by what was then called the barony of fferrenhynnell, the modern barony of Shelmaliere East. This area, of course, represents only the rump of land remaining to these families after the fourteenth-century southward advance of the Irish into northern Farnygenale. Cadet branches of the Roche family were once established in the parishes of Ballyvaldon and Ballyvaloo, indicating beyond doubt that this feudal barony shared the same area as that of the rural deanery of Fernagenall *alias* Rochesland. This deanery contained, in addition to all of Shelmaliere East, the parishes of Ballynaslaney, Kilmallock, St Nicholas, Skreen, Killisk, Castle Ellis, Ballyvaloo, Killila and Ballyvaldon.[1]

T180: *Fir na gCenél*
The cantred of Farnygenale derives from Fir na gCenél. This probably refers to Fir na gCenél of the Uí Chennselaig genealogies, said to derive from several sons of Énna Cennselach, although no pedigrees appear to survive. A reference to a king of Fir na gCenél occurs in a poem of around 900. This is (the *trícha* of) Ferneghenan (*sic*) of a charter of 1160 × 1162.[2]

95 Mac Shamráin, *Glendalough*, 103 (and cf. 209). **96** Flanagan, *Irish royal charters*, 286 (n. 5). **97** LL vol. i, p. 186. **98** O'Brien, *Corpus*, 48. **99** Orpen, *Song of Dermot*, l. 3074; RC 8/11, 39. **1** Brooks, *Knights' fees*, 53; Hore, *History of Wexford* vi, 147; MacCotter, 'Carew/Fitzstephen moiety of Desmond' ii, 104 (n.127). **2** O'Brien, *Corpus*, 88, 344; LL, 6627; Flanagan, *Irish royal charters*, 284. Flanagan's comments on Fir na gCenél (286, n.6) are the result of a misreading of a gloss. The king of Fir na gCenél mentioned in the Book of Leinster poem was named Ciarmac and not Lorcán Liamna as she states.

C181: *Shirebryn* (1375); *Shirbryn* (1412)
This cantred probably corresponds to the later deanery of Shelburne, equal to the modern barony of the same name and the parishes of New and Old Ross, Carnagh and Kilscanlan.[3]

T181: *Síl mBriain*
The origin of the cantred of Shirebryn is something of a mystery. This is certainly derived from Síl mBriain, but who these were is not clear. Byrne identifies them with a branch of the Loígis of that name. The territory of Bantry lay in the northern half of this cantred and Benntraige, a people found in several locations, are associated with the Loígis in the genealogies. A lineage, Uí Choscraig, who occur as lords of this Benntraige in twelfth- and fourteenth-century sources, are described in one pedigree as *Ríg Benntraige*. Accordingly, one may posit the existence of two related local kingdoms in Síl mBriain at one time, one each of Loígis and Benntraige.[4]

The cantreds of Wexford *inter Hibernicos*
No cantredal list survives for this northern half of Wexford as it was early overrun by the Irish, and reliance must be placed on the feudal and ruridecanal structures here which give some indication of the probable cantredal structure.

C182: *Dufthre* (1176), *Dufferth* (1247).[5]
This cantred must parallel the feudal barony and rural deanery of the same name (Duffir; Duffry). The *caput* of the barony was at Enniscorthy and lands in the parishes of St Mary's, St John's, Monart and Templeshanbo certainly lay within it.[6] These four also lay in the deanery, as did Templescoby, Rossdroit, Killann, and Newtownbarry.

T182: *Duibthír*
Another mysterious cantred is that of Duffir, from the Irish Duibthír. Ó hUidhrín names its rulers as Síol Brain, who give the later lineage O Breen (or O Brien).[7] Does this suggest some linkage with the Síl mBriain of Shirebryn (**T181**)?

*C183, *C184: (The remainder of northern Wexford *inter Hibernicos*)
The surviving evidence for the cantredal structure in this area is not sufficient to give a clear picture. Its pattern of sub-infeudation does give some clues, but these do not agree well with the later evidence for the ruridecanal structure here. The feudal structure consisted of one large fief held by service of five fees: the feudal barony of Shyrmall & Kenalahun; a few intermediate fiefs, and numerous small fees.

---

3 For the ruridecanal structure of Ferns I have relied on the source referred to in fn. 4, p. 127, above rather than on that published by Colfer in his 'Anglo-Norman Co. Wexford', 66, which is not based on the earliest lists and as such is defective. **4** Byrne, *Kings and high kings*, 132; O'Brien, *Corpus*, 31, 91–2; Atkinson, *The Book of Leinster sometimes called the Book of Glendalough*, 391b47; Flanagan, *Irish royal charters*, 265–6. **5** Orpen, *Song of Dermot*, l. 3215; Brooks, *Knights' fees*, 129. **6** Brooks, *Knights' fees*, 137–41. **7** Nicholls, 'Land of the Leinstermen', 553.

Shyrmall & Kenalahun was a Prendergast fee and seems to have included everything in the area not earlier given out to others. We can be fairly certain that it included lands in the parishes of Templeshannon, Clone and Kilbride, the former in the deanery of Shermale but the latter two in that of Oday. Again, this feudal barony seems to have included Crosspatrick, a parish shared by modern Wexford and Wicklow, and the Wicklow parish of Kilcommon, both of which lay in the deanery of Shillelagh.[8] There are, however, references to lands as lying in Kenalahun which were not part of this feudal barony, in the parishes of Kilnenor and Carnew, again both lying in the deanery of Shillelagh.[9] It would seem from this, therefore, that the territory of Kenalahun (*C183) as known to the colonists equated closely to that of the later rural deaneries of Shillelagh and Oday. Kenalahun was probably a cantred centered on the important seignorial manor of Ferns.

In regard to Shyrmall/Shermale (*C184), the parishes of Kilmuckridge and Killincooly were certainly part of the Boisrohard fee here, probably along with others in the eastern section of the deanery, a fee based on the *theodum* of Ofelimy. Another distinct (seignorial) fee here was that of Edermine in the west. This suggests that perhaps no more than half of the deanery of Shyrmall was part of the barony of Shyrmall & Kenalahun.[10] As toponyms, Oday ('Ode') and Shillelagh ('Sirlethi') were known to the colonists, but the surviving examples add nothing of relevance to the present discussion.[11] In light of the above it seems probable that the area under discussion had just two cantreds: Shyrmall (*C184), presumably similar in extent to the deanery of Shermale, and Kenalahun (*C183), similar in extent to the combined area of the deaneries of Shillelagh and Oday.[12] While one would need more evidence here to be sure of this conclusion, it is worth noting that in the lordship of Leinster where we find feudal baronies held of four fees or more, in most cases these bear the name of the cantred in which they are located.[13]

T183: *Síl nÉlóthaig*

From Fáelchú grandson of Silán mac Eógain of Uí Chennselaig come several later segments derived from his sons. Firstly Síl nÉlóthaig from Élóthach, a king of Uí Chennselaig (d. 732). This gives the later Shillelagh, a deanery and certainly a *trícha*.

8 Brooks, *Knights' fees*, 129–39; Nicholls, 'Carlow and Wexford', 34.   9 Brooks, *Knights' fees*, 131–2.   10 Ibid., 42–3, 45. Kilmuckridge and Killincooly were impropriate to Glascarrig, and the 'Glascarrig Document' (BL Add. 4789, f. 204) names their donor as one 'Borrgi', clearly a corruption of what must originally have read Borrard (Boisrohard), the name of the lords of Ofelimy. The Prendergast portion of Shyrmall must have included at least the parishes of Templeshannon and Ballyhuskard, impropriate to the priory of Enniscorthy (1622 Visitation).   11 Brooks, *Knights' fees*, 172; Nicholls, 'Carlow and Wexford', 35; Sheehy, *Pont. Hib.* i, p. 138.   12 The following is the composition of these deaneries. Shermale: Edermine, Templeshannon, Ballyhuskard, Kilcormick, Kilnamanagh, Kilmuckridge, Killincooly, and Meelnagh. Oday: Donaghmore, Kiltrisk, Monamulin, Kilbride, Toome, Ballycanew, Killenagh, Ardamine, Kiltennell, Kilmakilloge, Liskinfere, Kilnahue, and Kilcavan. Shillelagh: Ballycarney, Kilrush, Kilcomb, Kilnenor, Moyacomb, Carnew, Kilpipe, Crosspatrick, Kilcommon and Preban. (No listings for the cathedral parish of Ferns and for Rossminoge.)   13 This is true of Obargy, Odrone, Ofelimy (Tullow), Fernegenel, Overk, Offaly, Wicklow and Duffir. The only exceptions are Kilkea and Gowran.

Nine kings of Uí Chennselaig were of Síl nÉlóthaig between 732 and 965. The rulers of this *trícha* immediately before the Invasion would appear to have been Uí Brain of Uí Muiredaig (O Byrnes) who were probably planted here by Diarmait Mac Murchada, known for such political engineering.[14] While the cantredal structure of north Wexford is not clear the *trícha* of Síl nÉlóthaig probably lay in the probable cantred of Kenalahun (*C183), which also seems to have included the area of the deanery of Oday. The capital of twelfth-century Uí Chennselaig, Ferns, was located well inside this probable cantred. Experience of cantredal dynamics leads me to speculate that there may well have been two original cantreds here, Shillelagh and Oday, one of which bore the *alias* Kenalahun, and that both were united into a single cantred (of Kenalahun) by the early colonists. Kenalahun derives from Cenél Aitheamhain. This seems to refer to a *forsloinniud* of Uí Enechglais, Uí Aithemon Mestige, otherwise obscure.[15] The deanery of Oday derives from Uí Dega, for which see **T4**.

T184: *Síl Mella*

A segment first known as Síl nOnchon descended from Onchú, a brother of Élóthach. Between 865, when their first king of Uí Chennselaig reigned, and the mid-tenth century, when they came into exclusive possession of the kingship, this segment provided six kings of Uí Chennselaig. Sometime after 940 they changed their title to Síl Mella, perhaps as a propaganda exercise, Mella being the *cétmuinter* of Crimthann mac Énna Cennselaig. This collective name had earlier been applied to a branch of Síl Cormaic of Uí Chennselaig who appear to have fallen from power during the ninth century.[16] It is, therefore, not clear to whom the territorial designation, Síl Mella, applies. Síl Mella gives Shyrmall, a later deanery and probable cantred (*C184). The location of the original Síl nOnchon kingdom is thus uncertain.

   The final Uí Chennselaig segment were Uí Fhergusa, possible kings of whom were recorded in 887 and 909. The eponym was Fergus nephew of Eógan Caech. The location of this kingdom is unknown to me.[17]

14 O'Brien, *Corpus*, 348, Nicholls, 'Crioch Branach', 10–11.   15 TP, 40; O'Brien, *Corpus*, 68.
16 Ibid., *Corpus*, 10, 345–6, 348.   17 Ibid., 346, 351; AFM, 887; FIA, 909.

'How many triūchas in Ireland?'

Cā līn thriūc[h]a i *n*-Ēirind āin?
Cā līn leith-triūc[h]a comlāin?
Cā līn baile? – monor nglē –
Cā līn congbas gach baile?

How many triúchas in noble Ireland?
How many complete half-triúchas?
How many bailte – a bright toil –
How many does each baile sustain?

Cā līn baile is triūcha cēt
a nĒirind go n-ilarc[h]ēt?
Aderim rib – rādh ga *[l. go]* ngus –
gre(i)nd gach eolaigh a thomus.

How many bailte in the triúcha cét
In Ireland of the many hundreds?
I say to you – a sensible statement –
It is a challenge to every learned person to
measure it.

'Nā tabair mo gre(i)nd-sea fēin'
ar Fintan orfeil go cēill,
'uair is mē is eolc[h]u do chind
a nAlbain is a nĒirind'.

'Do not challenge me'
said most noble Fintan with sense
'I am the most learned of all
in Britain or in Ireland'.

'Deich mbaili sa triūc[h]a cē(i)t
ar .xx. baili, nī brēc;
gidh bec re n-āirem lindi
crīch adbul ar farsingi.

'Ten bailte in each triúcha cét
and twenty, no lie;
though small to count for us
their area forms a noble territory.

Baili congbus trī .c. bō
re taeb ocht seisreach, nī gō;
ceithri h-imirchi dōib de,
gan boin do buain rē chēle.

A baile sustains three hundred cows
with eight seisrecha, no falsehood
four full migrations may roam
with no cow of either touching the other

Āirmhim-sea ocht triūcha dēg
a crīch Midhi na mōrshēd;
deich triūcha fichet ele
a Connachta cūlbuidhe.

I count eighteen triúcha
in the territory of Meath of the great treasures
ten and twenty more triúchas
in Connacht of the yellow-haired.

Āirmhim-sea ocht triūcha dēg
ar fichit triūcha – nī brēch –
adeirim ribh – rādh gan ol –
itā i n-ollc[h]ūigead Uladh.

I count eighteen triúcha
and twenty triúcha – no lie –
I say to ye – a statement without fault –
in the great fifth of Ulster.

Aen triūcha dēc a Laignibh | Eleven triúchas in Leinster
is a .xx. go saidhbir | and twenty richly
ō Indbir Duiblinni ille | from Dublin's estuary hence
go Beluch na Bōromhe. | to the road of the cattle-tributes.

Deich triūcha itā san Mumain | Ten triúchas in Munster
is trī fichit gu cubaidh | and three twenties in accord
7 dā c[h]ōigedh go tend | and the two strong fifths
isan Mumain mōrfairsing. | in great spacious Munster.

I nĒrind ceithri triūcha dēg | In Ireland fourteen triúchas
ar .ix. fichit − nocho brēg; | and nine twenties − no lie;
gan esbaidh ar baili de, | without lack to any baile of them,
ar triūcha nā ar leathbaile. | In any triúcha, nor half a baile [i.e. nothing lacking].

Deich mbaili 7 cūig cēt | Ten bailte and five hundred
ar naī [= cūig] mīli − nocho brēc − | and nine [= five] thousand − without mistake −[1]
o da tsaites mari ind |
comlīn baile itā i n-Ērind. | total of bailte that are in Ireland.

Suidhecudh tellaigh Temrach | The settling of the manor of Tara
agum itā gu mebrach; | in that I am well-versed;
senc[h]as fear n-Ērend uli − | The history of all the men of Ireland
mōr in(n) obair aenduine. | great the labour for one man.

Senc[h]as fear n-Ērend uli | The history of all the men of Ireland
mar atā do rēir gach duini; | as it is according everyone
Fintan fīreolach go fir | Fintan the truly learned
is ē ros-āirim cā līn.' Cā. | he it is who counted how many.
(Book of Uí Maine, facsimile, 115^va56–^vb22).

Several MS copies are in existence. Printed (with translation) by O'Curry from TCD 1337, in *Cath Mhuighe Léana* (Dublin, 1855), pp 106–9. This, however, is clearly a later recension, with added verses dealing with the *baile biataig* and acres.

It will be noted that the numbers in the above poem do not total correctly. When the figures for each province are added together, the total number of *triúcha*s in Ireland comes to 187, yet in verse 10 the total is given as 194. Again, O'Curry's version differs in giving 35 for Ulaid as against 38 above. In verse 10 above, *naī* is certainly an error for *cūig* in the lost original.

1 The text is corrupt here; O'Curry reads *ó do shaidheas im a raind* and translates 'since I have taken to divide them'.

Atlas of the cantreds and *trícha céts* of Ireland, *c*.AD 1200

compiled by: Paul MacCotter. Cartography & GIS by: Mike Murphy,
Helen Bradley & Charlie Roche, Geography Dept., University College Cork

County Map

Miles
0   50

Donegal
Derry
Antrim
Tyrone
Fermanagh
Down
Armagh
Monaghan
Sligo
Leitrim
Cavan
Louth
Mayo
Roscommon Longford
Meath
Westmeath
Galway
Kingscounty
Dublin
Kildare
Clare
Queenscounty
Wicklow
Carlow
Limerick
Tipperary
Kilkenny
Wexford
Kerry
Waterford
Cork

Tir Luigda
Tir Boguine
Tricha Esa Ruaid
Ferr
Carbridrumclef
Dartry
Tyrearachmoye
Monterolis
Tyraulyf
Orrus
Luyne
Coran
Moylurg & Tyrelele
Bak & Glen
Trithweth
Fertyr & Clancowan
Sleoflow & the two Kerrys
Kerre
Cnyfertur
Sylmolron
Moyhee
Owyl
Conmacdonmor
Tyrmany
Conmacnekuly
Conmacnemar
Muntyrmurghyth
Clantayg
Clanferwyll, Gnomor & Gnobeg
Brunrath
Omany
Kenalgory
Cyllanwath

N

Inysowyn

Tir Luigdach

Tir Enna

Tricha Esa Ruaid

Tirkerin

Kennacht

Twescard

Dalrede

*Mahya

*Rathlowry

Kynilanmerach

Craglfergus

Maulyn

*Ardstraw

Clandermod

Tulacoch

Dalboing

Blathewyc

Clogher

Arde

Fermanach

Oveh

Lechayel

Erthyr

artry

Clonoys

*Breifne

Muderne

Machwercunuille

Coly

*Monterolis

Louedhe

Trithweth

*Muintir Mael Morda

*Gailenga & Luigne & Saitni

Ferros

Ferrard

*Munterangaly

*Cairpre Gabra

*Corkaree &

*Caille Follamain

*Brega

Tyrebeggan

*Tethba & Bregmaine

*Uí Thigernain

*Delvin

&

*Moyashel

Curkenie

Cenel Enda

*Laegaire

Fyngal North

*Deiscert Breg

Fyngal South

*Fartullagh & Farbill

*Crinagedach

y

*Clonmacnoise

Kenaleagh

Offelan

anwath

yons

Fercu

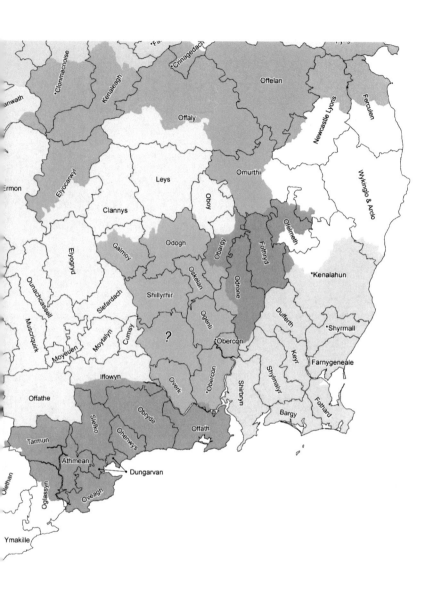

anwath

'Clonmachoise

Kenaleagh

'Crinagedach

'Fa

Offelan

Newcastle Lyons

Ferculen

Offaly

Ermon

Elyocanwyl

Leys

Omurthi

Wykinglo & Arclo

Clannys

Oboy

Elyogryd

Galmoy

Odogh

Obargy

Fothryd

Ofelmeth

'Kenalahun

Ounachcasseill

Slefardach

Shillyrhir

Oskelan

Odrone

Dufferth

Muscrquirk

Moyalyn

Cumsy

?

Ogenti

Obercon

'Shyrmall

Moyeuen

Shirbryn

Shylmalyr

Keyr

Farnygeneale

Iffowyn

Overk

'Obercon

Fothard

Offathe

Obryde

Bargy

Tarmun

Slefko

Ohenwys

Offath

Athmean

Dungarvan

Olethan

Oglassyn

Oveagh

Ymakille

Construction notes

The Atlas sets out to represent cartographically the cantreds and *trícha céts* of Ireland as they exist around AD 1200. In some parts of Ireland at this time these terms are still interchangeable, and always refer to the same unit. Hence the above title. The basic unit of construction in the atlas is the civil parish as mapped by the Ordnance Survey in the early nineteenth century, that is, where evidence merits the inclusion of a place in a particular cantred I have then included all of the parish in which that place lies in that cantred. In the dozen or so cases where the modern civil parish is an amalgam of two or more medieval parishes which are found to lie in different cantreds, the atlas attempts to portray the most likely line of division (just one was overlooked, see (7) below). The various coloured backgrounds illustrate the modern county structure. These were included to give perspective. For technical reasons accents are omitted from Gaelic names.

In most cases the divisions as mapped are derived from a consistency of evidence drawn from a number of sources (as illustrated in Chapter 2), and can be taken as accurate. However, there are a number of cases where an evidential shortfall renders the cartography somewhat speculative, in the sense that the precise borders of units are a 'best guess' even though, in nearly all such cases, the general outline is clear. This caveat applies to the following examples.

(1) In the lordship of Meath the cantredal structure is largely unrecoverable due to the early abandonment of the cantred as a unit of civil administration in favour of the feudal barony, as well as the lack of any relationship between cantred and rural deanery. Just two cantreds can be described. The Atlas deals with Meath by illustrating the probable outline of the pre-Invasion local kingdom/*trícha cét* structure. Those units which lie in the modern counties of Westmeath and Longford are derived from a firm evidential base although those in modern Co. Meath are somewhat less so. Again, the precise border between Muintir Máel Mórda (**133**) and Gailenga & Luigne & Saitni (**109**) is speculative.

(2) In Co. Kilkenny the original cantredal structure was subsequently altered by an extensive amalgamation where up to nine original cantreds were reduced to four administrative cantreds. The Atlas attempts a reconstruction of the original cantredal structure here and, while the general outline is certain, the detail is more speculative.

(3) The outline shape of the cantred of *Kenalahun (**183**) is certain but we cannot be sure that we are dealing with just one cantred here. (There may have been two.)

(4) In the case of the boundaries of the Waterford cantreds of Obryde (**172**) and Tarmun (**174**) there is again an element of speculation.

(5) The border between the Co. Kerry cantreds of Mayconkyn (**57**) and Orathath (**59**) is based on modern parish boundaries which may not reflect earlier medieval ones. These suggest that Mayconkyn may not have extended quite so far south.

(6) In Ulster the internal borders of the posited contiguous cantred group of ★Mahya (**145**), ★Ardstraw (**146**) and ★Rathlowry (**143**) are partly speculative, as is the total number of cantreds which may have existed on these lands.

(7) The east-north-eastern border between Ogenathy Donechud (**45**) and Alla (**46**) lies a little too far to the east in that it shows the modern parish boundaries and ignores the shape of the obsolete parish of Kilquane which lay in eastern Kilcummin and in Alla.

(8) In the case of Arech & Wetheni (**121**) its border with Ermon (**118**) may have lain somewhat farther north. The sources conflict and the map shows the minimalist position.

Most cantreds did not alter their boundaries or names throughout the Anglo-Norman period. In a small number of cases such alterations did occur. In such cases the pre-alteration situation is represented in the Atlas. I have published on such changes elsewhere.[1] Finally, we note the apparently unique situation in Offelan (**C65**), where what was certainly an original and singular cantred was divided into three abstract divisions at the time of its sub-infeudation. These divisions did not bear any relationship to Irish precursors, as was the norm elsewhere. These artificial cantreds did not last and something close to the original cantredal structure was re-established. The Atlas shows the original situation.

While the map portrays the results of my work its construction and design is largely the work of cartographer Michael J. Murphy of the Department of Geography, University College Cork, for whose assistance I am most grateful.

---

1 'Functions of the cantred', 323–4.

Críchad an Chaoilli

This document provides the fullest account of an Irish *trícha cét* in existence and, as such, deserves to be fully explored. What follows is, firstly, place-name identification and, secondly, a comparison of the boundaries thus revealed with those of the later cantred of Fermoy. *Críchad* is preserved in two fifteenth-century manuscripts, and has been published twice, each time with translation and commentary.[1]

DATING

The language of *Críchad* is early modern Irish. Various dates have been advanced for its composition.[2] The consensus in recent years has been to suggest a date in the early thirteenth century. This is largely based on Ó Murchadha's identification of a toponym in the text, *Muilinn Mairteil*, with the Anglo-Norman Martel family.[3] This identification is not certain, and there is no further evidence of colonial influence in the text. There are, however, indications that *Críchad*, as it has come down to us, is an early thirteenth-century recension of an older document, almost certainly composed during the years 1138–51. There are four elements to this suggested dating.

Firstly, the high level of toponomic and surname detail contained in *Críchad* cannot possibly be the result of some later antiquarian reconstruction and must represent a genuine pre-Invasion population survey, composed in all likelihood as some kind of rental or assessment record for taxation purposes, if not as some kind of military levy record. As a particular example one can quote the reference to Uí Fhinguine, a ruling family of Eóganacht Glennamnach, who only occur in annals of the eleventh century and in *Críchad*.[4] Secondly, if *Críchad* was composed around 1200, why is there no mention in it of the monastery of Fermoy and its extensive lands? This Cistercian foundation (*Castrum Dei*) has been given the traditional founding date of 1170 by Ware, in turn derived from the Cistercian filiation-tables.[5] Its colloquial name style, Mainistir Fhear Muighe, 'the monastery of the kingdom of Fermoy', indicates that the abbey was of pre-colonial foundation.[6] *Críchad*'s original

---

1 Power, *Críchad*; O'Keeffe, 'The ancient territory of Fermoy', passim. 2 For a discussion see Bhreathnach, 'Críchad an Chaoilli', 85–88. 3 Ó Murchadha, 'Cenn Ebrat, Sliab Caín' , 157n. 4 MacCotter, *Colmán*, 58–60. 5 O'Sullivan, 'St Mary de Castro Dei, Fermoy', passim; Mac Niocaill, *Manaigh Liatha*, 6. There is no evidence whatsoever as to whom Fermoy was founded by. 6 Cf. the Cistercian house of Abbeydorney, Mainistir Ua dTorna, in Co. Kerry.

can only have been composed before Fermoy's foundation. Thirdly, the reference to Cormac Cas, fictional ancestor to the Uí Briain, in the preamble,[7] can only make sense if the original was composed during a period of Uí Briain dominance of Fir Maige, the last such period being during the years 1138 × 1151. After 1151 Fir Maige was firmly in the Meic Carthaig sphere of influence. Finally, and crucially, the Book of Leinster contains a middle-Irish poem, certainly of pre-Invasion date, lauding Cathal mac Finguine, an early king of Eóganacht Glennamnach.[8] This mentions King Cathal's demesne *túath* (*secht mbali Cathail cen cháin*) and names its constituent *bailte*. These are the *bailte* of the *túath* of Glennamnach as listed in *Críchad*, demonstrating that the document is based on earlier pre-Invasion topographical material.

PLACE-NAME IDENTIFICATION

Power's efforts to identify the place-names in the document are remarkably poor and we are fortunate in being able to turn to Ó Buachalla's fine efforts which provide the foundation for the present identifications.[9] In the course of this work I have rechecked all Ó Buachalla's identifications, and confined comment to obvious mistakes. I have also added some new identifications. My comments are arranged under headings of individual *túatha*, following the arrangement of the original document. References to the '1301 List' below refer to the list of vills in the cantred of Fermoy of that date.

Eóghanacht Glennomnach
Rath Mór: this place occurs in 1301 in the possession of a branch of Cauntetons (later Condons) holding lands in northern Glanworth and Carrigdownane, but cannot be identified with more certainty.[10] Ceall Aenamhna: Killeenemer.[11]

Leathbhaile Uí Chonchubair
Ó Buachalla followed Power in identifying Ceall Garbháin with Kilcoran, an identification which is untenable. Both were probably misled by the seventeenth-century extent of Condons barony here, which included extensive lands south of the Blackwater which certainly did not form part of the earlier cantred of Fermoy. Neither can Cnocán Dúin Martan be Knockaunroe, as suggested by Ó Buachalla, while Airgetlaind clearly refers to the River Araglin and not the hamlet, as assumed by both. The original text is clearly corrupt here and the perambulation as described is impossible, conflicting as it does with that relating to Túath Ó Conaill. The only safe identifications in this section relate to Clondulane and Carrigatoortane.

Ó Cuain II (Íbh Máille Machaire)
Cúl Baedáin: this is the Colbadan which occurs twice as an *alias* for the manor of Ballyhindon.[12] Lis Donnchadha: references to this place in seventeenth-century doc-

---

7 Power, *Críchad*, 45. **8** LL, lines 19165–219. **9** Ó Buachalla, 'Placenames of North East Cork', passim; idem, 'Placename list', 39–44. See also O'Rahilly, 'Some Fermoy place-names', passim. **10** RC 7/8, 277. **11** PRC, 182. **12** RC 7/10, 319; 8/1, 119.

uments and maps suggest a location in northern Killeagh, which is confirmed by the earlier reference to 'Lesdon' as lying just south of Killeenemer.[13] Grealla hÍ Chuicneacháin: the lineage name survives in 'Ballymakinakin', the name given in the Down Survey barony map for the present Boherderroge and Loughnahilly. Laichi hÍ Fiaich: this is the Lathwok of 1280, when associated with Manning. Lynch identifies it with Labbacallee.[14]

Túath Ó Conaill

Lebglaisi: this rivulet is explicitly stated in *Críchad* to have lain east of Leitrim, a name equally explicitly used in a super-denominational sense as applying to the ridge formed by the high ground between the Blackwater and Araglin valleys, running eastwards to Lebglaisi. It seems a most logical supposition to suggest identification with the unnamed stream which runs down Carrigane Glen to meet the Blackwater and which is the eastern boundary of Leitrim parish and of the diocese of Cloyne as well. Feic Beg: Ó Buachalla's suggested identification of this place with Mount Rivers is given support by Anglo-Norman period references (to 'Fegbeg') which are numerous and occur in a similar geographical context. These also reveal the presence of weirs at Fegbeg, confirming its location on the Blackwater.

Uí Cúscraidh Shléibhe

Gleann Domain: see below.

Brí Gobann (first trian)

Carrac Cormaic: as Carrigcormyck etc., this place occurs in several pleadings relating to the St Michael family of Brigown before 1340, as well as in the '1301 List', all in contexts which suggest a probable location within the large townland of Mitchelstown.[15] Ceall Danáin: the old church site near the farmyard in Mitchelstown (*Críchad*, 72). Cluain Cairbreach: my reading of Ó Buachalla's evidence here would rather suggest an identification within the present Brigown for 'the two Clancarberyes'.[16] Ceall Bracáin: the modern Kilphelan and Kiltrislane are both versions of this toponym, which by extension must also have included the linking townland of Dromleigh; the actual church site is in Kiltrislane.[17] Craes Crú: this is well documented in a variety of forms before 1400, which reveal it to have lain 'in the mountains' and in possession of the senior line of the Caunteton lineage. These locators suggest an identification with Turbeagh, which was, along with its neighbours, an isolated pocket of chief Patrick Condon's land in 1612.[18] Tipra Grugáin: occurs as Tipergrogan – when associated with the St Michael family of Brigown – in 1296, and in the '1301 List' as Tybirgregan. The context of both references suggests a location in or near Brigown. Could the 'well' in question be that referred to in the 1901 O.S. edition as St Finnchú's Well, in eastern Brigown?[19] Dún Droignéin: Ó

13 PRC, 24; Petty's map of Cork. **14** RC 8/1, 117; JCHAS 26 (1921), p. 30. **15** RC 7/9, 5; NAI MS 2550, 91v. **16** RIA MS Cork Ordnance Survey Inqs. i, 295. **17** PRC, 26, 104, 185. **18** PRC, 26, 105, 241; CIPRJ, 194. **19** RC 7/5, 192.

Buachalla's location of Aithlis Cindfhaelad in Coolyregan indicates a location just to the east, in Carrigane.

Brí Gobunn (second trian)

Cúl Lughdach: this is certainly the seventeenth-century Kilcooldagh/Kilcoodooaghe, probably with the prefix *coill* or *cill*, which was located around the present Ardglare and Parknakilla.[20] Cnocán hÍ Chróingilla: I cannot accept Ó Buachalla's identification of this place with Knockanenabohilly, but cannot offer an alternative.

Brí Gobann (third trian)

Baili hÍ Mhaeilmórdha: Ó Buachalla was unaware of the continued existence of 'Ballymullmora' until 1637, in a context which locates it in modern Coolnanave.[21]

Ó Congangairm (first trian)

The eastern bounds of this *túath*, the 'river of Carker', must refer to the Ogeen River in Kilbrack.

Ó Congangairm (second trian)

Baili Meig Coirtéin: this is certainly the Balymacartan/Balymacorcon of 1301, which lay 'in [the parish of] Duncroith' *alias* Castletownroche.[22] This is probably the present Rathnacarton, in the western part of the parish. Note that the enumerator of *Críchad* is confused as to the Meig Coirtéin family, locating them in both the second and third *trians* of Ó Congangairm.

Ó Congangairm (third trian)

Cill Ó nGéibinnáin: Ó Buachalla is wrong in his identification of this lost toponym. Baile hÍ Ghormáin: Ó Buachalla is again incorrect here. This must be the modern Ballyviniter: in the thirteenth century the le Miniter family held the fee of Balygorman – which we know to have been extensive, just as Ballyviniter is in three townlands today – in the manor of Mallow.[23]

Ó Béce Abha

Áth an Chrainn: 'on both sides [of the river]'. The perambulatory context suggests an identification with Killavullen.

Ó Béce Uachtarach

Cluain Lochluinn: Power's identification of this place with Loughquinn has some merit. Gleann Tuircin: the perambulatory context suggests Annsgrove and Ballydoyle. Daire hÍ Cheinnéidig: a possible identification with the Daire of the 'Roche Charter', whose approximate location was in the area of Carrigleagh/Meadstown, has some merit.[24] Luimnech Beg: the perambulatory context suggests Ballinaltig. Taedán: certainly the present String (by translation), as suggested by

20 NAI Lodge MS Rolls, v, 480; Petty's map of Cork. **21** NAI Lodge MS v, 480. **22** RC 7/8, 404. **23** CDI, iv, 264; CJRI, iii, 288–9. **24** JCHAS 55 (1950), 93.

Power. Loch Luingi: to be identified with one of the lochs in the adjacent town-lands of Ballinvoher, Ballinaltig or Loughruane.[25]

Túath Ó Fiannadhuigh

Both Power and Ó Buachalla are mistaken here, their misidentification of Baile hÍ Ghormáin (which see Ó Congangairm, third trian, above) leading them to place this *túath* significantly too far to the west. While the only members identifiable today are Kilclousha and Ballyviniter, with the Blackwater as the southern border, the general lack of identifications from *Crichad* in the western parts of Mallow and Caherduggan parishes, when taken in conjunction with those identifications, leads to the clear conclusion that this *túath* lay substantially in western Mallow and Caherduggan.

Túath Ó nDuinnín

Cill Mainches: probably Farahy, the only significant ecclesiastical foundation in the area.

Uí Rosa

Cathair Gobunn: occurs regularly as Cathergan in Anglo-Norman pleadings, when in possession of the Synans of Doneraile. Process of elimination leads one to suspect this to be Castlepook.

COMPARISON OF IRISH AND COLONIAL FERMOY

Two *túatha* of Fir Maige as described in *Crichad* are significantly different from the other eight. The account of these does not list any families. They are also differentiated from the others by the description *fonn timchill*. These can be considered to be 'irregular'. The area of the eight 'regular' *túatha* of Fir Maige in *Crichad* all lay within the cantred of Fermoy. The single exception is Kilclousha, the church of Túath Ó Fiannadhuigh, which lies just outside of the cantred (Ballybeg West townland). Parts of the two 'irregular' *túatha* in *Crichad* also lay within the cantred.

   These 'irregular' *túatha* claimed for Fir Maige in *Crichad* provide further evidence of linkage between Fir Maige and Fermoy. These are described in *Crichad* as *fonn timchill*. O'Keeffe tentatively translated this term as 'border land'. He went on to point out that this term only applied to lands on the northern border of Fir Maige and was clearly not fully satisfied with his own suggestion.[26] Unfortunately this suggestion has not been questioned since and remains current, still being repeated as factual.[27] The term *fonn timchill* does not mean 'border land', but is the name of the Irish *trícha* and colonial cantred adjoining Fir Maige/Fermoy to the north (Fontymkyl: **C84, T84**).[28] One suspects that the final redactor of *Crichad* did not understand the

---

25 Power, *Crichad*, 12–13. **26** O'Keeffe, 'The ancient territory of Fermoy', 184. **27** Power, *Crichad*, 96; Bhreathnach, 'Crichad an Chaoilli', 92. **28** The compound *fonn timchill* is not found in DIL and appears to be unknown as a technical term.

material to hand. The disputed border between Fir Maige and Fonn Timchill was also that between the overkingdoms of Desmumu and Tuadmumu and thus a significant political divide for much of the twelfth century.[29] It is likely that these two 'irregular' *túatha* had been partly detached from Fir Maige by force during the Desmumu/Tuadmumu wars of the twelfth century and remained of indeterminate status when *Críchad*'s exemplar was written.

The first of these 'irregular' *túatha* was Uí Rosa. While this is claimed for Fir Maige in *Críchad*, it bears the name of the royal lineage of Déis Becc.[30] After the Invasion most of Uí Rosa remained part of 'Deesbeg' *alias* Tobernea, apparently divided into two fees. The present civil parish of Doneraile is an amalgam of no less than three earlier parishes, reflecting a similar secular divide in lordship here. The fee of Crogh *alias* Doneraile, essentially that part of Doneraile parish lying along both sides of the Awbeg, was held of the manor of Duncroith by the Synan family. The area of this fee was also that of the original parish of Doneraile. A second Synan fee, Dungleddy (an obsolete toponym), can be identified with Cloustoge and surrounding lands, that thin strip of Doneraile parish lying east of the Ogeen River. This identification is based on the possession of Dungleddy by the same Synan family, its association with the fee of Crogh in an early suit, and the early existence of a parish church there. While no parish of the name occurs in the Papal Taxation list of the deanery of Fermoy, there was a parish of Cloustoge.[31] In 1327 we find reference to the manor of Kilcolman, *Co. Limerick*, when the advowson of its corresponding parish, Rossagh, was in dispute. This represents the third original parish in what is now Doneraile. This parish survived until the turn of the seventeenth century, when absorbed by Doneraile. In 1327 Kilcolman was a sub-fee of the manor of Tobernea, and was the fee of Rossagh held of that manor by Brandon Synan in 1372. Two extents of the manor of Kylcolman *alias* Toghe ne Rossoghe (*Túath na Rossach*) survive from around 1600, which show it to have comprised the present Kilcolmans, Rossaghs, Streamhills, Rossaghroe, Ballyellis, Ardadam, Kilvicanese, Carrigeen, Ballyvonear, Inchnagree, Ballyshane, and, perhaps, Oldcourt.[32] Further east lay that fee held of Tobernea by David fitz Adam (Synan) in 1251 by an annual rent of one pound of pepper, and which again shows this rent in 1372. This fee seems to be that mentioned in related suits of 1295 and 1301 involving Maurice de Rochfort, lord of Tobernea, and Philip fitz William [Synan], which lists the lands of Cathirgon and Carikir. The former is, of course, the Cathair Gobhunn of *Críchad* – probably the present Castlepook – while the latter is Carker. In 1541 this rent of pepper was paid to the lord of Tobernea for the lands of 'Castell Fewke'. This fee must therefore have consisted of the four Carkers, both Castlepooks, both Skahanaghs, Ballinree, Garryhintoge, and Newtown.[33] Dungleddy was appendant to Duncroith and so

29 MacCotter, 'Rise of Meic Carthaig', passim; O'Rahilly, 'Some Fermoy place-names', 255–6. **30** Power, *Críchad*, 49. **31** RC 7/3, 170; 7/4, 121; 7/8, 372, 404, 428, 490; 7/9, 103; CDI, v, 276, 313, and see p. 84. **32** Nicholls, '*Red Book of Kildare*', 35, 62; Extent of Kilcolman, Desmond Survey Roll, NAI; RIA MS Cork Ordnance Survey Inqs. i, 163. **33** Nicholls, '*Red Book of Kildare*', 35.

probably lay in Co. Cork.[34] Therefore most, but not all, of the area of the *túath* of Uí Rosa lay outside of the cantred of Fermoy, in that of Fontymkyl. This is clearer in Figure 4.

The second 'irregular' *túath* was that of Uí Chúscraidh Sléibhe.[35] This appears to have been evenly divided between the colonial lords of Fermoy and Natherlach (a lordship in Fontymkyl cantred). Of the eleven places in Uí Chuscraidh listed in *Críchad* only five can be identified, three lying in modern Co. Cork and two in Limerick. Most of the unidentified places probably lay in modern Limerick. Here lay Cill Meithne (Kilbehenny) and Gleann Domain, both of which later occur as knights' fees held of the barony of Natherlach as well as chapels of the parish of Natherlach. The tenant of 'Glendowan' was the Caunteton lord of Fermoy and it is to be identified with the later Glencondon, whose approximate location can be shown to have lain in south-western Kilbehenny parish and whose church site may be that of Kilglass.[36] Further evidence of shared lordship or *condominium* can be seen in the knights' fee of Neynan (Templemolaga), whose military tenant held both of Natherlach and of the bishop of Cloyne.[37] While there is no direct evidence as to which county this fee lay in its later inclusion in Co. Cork and its continual presence in the diocese of Cloyne suggests Cork. Therefore it would appear that the *túath* of Uí Chuscraidh Sléibhe was evenly divided between Fermoy (Templemolaga and northern Marshalstown) and Natherlach (Kilbehenny). Thus the disputed status of this *túath* carried over into the post-Invasion period, when resolved by a partition. The above is illustrated in Map 2 (p 30).

The significant feature here is that of inheritance of border dispute by colonial lords from Irish pre-Invasion lords. Before the Invasion the *túatha* of Uí Rosa and Uí Chuscraidh Sléibhe were in dispute between the kings of Fir Maige and the polity of Fonn Timchill. Post-Invasion the area of both *túatha* was divided between the cantreds of Fermoy and Fontymkyl.

On the question of the relationship between *túath* boundaries and those of colonial parishes, it will be noticed that, internally, there is no evidence for any such relationship within Fermoy. Its parishes show no relationship whatsoever with the earlier *túatha*. There is, however, evidence to suggt that some of the parishes of Fermoy derive their shape from earlier indigenous *bailte*.[38] However,

Figure 4. Uí Rosa and Doneraile parish

Fee	Original Par.	County	Irish Túath
Crogh	Doneraile	Cork	Muighi Finne
Dungleddy	Cloustoge	Cork	Uí Rosa
Kilcolman	Rossagh	Limerick	Uí Rosa
Carker – Castlepook	Rossagh	Limerick	Uí Rosa

34 RC 7/8, 372. **35** Power, *Críchad*, 47–8. **36** CJRI, iii, 160; CCH, 39b; Mills, *Gormanston*, 115, 117; CIPRJ, 194; NAI Lodge MS Rolls, iv, 25, 483; Power, *Críchad*, 95–6. **37** Mills, *Gormanston*, 111; PRC, 26, 104. **38** See p. 84.

the external borders of the cantred largely reflect those of Irish Fir Maige as does the boundary between both halves of the *trícha* as indicated in *Críchad*, which follows closely the border between both chief manors of Glanworth and Castletownroche.[39]

39 Power, *Críchad*, 45.

The relationship between cantred and rural deanery

The thesis which forms the basis of this book contains a detailed statistical analysis of the relationship between cantred and rural deanery.[1] The results of this survey are given below. The survey is based on those cantreds, 109 in all, whose extent is sufficiently discernible to provide a basis for detailed comparison.

RESULTS

1 Cantreds coterminous or nearly so with deaneries, 49 (45 per cent).
2 Where two cantreds equal the area of one deanery, or two deaneries one cantred, 21 (18 per cent).
3 Where cantred and deanery are less closely related but still with significant areas of agreement, 16 (15 per cent).
4 Where there is no relationship between cantred and deanery, 24 (22 per cent).

INTERPRETATION

These figures reveal that the widely accepted correlation between cantred and rural deanery is not by any means as common as has been assumed. These figures suggest the following conclusions. About one half of all cantreds are matched by rural deaneries of similar area while in about one quarter of cases there is no discernible relationship. The remaining quarter consists of cases where there is a definite relationship between entities but where there are still significant differences or variables.

The survey also reveals the interesting pattern whereby each diocese generally has a single type of relationship between deanery and cantred. In the case of the dioceses of Ardfert, Armagh, Clonfert, Clogher, Down & Connor, Ferns, Emly, Killaloe, Leighlin, and Ross, most cantreds match closely the corresponding deaneries. At the other extreme we have the dioceses of Kildare, Limerick, Ossory, Tuam, and Waterford & Lismore, where we find, consistently, little relationship between both entities. Finally we have a middle group with varying relationships. The dioceses of Cashel, Cloyne, Cork, and Elphin show a pattern where most cantreds have corre-

---

1 'Cantred and Trícha Cét: medieval Irish political territorial denominations' (PhD, NUI, 2006), pp 214–20.

sponding deaneries but where there are some exceptions. This leaves just Dublin to consider, and here, a significant relationship between both entities exists over about half of the diocese. Those instances where no relationship exists between cantred and deanery raise the question as to just what template was used for the rural deanery there? This question remains to be investigated.

Bibliography

MANUSCRIPT SOURCES

Armagh Public Library
MS KH II 24 (17th-century transcripts of older material).
MS KH II 46 (17th-century transcripts of patent rolls).
National Archives of Ireland
MS 2550 (Molyneaux's transcripts of pleadings).
MS 5037 (Desmond survey, Co. Kerry).
Record Commissioners Calendar of Plea Rolls, volumes 1–13.
Record Commissioners Calendar of Memoranda Rolls, volumes 1, 6, 11.
Record Commissioners Calendar of Inquisitions post mortem, volume 15.
Record Commissioners Calendar of Exchequer Inquisitions, volumes 14, 16.
Record Commissioners Calendar of Chancery Inquisitions, volume 14.
Record Commissioners Calendar of deeds and wills in Chancery Inquisitions, volume 29.
Lodge's Repertory of the Rolls, volumes 1–4.
Ferguson MSS, volume 15.
Catalogue of Wadding deeds.
MS Kings Bench 2/5 (unpublished justiciary roll transcripts).
MS Calendar Roll of Justices Itinerant 33–34 Edward I, Co. Tipperary (Morrissey).
National Library of Ireland
MS 760 (Betham's notes from Exchequer pipe rolls).
MS 2509.
MS D.3331.
Genealogical Office
MS 190 (Betham's notes from plea rolls).
MS 192 (idem).
Trinity College Library
MS 1066 (17th century royal ecclesiastical visitations).
MS 1067 (idem).
MS 1366.
Royal Irish Academy Library
Ordnance Survey Inquisitions, Co. Cork (7 vols).
MS Book of Survey and Distribution, Co. Cork.
MS 12 D 9 (full transcript of Exchequer pipe roll of 1260–1).
MS 12 D 10 (notes from various Exchequer pipe rolls).
Boole Library, University College Cork
MS U/251 (quit rents, Co. Cork, early 18th-century).
Ordnance Survey Namebooks.

Curraghmore House
Curraghmore MSS.
Public Record Office of Northern Ireland
MS 3078/1/1/1 and 3 (Kildare papers).
Public Record Office, London
SP/63/45/35 (State papers, Ireland).
SC/6/1239/30 (Ancient petitions).
British Library, London
Additional MS 4789 (17th century transcripts, Bermingham Tower material).
Additional MS 4790 (idem).
Additional MS 4792.
Additional MS 4793.
Additional MS 6041 (Mortimer muniments, 13th–14th centuries).
Additional Charter 13598.
Harleian MS 2048.
Archiepiscopal Library, Lambeth Palace, London
Carew MS 606 (16th-century transcripts of 14th-century pleadings and other material).
Carew MS 619.
Cambridge University Library
Additional MS 3104.
Oxford University Library
Rawlinson MS B499 (transcript of new registry of St Thomas' abbey, Dublin).

ROLLS SERIES CALENDARS, ANNALS, AND OTHER PRINCIPAL PRIMARY SOURCES

Ancient laws of Ireland (Dublin, 1865–1901).
Appendices, *Reports of the Deputy Keeper of the Public Records in Ireland* (Dublin, 1869–).
Atkinson, R. (ed.), *The Book of Leinster sometimes called the Book of Glendalough* (Dublin, 1880).
Bain, J., *Calendar of documents relating to Scotland* i, (Edinburgh, 1881).
Best, R.I., M.F. O'Brien, O. Bergin, A. O'Sullivan (eds), *The Book of Leinster formerly Lebar na Núachongbála* (6 vols, Dublin, 1954–83).
Binchy, D.A. (ed.), *Corpus Iuris Hibernici* (Dublin, 1978).
Brewer, J., & W. Bullen (eds), *Calendar of the Carew manuscripts preserved in the archepiscopal library at Lambeth,* i (London, 1868); Miscellaneous volume (London, 1871).
Calendar of documents relating to Ireland (5 vols, London, 1875–1886).
Calendar of entries in the papal registers relating to Great Britain and Ireland (20 vols, London, Dublin, 1893–).
Calendar of inquisitions post mortem and other analogous documents preserved in the Public Record Office (London, 1904–).
Calendar of Irish patent rolls of James I [Dublin, 1966].
Calendar of patent rolls 1334–1338 (London).
Calendar of the justiciary rolls or proceedings in the court of the justiciar of Ireland, preserved in the Public Record Office of Ireland (3 vols, Dublin, 1905–1955).
Calendar of the patent and close rolls of chancery in Ireland, of the reigns of Henry VIII, Edward VI, Mary, and Elizabeth (2 vols, Dublin, 1861–2).
Calendar of the state papers relating to Ireland 1606–1608 (London, 1874).
Curtis, E. (ed.), *Calendar of Ormond deeds* (6 vols, Dublin, 1932–43).

Freeman, A.M., 'The annals in Cotton MS Titus A xxv', *Revue Celtique* 41 (1924), 301–30; volume 42 (1925), 283–305.

—— (ed.), *Annála Connacht: The Annals of Connacht (A.D. 1224–1544)* (Dublin, 1970).

Griffith, M. (ed.), *Calendar of Inquisitions formerly in the Office of the Chief Remembrancer of the Exchequer: prepared from the MSS of the Irish Record Commissioners* (Dublin, 1991).

Hardy, T.D. (ed.), *Rotuli Chartarum* i (London, 1837).

Hennessy, W. (ed.), *Chronicum Scotorum* (London, 1866).

—— (ed.), *The Annals of Loch Cé* (London, 1871).

—— & B. McCarthy (eds), *Annala Uladh: Annals of Ulster in Irish and English* (4 vols, Dublin, 1887–1901).

Hunter, J. (ed.), *Rotuli selecti ad res Anglicas et Hibernicas spectantes, ex archives in domo capitulari West-monasteriensi deprompti* (London, 1834).

Inquisitionum in officio rotulorum cancellariae Hiberniae asservatarum repertorium ii (Dublin, 1829).

Mac Airt, S. (ed.), *The Annals of Inisfallen* (Dublin, 1951).

Mac Giolla Choille, B. (ed.), *Books of Survey and Distribution* iii, County of Galway (Dublin, 1962).

Macalister, R., *Facsimiles in collotype of Irish manuscripts iv, The Book of Uí Maine* (Dublin, 1942).

Mulchrone, K. (ed.), *Facsimiles in collotype of Irish manuscripts ii, The Book of Lecan* (Dublin, 1937).

Murphy, D. (ed.), *The Annals of Clonmacnoise* (Dublin, 1896).

Ó hInnse, S. (ed.), *Miscellaneous Irish annals* (Dublin, 1947).

O'Donovan, J. (ed.), *The Annals of the Kingdom of Ireland by the Four Masters from the earliest period to the year 1616* (7 vols, Dublin, 1856).

Radner, J., *Fragmentary annals of Ireland* (Dublin, 1978).

Report of the commissioners appointed to take the Census of Ireland for the year 1841 (Dublin, 1843).

Simington, R. (ed.), *The Civil Survey, County of Tipperary, eastern and northern*, ii (Dublin, 1934).

—— (ed.), *The Civil Survey, County of Limerick*, iv (Dublin, 1938).

—— (ed.), *The Civil Survey, County of Waterford*, vi (Dublin, 1942).

—— (ed.), *The Civil Survey, County of Dublin*, vii (Dublin, 1945).

—— (ed.), *The Civil Survey, County of Kildare*, viii (Dublin, 1952).

—— (ed.), *Books of Survey and Distribution* i, County of Roscommon (Dublin, 1949).

—— (ed.), *Books of Survey and Distribution* ii, County of Mayo (Dublin, 1956).

Stokes, W. (ed.), 'The Annals of Tigernach', *Revue Celtique* 16–18 (1895–7).

The Book of Ballymote (Facsimile edition; Dublin, 1887).

The Irish fiants of the Tudor sovereigns (4 vols, Dublin, 1994).

Tresham, H. (ed.), *Rotulorum patentium et clausorum Cancellariae Hiberniae calendarium* [London, 1828].

ONLINE DATABASES AND OTHER SOURCES

Deutsches RechtsWörterbuch, Heidelberger Akademie der Wissenschaften, www.rzuser.uni-heidelberg.de/~cd2/drw.

Electronic Dictionary of the Irish Language, Royal Irish Academy & University of Ulster, www.dil.ie.

Ó Cíobháin, B., 'Cammas hUa Fathaid Tíre and the Vikings: Significance and Location', (accessed 2005), www.save@vikingwaterford.com.

Turner, S., 'Aspects of the development of public assembly in the Danelaw', *Assemblage: the Sheffield Graduate Journal of Archaeology*, issue 5 (2000), www.assemblage.group.shef.ac.uk.

SECONDARY WORKS

Andersen, P.S., *Samlingen av Norge og Kristningen av landet 800–1130* (Oslo, 1977).

——, 'When was regular, annual taxation introduced in the Norse islands of Britain?', *Scandinavian Journal of History* 16 (1991), 73–83.

——, 'Nordisk innvandring, bosetning og samfunnsdannelse på Isle of Man i middelalderen', *Collegium Medievale* 8:1 (1995), 5–49.

Anderson, M., *Kings and kingship in early Scotland* (Edinburgh, 1973).

Arthurs, J.B., 'Mourne', *BUPS* 1 (1952), 15–19.

Baillie, M., 'The dating of timbers from Navan Fort and the Dorsey, Co. Armagh', *Emania* 4 (1988), 37–41.

Bannerman, J., *Studies in the history of Dalriada* (Edinburgh, 1974).

Barnwell, P.S., 'The early Frankish *mallus*: its nature, participants and practices', in Pantos & Semple (eds), *Assembly places and practices* (2004), 233–46.

Barrow, G.W.S., *The kingdom of the Scots* (London, 1973).

Barry, Rev. E., *Barrymore: records of the Barrys of County Cork* (Cork, 1902).

Barry, T. (ed.), *A history of settlement in Ireland* (London, 2000).

Bateson, M. (ed.), 'Irish exchequer memoranda of the reign of Edward I', *EHR* 18 (1903), 497–513.

Begley, J., *The Diocese of Limerick Ancient and Medieval* (Dublin, 1906).

——, *The Diocese of Limerick in the sixteenth and seventeenth centuries* (Dublin, 1927).

Bernard, J.H., & M. Butler (eds), 'The charters of the Cistercian abbey of Duiske in the county of Kilkenny', *PRIA* 35 C (1918), 1–189.

Bhreathnach, E., 'Authority and supremacy: Tara and its hinterland', in *Discovery Programme Reports* 5 (Royal Irish Academy, Dublin, 1999), 1–23.

——, 'Críchad an Chaoilli: a medieval territory revealed', *JCHAS* 110 (2005), 85–95.

Binchy, D.A., *Celtic and Anglo-Saxon kingship* (Oxford, 1970).

—— (ed.), *Críth Gablach* (Dublin, 1979).

Bradley, J., 'The interpretation of Scandinavian settlement in Ireland', in Bradley (ed.), *Settlement and society* (1988), 49–78.

—— (ed.), *Settlement and Society in Medieval Ireland* (Kilkenny, 1988).

Brady, N., 'Labor and agriculture in early medieval Ireland: evidence from the sources', in A. Frantzen and D. Moffat (eds), *The work of work: servitude, slavery and labor in medieval England* (Glasgow, 1994), 125–45.

Broderick, G., 'Baile in Manx nomenclature', *BUPS* 2:1 (1978), 16–19.

——, 'Tynwald: a Manx cult site and institution of pre-Scandinavian origin?', *CMCS* 46 (2003), 55–94.

Brooks, E. St John, 'The grant of Castleknock to Hugh Tyrel', *JRSAI* 63 (1933), 206–20.

—— (ed.), *Register of the Hospital of St John Baptist, Dublin* (Dublin, 1936).

—— (ed.), 'Unpubished charters relating to Ireland, 1174–1182', *PRIA* 43 C (1936), 313–66.

——, *Knights' fees in counties Wexford, Carlow and Kilkenny* (Dublin, 1950).

——, 'The de Ridelesfords, i,', *JRSAI* 81 (1951), 115–38; ii, 82 (1952), 45–61.

—— (ed.), *The Irish cartularies of Llanthony Prima and Secunda* (Dublin, 1953).

——, 'A charter of John de Courcy to the abbey of Navan', *JRSAI* 63 (1963), 38–45.

Broun, D., 'The Seven Kingdoms in *De situ Albanie*: a record of Pictish political geography or imaginary map of ancient Alba?', in E. Cowan (ed.), *Alba: Celtic Scotland in the medieval era* (East Linton, 2000), 24–42.

Bugge, A. (ed.), *Caithreim Cellachain Caisil: the victorious career of Cellachan of Cashel* (Christiana, 1905).

Butler, W., *Gleanings from Irish history* (New York, 1925).

Byrne, F.J. (ed.), 'Clann Ollaman Uaisle Emna', *Studia Hibernica* 4 (1964), 54–94.

——, 'Historical note on Cnogba (Knowth)', *PRIA* 66 C (1968), 383–400.

——, 'Tribes and tribalism in early Ireland', *Ériu* 22 (1971), 128–66.

——, 'A note on Trim and Sletty', *Peritia* 3 (1984), 316–19.

——, 'The trembling sod: Ireland in 1167', in Cosgrove (ed.), *A new history of Ireland* ii (1991), 1–42.

——, & P. Francis, 'Two lives of St Patrick', *JRSAI* 124 (1994), 5–117.

——, *Irish kings and high kings* (Dublin, 2001).

Byrne, P., 'Ciannachta Breg before Síl nÁedo Sláine', in Smyth (ed.), *Seanchas*, 121–6.

Byrnes, M., 'The Árd Ciannachta in Adomnán's Vita Columbae', in Smyth (ed.), *Seanchas*, 127–36.

Cam, H., *The Hundred and the Hundred Rolls* (London, 1930).

Campbell, J., *The Anglo-Saxons* (London, 1991).

Carney, J. (ed.), *Topographical Poems by Seaán Mór Ó Dubhagáin and Giolla na Naomh Ó hUidhrín* (Dublin, 1943).

Carrigan, W., *History and antiquities of the diocese of Ossory* (4 vols, Dublin, 1905).

Caulfield, R., 'Early Charters relating to the city and county of Cork', *Gentleman's Magazine* 1865, 316–20, 449–452, 719–722.

—— (ed.), *The council book of the corporation of Youghal* (Guildford, 1878).

Charles-Edwards, T.M., 'Some Celtic kinship terms' *BBCS* 24 (1971), 105–22.

——, 'The seven bishop-houses of Dyfed' *BBCS* 24 (1971), 247–62.

——, 'Kinship, status, and the origins of the hide', *Past and Present* 56 (1972), 3–33.

——, 'Críth Gablach and the law of status', *Peritia* 5 (1986), 53–73.

——, *Early Irish and Welsh kinship* (Oxford, 1993).

——, et al. (eds), *The Welsh king and his court* (Cardiff, 2000).

Clinton, M., 'Settlement dynamics in Co Meath: the kingdom of Lóegaire', *Peritia* 14 (2000), 372–97.

Colfer, B., 'Anglo-Norman settlement in Co. Wexford', in K. Whelan (ed.), *Wexford: history and society* (Dublin, 1987), 65–101.

Colmcille, Fr., 'Where was Sliabh gCua?', *Decies* 46 (1992), 5–10.

Connor, R. & A. Simpson, *Weights and measures in Scotland: a European perspective* (Edinburgh, 2004).

Cooney, G., 'Reading a landscape manuscript: a review of progress in prehistoric settlement studies in Ireland', in Barry (ed.), *History of settlement* (2000), 1–50.

Cosgrove, A. (ed.), *A new history of Ireland* ii (Oxford, 1991).

Crawford, B., *Scandinavian Scotland* (Leicester, 1987).

Curtis, E. (ed.), 'Sheriff's accounts of the honour of Dungarvan,' *PRIA* 39 C (1929–31), 1–17.

——, *A history of medieval Ireland* (London, 1938).

—— (ed.), 'Feudal charters of the de Burgo lordship of Connacht' in Ryan (ed.), *Eóin Mhic Néill* (1940), 286–95.

Darvill, T., 'Tynwald Hill and the 'things' of power', in Pantos & Semple (eds), *Assembly places and practices* (2004), 217–32.

Davies, E., 'Treens and quarterlands: a study of the land system of the Isle of Man', *Trans. and Papers of the Institute of British Geographers*, 22 (1956).

Davies, O. & D. Quinn (eds), 'The pipe roll of 14 John', *UJA* 1941 (supplement), 1–76.

Davies, R., *Conquest, coexistence and change in Wales 1063–1415* (Oxford, 1987).

Davies, W., *An early Welsh microcosm: studies in the Llandaff charters* (London, 1978).

——, *Patterns of power in early Wales* (Oxford, 1990).

Dillon, C. & H. Jefferies (eds), *Tyrone: history and society* (Dublin, 2000).

Dillon, M. (ed.), *Lebor na Cert* (Dublin, 1962).

—— (ed.), 'Ceart Uí Néill', *Studia Celtica* 1 (1966), 1–16.

Dobbs, M. (ed.), 'The history of the descendants of Ir', *ZCP* 13 (1921), 308–60; vol. 14 (1923), 44–144.

—— (ed.), 'The genealogies of the Southern Uí Néill', *ZCP* 20 (1926), 1–29.

—— (ed.), 'The Ban-Shenchas', *Revue Celtique* 48 (1931), 163–234.

——, 'The territory and people of Tethba', *JRSAI* 68 (1938), 241–59; 71 (1941), 101–10; 72 (1942), 136–48.

——, 'The Dál Fiatach', *UJA* 8 (1945), 66–79.

——, 'A poem on the Uí Dega', *Journal of Celtic Studies* 1 (1949/50), 227–31.

Doherty, C., 'The Vikings in Ireland: a review', in H. Clarke et al. (eds), *Ireland and Scandinavia in the early Viking age* (Dublin, 1998), 288–330.

——, 'Settlement in early Ireland: a review', in Barry (ed.), *History of settlement* (2000), 50–80.

Duffy, J., *Clogher Record album: a diocesan history* (Monaghan, 1975).

——, 'Medieval Monaghan: the evidence of the Place-names', *Clogher Record* 16:3 (1999), 7–28.

Duffy, P.J., 'The territorial organization of Gaelic landownership and its transformation in Co. Monaghan', *Irish Geography* 14 (1981), 1–26.

——, *Landscapes of South Ulster* (Belfast, 1993).

——, 'Social and spatial order in the MacMahon lordship of Airghialla' in Duffy et al. (eds), *Gaelic Ireland* (2001), 115–137.

—— et al. (eds), *Gaelic Ireland c.1200–c.1650: land, lordship and settlement* (Dublin, 2001).

Duffy, S., 'Ostmen, Irish and Welsh in the eleventh century', *Peritia* 9 (1995), 378–96.

Duncan, A., *Scotland: the making of the kingdom* (Edinburgh, 1975).

Dwyer, P., *The diocese of Killaloe from the Reformation to the nineteenth century* (Dublin, 1878).

Egan, P., (ed.), 'Obligationes pro Annates Clonfertenses Dioceses', *Archivium Hibernicum* 21 (1958), 52–74.

Elrington, C., (ed.), *The whole works of the Most Reverend James Ussher DD*, i (Dublin, 1847).

Empey, C.A., 'The cantreds of Medieval Tipperary', *NMAJ* 13 (1970), 22–9.

——, 'The cantreds of the medieval county of Kilkenny', *JRSAI* 101 (1971), 28–134.

——, 'The settlement of the kingdom of Limerick', in J. Lydon (ed.), *England and Ireland in the Later Middle Ages* (Dublin, 1981), 1–25.

——, 'The Norman period, 1185–1500', in Nolan (ed.), *Tipperary: history and society* (1985), 70–91.

——, 'Anglo-Norman settlement in the cantred of Eliogarty', in Bradley (ed.), *Settlement and society* (1988), 208–228.

——, 'County Kilkenny in the Anglo-Norman period', in W. Nolan and K. Whelan (eds), *Kilkenny: history and society* (Dublin, 1990), 75–96.

——, 'Anglo-Norman Co. Waterford: 1200–1300', in W. Nolan and T. Power (eds) *Waterford: history and society* (Dublin, 1992), 131–46.

Falkiner, C.L., 'The counties of Ireland: an historical sketch of their origin, constitution, and gradual delimitation', *PRIA* 24 C (1903), 169–194.

Feehan, J., *Farming in Ireland* (Roscrea, 2003).

Fick, A., *Worterbuch der Indogermanischen Sprachen* (Gottingten, 1870).

Finberg, H., 'Anglo-Saxon England to 1042', in Finberg (ed.), *Agrarian history* (1972), 385–507.

—— (ed.), *The agrarian history of England and Wales*, i, (Cambridge, 1972).

FitzPatrick, E., 'Assembly and inauguration places of the Burkes in late medieval Connacht', in Duffy et al. (eds), *Gaelic Ireland* (2001), 357–76.

——, 'The gathering place of Tír Fhiachrach?', *PRIA* 101 C (2001), 67–105.

——, 'Royal inauguration mounds in medieval Ireland', in Pantos & Semple (eds), *Assembly Places and Practices* (2004), 44–72.

Flanagan, D., 'Common elements in Irish place-names: *Baile*', *BUPS* 2:1 (1978), 8–13.

——, 'Transferred population or sept-names: Latharna', *BUPS* 2:2 (1979), 23.

Morton, D., (= Flanagan, D.), 'Tuath-divisions in the Baronies of Belfast and Massereene', *BUPS* 4 (1956), 38–44; vol. 5 (1957), 6–11.

Flanagan, M.T., 'Mac Dalbaig, a Leinster chieftain', *JRSAI* 111 (1981), 5–13.

——, 'Henry II and the kingdom of Uí Fáeláin', in Bradley, (ed.), *Settlement and Society* (1988), 229–40.

——, *Irish Society, Anglo-Norman settlers, Angevin kingship* (Oxford, 1989).

——, 'The castle of Telach Cail in Delbna', *IHS* 28 (1993), 385–90.

——, 'Historia Gruffud vab Kenan and the origins of Balrothery', *CMCS* 28 (1994), 71–94.

—— (ed.), *Irish royal charters: texts and contexts* (Oxford, 2005).

Frame, R., 'Commissions of the Peace in Ireland 1302–1461', *Analecta Hibernica* 35 (1992), 1–44.

Fraser, J., P. Grosjean, J. O'Keeffe (eds), *Irish Texts* i (London, 1931).

Freeman, A.M. (ed.), *The Compossicion Booke of Conought* (Dublin, 1936).

Geiriadur Prifysgol Cymru: a dictionery of the Welsh language (Cardiff, 1950–67).

Gerriets, M., 'Kingship and exchange in pre-Viking Ireland', *CMCS* 13 (1987), 39–72.

Gibson, D., 'Chiefdoms, confederacies and statehood in early Ireland', in J. Arnold and D. Gibson (eds), *Celtic chiefdom: Celtic state* (Cambridge, 1995), 116–28.

Gilbert, J.T., *A history of the city of Dublin* i (Dublin, 1854).

—— (ed.), *Chartularies of St Mary's Abbey Dublin*, i and ii (London, 1884).

—— (ed.), *Register of the Abbey of St Thomas, Dublin* (London, 1889).

—— (ed.), *Crede Mihi* (Dublin, 1897).

Grant, A., 'Thanes and thanages from the eleventh to the fourteenth centuries', in Grant and Stringer (eds), *Medieval Scotland: crown, lordship and community* (Edinburgh, 1993), 39–81.

Gwynn, A., *The medieval province of Armagh* (Dundalk, 1946).

—— & D. Gleeson, *A history of the diocese of Killaloe* (Dublin, 1962).

—— & R. Hadcock, *Medieval religious houses Ireland* (London, 1970).

Gwynn, E.J. (ed.), 'An Irish penitential', *Ériu* 7 (1914), 121–95.

Hamlin, A., 'The early church in Tyrone to the twelfth century', in Dillon & Jefferies (eds), *Tyrone* (2000), 85–126.

Handford, S. (ed. and trans.), *The Agricola and the Germania of Tacitus* (London, 1967).

Hardiman, J., *The history of the town and county of Galway* (Dublin, 1820).

—— (ed.), 'Ancient deeds and chief writings', *TRIA* 15 C (1828), 1–95.

—— (ed.), *A chorographical description of Iar-Connaught* (Dublin, 1846).

Harris, W., *Hibernica* (Dublin, 1770).

Haskins, C., *Norman institutions* (Cambridge, 1925).

Helle, K. (ed.), *The Cambridge history of Scandinavia* i (Cambridge, 2003).

Hellquist, E., *Svensk Etymologisk Ordbok* (Stockholm, 1922).

Hennessy, M., 'Parochial organization in medieval Tipperary' in Nolan, *Tipperary* (1985), 60–70.

Hennessy, W. (ed.), *The Book of Fenagh* (Dublin, 1875).

Hogan, E., *Onomasticon Goedelicum locorum et tribuum Hiberniae et Scotiae* (Dublin, 1910).

Hogan, J., 'The tricha cét and related land measures', *PRIA* 38 C (1929), 148–236.

——, 'The Uí Briain Kingship in Telach Óc', in Ryan (ed.), *Eóin Mhic Néill* (1940), 406–44.

Hore, P., *History of the town and county of Wexford* (6 vols, London, 1900–11).

Hull, V., 'Conall Corc and the Corco Luigde', *Publications of the Modern Language Association of America* 62 (1947), 897–909.

Jackson, K., *The Gaelic notes in the Book of Deer* (Cambridge, 1972).

Jaski, B., *Early Irish kingship and succession* (Dublin, 2000).

Jefferies, H., 'The founding of Anglo-Norman Cork', *JCHAS* 91 (1986), 26–48.

——, 'Derry diocese on the eve of the Plantation' in O'Brien (ed.), *Derry & Londonderry* (1999), 175–204.

Jenkins, P., 'Regions and cantrefs in early medieval Glamorgan', *CMCS* 15 (1988), 31–50.

John, E., *Reassessing Anglo-Saxon England* (Manchester, 1996).

Jones, D., *Graziers, Land reform and political conflict in Ireland* (Washington, 1995).

Jones, G., 'Post-Roman Wales', in Finberg (ed.), *Agrarian history* (1972), 283–384.

——, 'Multiple estates and early settlement', in P. Sawyer (ed.), *Medieval settlement: continuity and change* (London, 1976), 15–40.

——, 'Continuity despite calamity: the heritage of Celtic territorial organization in England', *Journal of Celtic Studies* 3 (1981/2), 1–31.

Kelleher, J.V., 'Early Irish history and pseudo-history', *Studia Hibernica* 3 (1963), 113–27.

——, 'Uí Maine in the annals and genealogies to 1225', *Celtica* 9 (1971), 61–107.

Kelly, F., *A Guide to early Irish law* (Dublin, 1988).

——, *Early Irish farming* (Dublin, 2000).

Knox, H.T., 'The manor of Admekin (Headford) in the thirteenth century', *JGAHS* 1 (1900), 168–183.

——, 'An identification of places named in Tirechan's Collections', *JRSAI* 31 (1901), 24–39.

——, 'Occupation of Connacht by the Anglo-Normans after 1237', *JRSAI* 32 (1902), 132–8, 393–406; vol. 33 (1903), 58–74, 179–89, 284–94.

——, *Notes on the early history of the dioceses of Tuam, Killala and Achonry* (Dublin, 1904).

——, *History of the county of Mayo to the close of the sixteenth century* (Dublin, 1908).

——, 'Kilcolgan', *JGAHS* 9 (1915), 129–177.

Kraft, J., *Hednagudar och hövdingdöme i det gamla Skandinavien* (Upplands-Bro, 1999).

——, *Tidiga spår av Sveariket* (Upplands-Bro, 2001).

——, *Ledung och sockenbildning* (Upplands-Bro, 2005).

Lacey, B., 'County Derry in the early historic period' in O'Brien (ed.), *Derry & Londonderry* (1999), 115–48.

Langrishe, R., 'Notes on Jerpoint abbey, County Kilkenny', *JRSAI* 36 (1906), 179–97.

Latham, R.E., *Revised medieval Latin word-list from British and Irish sources* (London, 1965).

Lawlor, H.J. (ed.), 'Calendar of the *Liber Ruber* of the diocese of Ossory', *PRIA* 27 C (1908), 159–208.

Leister, I., *Peasant openfield farming and its territorial organization in Co. Tipperary* (Marburg, 1976).

Lennard, R., 'The origins of the fiscal carucate', *Economic History Review* 16 (1944), 51–63.

Lexikon Des Mittel Alters (Munich, 1991).

Liber Cartarum Prioratus Sancti Andree in Scotia (Bannatyne Club, 1841).

Livingstone, P., *The Monaghan story* (Enniskillen, 1980).

Lloyd, J.E., *A history of Wales* i (London, 1912).

Loyn, H.R., *The making of the English nation* (London, 1991).

Lucas, A., *Cattle in ancient Ireland* (Kilkenny, 1989).

Mac Cana, P., 'Aspects of the theme of king and goddess in Irish literature', *Études Celtiques* 7:1 (1955), 76–114.

Mac Giolla Easpaig, D., 'Placenames and early settlement in Co. Donegal' in Nolan et al. (eds), *Donegal: history and society* (Dublin, 1995), 149–82.

Mac Ivor, D., 'The Knights Templars in Co. Louth', *Seanchas Ardmhacha* 4 (1961), 73–91.

Mac Iomhair, D. (=Mac Ivor, D.), 'The boundaries of Fir Rois', *CLAJ* 15 (1961–4), 144–79.

Mac Niocaill, G., *Na Manaigh Liatha in Éirinn* (Dublin, 1959).

—— (ed.), *The Red Book of the earls of Kildare* (Dublin, 1964).

——, 'The origins of the *Betagh*', *Irish Jurist* 1:1 (1966), 292–8.

——, 'Tír cumaile', *Ériu* 22 (1971), 81–6.

—— (ed.), 'The Irish 'charters'', in P. Fox (ed.), *The Book of Kells: commentary* (Luzern, 1990), 153–166.

Mac Shamhráin, A., *Church and polity in pre-Norman Ireland: the case of Glendalough* (Maynooth, 1996).

——, 'The making of Tír nEógain', in Dillon & Jefferies (eds), *Tyrone* (2000), 55–84.

Mac Síthigh, M., 'Cairteacha meán – aoiseacha do Mhainistir Fhobhair', *Seanchas Ardmhacha* 4 (1961), 171–5.

Macalister, R., *Corpus Inscriptionum Insularum Celticarum* i, (Dublin, 1945).

MacCotter, P., 'The Carews of Cork, i', *JCHAS* 98 (1993), 61–74.

——, 'The Carews of Cork' (unpublished MA thesis, NUI, 1994).

—— & K.W. Nicholls (eds), *The pipe roll of Cloyne: Rotulus Pipae Clonensis* (Cloyne, 1996).

——, 'The sub-infeudation and descent of the Carew/Fitzstephen moiety of Desmond', *JCHAS* 101, (1996), 64–80, vol. 102 (1997), 89–106.

——, 'A history of the Sall(e) family of Cashel', *Irish Genealogist* 10:2 (1999), 215–33.

——, 'The cantreds of Desmond', *JCHAS* 105 (2000), 49–68.

——, *Colmán of Cloyne: a study* (Dublin, 2004).

——, 'Lordship in Anglo-Norman Kerry 1177–1400', *JKAHS* 2:4 (2004), 39–85.

——, 'Functions of the Cantred in Medieval Ireland', *Peritia* 19 (2005), 308–332.

——, 'The rise of Meic Carthaig and the political geography of Desmuma', *JCHAS* 111 (2006), 59–76.

——, 'Townland development in Munster', forthcoming.

——, 'Irish rural deaneries', forthcoming.

MacNeill, J., 'Early Irish population-groups: their nomenclature, classification and chronology', *PRIA* 29 C (1911), 59–109.

——, 'The Vita Tripartita of St Patrick', *Ériu* 11 (1932), 1–41.

MacQueen, H., 'The laws of Galloway: a preliminary survey' in R. Oram and G. Stall (eds), *Galloway: land and lordship* (Edinburgh, 1991), 131–43.

Masterson, R., 'The diocese of Kilmore and the priory of Fore: 1100–1450', *Bréifne* (2003), 1–20.

McErlean, J., 'The synod of Ráith Breasail: boundaries of the dioceses of Ireland', *Archivium Hibernicum* 3 (1914), 1–33.

McErlean, T., 'The Irish townland system of landscape organization', in T. Reeves-Smyth and F. Hamond (eds), *Landscape archaeology in Ireland* (BAR British Series 116, 1983), 315–40.

McGowan, K., 'The Four Masters and the governance of Ireland in the Middle Ages', *Journal of Celtic Studies* 4 (2005), 1–42.

McKerral, A., 'Ancient denominations of agricultural land in Scotland', *Proceedings of the Society of Antiquarians of Scotland* 78 (1944), 39–80.
——, 'Land divisions in the West Highlands of Scotland', *Isle of Man Natural History and Antiquarian Society* 5:2, 12–20.
McLeod, N., 'Interpreting early Irish law: status and currency', *ZCP* 41 (1986), 46–65; vol. 42 (1987), 41–115.
McNeill, C. (ed.) *Liber Primus Kilkenniensis* (Dublin, 1931).
—— (ed.), *Calandar of Archbishop Alen's Register* (Dublin, 1950).
—— (ed.), *Registrum de Kilmainham* (Dublin, n.d.).
McNeill, T.E., *Anglo-Norman Ulster* (Edinburgh, 1980).
'Mansfield Papers', *Analecta Hibernica* 20 (1958), 91–125.
Megaw, B., 'Norsemen and native in the kingdom of the Isles', *Scottish Studies* 20 (1976), 1–44.
——, 'Note on "Pennyland and Davoch in south-western Scotland"', *Scottish Studies* 23 (1979), 75–7.
Meyer, K., *Betha Colmáin maic Lúacháin* (Todd Lecture Series xvii, Dublin, 1911).
—— 'The Laud genealogies and tribal histories', *ZCP* 8 (1912), 291–338.
Mills, J., 'The Norman settlement in Leinster – the cantreds near Dublin', *JRSAI* 24 (1894), 161–75.
—— & M. McEnery (eds), *Calendar of the Gormanston Register* (Dublin, 1916).
Murray, A.C., 'The position of the graphio in the constitutional history of Merovingian Gaul', *Speculum* 6 (1986), 787–805.
——, 'From Roman to Frankish Gaul: *centenarii* and *centenae* in the administration of the Merovingian kingdom', *Traditio* 44 (1988), 59–100.
Murray, L., 'A calendar of the Register of Primate George Dowdall', *CLAJ* 6 (1925–8), 90–100, 147–58, 213–28, vol. 7 (1929–32), 78–95.
——, 'The Pictish kingdom of Conaille Muirthemne', in Ryan (ed.), *Eóin Mhic Néill* (1940), 445–53.
Ní Dhonnchadha, M., 'The Guarantor List of Cáin Adomnáin, 697', *Peritia* 1 (1982), 178–215.
Ní Ghabhláin, S., 'The origin of medieval parishes in Gaelic Ireland: the evidence from Kilfenora', *JRSAI* 126 (1996), 37–61.
Ní Mhaonaigh, M., '*Nósa Ua Maine*: fact or fiction?', in Charles-Edwards et al. (eds), *The Welsh king and his court* (2000), 362–81.
Nicholls, K.W., 'Some place-names from the Red Book of the Earls of Kildare', *Dinnseanchas* 3 (1969), 25–37, 61–3.
——, 'The Butlers of Aherlow', *Journal of the Butler Society* ii, (1969), 123–8.
——, 'Some placenames from *Pontificia Hibernica*', *Dinnseanchas* 3:4 (1969), 85–98.
——, 'The episcopal rentals of Clonfert and Kilmacduagh', *Analecta Hibernica* 26 (1970), 130–43.
——, 'Miscellanea: Counties Carlow and Wexford', *Dinnseanchas* 4:2 (1971), 33–7.
——, 'Rectory, vicarage and parish in the western Irish dioceses', *JRSAI* 101 (1971), 53–84.
——, 'Inquisitions of 1224 from the Miscellanea of the Exchequer', *Analecta Hibernica* 27 (1972), 103–112.
——, 'Some unpublished Barry charters', *Analecta Hibernica* 27 (1972), 113–19.
——, 'A charter of William de Burgh', *Analecta Hibernica* 27 (1972), 120–4.
——, 'The Register of Clogher', *Clogher Record* 7 (1972), 361–431.
——, 'Some Patrician sites of eastern Connacht', *Dinnseanchas* 5:4 (1973), 114–18.
——, 'Anglo-French Ireland and after' (review article), *Peritia* 1 (1982), 370–403.

——, 'A charter of John, Lord of Ireland, in favour of Matthew Ua Hénni, Archbishop of Cashel', *Peritia* 2 (1983), 267–76.

——, 'The land of the Leinstermen' (review article), *Peritia* 3 (1984), 535–58.

——, 'Medieval Anglo-Ireland' (review article), *Peritia* 3 (1984), 579–84.

——, 'A charter of John, lord of Ireland, in favour of Baltinglass', *Peritia* 4 (1985), 187–206.

——, 'Abstracts of Mandeville deeds, NLI MS 6163', *Analecta Hibernica* 32 (1985), 1–26.

——, 'Three topographical notes', *Peritia* 5 (1986), 409–15.

——, 'Gaelic society and economy in the high Middle Ages', in Cosgrove (ed.), *A new history of Ireland* ii (1987), 397–435.

——, 'The development of lordship in County Cork, 1300–1600', in O'Flanagan and Buttimer (eds), *Cork* (1993), 157–211.

——, 'Crioch Branach: The O'Byrnes and their country', in C. O'Brien (ed.), *Feagh McHugh O'Byrne* (Rathdrum, 1998), 7–39.

——, 'The Anglo-Normans and beyond', in J. Crowley (ed.), *Atlas of Cork City* (Cork, 2005), 104–11.

Nolan, W. (ed.), *Tipperary: history and society* (Dublin, 1985).

Ó Buachalla, L., 'The Uí Liatháin and their septlands', *JCHAS* 44 (1939), 28–36.

——, 'The Uí Meic Caille in pre-Norman times', *JCHAS* 50 (1945), 24–7.

——, 'The placenames of North East Cork' *JCHAS* 54 (1949), 31–4, 88–91; vol. 55 (1950), 46–9, 91–5.

——, 'Contributions towards the political history of Munster' ii, *JCHAS* 57 (1952), 67–86.

——, 'Townland development in the Fermoy area', *Dinnseanchas* 1:4 (1965), 87–93.

——, 'An early fourteenth-century placename list for Anglo-Norman Cork', *Dinnseanchas* 2 (1966–7), 1–12, 39–50, 61–7.

Ó Canann, T., 'Trí Saorthuatha Mhuinntire Chanannáin: a forgotten medieval placename', *Donegal Annual* 38 (1986), 19–46.

——, 'Aspects of an early Irish surname: Ua Canannáin', *Studia Hibernica* 27 (1993), 113–144.

Ó Ceallaigh, S., *Gleanings from Ulster history* (Cork, 1951).

Ó Conbhuí, C., 'The lands of St Mary's abbey, Dublin', *PRIA* 62 C (1962), 21–85.

Ó Corráin, D., 'Studies in West Munster history', *JKAHS* 1 (1968), 46–55; vol. 2 (1969), 27–37.

——, 'Irish regnal succession: a reappraisal', *Studia Hibernica* 11 (1971), 9–18.

——, 'Dál Cais – church and dynasty', *Ériu* 24 (1973), 52–63.

——, 'Nationality and kingship in pre-Norman Ireland' in T.V. Moody (ed.), *Nationality and the pursuit of national independence* (Belfast, 1978), 1–36.

——, 'The Uí Chobthaigh and their pedigrees', *Ériu* 30 (1979), 168–71.

——, 'Irish kings and high kings' (review article), *Celtica* 13 (1980), 150–68.

——, 'Studies in the history of Dalriada' (review article), *Celtica* 13 (1980), 168–82.

——, 'The early Irish churches: some aspects of organization' in Ó Corráin (ed.), *Irish antiquity: essays and studies presented to M.J. O'Kelly* (Cork, 1981), 327–41.

——, 'Corcu Lóigde: land and families' in O'Flanagan and Buttimer (eds), *Cork* (1993), 63–81.

——, 'Hogan and early medieval Ireland' in Ó Corráin (ed.), *James Hogan: revolutionary, historian and political scientist* (Dublin, 2001), 89–115.

——, *Ireland before the Normans* (second edition, forthcoming).

Ó Cróinín, D., *Early medieval Ireland 400–1200* (New York, 1995).

Ó Donnchadha, T. (ed.), 'Advice to a prince', *Ériu* 9 (1921–23), 43–54.

—— (ed.), *An Leabhar Muimhneach maraon le suim aguisíní*, (Dublin, [1940]).

Ó Dufaigh, S., 'Notes on the McKennas of Truagh', *Clogher Record* 8 (1973–5), 221–7.

Ó Duíbhgeannáin, M., 'The Uí Briúin Bréifne genealogies', *JRSAI* 64 (1934), 90–137, 213–56.

——, 'Notes on the history of the kingdom of Bréifne', *JRSAI* 65 (1935), 113–40.

Ó Fiaich, T., 'The kingdom of Airgialla and its sub-kingdoms' (PhD, NUI, 1950).

O'Flanagan, P., & C. Buttimer (eds), *Cork history and society* (Dublin, 1993).

Ó Floinn, R., 'Freestone Hill, Co. Kilkenny: a reassessment', in Smyth (ed.), *Seanchas* (2000), 12–29.

Ó hÓgáin, S., *Conntae an Chláir: a triocha agus a tuatha* (Dublin, 1938).

Ó Mórdha P., 'The medieval kingdom of Mugdorna', *Clogher Record* 7 (1972), 432–46.

Ó Mórdha, E., 'The Uí Briúin Bréifne genealogies and the origins of Bréifne', *Peritia* 16 (2002), 444–50.

Ó Muraíle, N., 'Some early Connacht population groups', in Smyth (ed.), *Seanchas* (2000),161–77.

——, 'Settlement and placenames' in Duffy et al. (eds), *Gaelic Ireland* (2001), 223–45.

——, (ed.), *The great book of Irish genealogies: compiled by Dubhaltach Mac Fhirbhisigh* (5 vols, Dublin, 2003).

Ó Murchadha, D., 'The castle of Dún Mic Oghmainn and the overlordship of Carbery', *JCHAS* 93 (1988), 73–82.

——, 'Odhbha and Navan', *Ríocht na Midhe* 8 (1992–3), 112–23.

——, 'Cenn Ebrat, Sliab Caín, Belach Ebrat,' *Éigse* 29 (1996), 153–71.

——, 'The origins of Clann Bhruaideadha', *Éigse* 31 (1998), 121–31.

——, 'Early history and settlements of the Laígis', in P. Lane and W. Nolan (eds), *Laois History and Society* (Dublin, 1999), 35–62.

——, 'The formation of Gaelic surnames in ireland: choosing the eponyms', *Nomina* 22 (1999), 25–44.

——, (ed.), 'The Cork decretal letter of 1199', *JCHAS* 106 (2001), 79–100.

Ó Raithbheartaigh, T. (ed.), *Genealogical tracts* i, (Dublin, 1932).

Ó Riain, P. (ed.), *Corpus Genealogiarum Sanctorum Hiberniae* (Dublin, 1985).

——, D. Ó Murchadha, K. Murray (eds), *Historical dictionary of Gaelic placenames*, Fascicle 1 (ITS, London, 2003).

O'Brien, G. (ed.), *Derry & Londonderry: history and society* (Dublin, 1999).

O'Brien, M.A. (ed.), *Corpus Genealogiarum Hiberniae* i, (Dublin, 1962).

O'Connell, J., 'Obligationes pro annatis Dioceses Ardfertensis', *Archivium Hibernicum* 21 (1958), 1–51.

O'Curry, E., *Cath Mhuighe Léana* (Dublin, 1855).

O'Daly, J., 'Inauguration of Cathal Crobhdhearg O'Conor', *Journal of the Kilkenny Archaeological Society* 1852–3, 335–47.

O'Doherty, J., 'Obligationes pro annates Provinciae Tuamensis', *Archivium Hibernicum* 26 (1963), 56–117.

O'Donovan, J. (ed.), *The tribes and customs of Hy Many commonly called O'Kelly's country* (Dublin, 1843).

—— (ed.), 'Geinealach Chorca Laidhe', *Miscellany of the Celtic Society* (Dublin, 1849).

O'Flaherty, R., *Ogygia* (London, 1685).

O'Grady, S.H. (ed.), *Caithréim Thoirdhealbhaigh* (2 vols, ITS, London, 1929).

O'Keeffe, J.G. (ed.), *Buile Suibhne* (ITS, London, 1913).

——, 'The ancient territory of Fermoy', *Ériu* 10 (1926–8), 170–89.

O'Nolan, T.P., 'Mór of Munster and the tragic fate of Cuana son of Cailchín', *PRIA* 30 C (1912), 261–82.

O'Rahilly, T.F., *Early Irish history and mythology* (Dublin, 1946).

——, 'Some Fermoy place-names', *Ériu* 12 (1934–8), 254–6.

O'Reilly, T., 'Historia et Genealogia Familiae de Burgo', *JGAHS* 13 (1929), 50–60, 101–38.

O'Sullivan, D., 'The Cistercian abbey of St Mary de Castro Dei, Fermoy, Co. Cork', *JCHAS* 51 (1946), 170–81.

O'Sullivan, W. (ed.), *The Strafford Inquisition of Co. Mayo* (Dublin, 1958).

Orpen, G.H. (ed.), *The Song of Dermot and the Earl* (Oxford, 1892).

——, *Ireland under the Normans* (4 vols, Oxford, 1911–1920).

——, 'Some Irish Cistercian documents', *EHR* 27 (1913), 303–13.

——, 'The earldom of Ulster' *JRSAI* 43 (1913), 30–46, 133–43; 44 (1914), 51–66; 45 (1915), 123–42.

——, 'Inquisition touching Le Wastyn, Co. Westmeath', *JRSAI* 50 (1921), 167–77.

Otway-Ruthven, A., 'Anglo-Irish shire government in the thirteenth century', *IHS* 5 (1946), 1–28.

——, 'Dower charter of John de Courcy's wife', *UJA* 12 (35) (1949), 77–81.

——, 'The medieval county of Kildare', *IHS* 11 (1958–9), 181–99.

——, 'Knight service in Ireland', *JRSAI* 89 (1959), 1–15.

——, 'Knights' fees in Kildare, Leix and Offaly', *JRSAI* 91 (1961), 163–82.

——, 'The partition of the Verdon lands in Ireland in 1332', *PRIA* 66 C (1967), 401–55.

——, *A history of medieval Ireland* (London, 1968).

Pantos, A., & S. Semple (eds), *Assembly places and practices in medieval Europe* (Dublin, 2004).

Patterson, N.T., *Cattle lords and clansmen: the social structure of early Ireland* (London, 1994).

Pender, S. (ed.), *Déssi genealogies* (Dublin, 1937).

—— (ed.), *A census of Ireland circa 1659* (Dublin, 1939).

—— (ed.), 'The O Cleary Book of Genealogies', *Analecta Hibernica* 18 (1951).

Petty, W., *Hibernio Delineatio: Atlas of Ireland* (1685: rep. Newcastle-upon-Tyne, 1968).

Pollock, F., and F. Maitland (eds), *The history of English law before the time of Edward I*, i (Cambridge, 1968).

Poppe, E., 'A new edition of Cáin Éimíne Báin', *Celtica* 18 (1986), 35–52.

Power, P., (ed.) *Crichad an Chaoilli being the Topography of Ancient Fermoy* (Dublin, 1932).

Price, L., 'Placenames of the barony of Arklow, County of Wicklow', *PRIA* 46 C (1940), 237–86.

——, *The place-names of Co. Wicklow* iv (Dublin, 1953), v (Dublin, 1957), vii (Dublin, 1967).

——, 'A note on the use of the word *baile* in place-names', *Celtica* 6 (1963), 119–126.

——, 'The origin of the word *Betagius*', *Ériu* 20 (1966), 187–190.

Reeves, W., *Ecclesiastical antiquities of Down, Connor and Dromore* (Dublin, 1848).

Rennison, W., 'Joshua Boyle's accompt of the Temporalities of the Bishoprick of Waterford', *JCHAS* 32 (1927), 42–9; vol. 35 (1930), 26–33; vol. 36 (1931), 20–24.

Richards, M., 'Early Welsh territorial suffixes', *JRSAI* 95 (1965), 205–12.

——, *Welsh administrative and territorial units* (Cardiff, 1969).

Richardson, H., & G. Sayles (eds), *Parliaments and councils of medieval Ireland* (Dublin, 1947).

Ross, A., 'The dabhach in Moray: a new look at an old tub', in A. Wolf (ed.), *Landscape and environment* (St Andrews, 2006), 57–74.

Russell, P. (ed.), 'Nósa Ua Maine: 'The Customs of the Uí Mhaine'', in Charles-Edwards et al. (eds), *The Welsh king and his court* (2000), 527–551.

Ryan J. (ed.), *Féil-sgribhinn Eóin Mhic Néill* (Dublin, 1940).

Sawyer, B., & P. Sawyer, *Medieval Scandinavia: from conversion to reformation* (Minneapolis, 1993).

Scott, A.B., & F.X. Martin (eds), *Expugnatio Hibernica: The Conquest of Ireland* (Dublin, 1978).

Sellar, W.D., 'Celtic law and Scots law: survival and integration', *Scottish Studies* 29 (1989), 1–27.

Sharpe, R., 'Churches and communities in early medieval Ireland: towards a pastoral model' in Sharpe & Blair (eds), *Pastoral care before the parish* (Leicester, 1992), 81–109.

Sheehy, M.P. (ed.), *Pontificia Hibernica: medieval papal chancery documents concerning Ireland: 640–1261*, (2 vols, Dublin, 1962–5).

Simms, K., 'The medieval kingdom of Lough Erne', *Clogher Record* 9 (1977), 126–41.

——, 'The O'Hanlons and the O'Neills and the Anglo-Normans in thirteenth-century Armagh', *Seanchas Ardmhacha* 9 (1978), 70–94.

——, 'The origin of the diocese of Clogher', *Clogher Record* 10 (1980), 180–98.

——, 'Gabh umad a Fheidhlimidh', *Eriú* 31 (1980), 132–45.

——, *From kings to warlords* (Woodbridge, 1987).

——, 'Tír Eógain north of the mountain' in O'Brien (ed.), *Derry & Londonderry* (1999), 149–74.

Skene, W., *Celtic Scotland: a history of Ancient Alban* iii (Edinburgh, 1890).

Smith, L. (ed.), *The Itinerary of John Leland* iv, (rep., Carbondale, 1964).

Smyth, A. (ed.), *Seanchas: studies in early and medieval Irish archaeology, history and literature in honour of Francis J. Byrne* (Dublin, 2000).

Stenton, F., *Anglo-Saxon England* (Oxford, 1971).

Stokes, W. (ed.), *The Tripartite Life of Patrick with other documents relating to that saint*, (2 vols, London 1887).

—— (ed.), *Lives of the saints from the Book of Lismore*, Anecdota Oxoniensia (Oxford, 1890).

—— (ed.), *Félire hUí Gormáin: The Martyrology of Gorman* (London, 1895).

——, 'The Bodleian Amra Choluimb chille', *Revue Celtique* 20 (1899), 30–55, 132–83, 248–87, 400–37.

—— (ed.), *Félire Oengusso Céli Dé: The Martyrology of Oengus the Culdee* (London, 1905).

Stout, M., 'Ringforts in the south-west midlands of Ireland', *PRIA* 91 C (1991), 201–43.

Swift, C., 'Óenach Tailten, the Blackwater Valley and the Uí Néill kings of Tara', in Smyth (ed.), *Seanchas* (2000), 109–20.

——, 'Royal fleets in Viking Ireland', in J. Hines, A. Lane and M. Redknapp (eds), *Land, sea and home* (Maney, 2004), 189–206.

Taylor, S., 'Generic-element variation, with special reference to eastern Scotland', *Nomina* 20 (1997), 5–22.

Thompson, A. H., 'Diocesan organization in the Middle Ages: archdeacons and rural deans', *Proc. of the British Academy* 29 (1943), 153–94.

Thorpe, L. (trans.), *Gerald of Wales, Journey through Wales and the Description of Wales* (London, 1978).

Todd, J., *Cogadh Gaedhel re Gallaibh: The War of the Gaedhil with the Gaill* (London, 1867).

Walsh, A., 'Excavating the Black Pigs Dyke', *Emania* 3 (1987), 5–11.

Walsh, P., *Leaves of history* (Drogheda, 1930).

——, *The placenames of Westmeath* (Dublin, 1957).

——, *Irish leaders and learning through the ages*, ed. N. Ó Muráile (Dublin, 2003).

Ware, J., *The antiquities and history of Ireland* (Dublin, 1705).

Warner, R., 'Clogher: an archaeological eindow' in Dillon et al. (eds), *Tyrone* (2000), 39–54.

——, 'Notes on the inception and early development of the royal mound in Ireland', in Pantos & Semple (eds), *Assembly places and practices* (2004), 27–43.

Watson, W., *The history of the Celtic place-Names of Scotland* (Edinburgh, 1926).

Westropp, T., 'The historic character of the 'Wars of Turlough'', *TRIA* C 32 (1902), 139–97.
——, 'On certain typical earthworks and ring-walls in County Limerick', *PRIA* 33 C (1916), 9–42.
White, N.B. (ed.), *The Red Book of Ormond* (Dublin, 1932).
—— (ed.), *Irish monastic and episcopal deeds 1200–1600* (Dublin, 1936).
—— (ed.), *Extents of Irish monastic possessions* (Dublin, 1943).
—— (ed.), *The Dignitas Decani of St Patrick's cathedral, Dublin* (Dublin, 1957).
Williams, D.G.E. (=Williams, Gareth), 'Land assessment and military organization in the Norse settlements in Scotland' (PhD, University of St Andrews, 1997).
——, 'The dating of the Norwegian *leiðangr* system: a philological approach', *Nowele* 30 (1997), 21–5.
Williams, Gareth, 'Ship-levies in the Viking age', in A. Nørgård et al. (eds), *Maritime warfare in Northern Europe* (Copenhagen, 2002), 293–308.
——, 'The dabhach reconsidered: pre-Norse or post-Norse?', *Northern Studies* 37 (2003), 17–31.
Williams, Glanmor, *The Welsh church from conquest to reformation* (Cardiff, 1976).
Zupko, R., 'The weights and measures of Scotland', *SHR* 56 (1977), 119–45.

Index

Page numbers occur in **bold** where the primary account of cantreds and *trícha*s occurs. To avoid excessive and unnecessary repetition parish names occurring in the gazetteer, and townland names occurring in the footnotes of chapter 5, are not indexed. The reader is directed to the atlas as a guide to the location of interest. The following abbreviations are used.

b. = barony	f.b. = feudal barony
c. = county	m. = manor
can. = cantred	r.r. = rural rectory
d. = rural deanery	r. = river
dio. = diocese	t. = town or city

Uaithne, 98, 213
Ualgarg Ua Ruairc, 221
Ubulc & Berre, 151
Uhegeni, 242
Uí *Choisduibh, 114
Uí Áeda Odba, 205
Uí Áeda of Uí Dega, 130n
Uí Áeda of Uí Beccon, 202
Uí Ágda, 201
Uí Aichir, 193
Uí Ailello, 100, 209–11
Uí Airt, 200
Uí Aithemon Mestige, 100, 254
Uí Amalgado, 145
Uí Anluain, 239–40
Uí Anmchada, 162
Uí Badamna (**T43**), **159**
Uí Baígelláin, 241
Uí Báirrche, 128, 251
 (**T179**), 101, 251
Uí Bairrche Mara, 101
Uí Bairrche Tíre (**T2**), **128**
Uí Beccon, 202
Uí Bercháin, 158
Uí Berchon (**T74**), **183**
Uí Bergda, 182
Uí Blait (**T89**), 191, **192**
Uí Blaithmeic, 158
 (**T152**), 50, **233**
Uí Bráein, 199–200
Uí Brain (of Uí Muiredaig), 254
Uí Brecáin, 195
Uí Bresail, 240
Uí Briain kings of Tuadmumu, 43, 96, 145,
 185, 187, 189, 266
Uí Briain of Aherlow, 189
Uí Bric, 245
Uí Brigte, 246
 (**T172**), **247**
Uí Briuin Aí, 100, 102, 148, 207–9
Uí Briúin Archaill, 224
Uí Briúin Bréifne, 133, 200, 218–19, 221
Uí Briúin Cualann, 164–5
Uí Briúin Rátha (**T7**), 43, **132**,
Uí Briúin Seola, 102, 134–7, 143
 regional kingdom, 143
Uí Briúin Umaill, 146
Uí Briúin, 134, 143, 219
Uí Buide (**T3**), **128–9**
Uí Builc, 151–2, 162
Uí Caellaide, 183
Uí Cathniad, 145

Uí Chaím, 152
Uí Chaíndelbáin, 206
Uí Chairpre Íochtarach (**T77**), 46, 48, **185–6**
Uí Chairpre Uachtarach (**T76**), 50, **185–6**
Uí Chairpre, 185
Uí Chaissíne (**T90**), 192, **193**
Uí Chathail, 145
Uí Chatháin, 225–6
Uí Chathaláin, 213–14
Uí Chathasaig, 165
Uí Chellaig (of Clann Echdach), 228
Uí Chellaig Cualann, 164–5
Uí Chellaig Brega, 205
Uí Chellaig Uí Maine, 141, 207–8, 222
Uí Chennétig, 211–12
Uí Chennselaig, 40, 100–2, 128, 130–1,
 249–51, 253–4
Uí Cherbaill Airgialla, 236, 238, 241
Uí Cherbaill Éli, 212
Uí Chérín, 212
Uí Chernaig Breg, 205
Uí Chernaig, 89
Uí Chéthig, 17, 176
Uí Chiarda, 177, 201
Uí Chinn Fháelad, 186
Uí Chléirchín, 185
Uí Chobthaig, 162
Uí Chonaill of Uí Fhidgente, 185–7, 193
Uí Chonaill Corcu Loígde, 162
Uí Chonaing, 204, 236
Uí Chonchobair (of Ciarraige), 168
Uí Chonchobair (of Connacht), 96, 136, 144
Uí Chonfhiacla, 200
Uí Chongalaig, 205
Uí Chonlígáin, 95
Uí Chorcráin, 95
Uí Chormaic of Uí Fhidgente, 193–4
Uí Chormaic Loisc, *see* Dál Cormaic Loisc
Uí Chormaic Tuirbe, 166
Uí Choscraig, 252
Uí Chremthainn, 241–4
Uí Chúain, 68
Uí Chuanach, 190
 (**T124**), 214, **215**
Uí Chuiléin, 186
Uí Chuillín, 183
Uí Chuirb Liatháin (**T44**), **159**
Uí Chuirc, 17–18
Uí Chúscraidh Sléibhe, 271
Uí Crimthannáin, 173
Uí Cruinn, 240
Uí Dedaid, 215